Soviet Psychology

Soviet Psychology

PHILOSOPHICAL, THEORETICAL, AND EXPERIMENTAL ISSUES

Levy Rahmani

INTERNATIONAL UNIVERSITIES PRESS, INC.

NEW YORK

Library of Congress Catalog Card Number: 72-182041
ISBN: 0-8236-6110-5

Manufactured in the United States of America

To my wife, Rodica,
and my children, Eliana and Amir

Acknowleagmenis

I am indebted to many individuals, over three continents, who have encouraged and helped me to obtain needed materials, and who were instrumental in seeing that these materials followed me in my peripatetic movements. I am particularly indebted to those who patiently read the successive drafts, critically influencing my approach to the subject matter of this book. It is due largely to their efforts on my behalf that the original rough sketch is hardly recognizable in the book as it now reads.

It would be impossible for me to mention all those to whom I owe thanks, but I would like to single out a few. Josef Brožek has contributed enormously, both directly and indirectly, to the accomplishment of my task. He assisted me in every possible way. John Sullivan spared no effort in helping me find publication channels, and the late George Klein was responsible for my introduction to International Universities Press. Neil O'Connor made valuable suggestions for the chapter, Thinking and Language.

It was Dr. Abram Kagan and Irene Azarian of I.U.P. who, after seeing an earlier version of the manuscript, foresaw that a final reworking would make the book more readable and accepted it for publication. Norma Fox has done for this book much more than an editor usually does. It is to her that the reader owes the acceptable style of the book's language, which she transformed from my own cumbersome non-native English. I am to be held responsible for any awkwardness which has survived her hand.

Above all, I am grateful to my family who had to bear my intense preoccupation and seclusion during the many hours of writing and research. To them I dedicate this book.

Contents

CONTENTS

Foreword

Books have their history. The full story of the genesis of the present volume would make for fascinating reading, reflecting the intellectual and human drama of Eastern Europe during the last quarter of a century. However, the human aspects—a saga of struggle for survival, physical and intellectual, against odds that at times must have appeared overwhelming—will not be touched upon here. The book should be judged in terms of its intrinsic merit. An occasional missing page reference, in a work that is otherwise meticulously documented, reflects the fact that some of the original notes may have been lost during the long and turbulent passage from Bucharest to Boston via Jerusalem. The need to shift languages twice in mid-stream certainly did not lighten the demands made on the writer.

While living as a young man in Roumania, Levy Rahmani was reared, as it were, on Soviet psychology. The official textbook he studied in 1949, in preparation for examinations for admission to the university, was the work by Kornilov, Smirnov and Teplov (1948), *Psychology*. Later, he was deeply impressed by S. L. Rubinshtein's (1946) informed, theoretically oriented *Foundations of General Psychology*. After all these years, Dr. Rahmani still remembers the book's call number in Bucharest's Library of the Association for Roumanian-Soviet Friendship.

In 1950 the author became aware, first through reports in the press, of the events at the Joint Session of the USSR Academy of Sciences and the Academy of Medical Sciences. The intent of the Session was to install Pavlov's views as the basis for all biomedical sciences, including psychology. At that time, in view of the author's interest in medicine, the proposals made at the conference appeared to make good sense to him. It took time and critical thought before he saw in perspective the potentially dangerous consequences for psychology.

Dr. Rahmani's thorough grounding in Soviet psychology is reflected positively in the authentic Soviet "flavor" of the present work, down to the sequence and the terminology of the chapter headings (cf. "Will and Voluntary Activity," where a "Western" author would speak of "motivation"). Rejecting the roles of either a blind protagonist or an equally blind antagonist, he has chosen the approach of an interested observer, a dependable reporter, and an honest critic.

As a result, the volume constitutes a needed and unique contribution to the growing Western literature on Soviet psychology, its past and its present. Earlier, Dr. Rahmani (1966) contributed a chapter to a volume in which several aspects of recent Soviet psychology were discussed, as well as an informative review (Rahmani, 1965) of the proceedings of the important 1962 conference. The present work provides a detailed portrait and synthesis of selected aspects of Soviet psychology, with emphasis on the events and achievements of the past two eventful decades.

The substantial introductory chapter provides historical background in the form of an overview of the developments from 1917 to 1950. In the body of the text, three topics are treated in depth: the nature of mind, sensory cognition, and thought and language. Less extensive treatment is accorded to memory; a reader interested in this topic will wish to familiarize himself with two Soviet monographs recently made available in English (Beritashvili, 1971; Luria, 1968). Three brief chapters are devoted to personality and the related topics of affective processes and voluntary activity.

In the lengthy chapter on the "Nature of the Mind" the author analyzes in detail the two-fold requirement that Soviet psychology be based philosophically on dialectical materialism and scientifically on I. P. Pavlov's physiology of highest nervous activity. Special attention is given to recent developments associated with the introduction of cybernetics. The changing relationships between Pavlovian physiology and psychology are outlined, taking into account both the earlier controversies and the recent advances in the interpretation of the mechanisms of brain function typified by the work of such innovators as Anokhin and Bernshtein.

Topically, the book has certain features in common with the two volumes entitled *The Science of Psychology in the USSR,* published in Russian in 1959 and 1960 and in an updated English edition 10 years later (Cole and Maltzman, 1970). However, in comparison with a whole corps of writers who contributed to that work, Rahmani's monograph is indeed a remarkable one-man opus. Although there are understandably certain limitations, especially in the selection of topics, since it is virtually impossible for one person to be expert in the many areas constituting current scientific psychology ("psychological sciences," in Russian parlance), there is, as is apparent in the current volume, the important advantage of a consistent approach, uniform framework and integrated presentation.

An outstanding characteristic of this opus is its thorough documentation, including well-chosen, direct quotations from the works of the authors being discussed.

Except for the overview covering the pre-1950 developments, the work is not a history of psychology, in any traditional sense. Within each chapter the orientation is "developmental" rather than historical, with interconnections between events—ideas and experimental findings being viewed as more important than chronological sequences. The author's interests are centered on scientific psychology's theories, considered in connection both with the experimental findings and the metatheoretical (philosophico-ideological, methodological, in Soviet terminology) "foundations."

Dr. Rahmani's work will be an effective "introduction" to Soviet psychology by providing a survey of the field, with emphasis on the basic issues, fundamental positions and main trends of development.

JOSEF BROŽEK

Lehigh University

REFERENCES

Beritashvili, I. S. (1971), *Vertebrate Memory: Characteristics and Origin* (Transl. from the 1968 Russian edition). New York: Plenum Press.

Cole, M. & Maltzman, I., eds. (1969), *A Handbook of Contemporary Soviet Psychology.* New York: Basic Books.

Kornilov, K. N., Smirnov, A. A. & Teplov, B. M., Eds. (1948) *Psikhologiya.* Third edition. Moscow: Uchpedgiz.

Luriya, A. R. (1968), *The Mind of a Mnemonist.* (Transl. from 1968 Russian edition.) New York: Basic Books.

Rahmani, L. (1965), Review of F. N. Fedoseev (Chief Ed.): Philosophical problems of the physiology of highest nervous activity and psychology (in Russian). *Contemp. psychol.,* 10:249-250.

_____ (1966), Studies on the mental development of the child. In: *Present-day Russian Psychology,* ed. N. O'Connor. Oxford, England: Pergamon Press, pp. 152-177.

Rubinshtein, S. L. (1946), *Osnovy obshchei psikhologii* [Foundations of General Psychology]. Second edition. Moscow: Uchpedgiz.

1

Soviet Psychology: a Historical Overview

During recent years the study of psychology in the Soviet Union has undergone significant changes. The narrow, conformistic approach arising out of the conference held in 1950 on the development of Pavlovian theory has gradually been replaced in the 1960's by a diversity of empirically tested theories. Deeply rooted beliefs in such theories as Pavlov's reflexology have been challenged while concepts like Vygotskii's cultural-historical view, not long ago rejected by the official psychology, are now widely discussed. Furthermore, areas of study once thought to represent the "decadent imperialist" ideology—witness cybernetics—have come to be accepted as worthy of investigation. Although contemporary Soviet psychology consists of a relatively stable system of ideas which characterizes it as a distinctive school, this newest phase in its history is definitely marked by an endeavor to incorporate some facets of Western thinking into its theoretical framework.

A consideration of the development of psychology in the USSR since 1917 leads naturally to a more comprehensive understanding of the current scene. This chapter does not seek to offer a strictly chronological account; rather, the major theories emerging between 1917 and 1950 will be presented. The various developments will be viewed in terms of their substantiation of Marxism and their consequent successive acceptance and rejection by political institutions such as the Central Committee of the Communist Party and the Communist Cell of the Moscow Institute of Psychology. Such a presentation is limited to the extent that it cannot encompass the details of the social and political background underlying the changes occurring in Soviet psychology during this period. [1]

ATTEMPTS TO BUILD A MARXIST PSYCHOLOGY

The Attack on Bourgeois Psychology

In the aftermath of the October 1917 revolution, Soviet institutions faced the overwhelming task of fundamental reorganization. To meet the pressing ideological and practical demands of their new society, especially in the area of education, Soviet psychologists immediately attempted to formulate an objective and materialist psychology. The Western European tradition in psychology was naturally attacked for representing the bourgeois ideology, for being dominated by idealism, metaphysics, and subjectivism. But what particularly marked this period was the tendency to evaluate all fields of "bourgeois" scientific study in terms of a "crisis." This mode of criticism was initiated in *Materialism and Empirio-Criticism* where Lenin (1909) argued that the study of physics in capitalist countries was in a state of profound confusion. Unable to assimilate the new discoveries, it had resorted to the theory of "vanishing matter."

Psychology's crisis was seen to lie in the contradiction between experimental psychology, which implied a spontaneously materialist approach, and the subjective view of the

---

[1] The interested reader is referred to Bauer's (1952) comprehensive analysis of the social events behind the evolution of the Soviet concepts of man and his development.

psyche grounded in the philosophy of Descartes and Locke (Yaroshevskii, 1970). P. M. Rubinshtein (according to Petrovskii, 1967) stated that the various Western schools which were developed during this period began in reaction to Wundt's formulations. Whereas behaviorism was a reaction to the method of introspection, the Gestalt school was directed against Wundt's emphasis on the elements of mind. The psychology of personality and individual differences, including psychoanalysis, contrasted with the formulation of universal laws governing the human mind. Finally, the development of tests for vocational guidance and selection was a step beyond Wundt's disregard for the practical demands of society.

Wundt's importance in the history of psychology is currently recognized by Soviet psychologists. Ramul (1971), a distinguished Gruzinian psychologist—he is 90 years old—wrote:

> The name of Wilhelm Wundt is most closely linked to one of the most important events in the whole history of psychology: its transformation in the last quarter of the 19th century from an inexact "empirical" psychology into a far more exact experimental psychology [p. 114].

Fifty years ago, Soviet psychologists regarded Wundt primarily as "the father of European bourgeois psychology." Consequently, counterresponses to his views were regarded as "progressive" and came to have a sort of "fellow-traveller" appeal to the Soviets who were searching for their own psychology. Close connections developed between Watson and the Soviet psychologists. Watson (1927) authored the article on behaviorism for the first edition of the *Large Soviet Encyclopedia*. The Gestalt theory was also regarded favorably. Its concept of wholeness appeared compatible with the dialectic method. Luriya (1928) wrote:

> The new German psychology *(Gestaltpsychologie)* proceeded from a criticism of associationism and of the "mosaic" concept of the old psychology and studied a series of basic rules of the integral behavior,

emphasizing the specific quality of its most complex forms. While American psychology stressed the need for an objective, materialist study of the psyche but was actually limited to a purely mechanistic approach, the new German psychology . . . emphasized that aspect of the most complex forms of behavior which we label dynamic, dialectic. Clearly, the task of contemporary Russian science is to take account of the achievements of this new Western trend and, while avoiding its mistakes, build a system of its own, based on an objective and dynamic approach to the psyche [p. 60].[2]

Psikhologiya published a paper by Koffka (1932) in which he criticized the mechanistic and vitalistic trends in the psychology of that time. An editorial footnote mentioned the ". . . healthy tendency among the best bourgeois psychologists to surmount vitalism and mechanicism in science."

Gestalt psychology did not escape severe criticism. Vygotskii was willing to admit the usefulness of "structure" and although he appreciated the attempt to give it a materialist interpretation, he strongly rejected the tendency to link it with the German *Naturphilosophie.* The Gestalt criticism of the mechanistic approach, he claimed, only dealt with superficial aspects while failing to analyze its essential nature. Teplov (1947) noted that the position taken by the Gestalt school against the mechanistic approach obscured its idealistic and metaphysical conception. Finally, it was Pavlov's (1934) thinking which significantly contributed to the later rejection of the Gestalt theory as an idealistic and metaphysical conception. Strongly opposed to the Gestalt denial of the role of the compounding elements of a mental structure, Pavlov stated bluntly that this theory contributed nothing to psychology.

To the reader familiar with the negative Soviet attitude toward psychoanalysis, it may be of interest to learn that in the early 1920's Russian philosophers and psychologists found common points between Marxism and psychoanalysis. Psycho-

[2] *Editorial Note:* This quotation has been translated into English by the writer. Hereinafter, unless otherwise specified, it is to be understood that throughout the present volume, all quoted material requiring translation has been translated by the writer.

analysis was suggested as the methodological application of historical materialism [3] to the study of the psyche. Reisner (1923, 1924a,b, 1925), an expert in the theory of law who became interested in psychology, proposed reforming this discipline along psychoanalytic lines. He believed that such revision was the sole answer to the problems raised by historical materialism. Bykhovskii (1923), too, proposed investigating the methodological premises of psychoanalytic theory in the light of dialectical materialism. And the philosopher Varyash wrote that psychoanalysis might have positive results if practiced by Marxist physicians expert in it (quoted by Petrovskii, 1967, p. 87). Obviously, there was criticism of psychoanalysis, as well. *Pod Znamenem Marksizma (Under the Banner of Marxism)* published an extensive criticism of psychoanalytic theory (Yurinets, 1924) and *Vestnik Kommunisticheskoi Akademii*, while publishing Reisner's (1924a) paper, expressed its disagreement with the author's Freudian "deviation." These criticisms notwithstanding, there were no attempts at an antianalytic campaign.

By the end of the decade attitudes had shifted sharply. In 1925 Clara Zetkin, a German socialist, published, in Russian, her memories of Lenin, who died the previous year. He was reputed to have said:

> The extension on Freudian hypotheses seems "educated," even scientific, but it is ignorant, bungling. Freudian theory is the modern fashion. I mistrust the sexual theories of the articles, dissertations, pamphlets, etc., in short, of that particular kind of literature which flourishes luxuriantly on the dirty soil of bourgeois society. I mistrust those who are always contemplating the sexual questions, like the Indian saint his navel. It seems to me that these flourishing sexual theories which are mainly hypothetical, and often quite arbitrary hypotheses, arise from the personal need to justify personal abnormality or hypertrophy in sexual life before bourgeois morality, and to entreat its patience. This masked respect for bourgeois morality seems to me just as repulsive as poking about in sexual matters. However wild and revolu-

---

[3] Historical materialism is the application of dialectical materialism to the study of society.

tionary this behavior may be, it is still really quite bourgeois. It is, mainly, a hobby of the intellectuals and of the sections nearest them. There is no place for it in the Party, in the class conscious, fighting proletariat [p. 45]. [4]

Pravda was quick to reproduce these remarks and to point out that Lenin was addressing himself to the attempt to unify Marxism and psychoanalysis. This marked the beginning of a series of antipsychoanalytic articles in political and professional journals. Shortly after the article in *Pravda,* Bammel, a philosopher, wrote an article entitled "Lenin's philosophical method and certain features of the contemporary revisionism" in which he criticized Varyash's attempt to bring together the views of Marx and Engels, on the one hand, and Freud's, on the other. Bammel stated that the interpretation of the psychoanalytic theory of the unconscious as a translation of the social laws formulated by Marx and Engels into a psychology of the individual, represented a distortion not only of Freud's concept of the unconscious, but also of the Marxist view of history (according to Petrovskii, 1967).

In 1926, Bykhovskii retracted his original position, claiming that Freudian theory was but one of many attempts to approach social phenomena from a purely biological point of view. A number of articles appeared which concerned themselves with the criticism of psychoanalysis from the Marxist perspective (Sapir, 1926, 1929; Reich, 1929). The opposition to psychoanalysis was even linked to Trotsky's revision of Marxism (Shemyakin and Germonovich, 1932).

The criticism of psychoanalysis during this period, as well as in subsequent years, led to its total rejection. However, at this time there was no suppression of publication regarding psychoanalysis. The most illustrative example of this policy was the Reich paper of 1929, which was followed by Sapir's critical paper attacking Reich's Marxist interpretation of psy-

[4] Translated by International Publishers in 1934.

choanalytic views. Moreover, such criticism amounted to the denial of the very problems raised by Freud and his followers. Only in recent years have attitudes begun to change.

Russian psychology before the revolution was understandably regarded by Soviet psychologists as part of the bourgeois ideology. This helps to explain the frequent use of such terms as "ideological front" and "the victory of materialism over idealism" in the field of psychology, during the early phases of the endeavor to create a Soviet psychology. Papers criticizing idealism and metaphysics in psychology were published in political journals such as *Under the Banner of Marxism* and *Voinstvuyushchii Materialist (The Militant Materialist)*. Psychology in Russia prior to 1917, as in Western Europe, was also said to be in a state of crisis stemming from the dichotomy between the experimental approach to the psyche and the underlying subjective view of it. This conflict was apparent in the work of Chelpanov (1863–1936). The author of several philosophical and psychological books, among which were *Brain and Psyche* in 1912 and *Introduction to Experimental Psychology* in 1924, as well as the founder and first director of the Moscow Institute of Experimental Psychology in 1912, Chelpanov accepted both Wundt's physiological psychology and the introspective method of the Würzburg school. Unlike several philosophers who were expelled from Russia in 1921, among whom were Lopatin (1855–1920) and Losskii [5] (1870–1965), Chelpanov did not lose his position and consequently bore the brunt of the assault against the "bourgeois" psychology in Russia.

Nevertheless, certain thinkers of the late nineteenth century were held in high regard. The "revolutionary democrats" —Chernyshevskii, Belinskii, Dobrolyubov—were considered representative of the materialistic and progressive traditions

---

[5] Losskii was professor of philosophy at the Moscow University. In 1922 he emigrated to Czechoslovakia and in 1946 to the United States, where he taught at the St. Vladimir Russian Orthodox Seminary in New York City. In 1951, he published a history of Russian philosophy.

of Russia at its best. Gertsen was commended for his ideas on education, and the Pedagogical Institute of Leningrad was named after him. Ushinskii, whose work was published in a multivolume edition in the Soviet Union, was honored for having expressed the idea that logic is only the reflection of objective relationships.

Finally, of note, was a group of biologists whose ideas have been very influential in Soviet psychology. Among them was Sechenov (1829–1905), "the father of Russian physiology," whose works *Reflexes of the Brain* (1863) and *The Elements of Thought* (1878) [6] were of particular importance. Sechenov postulated that "the organism cannot exist without its supporting external environment; hence a scientific definition of the organism should include also the environment which influences it" (Koshtoyants, 1965). He viewed the workings of the mind not as a spontaneous phenomenon, but as the result of constant stimulation of the nervous system. Psyche implies a reflex activity combining the external influences upon the organism with its response as a reverse action upon the stimulus in the form of muscular movement or speech. For Sechenov, thought was an act of confrontation between the various elements of knowledge, namely perceptions, images, concepts. Thought consists of man's orientation among objects, space, and time, and of establishing relationships in all the three spheres. It operates according to the reflex mechanism, but need not be expressed in movement due to the central inhibition. In Rubinshtein's (1957c) view, Sechenov's theory of the psyche was the axis on which revolved the ideological struggle between materialism and idealism during the entire course of Russian psychology from 1863 until the eve of the 1917 revolution.

The Reflexological Orientation

The major role in the attempt to substantiate that tenet of

---

[6] A revised and enlarged edition was published in 1903.

Lenin's philosophy which sees mental phenomena as having a material, objective basis in cerebral processes has been shared by two individuals: Bekhterev and Pavlov. Despite significant differences between them, both may be considered as followers of Sechenov's thinking.

Bekhterev (1857–1927) published about 600 works in the fields of the anatomy and physiology of the nervous system, clinical neurology and psychiatry, psychology and pedagogy. Among his contributions to neurology were the description of several normal and pathological reflexes, the discovery of certain nuclei and conduction paths in the brain, the discovery of centers which regulate the secretion of inner organs and the demonstration of the role held by the cortical motor areas for movements acquired during individual development. Furthermore, Bekhterev elaborated the method of associative motor reflexes. Some of his works were translated in more than one edition such as *Nerve Paths in the Brain and Spinal Cord, The Fundamentals of Cerebral Functions, Psyche and Life, General Principles of Human Reflexology* (1917). In 1893 Bekhterev became professor at the Military Medical Academy in Petersburg. He founded, in 1908, the Psychoneurological Institute, which was reorganized after the 1917 revolution in the State Psychoneurological Academy. In 1918 Bekhterev was appointed director of the State Institute for Brain Research which is currently bearing his name. While teaching at the Leningrad Medical School, he headed a sizable team of coworkers in Leningrad and Kharkov. [7] His "objective psychology" was initially presented in a paper in 1904 in the *Bulletin of Psychology, Criminal Anthropology and Hypnosis,* which he edited. Bekhterev extensively exposed his theory in *Objective Psychology* (1907), *General Principles of Human Reflexology* and *Collective Reflexology* (1918).

Employing a "biosocial" perspective, Bekhterev felt he was working toward a scientific study of personality. His theory

[7] A comprehensive summary of Bekhterev's work, in English, was done by Shnirman (1928, 1930), a coworker of Bekhterev's.

was concerned with both elementary and complex aspects of mental activity. He sought to study the effect of physical, biological and social factors on psychic functioning, in a strictly objective manner, by recording the external reactions, including facial expressions, gestures and speech, and relating them to their current and prior stimuli. Bekhterev continually emphasized his conviction that no conscious or unconscious phenomenon exists which is not manifest, sooner or later, in external behavior. This naturally led to his insistence upon studying man in his social environment.

Although his position was close to being behaviorist, Bekhterev did speculate about the neurological basis of psychic functioning. He posited that mental and physical phenomena represent a single neutral process. The obstacles met by the waves of ions produced by external stimulation, and intensified in the brain, result in a tension responsible for the "subjective tint" of the nervous current.

The official evaluation of Bekhterev and his views was ambivalent. He was appreciated for his political attitudes, for which he had been on bad terms with the Tsarist regime. After the revolution, Bekhterev embarked on an intensive work for public health. Kalinin, the Chairman of the Presidium of the Supreme Soviet of the USSR, praised him in his obituary in *Izvestiya* for his contribution to the rapprochement between labor and science. An editorial footnote to a paper published by Bekhterev (1926) in *Pod Znamenem Marksizma* emphasized the acceptance of dialectical materialism by a scientist. The 40th anniversary of Bekhterev's activity was celebrated by a festive volume (*Volume*, 1926). Recent writers also pointed out his merits (Shein, 1963). Yet at the same time, some of his statements which expressed an extreme mechanistic tendency were rejected. *Pod Znamenem Marksizma* published a sarcastic criticism of Bekhterev's theory (Nevskii, 1922).

By the late 1920's, and particularly after Bekhterev's death, the tendency to reject his views prevailed (Cheranovskii,

1928; Kurmanov, 1929). In 1928 the Leningrad Society of Reflexology, Hypnosis, Neurology and Biophysics set up a special panel for methodological problems, whose task it was to reorient reflexology on the basis of dialectical materialism. The next year a conference was held on the topic "reflexology or psychology." The proceedings marked the end of reflexology as a dominant trend in Soviet psychology on the strength of its finding that most of its basic propositions were incompatible with Marxism. In 1929 the Second All-Union Conference of Marxist-Leninist Research Institutes concluded that reflexology was a "revisionist" trend which deviated from the true Marxist-Leninist position (Editorial, 1929). In the early 1930's, the criticism of reflexology was a major topic in Soviet psychology (Belyaev, 1930; Mogendovich, 1931; Dobrynin, 1931; L. M. Shvarts, 1931; Ananev, 1931). Ananev and Myasishchev, two leading psychologists, who at that time were Bekhterev's coworkers, were among those who criticized reflexology.

The reversal of attitude toward Bekhterev's school can be linked to two factors. First, the fate of his work, as with that of numerous other Soviet scholars, rested upon its satisfaction of ideological demands. Conjectures originally deemed correct were supplanted as supposedly more suitable theories arose. Right after the revolution, the search for a materialistic psychology made any mechanistic approach acceptable, and it was Bekhterev who provided such an explanation of mental phenomena. As a more sophisticated approach to mental activity, in particular to consciousness, was felt to be needed, support for Bekhterev's theories declined since they were regarded as retarding the development of a Marxist psychology. The second reason for this change of attitude can be found in the evolution of Bekhterev's theory itself. In his early works, he spoke about an "objective psychology" and his criticism of subjective psychology seemed to be directed against the idealistic psychology and not against psychology as such. In line with this, he had worked out methods considered essential for a materialist psychology, including the technique for motor associations which was given much credit for its use in the objective investigation of the brain's functioning.

But in the period immediately following the revolution, Bekhterev turned to "reflexology." More than a mere change of label, it was intended to express his dissatisfaction with psychology in general. This time Bekhterev identified "observational" psychology with experimental psychology and claimed that both were aimed at the study of man's inner world. Reflexology became even more antagonistic to Soviet ideological requirements when Bekhterev emphasized that his study of the associative-reflex activity did not relate to a direct investigation of the functioning of the brain. In this he sharply disagreed with Pavlov's approach for, paradoxically, he was implying that the brain is inaccessible to any objective study. Reflexology was defined as the biological investigation of personality regarded as a biosocial entity. Bekhterev and Shchelovanov (1924) also introduced the concept of a developmental reflexology. Memory, feelings, volition, etc. were seen as little more than metaphysical concepts. Thus Bekhterev was at odds with the Marxist proposition that mental phenomena reflect objective reality.

The official furor against Bekhterev seems, however, to have been intensified by two statements which contradicted the foundations of dialectical materialism. First, he stated—recalling the views of Oswald, a target of Lenin's (1909) criticism—that energy exists beyond material and mental phenomena. Matter and mind were seen as identical. This was a shift from his earlier view that mental phenomena parallel cerebral processes. In the reflexological period, having suggested that both matter and mind evolved from energy, Bekhterev went on to try and reduce all phenomena to mechanical laws. Both nature and society had evolved in a similar way. According to Budilova (1960), Bekhterev's work of 1904 already implied this theory. But in later works, when he presented it as a Marxist proposition, he ran into unavoidable criticism.

Second, Bekhterev admitted, inconsistently with his earlier views, that self-observation was a necessary method in psychology. He pointed out that the study of reflexology and of subjective psychology were compatible since they both deal essentially with the same phenomena: the first, phenomena in their objective manifestations, the second, in their more limited, subjective form. While Bekhterev accepted the proposition that consciousness is simply a function of the brain, he was ready to consider any hypothesis other than the purely metaphysical. Actually, he stated that the task of reflexology was to study the correlation between the objective processes underlying the psychical phenomena, and the subjective phenomena discovered by the subject himself through self-observation. Thus it turned out that Bekhterev found himself closer to Chelpanov than to Pavlov.

Stressing the contradictions in Bekhterev's theory, Chelpanov (1924, 1925, 1926) regarded reflexology as a danger for psychology in Russia. He remarked that reflexology was not a subjective psychology, but neither was it a Marxist psychology. Eventually, he contributed to the attack on reflexology when he wrote ". . . reflexology itself does not exclude subjective psychology as some people think. It only limits the area of its study mainly to self-analysis as fully as possible, as it is already practised by the so-called Würzburg school" (1925, pp. 18-19).

For several reasons Pavlov's (1850-1936) theory has played quite a different role in Soviet psychology. First, by appearing to offer a methodology for investigating the cerebral basis of the human psyche, Pavlov's work satisfied ideological needs as is revealed for instance by the following statement by Fingert in 1930 (quoted by Petrovskii, 1967).

The theory of conditioned reflexes represents one of the greatest achievements of scientific thought, when considered within its own limits. By discovering the mechanism underlying the higher nervous activity of animals, the theory of conditioned reflexes implicitly discovers the origin of the individually acquired experience and its relationships to the inherited experience of the species. Thus it is a sort of continuation of Darwin's theory. Furthermore, by discovering the role of the higher areas of the central nervous system, the theory of conditioned reflexes . . . indicates the way for solving the problem of the objective substratum of psyche, i.e., the problem of the level of organization of matter, at which psyche occurs. Finally, the theory of conditioned reflexes offers an invaluable methodology for a scientific, Marxist, materialist psychology of man [p. 116].

Second, unlike Bekhterev, Pavlov attempted no philosophical speculations and thus avoided any ideological dispute. He did not refer to Marxism in his work as Bekhterev did. Pavlov was regarded as a "spontaneous materialist," the term reserved by Soviet ideology for scientists who take a materialist approach but not in a conscious, deliberate way. An editorial in *Pod Znamenem Marksizma* (according to Petrovskii) stated that "Marxism welcomes any creative attempt in every scientific area, if it corresponds to a materialistic, that is to say scientific, conception. Such an attempt in the area of psychophysiology is, for instance, the theory of conditioned reflexes" (p. 299). This is not to imply that Pavlov did not explore other areas. For instance, he spoke about a "reflex of purpose" related to an irresistible tendency to possess the stimulating object. This was supposed to derive from the feeding reflex which, in the course of evolution, had turned into a generalized haptic reflex, which in its turn, became a reflex of purpose. The collector's passion was interpreted as a reflex of purpose, while suicide was said to result from the inhibition of this reflex. Pavlov (1916) even went so far as to speculate about the Anglo-Saxon character which he regarded as the highest personification of the reflex of purpose. A year later (Pavlov, 1917) he was writing about a "freedom" reflex. Such speculation was criticized in the press, where it was explained as a limitation of "spontaneous" materialism. Pavlov, however, was generally cautious in applying his animal laboratory findings directly to human physiology. Meanwhile, the official appreciation of his work was overwhelmingly positive and the publication, in 1923, of the first collection of his writings, was celebrated in the political press with such glowing titles as "a victory of materialism."

Another reason for Pavlov's central position in Soviet psychology was his restraint from overtly attacking psychology. His criticism of psychology could readily be interpreted as being directed against the "old" introspective psychology and he was sympathetic to psychological trends, such as behaviorism, which clearly rejected subjective and anthropomorphic interpretations. Furthermore, Pavlov favored the concept of association which he equated with that of the conditioned reflex. In the final years of his life he seemed to entertain a broader understanding of psychology. Anokhin (1949a), one of his most widely known coworkers, suggested that Pavlov's original rejection of psychological concepts was more a matter of strategy than of his conviction that the study of subjective experience was irrelevant. Apparently, Pavlov had even considered setting up a psychological laboratory.

Soviet psychologists had mixed feelings about Pavlov's theory. On the one hand, feeling that the existence of psychology as an independent science in Soviet Russia was threatened by Pavlov's physiological approach, they were hostile, or at least ignored his work. On the other hand, they did make use of some of Pavlov's statements to strengthen their own position. For instance, in 1924, Kornilov was openly critical of Pavlov's theory. But three years later he wrote that Soviet psychologists regarded the physiology of higher nervous activity as highly relevant to their own work.

Finally, Pavlov's extension of his theory to the area of thought and language also may account for his stable position in Soviet psychology. His idea that words form a special system of conditioned stimuli apt to signal all the other stimuli has inspired extensive work in psycholinguistics (Slobin, 1966). Pavlov (1935) wrote:

> To an animal, reality is signalled almost exclusively merely by the stimulations . . . which converged directly to the special cells of the visual, auditory, and other receptors of the organism. This is what we likewise possess in the form of impressions, sensations and conceptions of the environment. . . . This first system of signalling reality is the same in our case as in the case of animals. But words have built up a second system of signalling reality, which is peculiar to us, being a signal of the primary signals. The numerous stimulations by word have, on the one hand, removed us from reality, a fact we should constantly remember so as not to misinterpret our attitude towards reality. On the other hand, it is nothing other than words which has made us human. However, it is beyond doubt that the essential laws governing the work of the first system of signalling necessarily regulate the second system as well, because it is work done by the same nervous tissue [p. 179]. [8]

This statement, and the studies which emerged from it, have been interpreted as support for the Marxist proposition that language and thought reflect objective reality. Interestingly enough, Pavlov's hypothesis of a second signal system, unlike all his other hypotheses, was not based on experimental findings. He advanced this hypothesis in 1927, after having become interested in the psychiatric clinic. It was inspired, primarily, by the observation of pathological cases. As a matter of fact, Pavlov had little understanding of the social nature of language (Dobrogaev, 1947). In summary, he had merited recognition in the Soviet literature for substantiating the hypotheses which Sechenov had advanced but was unable to implement experimentally.

It should be mentioned that in the 1920's there was a strong interest in neurophysiological study in Russia. The studies of Lazarev (1923) and Ukhtomskii (1925) were very

[8] Translated by W. Horsley Gantt.

influential. Furthermore, much work was done in the field of comparative psychology from a biological perspective, forming part of the background of later studies. Severtsov's (1866-1936) works, in particular his influential *Evolution and Psyche* published in 1922, can be used as an illustration. Severtsov actually laid the foundation of the evolutionary morphology of animals as an independent science. He founded, in 1930, a laboratory of evolutionary morphology at the Academy of Sciences, where he had been a member since 1920. This laboratory was the basis of the Institute of Animal Morphology, founded in 1935, which is currently bearing Severtsov's name. Severtsov advanced hypotheses about the directions and ways of the morphophysiological progression and regression, about the types of phylogenetic changes of organs and the phylogenetic correlations. According to his theory of "phyloembryogenesis," the evolution takes place through the modification of the course of ontogenesis. New characteristics occur in the course of evolution in the form of new structures which change the course of ontogenesis, in different stages of individual development from birth to death. Phylogenesis represents a series of ontogeneses changing under the influence of natural selection. Furthermore, Severtsov described a type of adjustment of animals consisting of behavioral modifications without morphological changes, as well as two evolutionary directions this type of adjustment has taken. In arthropoda, there was a dominant evolution of instincts which have attained a high degree of complexity in insects. In vertebrates there was a predominant development of individual adjustive changes in behavior. This evolution is maximal in man whose artificially created environment of culture and civilization bears witness to his capacity to adapt to any condition.

The work of Vagner (1849-1934), another biologist, has served as inspiration for many Russian students of animal behavior. Vagner headed the laboratory for animal studies of the Institute of Brain Research, in Leningrad, and was known for his two-volume work, *Biological Foundations of Comparative Psychology* (1910–1913). In 1923, he published another major work, *Biopsychology and Related Sciences*. Vagner's belief was that any biological science of man has to be based on comparative study, i.e., comparative anatomy, comparative physiology and so forth. In the same vein, he made a strong plea for the study of comparative psychology. Vagner was critical of two prevalent and conflicting tendencies. The first was the proposition that there is nothing in the human psyche which does not exist in the animal psyche. Adherents of this theory thus spoke of an animal consciousness, will and reason. Vagner criticized this position of Wundt and Romanes, among others, and dismissed such tendencies as "monism upside down." At the same time, he argued that Loeb's proposition that mind consists essentially of automatic reactions was equally wrong, and rejected it as "monism right side up."

Vagner's own view was that instinctive actions represent a hereditary response to a sum of stimulations and that underlying these actions are reflexes. Rational behavior also has a reflex origin, but there is no direct relation between the instinctive and the rational behaviors, each representing a different line of evolution. Even instincts were not to be reduced to reflexes. "It is not more warranted," he wrote, "to state that instincts are reflexes than to state that the wing of a butterfly, a dragonfly, a bird, or an airplane are the same thing. Indeed, they are similar regarding the adjustment for flight, but they are utterly different in their substance" (1923, p. 36). Both instinct and reflex are hereditary and have some similar features, but the study of the reflex mechanism is insufficient for the understanding of instinctive behavior. Vagner stressed the individual variability of instinctive behavior within the parameters imposed by heredity. Thus, new instincts may develop by way of mutation, as well as through individual variation.

Vagner's distinction between instinct and reflex ran counter to the assumption of Frolov (1936, 1937, 1938, 1952), a co-worker of Pavlov, that the instinct is a chain of reflexes. This view was quite popular with Pavlov's school. Vagner was also in disagreement with Borovskii (1928a,b, 1932), the head of the laboratory of comparative psychology at the Moscow Institute of Psychology. Borovskii argued for a "comparative reflexology" and ascribed no significance to the subjective aspect of man's reactions. In his view, the formation of habits in man is only a particular case of the elaboration of habits in animals; the learning curves for both are the same. Borovskii concluded that the paramount task of pedagogy is the study of the laws of habit formation and that the educator who is interested in animal psychology become familiar with methods which are essentially the same in the study of children and animals.

The Sociogenetic Approach

A great deal of effort was expended by Russian psychologists after the 1917 revolution to formulate a theory compatible with the Marxist tenet that the human psyche is a reflection of an objective reality, in particular the social environment. They had also to cope with the task of building a theory of education applicable to the "new" man. The problem of relationships between collective psychology and individual psychology was a major concern of the Soviet psychologists of the 1920's. They faced the following dilemma: is social psychology a legitimate branch of psychology, or should all the manifestations of the individual's psychology be regarded in terms of his social and, particularly, class position. In the light of the theory of historical materialism, they were inclined to the second solution. There was an additional reason for this tendency. Insofar as "bourgeois" psychology was regarded primarily as a psychology of individualism, a social psychology which purported to be concerned with the psychology of the "builder of communism" had to be opposed to an individual psychology. Hence there developed a sociogenetic trend which reflected the prevailing *Zeitgeist* in view of the extremist approach of its proponents. Zalkind (1924a,b), a psychologist affiliated with the Institute of Communist Education, published a collection of papers and speeches entitled *Essays of a Culture of a Revolutionary Time.* He was concerned with child psychology as well as with psychopathology, and to both areas he brought his ideas which a critic termed "pathological Marxism" (Vainshtein, 1924a,b). Zalkind went so far as to claim that the physiology of human beings is directly conditioned by the social class to which they belong. As man's social role increases historically, the influence of the natural environment becomes weaker. Thus with the development of man's productive capacity, there occurred a division into classes, each having its own psychophysiology determined by its role vis-à-vis the means of production in society. In short, we have not only a class consciousness but also a class physiology. Zalkind speculated further that people were unable to consolidate their newly acquired reflex associations into a hereditary factor because of the rapid changes in the social environment. Concluding that the Soviet anthropophysiologists should take into account both the organizing and disrupting roles of the socioeconomic factor, Zalkind argued that the aim of a communist pedagogy should be the attainment of a stable system of reflexes. He wrote:

> The society divided into classes with its lack of organization in the current historical period . . . is to a large extent a pathological phenomenon and needs educational treatment . . . The principles of our pedagogy, namely the dialectic materialism, the revolutionary activism . . . and the proletarian collectivism, constitute a therapeutic approach to all the deficiencies of contemporary human psychophysiology [pp. 124–125].

Zalkind felt that it was necessary to replace the "class physiology" with a unitary physiology of all mankind. This could be accomplished only in a socialist state where there is a rational distribution of jobs.

The sociogenetic approach was opposed to reflexology and yet both shared the one-sided position regarding human psychology. Zalkind's contentions of a class physiology matched Bekhterev's reduction of all mental phenomena—including the psychology of groups—to physical laws such as the law of inertia. Both responded to the demands of their time and both inevitably came to be rejected later.

Kornilov's Reactology

The "reaction" theory proposed by Kornilov (1879–1957) in the 1920's was the first attempt in Soviet psychology to bring together the biological and social factors determining the human psyche. To be sure, the theories presented so far also attempted a synthesis. But in the other cases, one factor was given a strong preponderance over the others. Kornilov produced an essentially balanced, two-factor theory which might be regarded as the first draft of a Soviet psychology.

During his long career, he displayed the distinctive ability to adjust his thinking as the times changed. Originally a student of Chelpanov, after the revolution he became his fierce opponent. In 1921, he favored the separation of psychology from philosophy, but in January 1923, in his address to the First All-Union Congress of Psychoneurology, he was already speaking about the need to apply the Marxist philosophy to psychology. In 1921, he had defined psychical phenomena as purely physical energy. "Psychology is not more than a part of physics; what we label psychical processes are little more than a particular kind of physical energy" (p. 142). Yet in his 1923 address, he accepted Lenin's much quoted statement that the psyche is a property of the most highly organized form of matter, the brain. This was little more than the endorsement of an accepted formula, since Kornilov had apparently only a superficial knowledge of Marxist philosophy. But he did appear as a pioneer of Marxist psychology at a congress whose proceedings were reported in *Pravda* and *Izvestiya*. And by the end of 1923, he was appointed the director of the Institute of Psychology. The occasion marking Chelpanov's replacement —actually Chelpanov had been reappointed by the Soviet authorities in 1921 when the Institute was reorganized—was celebrated as a political event. "Starting from 1923, Soviet psychology freed itself from the influence of Chelpanov's empirical approach and adopted the methodology of dialectic materialism, deliberately facing the task of building a Marxist psychology" (Petrovskii, 1967, p. 59).

At the Second Congress of Psychoneurology, Kornilov (1924) enumerated, in a paper entitled "The Dialectic Method in Psychology," the following principles: continuous variability of nature, universal connections between phenomena, universal determinism, development by leaps with transitions from quantity to quality, and progressive development. The application of dialectical materialism to psychology became the major issue of Kornilov's following works (Kornilov, 1926, [9] 1927, 1928, 1929, 1930). He saw in his concept of reaction, *dialektizatsiya* of psychology: the subjective state is the thesis; the reflexes are the antithesis; and the reaction is the synthesis. The concept of reaction was said to differ from that of reflex in three respects: (a) it was universal, i.e., referred to all the response movements of the organism, including the unicellular; (b) it meant a reponse of the whole organism and not of a single organ; (c) it included the subjective side of a response. Kornilov (1930) wrote in an article appearing in Murchison's *Psychologies of 1930:*

Reactions are a *biosociological* conception, under which it is possible to group all the phenomena of the living organism, from the simplest to

[9] This was a polemical article in reply to Struminskii (1926), who disagreed with Kornilov's interpretation of Marxism in psychology.

the more complicated forms of human behavior in the conditions of social life. The reactions of man in connection with his social relations
acquire a social significance. In this we observe the main distinction
between psychology and physiology. The latter also studies the reactions
of man, but studies them without any reference to his social relations,
while in psychology these relations constitute the principal content of
the reactions studied. This is why we regard psychology as a social science rather than a branch of natural science [p. 268].

Thus, Kornilov defined behavior as an assembly—not an arithmetic sum—of reactions, a result of complex relations either of
cooperation or of conflict, of reciprocal inhibition between
reactions. Following the same line of reasoning, Kornilov
thought he had achieved a synthesis between the objective
and the subjective approaches in psychology. This was the
purpose of his 1925 *Manual of Psychology Presented from the
Point of View of the Dialectic Materialism,* apparently the first
textbook of Soviet psychology. As a matter of fact, his approach was an application of Hegel's triad, which was favored by
Soviet philosophers of that time. A. A. Smirnov (1960) admitted
that the study of reactions proposed by Kornilov was not new
at all, and that it could be traced back to the works of Wundt
and Titchener. He saw Kornilov's contribution to be the discovery of a relationship between the speed of reaction and the
nature of the task, as well as between its intensity and the
kind of activity performed by the subject. Using a self-
designed apparatus, the dynamometer, Kornilov combined
measures of reaction time with intensity of response. He
found that when subjects were given instructions to respond
in what for them would be the most convenient way, so-called
natural reactions, some of them tended to respond rapidly (a
reaction time of 130–170 msec.), while others gave slow reactions (a reaction time of 214–367 msec.). Some subjects had
a higher expenditure of energy, while others expended less.
There was no relationship between the latency and the intensity of the reactions. But when subjects were required to

respond with either an accelerated or a delayed reaction (e.g., they were asked to discriminate stimuli), inverse relations were induced between the latency and the intensity of the reactions. In the case of accelerated reactions, the expenditure of muscular energy was increased, while in the case of delayed reactions, the expenditure was reduced. Kornilov related the increase in reaction time to an interference with the central psychological link of the reaction. He interpreted these findings in terms of the psychodynamic principle of a monopolar expenditure of energy. In turn, this principle was derived from two general laws of neurophysiology: (1) the law of inhibition between centers in the brain and (2) the facilitation law.

Despite his ascribing a certain, albeit limited, role to consciousness, there was a singular lack of psychological terminology in Kornilov's works. For example, in his textbook there was no chapter devoted to sensations and perceptions. The physiological basis of sensations and the traditional experimental methods used for their study at the Moscow Institute of Psychology were discussed in the chapter, "The Nervous System; Reception Mechanisms." Feelings—which Bekhterev called "mimico-somatic" reflexes—were regarded as instinctive-emotional reactions, which indicated the satisfaction or lack of satisfaction of vital needs. Will, or voluntary activity, which was Kornilov's main concern before the revolution, was not mentioned at all. Kornilov spoke only about the "concluding stage of a reflex act."

In 1930 the First All-Union Conference for the Study of Man's Behavior took place. Although it supported the reaction theory, during the same year and in 1931, a critical discussion of reactology was initiated by the Communist Cell of the Moscow Institute of Psychology. The feeling was that this theory lagged behind the development of Marxist theory in the biological and social sciences. It was subsequently concluded that Kornilov was hostile to Marxist theory, that he was an agnostic who altered the Marxist-Leninist theory of reflection in the spirit of Kant's philosophy, that he was responsible for the divorce of psychology from practice, and that the journal which he edited, *Psikhologiya,* [10] did not differ from any bourgeois psychological publication (Kornilov, 1931; [11] Zalkind, 1931; Talankin, 1931; Conclusions, 1931). The resolution issued by the General Assembly of the Communist Cell stated that neither the concept of reflex nor that of reaction were acceptable for Marxist psychology because: they (a) are based on the "equilibrium" theory and disregard the process of "self-motion"; (b) approach behavior in an abstract way, i.e., do not regard man as the product of a historical development; (c) imply a reduction of the complex psychical processes to simple responses to stimulation.

The current evaluation of Kornilov's work is more objective (Ananev, 1960; Teplov, 1960; Samarin, 1962). Kornilov is appreciated as the first Soviet psychologist who realized that a scientific psychology has to be based on Marxist philosophy. He is credited with the selection of the basic propositions of Marxist philosophy relevant for psychology. It was he who first confronted the idealistic as well as the vulgar-materialistic tendencies in psychology. However, his theory of reactions is regarded as an eclectic combination of Marxist principles with "mechanical" and "energetical" propositions. His synthesis of objective and subjective psychology was superficial, based on a compromise between them and not on their analysis. Furthermore, it was remarked that the concept of reaction, like Bekhterev's concept of reflex, had too broad a meaning. Kornilov contended, for example, that both inorganic and organic worlds possess the property of reactivity. By the same token, the concept of reaction was applicable to biological as well as to social phenomena. Finally, it was objected that

[10] Kornilov edited *Psikhologiya* between 1928 and 1931, and Kolbanovskii, between 1931 and 1932 when its publication was discontinued. Between 1932 and 1955, when *Voprosy Psikhologii* (Questions of Psychology) began publication, there existed no psychological periodical.

[11] A reply to Talankin's criticism.

he did not realize the dialectical unity between the innate and the acquired features of behavior. He stated that man has as many instincts as animals do, but in the former they are latent, being masked by socially acquired reactions. The critic claimed that Kornilov failed to understand that the innate features of behavior do not merely coexist with the acquired features, but rather are transformed by them. In Kornilov's defense, it is said that at the end of the 1920's, Soviet psychologists were under the influence of Plekhanov, a leading Marxist theorist, who conceived of psyche and physiological phenomena as two sides of the same process. The concept of the psyche as a reflection of the external reality had not yet been well established in the Soviet ideology. In addition, it was conceded that the views of Deborin (1929), another Marxist theorist, which prevailed at the time of Kornilov's writings, were only later judged as representing a mechanistic deviation from dialectical materialism. Indeed, the decline of reactology was closely linked to the resolution of the Party Cell of the Institute for Red Professors in Philosophy and Natural Sciences, in December 1930 (Aus der Resolution, 1930; Mitin, 1931; Kolbanovskii, 1932; Talankin, 1932).

Kornilov was replaced by Kolbanovskii, a leading psychologist until his recent death in 1971. He belonged at that time to a group of young psychologists affiliated with the Moscow institute. But in 1939, Kornilov was reappointed director of the institute and when the RSFSR Academy of Pedagogical Sciences was founded in 1943, he became its vice-president, a position which he held until his death. Kornilov published a high school textbook in 1946 and coauthored with Smirnov and Teplov a textbook for pedagogical institutes the third edition of which appeared in 1948 and was the only manual to be used, officially, before a new manual was published in 1956.

Blonskii and Pedology

The study of mental development of the child was one of the major areas of Soviet psychology in the 1920's and the 1930's; it was largely in this field that the drive for a new psychology became manifest. In the 1920's, the biogenetic law according to which ontogeny recapitulates phylogeny was of central importance (Vygotskii, 1927). Even later, *Pod Znamenem Marksizma* published an article (Matveev, 1934) which stated that "the biogenetic law is still an important method for the study of the process of evolution" (p. 77). This concept implied that the child's mental growth is spontaneous and largely independent of education which could, at most, either accelerate or inhibit the manifestations of the innate qualities of the psyche. The study of the child was the domain of pedology, a vaguely defined field. [12] Blonskii described pedology as the study of growth, behavior and constitution of the child throughout his various stages. As a study of "age syndromes," it synthesized anatomical, physiological and psychological characteristics of the child. In Blonskii's view, pedagogy was the applied science which made use of the pedological findings. For example, the educator has to take into account certain atavistic traits of children. The relation of pedagogy to pedology was likened to that of gardening to botany, or cattle breeding to zoology.

Various positions existed within pedology regarding the relationships between the two determining factors of growth, the biological and the social. While some authors favored the biogenetic principle, this theory was opposed by members of the sociogenetic school. Along with Zalkind, Molozhavyi and Zaluzhnyi regarded the environment, and above all the social environment, as almost the sole determining factor of development. An adequate analysis of its structure was

---

[12] A journal entitled *Pedologiya* was published until 1932, edited by Zalkind.

regarded as sufficient for the understanding of man. "The child's environment," wrote Molozhavyi, "and first of all the industrial environment, determines all the processes and functions of adjustment. It is here where his constitution takes shape, once and for all, where the mechanisms of his behavior, the habits and the ways of acting are elaborated" (quoted by Petrovskii, 1967, pp. 233–234). He stated that any action, elementary or complex, performed by animals or man, can be explained as an endeavor to restore the disturbed equilibrium with the environment. Zaluzhnyi claimed simply that the laws of the behavior of a group of children are identical with the laws of sociology. Zalkind was among the outspoken critics of the biogenetic principle. He argued that it implied reverting to the distant past, while class education demanded an orientation toward the present. Whereas the pedagogical postulate of the biogenetic law specified "nonintervention" in the child's life, Zalkind stated that man actually frees himself increasingly from the direct influence of nature by becoming subject to the influence of the social milieu. In turn, he changes his milieu with its economic structure. Zalkind (1930) divided the child's biological endowment into three parts: old, preindustrial elements; new experiences, mainly acquired in the period of industrial development; and the most recent biological features which develop in the individual's life. He concluded that

> . . . due to the plasticity of his makeup, man's ability to be educated increases. For the Soviet Union, the cycle of biological and mental change is of primary importance. While the role of heredity cannot be denied, we are opposed to a fatalistic attitude. The cerebral cortex can be influenced by organizing the social environment. In a short time, man's energy can be directed in a new way which corresponds to the interest of the working class. Finally, the constitutional elements should not be used apolitically but in close coordination with the revolutionary purposes of our epoch" [p. 84].

Basov (1931) was another pedologist whose main contention was that while heredity and environment are the determining factors of human growth, their roles change from one stage of development to the other: when one phase is dominant, the other has a lesser impact. Since the influences of environment and of learning are consistent with the goals of education, the effects of enriching one's knowledge are potentially unlimited. Any limitations that may exist are of an external nature, i.e., in relation to the social environment. On the other hand, the innate factor is capable of little change. That is to say, the constitution of the individual allows for only small modifications.

Finally, Pinkevich's (1929) account of human development is worth quoting, since it is an instructive illustration of the pedological points of view.

> Human behavior . . . is fully determined by the environment, above all by the social environment. Instincts and unconditioned reflexes represent the first large group of more or less homogeneous phenomena, while the conditioned reflexes and, generally, the newly acquired reactions form the second group. Finally, to a third group belongs the behavior associated with thinking (consciousness) which is generally called intellect. The emotions, as a reaction of the second order, are present in all these groups. The second and the third groups are the most important ones regarding pedagogy. While the first group cannot be made use of directly, it forms the basis for all sorts of skills, abilities, habits, etc., via conditioned reflexes and associations. These processes are formed through practical education, socially organized activity, study or work. Some skills are acquired automatically, while others need intellectual effort. But the main conditions for the successful acquisition of skills are interest and satisfaction . . . The pedagogical task is to organize the development in such a way as to make upbringing and education, the formation of conditioned reflexes and associations, the child's volition and thinking gratifying and highly interesting [pp. 55–60].

The following is Pinkevich's formula of development: human development = C (constitution) × E (environment, social and physical); the pedagogical process = C × OE (organized environment); education = GT (genotype) + PT (phenotype) × OE; upbringing = (GT + PT) × OE (in particular social environment).

Blonskii (1884-1941) was the most prominent pedologist. Actually, the scope of his work went beyond the concern of pedology. He was a student of Chelpanov and, in terms of Soviet ideology, belonged to the idealistic camp before the revolution. His original interest was in philosophy and he was well enough acquainted with the philosophical schools of his time to have written a book discussing them. Blonskii shifted to specific studies in psychology only after 1930 when he joined the Moscow institute lead by Kornilov. In his last year of life, he headed the institute's laboratory of thought and speech.

The transition to Marxism was not without difficulty for Blonskii. A historian of Russian psychology (Petrovskii, 1967) wrote:

> The development of Blonskii's theories was complex and contradictory. But it was a natural expression of the ideological development of the bourgeois intelligentsia when it adopted the political stand of the proletariat . . . and contributed to the creation of the culture of the new society, gradually assimilating Marxism and freeing itself from the erroneous theoretical positions [p. 103].

The first signs of Blonskii's move toward Marxist philosophy were evident when he attempted to integrate the "philosophy of action" with Marx's economic and social theory, in *The Reform of Science* in 1920. But the turning point came the following year in his *Essay of Scientific Psychology*. Teplov (1947) recognized it as the first genuinely militant statement against idealistic psychology and the first real attempt to construct a new psychology on the principles of dialectical materialism. Blonskii demonstrated somewhat greater sophistication than Chelpanov, Kornilov and others who spoke of a social psychology, when he analyzed the effect on the individual of the various forms of social consciousness such as religion, science, art and ethics. In this work, Blonskii outlined his genetic-comparative approach to the study of psyche and proposed that man's behavior be viewed in the light of the interests of his social class. However, at this stage, he had not yet fully elaborated his developmental approach, nor could he say more than that:

> Up to the present we were biologists . . . in that we drew together human and animal behavior. This was a one-sided view. Now the field should be enlarged to include the sociological aspect as well. Mankind traveled a long way in its social development which unavoidably influenced its emotional and instinctive behavior. With the impact of social adjustment and of education, some basic instincts astrophied, others were stimulated, while still others were transformed [p. 103].

However, in his *Developmental Pedology* in 1930, Blonskii articulated a clear-cut biological position. At that time, he saw mental life as a successive series of stages from the lethargic, to the partially alert, to the fully alert. The evolution of animal behavior was naively presented as being dependent upon the gradual prevalence of wakefulness as we go up the evolutionary ladder. The prevalence of the intellectual over the emotional processes and the development of voluntary behavior were regarded as typical for the alert period. All the features of infantile behavior, "the age syndrome," were explained by the increase of the mass of the organism. Thus childhood was characterized as a period when $m(t-1) < mt$, where m = mass, the quantity of matter in the organism, t = time. In adulthood, m is constant, while in aging people $mt-1 > mt$. Blonskii divided the child's development into periods according to the growth of teeth (without teeth, with milk-teeth, with permanent teeth). In *Developmental Pedology* (1930) he wrote:

> The childhood of stable teeth may be considered as the age of civilization, when the child assimilates the contemporary technique. Civiliza-

tion is a too recent achievement of mankind to be transmitted by heredity. This is why learning plays a considerable role in the life of the stable-teeth child [Petrovskii, 1967, p. 188].

Discussions which took place in the early 1930's regarding the object of psychology (Vedenov, 1932), in particular Vygotskii's works, undoubtedly played a role in the development of Blonskii's thinking. Between 1935 and 1941, he wrote three books which marked a significant change in his genetic conception: *Memory and Thought* and *The Development of Thought in the School-child*, both in 1935, and *The Psychological Analysis of Remembering*, in 1940. The leitmotiv throughout his works was the development of the relationships among perception, memory and thinking. His purpose was to resolve the conflict between the theory of memory as a universal function of organized matter, and the theory of memory as a strictly human capacity. He conceived of memory as a biological phenomenon, a property of the brain, available at various levels of evolution. At the same time, however, memory was seen not only as a means of biological adaptation, but also as a tool for the transmission of acquired social experience. Thus, Blonskii turned to the study of the evolution of memory, in particular, its social roots. He regarded the four kinds of memory—motoric (the memory of habits), affective, pictorial and logical—as stages, or levels, of its phylo- and ontogenetic development. For instance, the affective memory is stable, possessing both biological and social attributes. Pictorial memory, such as visual imagery, is a primitive mnemonic process, appearing in drowsy states, etc. With the evolution of language, logical memory came into being, enabling the formation of connections between memory and thought. Verbal memory, Blonskii suggested, is a tool of logical memory, controlling the formation of associations. At the same time, it is an instrument of thought which is based on memory.

At this stage of his work, Blonskii had taken an avowedly dialectical position. He felt that the various theories of memory could be reduced to two divergent positions: (a) memory is a general function of the organized matter; (b) memory is a purely human function which is not even present in all humans. This antagonism, Blonskii concluded, was a result of the failure to take a dialectical approach to the different aspects of memory. The extent of Blonskii's change of mind becomes obvious when this analysis is compared with what he had to say about memory in 1927. In *Psychological Essays* he wrote:

> Very little is said about memory in my book. To me, the problem of memory can be reduced to the problem of reception of visual images (in this instance, we apparently have to accept Loeb's photographic theory . . .) and first of all, to the problem of occurrence and reinforcement of manifest and of latent verbal habits (I refer to Watson's *Psychology*). . . . That means that one has to distinguish between "memory of pictures" and "verbal memory." The problem of the "pictorial memory" consists of the history of the image: (1) image-copy; (2) consecutive image; (3) pictorial image . . . as well as of the problem whereby stimuli primordially reactivate the images. . . . The problem of "verbal memory" consists of the problem of latent verbal habits [p. 162].

But Blonskii's concern with the complex aspects of memory and thinking made him reluctant to accept the Pavlovian approach to these processes. Whereas in 1927 he wrote that the development of purposeful behavior represents, to a large extent, a chain of conditioned reflexes, by 1935 he admitted the validity of Pavlov's theory only for elementary processes.

Blonskii further concluded, on the basis of his experimental studies with young schoolchildren, that thought is not an a priori activity and cannot emerge from an empty intellect. He stressed the relationship between the child's thinking and his activity, and maintained that the development of the child's concepts is a direct reflection of the evolution of his activities of play and learning. His statement that the theory of behavior should be a theory of the history of behavior became the kernel of Vygotskii's cultural-historical conception. Vygotskii cited this statement and regarded it as a genuine dialectical position in psychology.

CRYSTALLIZATION OF SOVIET PSYCHOLOGY

The "battle for consciousness" in the 1930's marked a turning point in the history of Soviet psychology. The effort to define man primarily as a conscious and active being has given rise to basic postulates underlying current Soviet psychology. The development of these ideas was not unhampered, but they have survived the vicissitudes of politics and ideology, thereby forming what is essentially the nucleus of the contemporary Soviet approach to thought, language, memory and so forth. The work of two men, Vygotskii and Rubinshtein, played the most prominent role in this development of a Soviet psychology of consciousness.

Vygotskii's Cultural-Historical Theory

Unlike Kornilov and Blonskii, who were active before the revolution, Vygotskii (1896–1934) came in contact with psychology only in the *Sturm und Drang* years after the revolution. His first appearance as a psychologist was in 1924 at the Second Congress of Psychoneurology. In a paper appearing in a volume entitled *Psychology and Marxism*, edited by Kornilov in 1925, Vygotskii included as an epigraph a quotation from Marx (1897) the essence of which became the leitmotiv of his later work.

A bee in her construction of wax cells puts to shame some human architects. But even the worst architect differs from the best of the bees from the very outset because before constructing a cell from wax he has already constructed it in his head. In the end of the work process a result is achieved, which even before the start of this process existed as an idea, that is in the imagination of the worker [p. 198]. [13]

The paper made a strong plea for the study of consciousness in Soviet psychology:

> In that psychology ignores the problem of consciousness, it blocks itself off from access to the investigation of complicated problems of human behavior, and the elimination of consciousness from the sphere of scientific psychology has as its major consequence the retention of all the dualism and spiritualism of earlier subjective psychology [p. vi]. [14]

Vygotskii argued that relevant aspects of mental life, such as inner speech, had been ignored because of the avoidance of the study of consciousness. This, in turn, prevented an understanding of the essential differences between animal and man. Opposed to reflexology, he argued that man's behavior cannot be studied independently of his mind, and that to consider the psyche as an epiphenomenon results in a biological absurdity. Vygotskii also objected to the contention that human behavior is simply a sum of reflexes. "It is true," he wrote, "that the reflex is the foundation, but from it you can learn nothing about the building which will be constructed" (p. 181). While admitting that sensations, speech, instincts and emotions are reflexes, he nonetheless maintained that when the concept of reflex was given a universal meaning, it lost its psychological significance.

At this point, however, Vygotskii was still close to behaviorism (Shein, 1965). He regarded behavior as being composed of movements and reactions, with the most complex mental activities representing very fine movements. He rejected introspection as a legitimate psychological method, though he did concede that a subject's verbal report could be useful.

[13] Translated from German by Samuel Moore and Edward Aveling.
[14] This translated quotation is part of Bruner's introduction to the English translation of *Thought and Language*.

Mental processes are similar to all other human processes, he rationalized, and are therefore subject to the same laws. In Vygotskii's opinion, psychology could be described as a biosocial science: as a biological science, since behavior is one of the most important factors of adaptation; as a social science, since the social environment is the most relevant factor of human behavior.

Vygotskii was also close to the position of James when he stated that consciousness was a second experience, an experience of experience *(perezhivanie perezhivaniya)*. The conscious act consists of the transfer of a reflex from one system to another one. The experience *(perezhivanie)* of objects, which is a reflex, becomes the stimulus for a new reflex, for a secondary experience. In his later works, however, Vygotskii undertook a critical analysis of various trends in psychology, in particular of two tendencies, those referred to as "explanatory" and "descriptive." Explanatory psychology, which had as its model the natural sciences, tended toward physiology. It was not apt to tackle the problem of consciousness. The descriptive or comprehensive psychology aimed at an understanding of man's inner world but its methodology was idealistic and vitalistic. Although German Gestaltists, Wertheimer, Köhler and Koffka, attempted to surmount this dualism, their effort proved to be a failure and vitalistic as well as mechanistic elements were retained in their theories. Vygotskii concluded that the very foundation of psychology had to be rebuilt. Accordingly, he recommended that psychology apply itself to studying the meaningful and "systemic" structure of psychical activity, both in its formation and disintegration. In his view, consciousness, by which he meant precisely that system of relationships among the psychical functions, should be the major topic of Soviet psychology. Given the background of the conflict between the biological and the sociological approaches, as well as the history of the "two fronts" battle against idealism and mechanism, the plea for the study of consciousness was very significant.

Vygotskii extended his theory even further to incorporate Engels' concept of the role of labor in the evolution from monkey to man. Engels had assumed that the tools used by the primitive man led to the transformation of the animal mind into human consciousness, a proposition which Vygotskii developed in his theory of mediation. He assumed that in the same way that the implements created by the primitive man transformed the natural functioning of human organs, signs and symbols have been produced as artificial conditioned stimuli to enable the monitoring of behavior. The difference between implement and sign is one of orientation: while implements are oriented toward external objects, signs are directed toward man's actions themselves. In the same way that the use of a certain implement determines the character of an action with an object, the quality of a sign determines the character of the psychical function. The mastering of nature, i.e., the ability to change objects in accordance with man's needs, and the mastering of behavior are closely related.

Vygotskii saw the genesis of signs as a process of internalizing the means of social communication. He formulated a general genetic principle of cultural development according to which during the cultural development of the child, each function shows up twice: first, on the social level, then on the psychological level; first, as an interpsychical category in connection with the relations between people, then as an intrapsychical category. The development of each higher psychical function necessarily passes through an external stage since it originally has a social function. There are three phases of the process of internalization, as illustrated in the development of speech. In the first phase, words express the relation of the child to objects. In the next phase, the relation between word and thing is used by the adult as a means of communication with the child. In the final stage, words become intrinsically meaningful to the child.

Hence, words, as signs, are a sort of social tool which help man to control the "lower," "natural" mental functions.

These inferior functions develop into "cultural" functions due to the organizing role of the signs. Vygotskii saw therefore an essential difference between his own approach and Piaget's assumption that the development of the child's thought is a self-contained shift from egocentrism to a socialized attitude. Consistent with his goal of a materialistic and objective psychology, Vygotskii's theory of internalization meant that the source of man's consciousness is outside the individual himself and consists of the internalization of signs as a means of communication.

The concept of "sign" was assumed to provide a resolution of the social-biological dilemma. Signs enable man to master the lower, psychobiological functions and elevate them to the level of the cultural functions. Thus, the higher functions are the inferior functions plus their organization, or orientation. For instance, an intellectual reaction represents a *system* of habits; thought is representation plus will. In 1934 Vygotskii wrote:

> Concept formation is the result of a complex activity in which all the basic intellectual functions take part. The process cannot, however, be reduced to association, attention, imagery, inference, or determining tendencies. They are all indispensable, but they are insufficient without the use of the sign, or word, as the means by which we direct our mental operations, control their source, and channel them toward the solution of the problem confronting us [p. 58]. [15]

Vygotskii proposed the "experimental-genetical" method, which he also termed the "instrumental" method. Its aim was to discover how relationships developed among the constitutive elements of higher psychical functions. Vygotskii (1934) expressed the purpose of a developmental study as one which would be able

> . . . to fuse any congealed . . . psychological form, to transform it into a running stream of interchangeable moments. Briefly, the aim of such

[15] Translated by Eugenia Hanfmann and Gertrude Vakar.

an analysis is to study experimentally any higher form of behavior, not as a thing, but as a process . . . not from a whole thing to its parts, but from a process to its different moments [p. 132].

For Vygotskii, the study of the natural development of the child as a unitary process includes a study of his education. In his own words, ". . . the instrumental method is a manner of studying behavior and its development by discovering the psychological implements of the behavior and the *structure* of the instrumental acts produced by them" (pp. 230–231).

Three phases may be distinguished in the development of Vygotskii's theory of signs (Brushlinskii, 1966). In the first phase, he stressed the role of signs independently of their meaning, that is to say in a formal sense. Signs were said to change nothing in the object itself, but rather implied a sort of self-stimulation to direct one's behavior. His experimental studies on the formation of artificial concepts belonged to that phase. Vygotskii himself later realized that such studies could not shed light on the connection between stages of development.

In the second phase, Vygotskii was concerned with the meaning of signs, as illustrated by chapter 5 of *Thought and Language* (1934). In the final phase, Vygotskii deemphasized the concept of sign itself and, instead, placed the stress on the concept of meaning. Shif's (1935) study of the formation of concepts is representative of the new point of view and chapter 6 of Vygotskii's book illustrates this evolution.

Predictably, Vygotskii also tackled the complex problem of the relationship between development and learning. He disagreed both with Piaget's view that maturation is a prerequisite to learning, and with Koffka's proposition that development is independent of learning, but learning itself is identical with development, which he rejected as dualistic. In Vygotskii's view, although learning is the propelling force of development, the *forms* of learning are contingent upon the stages of development. The acquisition of knowledge has an impact on the structure of the psychical processes, resulting in new kinds of voluntary and conscious activity. Thus, the assimilation of mankind's experience, through learning, is a specifically human form of mental development.

Conceiving of the child's mental growth in this way, Vygotskii proposed as a method of investigation establishing "the zone of proximal development," that is, to determine how a child solves a problem independently, and how he solves it with the adult's help. The discrepancy between the results obtained in the two situations would indicate the diagnosis and the prognosis of the child's development. Luriya (1961) offered an instructive application of this method to the study of mentally retarded children.

In view of the complexity of Vygotskii's work, it is not surprising that its evaluation has been a subject of live controversy in Soviet psychology. From the perspective of a dogmatic Marxian approach, it was regarded as heresy in that Vygotskii did not merely reproduce what Marx and Engels had said, but rather elaborated upon a number of their views in a sophisticated psychological theory. Two years after its publication in 1934, *Thought and Language* was suppressed. [16] The work was said to be antimarxist; Vygotskii's theories were labeled "bourgeois" and lumped in the same category with those of Levy-Bruhl, Durkheim and others. However, Vygotskii's work has been subjected to a more searching criticism, in particular by Rubinshtein and by some of Vygotskii's own followers who have extended his arguments.

First, it was pointed out that Vygotskii assumed that the inferior processes are merely organized or structured by the higher "cultural" processes. Again, the uncritical acceptance of Hegel's triad accounted for this, since it implied the negation but not the annihilation of an inferior process. Furthermore, it was not even clear what Vygotskii meant by "inferior"; the

[16] A collection of Vygotskii's works was first published in 1956 with an instructive introduction by Leontev and Luriya. A second volume was published in 1960.

term could also imply physiological processes. It was further objected—this was strongly emphasized by Rubinshtein—that Vygotskii conceived of the social factor as an interaction between the adult and the child. Consciousness appeared then to be a direct expression of the individual's inner experiences, and not to be contingent upon "material practice," i.e., on the objects of people's actions. This was said to leave the door open for idealism, since the source of the development of the psyche was seen to reside in the interaction of subject and subject, rather than in the interaction of subject and object. The evolution of Vygotskii's theory on the nature of signs was related to this argument, but on this point his concepts remained essentially unchanged.

Finally, Vygotskii's notion about the relation between concepts and words caused Rubinshtein (1946) to remark that in Vygotskii's theory the role of speech was elevated to that of creator of thought. What Vygotskii understood to be a means for the expression of thought, actually turned out to be regarded as its ultimate cause. Not merely a theoretical position, this conception led to a certain methodology. Thus Vygotskii conducted experiments to discover the gradual acquisition of the intellectual functions, in particular the role of speech, as well as other signs. "Thought," wrote Rubinshtein (1946), "appeared not so much as a reflection of the objective world in unity with speech on the basis of social practice, but rather as a derivative function of verbal signs" (p. 339).

Leontev, a close collaborator of Vygotskii, has contributed much to the development of his teacher's theory with respect to the points mentioned above. In one of his early works, done in 1931, he followed Vygotskii's thinking very closely. Leontev assumed that memory, like any other mental process, undergoes a twofold development, biological and cultural. As a consequence, two forms of memory have developed: (1) an inferior, natural, nonmediated and involuntary memory, and (2) a superior, voluntary memory. Leontev's experimental studies were designed to test this assumption, using Vygotskii's method of double stimulation.

Subjects were presented with two kinds of stimuli: objects to be memorized and mnemonic devices. In one experiment, the subjects had to memorize 15 names of objects, while in another experiment, they were also requested to choose from a number of pictures those which represented the named objects. The pictures were said to serve as a means of memorization. There were three groups of subjects: nursery school children, students of the 5th and 6th grade, and adults. The young children were found unable to take advantage of the mnemonic devices, for the extent of memorization on the two experiments was the same. The performance of the school-children was considerably improved in the second experiment. But in the adults, there was again no significant difference between the two experiments.

Leontev concluded that the nursery school children were unable to make use of the external means and were unable to draw upon previous inner experiences for the purpose of remembering. The different results obtained by the students were explained as reflecting a transition from "externally oriented" to "internally oriented" memorization. The result obtained in the adult group was interpreted as evidence that at this stage the role of external means takes the form of words so that there is no difference between the presence or absence of mnemonic means. A later critic (Zinchenko, 1961) has pointed out that this interpretation actually implied a refutation of the basic view held by Vygotskii and Leontev themselves that inferior and higher forms of memory should be regarded as a single entity. The development of memory was now simply reduced to an appropriate assimilation of various mnemonic devices. Furthermore, the process of mediation appeared to be directly dependent upon the understanding of the meaning of words. Hence, memory was in fact regarded as a mere aspect of thought. It was also totally included in the realm of consciousness. The possibility of an idealistic approach to logical memory was not ruled out, since the latter, in fact, was separated from both associative and physiological memory.

A. N. Leontev's (1940) doctoral dissertation on the development of the psyche, a monograph in 1947 on the same topic, as well as an article in 1945 on the child's mental growth marked a significant development of his thought. His major thesis was that psychical processes represent a particular form of activity and derive from people's concern with external objects. Psyche is a result of the transformation of the external, material activity, into an internal activity during the course of man's historical development. In this, Leontev, while following Vygotskii's thinking, was at variance with his teacher's approach—which was regarded as intellectualistic—when he postulated that the child's meaningful activity was determined by the level of his mental growth and not by the interaction between his consciousness and that of the adult. Leontev also disagreed with Vygotskii's view of the role played by the development of concepts for the child's mental growth.

Leontev felt that Soviet psychology had two major tasks. The first, to define the structure of man's activity through an analysis of the relationships between activity as a whole, actions and operations. The structure of the internal, psychical activity was assumed to be essentially the same as that of the external activity. The second task should be to clarify the concept of meaning. This was seen as a prerequisite to the full understanding of consciousness as a reflection of external reality. For Leontev, the critical issue was the relationship between meaning and significance. Meaning was seen as a generalized reflection of objective reality in human consciousness, as elaborated by mankind and consolidated in concepts and abilities. As such, it is independent of the individual's attitude towards the external world. Significance was defined as the reflection of the relation between the motive of the individual's activity and its object, or its representation in the individual's mind. Accordingly, Leontev speculated about the history of human consciousness in terms of the structure of people's activity which, in turn, was seen as an expression of the changing structure of the society. Thus, in the primitive society, which was not divided into social classes, meaning and significance coincided, this constituting the main feature of primitive consciousness. Meaning and significance became separated with the disintegration of the homogeneous primitive society and the occurrence of social classes. This separation was caused by the alienation of the product of labor from the labor itself as performed by one segment of the society, namely, the slaves. In the subsequent class societies this separation was perpetuated, but in the socialist society the meaning and the significance of things were expected to be again welded together. That is, the objective result of an activity would coincide with its subjective significance. With this line of reasoning, Leontev approached the child's mental development in terms of the evolution of his activity. The three successive types of dominant activity—play, learning and work —represent essentially different kinds of relationships to the external world. They are manifestations of different structures of psychical activity. One may obtain a deeper insight into the processes of perception, thought and volition, if they are approached from the perspective of the child's dominant type of activity.

Rubinshtein's Theory of Consciousness

A strong plea for Soviet psychology to become a psychology of consciousness was also made by Rubinshtein (1889-1960). A student of philosophy in Germany and acquainted with Hegel's system (1914), Rubinshtein applied this knowledge in his endeavor to provide the foundation for Soviet psychology in the 1930's. Thus, only in the last years of his life was he particularly concerned with experimental studies (1958, 1960a).

Rubinshtein's first significant publication for Soviet psychology was a paper, in 1934, which dealt with psychological issues in the works of Marx. As Leontev (1959b) noted, it did not receive the attention it deserved. In 1935, he published *Foundations of Psychology.* This was a major work in which Rubinshtein advanced the thesis of a close relationship between consciousness and activity. However, it would appear that his formulations were not entirely clear and, in particular, his proposition that consciousness is manifest only in activity was not readily understood (Leontev, 1959b). In a revised and expanded volume, *Fundamentals of General Psychology,* Rubinshtein (1946), formulated three tasks for Soviet psychology. First, it had to overcome fatalistic views regarding the development of personality and of consciousness. In supporting this position, Rubinshtein made use of much biological material, including some of Severtsov's findings, with which he formulated the dialectic of child development: the child develops *through* education and learning. The second task was to discover the relation between the external reality and consciousness. This meant overcoming the view that consciousness is passive, a prominent feature of traditional psychology. Rubinshtein's (1946) position became a classic for Soviet psychology:

> All psychical processes . . . exist as facets, as moments of play, learning, work etc., that is, of one of the forms of activity. They exist only in the interconnections, interpenetration of all sides of consciousness within a concrete activity, are formed in the realm of an activity and are determined by it. . . . The Marxist-Leninist thesis about the unity of psyche and activity . . . makes possible the discovery of the real causes of the facts and processes studied by psychology [p. 109].

The third task was to overcome abstract functionalism.

Rubinshtein's textbook was subjected to wide-ranging discussion[17] and in 1941 was awarded a Stalin prize. However,

[17] It was discussed at the All-Unional Conference for Pedagogical Sciences—the largest gathering of psychologists and educators at that time—as well as at the psychology department of the "Gertsen" Pedagogical Institute in Leningrad.

it was criticized for having failed to fulfill its "supertask," namely, to build a system of Marxist psychology. As a matter of fact, it had also been the intention of Rubinshtein to lay the foundations for the psychological theory of Soviet pedagogy. In 1943, he made a further step in developing his views and formulated the following theoretical principles of Soviet psychology. (1) The principle of psychophysical unity: mind is not only a function of matter, but also a reflection of the external, material reality. (2) The principle of dialectic development of psyche. Human psyche is a product of an historical evolution and has a capacity for change. Psychical functions and functions of the brain exist in a complex unity with reciprocal interaction. Thought and behavior are also in unity with interaction. Behavior is primarily conditioned by the economic structure and relationships of production. (3) The historicalism principle: psychology is not only a biological, but also a social-historical science. The laws of human psychology are capable of change and socialist man is different from capitalist man. There are no universal laws of human psychology. (4) The principle of unity of theory and practice. (5) The principle of unity of consciousness and activity. The content of thought derives from man's experience. Consciousness is a human attribute which develops as a result of learning and experience. Rubinshtein (1943) believed that these principles already underlay Soviet psychology. He concluded confidently:

> The fundamental task was that of translating the general methodological theses into the concrete substance of a psychological theory. This task has essentially been fulfilled. As a result of the theoretical and experimental work of the last years, the basic features of the system of Soviet psychology have already been formulated [p. 47].

The second edition of the *Fundamentals of General Psychology* (1946) again gave rise to considerable discussion. As a matter of fact, this is quite understandable, since—to the writer's knowledge—it remains the only extensive Soviet textbook of psychology and is unmatched by any of the university textbooks, prepared for the pedagogical institutes. In 1948, both Leontev's and, in particular, Rubinshtein's views were subjected to sharp criticism. This followed the suppression in 1947, of Aleksandrov's *History of Western European Philosophy* (1946), an event marking the start of the "anticosmopolitic" campaign, and the controversy in biology, in 1948, which resulted in the condemnation of the Weissman-Morgan school of genetics and the "victory" of Lysenko's views. These events were reflected in the criticism of Rubinshtein and Leontev. Thus, a critic (Chernakov, 1948) [18] alluded to Rubinshtein's reference to the work of Shmalkhausen, an opponent of Lysenko:

> This courtesy towards the man who only recently was the leader of the Weismann-Morgan trend in our biology is no accident on the part of S. L. Rubinshtein. It is no accident that S. L. Rubinshtein in discussing problems of heredity in his book does not criticize the reactionary theory of the Weismann-Morganists, and that he does not, moreover, try to divorce himself from it. In Prof. Rubinshtein's book, as in Shmalhausen's book, we find the same kind of verbal declarations of devotion to dialectical materialism, but in reality we observe a compromise with reactionary and idealist theories [p. 263].

Another critic (Kolbanovskii, 1948) merely reproduced Zhdanov's (1947) [19] criticism of Aleksandrov for not having presented the history of philosophy as the history of the struggle between materialism and idealism, but instead taking an "objectivist" position. In reference to Rubinshtein, it thus could be said:

> The author does not criticize the psychological conceptions of various philosophers and psychologists but merely records their theories. . . . Rubinshtein mentions only in a very general way the struggle between materialism and idealism. He does not criticize the reactionary concep-

---

[18] Translated in: Wortis, J. (1950), *Soviet Psychiatry.*
[19] Zhdanov was a member of the Politburo and was responsible for propaganda.

tions of the modern bourgeois psychologists . . . His work lacks that definite partisanship with which Marxists must approach the heritage of the past and the analysis of the theories produced by the ideologists of the modern bourgeoisie [p. 287]. [20]

Nor did Leontev escape criticism for having taken an apolitical and objectivist approach (Maslina, 1948). Some of his positions were accepted. The critics agreed with his view that each historical period creates its specific form of consciousness, that psychology must study concrete man, in particular socialist man, and that the consciousness of people reflects the character of their activity. But Leontev was said to be inconsistent, to have oversimplified some issues, and to have used vague language. Thus, in analyzing the role of work in the formation of the human psyche, he overestimated the role of the technical division of labor. His view of the objectivity of meaning confused the issue of the class character of the worker's consciousness. Finally, Leontev's description of Soviet man was said to be poor, failing to emphasize his high moral qualities.

Several more specific objections were raised regarding Rubinshtein's work. First, it was argued that implicit in the distinction which he made between two aspects of consciousness, namely, knowledge and experience, or the immediately given, was the claim that only knowledge is a reflection of outside reality. This appeared to ignore the objective source of subjective experiences. Furthermore, the distinction between consciousness in the psychological sense and consciousness in the philosophical sense was said to mean the denial of the social nature of consciousness, the exclusion of the problem of individual and social consciousness from psychology, and the denial of the role of class ideology in the formation of individual consciousness.

Rubinshtein was also charged with actually accepting Freu-

[20] In Wortis, J. (1950), *Soviet Psychiatry.*

dian theory under the guise of criticizing it. It was charged that although correct in his opposition to an abstract intellectualism, he was led subsequently to the erroneous position that one had to distinguish between the psychological and ideological meaning of consciousness. This view was said to be close to those of Freud, Lewin, and other "reactionary" psychologists. Rubinshtein was accused of having failed to realize that the organic reactions resulting from the external manifestations of emotions, are a result of the individual's awareness of external conditions. His distinction between the nature of perception and feeling brought him close to Chelpanov. The critics also referred to Rubinshtein's conception of will as it related to drives. Excerpts from his work and from Freud's writings were compared to show that, despite Rubinshtein's rejection of Freud's pansexualism, he did accept the underlying premises of psychoanalysis.

Soviet Psychology after 1936

Soviet psychologists and "Sovietologists" agree that the resolution taken on July 4, 1936, by the Central Committee of the Communist Party "on pedological distortions in the commissariats of education" marked a turning point in the history of Soviet psychology and pedagogy. But this is the extent of their agreement. While the Soviets have emphasized the positive results of the resolution—along with the acknowledgment in recent years of its dogmatism—Western students of the history of Soviet psychology recorded it as decidedly a negative event.

The resolution mentioned that the responsibility given to pedologists to set up classes and to arrange the school program while representing an organization separate from the teachers was harmful. The pedologists were out of touch with the social reality, ignored the political goals of the school, relied on pseudoscientific experiments, and decided arbitrarily the future of many students with negative consequences not only for them but for their families and environment as well. The establishment of a broad network of "special" schools was regarded as a deleterious result of the pedological practice.

At this point it should be mentioned that the early 1930's saw the extensive development of psychological testing for assessing the intellectual level of students, as well as for professional career orientation and personnel selection. Numerous tests, many of which were constructed by Russian psychologists, for the child's mental and intellectual development, "constitutional" tests, tests for professional suitability, etc., were widely used. *Psikhofiziologiya Truda i Psikhotekhnika* [21] (Psychophysiology of Work and Psychotechnique) published many articles on testing. However, the theory and practice of testing was a subject of controversy. Blonskii, Rossolimo (1922), the author of a well-known personality "profile," and many others favored testing, but Bassov, Zalkind, Molozhavyi and, in particular, Krupskaya, Lenin's wife, who was very active in the field of education, opposed it. In April 1927, The First Pedological Conference identified the role of testing, and a month later the association of Moscow testologists was founded. But a conference on the evaluation of the progress of students in school, organized the same year by the Commissariat of Education, concluded that the use of tests was inappropriate in the general school setting and that they should be used strictly for research purposes in a few selected schools. Kornilov (1928) expressed adequately the conflict between the two positions when he wrote:

> The method of testing is a double-edged sword: if it is well founded, it can be very valuable; conversely, when it is lacking a solid preliminary foundation, the method of testing becomes a pseudo-scientific game of chance which quite often can produce considerable damage since on the basis of tests results, the life of an adult as well as of a child is frequently changed and sometimes simply spoiled [p. 27].

[21] This periodical was published until 1934 and since 1932 was named *Sovetskaya Psikhotekhnika.*

Other writers were also critical of the testing method and regarded it as an influence of "bourgeois" psychology which was in "crisis" (Strakhov, 1930; Vedenov, 1932; Luriya, 1932; Rudik, 1932). Justifying the 1936 resolution, Petrovskii (1967) wrote:

> Whatever the critical remarks of the tests were, unfortunately they failed to be a sufficient obstacle to the wide penetration in practice of ill-founded tests at the beginning of the 1930's. The tests produced considerable damage to Soviet schools and their harmful influence was felt in several areas of the socialist construction. All this justified the stern evaluation of the irresponsible use of tests in pedology by the Central Committee of the Party [p. 160].

Another important part of Soviet psychology before 1936 was the psychology of work or psychotechnique. There was much interest in the rational organization of work, urged by Lenin himself. Obviously, he regarded Taylor's system as designed to increase worker exploitation, but he acknowledged its scientific aspect. The first conference on the scientific organization of work, presided over by Bekhterev, took place in 1921. In 1927, the All-Union Society for Psychotechnique and Applied Psychophysiology was founded, with its own journal. A Central Institute was founded, as well as several psychotechnical institutes in Leningrad, Kharkov, Tiflis and other cities. A large number of studies were conducted concerning professional orientation and selection in industry, transportation, army and school, the causes of accidents in factories, the factors of fatigue, etc. The works of Shpilrein (1923a,b, 1928, 1930a,b, 1931a,b,c) and Gellershtein (1930a,b) were fairly well-known outside the Soviet Union as a result of presentations at international congresses. By the end of the decade, large numbers of persons were being tested and, according to Petrovskii, about 1,000,000 were tested in the single year of 1931.

However, by the beginning of the 1930's a conflict had arisen between Russian students of the psychology of work and Soviet ideology, apparently as a result of an antagonism between professional selection and political aspects of the drive for industrialization. It was charged that the work-psychologists considered themselves "technical" experts and, thereby, remote from any theoretical polemics. Shpilrein, in particular, was said to have failed to take a critical stand against Stern's personalistic theory, which he regarded as a reaction to Wundt's ignorance of the problem of individual differences. In 1931, a year marked by polemics all along the ideological front, Shpilrein retreated from his earlier position and acknowledged his mistakes. Again, this was a case of self-criticism where it is hard to distinguish between a real change of mind and compliance with authoritarian requirements. Here is Petrovskii's (1967) reaction to a statement by Bauer:

> In vain speaks Bauer . . . ironically about the fact that Shpilrein was as if forced to repudiate his teacher and to paste on him the tag of an idealist. Shpilrein's rejection of his personalistic mistakes was a natural rejection by a communist of his idealistic mistakes which he has become aware of. Shpilrein's criticism of Stern was not the pasting of a tag, but a consistent and conclusive analysis of Stern's mistakes [p. 276].

The 1936 resolution regarded the static approach of pedology and its law of the dependence of child development on heredity and social factors, the so-called two-factor theory, as anti-Marxist. Pedology uncritically accepted principles of its bourgeois counterpart aimed at the preservation of the ruling class. It was decided that the teaching of pedology be abolished, pedological practice in schools be ended, and all books on pedology be sharply criticized.

The interpretation of this document went far beyond its ostensible concern. Within a few months, the general assembly of the Moscow Psychological Association had issued a resolution of its own, based on the resolution of the Central Committee of the Communist Party. It stated (according to Petrovskii, 1967):

We must put an end to the attempts to build a Soviet psychology through declarations and references to the principles of Marxism-Leninism. The Association considers it necessary to implement the principles of Marxism-Leninism in psychology in specific investigations. . . . The Assembly considers the most important task to study intensively, both theoretically and experimentally, a series of basic problems. Among them are: (a) a Marxist history of psychology and a theoretical analysis of the contemporary theories in psychology; (b) a concrete study of the material basis of the psyche in relation with the current theory of the structure, functions and pathology of the brain; (c) the study of the child's mental development in relation to learning; (d) the study of personality and the theory of psychical functions; (e) the problem of individual differences. . . . The Assembly ascribes an exceptional significance to the indication given by the Central Committee of the Communist Party regarding the creation of a Marxist science of children and considers the most important task of psychologists the theoretical elaboration and the specific investigation of the problems related to upbringing and education. This work has to be carried out in close contact with the pedagogists. The Assembly considers it necessary to study the psychology of work [p. 294].

The resolution on pedology inhibited the development of those areas of study to which it referred. Important works on child psychology, including those of Blonskii and Vygotskii were suppressed. Between 1936 and the 1950's, there was no Soviet psychology of work (or by its modern name, industrial psychology). The activity of all the psychotechnical laboratories was ended. [22] An authoritarian atmosphere prevailed in every sphere of study which dealt with the heredity-environment problem (Mitin, 1939; Conference, 1939). It became even less tolerant after the imposition of Lysenko's line in biology in 1948. Kostyuk (1949), a Ukrainian psychologist concerned with pedagogical problems, made explicit the official view.

Kostyuk noted two opposing theories regarding the applica-

[22] In this context, the following recent statement by Lomov (1971) has a particular significance. In an article discussing the meaning of the decisions of the 24th Congress of the Communist Party of the USSR for psychology, he wrote: "It is reasonable to assume that before long, in many practical areas of the construction of communism there will be created positions for psychologists" (p. 11).

tion of Michiurin-Lysenko's principles to man. While some claimed that this did not bear any relationship to the problem of the role of heredity for human development, others were in favor of its direct application to pedagogy. Neither approach, in Kostyuk's view, is acceptable. The essential difference between animal and man is that man has a need to forge the means of his existence himself. In this historical process, men changed their environment and, at the same time, transformed their own nature. These changes were transmitted, not only as a result of biological evolution, but also during the course of historical development. This position, Kostyuk argued, is fully in agreement with Michiurin who regarded heredity as a product of development. Lysenko's emphasis on the physiological nature of heredity is also applicable to man since, despite its complexity, the mechanisms of human heredity are only physiological. To speak of psychological heredity would be Lamarckism or, more precisely, psychoneo-Lamarckism, and would be a deviation from dialectical materialism. This had been the theoretical basis of pedology, despite the obvious fact that children's habits, interests, and the like are not of a hereditary nature. The remnants of capitalism in the child's mind cannot be accounted for by heredity but stem rather from the consciousness of the adult who influences the child's consciousness. Concepts and sensations are not inherited; man inherits only anatomical and physiological characteristics, as well as the primary and secondary needs which have evolved in the course of history. Such individual features are only the seeds for subsequent development of a specific personality. Thus, for instance, while hereditary properties do play some role in the formation of certain features of the personality, the effect of social relations is the primary element of this process. Moreover, during the course of history, heredity was modified with the occurrence of new natural possibilities. The extent to which the natural possibilities were developed depended upon the historical epoch and upon the nature of relationships between people. The child's development depends on the inner struggle between the level of development already attained, and the new demands made by society in general, particularly by the process of education. Mental growth consists in meeting these demands, in raising the intellectual processes and the abilities to the level of the new tasks, in developing new dimensions of consciousness and self-consciousness, in the rejection of old features of the psychical life. It is instructive to compare Kostyuk's argument in 1949, with his position in 1969. In his recent articles on the same topic, he heavily relied on Leontev's work.

However, while the framework of studies in those areas related to the child's development was quite rigidly shaped, several other fields of study were able to develop in the 1930's and the 1940's, rather free of interference. Thus, for instance Teplov (1896–1965) initiated during this time his extensive studies on the development of abilities and of individual differences. Usnadze (1886–1950) advanced the concept of "set," currently developed by his Georgian followers. The works of Orbeli (1945, 1962), Bernshtein (1947), Anokhin (1949b) and Beritov (1947), in particular, opened new paths in neurophysiology. In these studies, there was an obvious departure from the earlier attempts of Bekhterev and Pavlov to substitute psychological concepts with a physiological terminology. Conversely, the investigation of the complex forms of animal behavior led to the acceptance of psychological notions. Furthermore, while Pavlov's approach was basically analytic, these scholars have been more in favor of a synthetic conception of the functioning of the central nervous system.

Hence, during this period, unrestricted "deviations" from Pavlov's theory were possible despite the high official sanction it received. In June 1950, the Joint Session of the Academy of Sciences of the USSR and of the Academy of Medical Sciences of the USSR Dedicated to the Development of I. P. Pavlov's Teaching, put an end to this situation. Its purpose was explicitly stated as that of undertaking a critical and self-critical examination of how matters stand with regard to the development of Pavlov's legacy in the Soviet Union. In two major addresses delivered to the session, large portions of which appeared in *Pravda,* a critical survey was made of the state of Pavlov's teaching in the biological and medical sciences, including psychology. The speakers, Bykov and Ivanov-Smolenskii, referred to a pre-Pavlovian era and a Pavlovian era. Pavlov's theory was to become the only scientific approach. The aim of the session was to stamp out any Western influence in the concerned areas. Thus it was an expression of the anticosmopolitic campaign. As a matter of fact, it appears that the conference had been inspired by Stalin himself (Tucker, 1963). Along with Stalin's (1950) work on Marxism and linguistics, published at the same time, the conference constituted part of the drive to create a pure Soviet Marxist science. Two years later, Stalin (1952) published another work, this time about Marxism and the economic problems of socialism, which contained some new formulations for the Soviet ideology. In the current jargon, this literature was an expression of the "personality cult." The Pavlovian session was the final time in the history of Soviet psychology that an event with clear political implications, such as an editorial in a political journal, or a resolution of a political organization changed the course of its development.

2

The Nature of Psyche

Following the 1950 Pavlovian Conference, much effort was devoted to formulating the subject matter of psychology which involved a definition of the nature of psyche, to be consonant with the dialectical materialism and with Pavlovian principles. The editorial introduction to the two-volume work, *Psychological Science in the USSR*, published in 1959–1960, stated:

> The natural-scientific approach consists of the reflex theory of the psyche propounded by Sechenov and developed by Pavlov. Soviet psychologists see psyche as the functioning of the brain, as a property of the most highly organized matter, capable of reflecting reality [p. 4].

As in the early years after the revolution, and again following the 1936 resolution, there was a strong demand for reassessment in Soviet psychology. Psychologists whose views had been previously criticized also took part in this campaign. [1] Thus Leontev stated in 1952 that

[1] Aleksandrov, whose *History of Western European Philosophy* was a target of Zhdanov's anticosmopolitic attack in 1947, was in 1950 an outspoken critic of the "deviations" from Pavlov's teaching. Later, he was said to have levelled unfounded criticism against Orbeli, Bernshtein, Anokhin and others (Mitin, 1963).

. . . the concepts and methods of the subjective psychology are inconsistent with the strictly scientific concepts and objective methods of the Pavlovian physiology of the higher nervous activity [p. 55].

He argued that the way mental processes like perception, memory, etc., were discussed in Soviet texts differed little from their Western counterparts, that is the terms used were those of subjective psychology. A textbook by Kornilov (1946) read:

> The peculiar feature of human psyche consists in man's ability to perceive his own experience. . . . People can only guess the experience of others, but only the individual himself can recognize and "subjectively" understand his own feelings, thoughts and wishes. However, these experiences cannot be seen as being manifested only subjectively; they are also always combined with physical and physiological processes taking place simultaneously in the organism [p. 114].

Such was the practice of textbooks during this period. Each chapter on a specific mental process concluded with a paragraph about the underlying "physiological basis," which was usually a restatement of a Pavlovian concept with little variation from one chapter to the next. Rubinshtein wrote in 1955:

> The reconstruction of Soviet psychology along Pavlovian lines requires the resolute rejection of idealistic concepts which still exist in psychology and the creative elaboration of a new psychological theory in keeping with the spirit of Marxism-Leninism and Pavlov's teaching. . . . Soviet psychologists have not yet assimilated the spirit of creative Marxism and failed to work out a genuine Marxist-Leninist psychology. The influence of idealistic psychology . . . has not been surmounted and psychology has not become an efficient science contributing its share to the building of communism [pp. 194–197].

Clearly, his prediction, expressed in 1943, that a new Soviet psychology was just around the corner, had yet to be realized in terms of Soviet ideology.

Authoritative publications expressed the belief that insofar as Russian psychologists possessed the basic prerequisites for developing a genuine Soviet psychology, namely the teachings of the "classics of Marxism" and the work of Pavlov, they were to be held responsible for their failure to substantiate these propositions in specific concepts. In 1954, *Voprosy Filosofii,* the publication of the Institute of Philosophy of the USSR Academy of Sciences, ran an editorial which concluded a lengthy debate on the philosophical problems of psychology by stating:

> Regardless of their joint efforts to take dialectical materialism as a guide in their study of psychical phenomena, psychologists so far have failed to achieve the creative application of Marxist philosophy and thus put an end to the backwardness of psychology [p. 182].

Although Soviet psychologists had essentially accepted Lenin's proposition that the psyche is a reflection of external reality, they, naturally, disagreed when it came to elaborating specific definitions. During the early 1950's, the debate generally focused on varying interpretations of Marxist and Pavlovian propositions. At times, the same statements by Engels or Lenin were used in the argument (Arkhipov, 1954; Mikhailov, 1954; Namitokov, 1955; Vatsuro, 1951; Blagonadezhina, 1952; Zankov, 1951b; Boiko, 1952; Avramenko, 1954; Khromov, 1952; Mansurov, 1952, 1955; Editorial, 1955).

The quality of the discussion has remarkably improved in recent years. Instead of mere exegesis of what Lenin or Pavlov said, there is now a search for factual evidence in support of specific propositions. This was obvious at a number of conferences organized to discuss philosophical problems related to contemporary natural sciences (Kolbanovskii et al., 1964; Konstantinov et al., 1966a). Soviet writers themselves have admitted the futility of their earlier polemics (Ponomarev, 1960). Whether or not there exists a unitary Soviet conception of mind as a reflection of reality and as a reflex activity remains an important question. It is safe to state that beyond certain significant differences among authors there is a sharing of basic ideas which makes Soviet psychology a distinctive school with a unique approach to the problem of mind.

THE CONCEPT OF REFLECTION

Lenin's (1908) proposition that ". . . it is logical to assume that the whole of matter possesses a property essentially similar to sensation, namely the property of reflection" (pp. 80–81), is basic to Soviet psychology. Quoted countless times, this statement has initiated endless polemics. The following passage from a major textbook (Kovalev et al., 1966) [2] expresses the view of psyche which is generally held.

> Human psyche is a property of highly organized matter and is the result of a very long development. The origin and development of psyche is linked to the origin and development of the organic nature. Psyche develops from elementary, primitive forms to complex phenomena of logical thought and consciousness in man. The formation of psyche in both phylogenesis and ontogenesis is a process of qualitative transformation: the occurrence and development of new, ever more improved forms of reflection of the world, organically connected with the development of the nervous system. This is a law-governed process in which each stage prepares the next one. Psyche gets an ever-growing role of *control* of the behavior and vital activity of animals and, particularly, of man. . . . It would be wrong to think that sensation appears "from nothing." Certainly, the appearance of sensation was possible only because the inorganic nature has properties similar to those of animated matter. . . . One of the joint properties of inorganic and organic matter is the property of reflection. *Reflection is the property of matter to change as it is affected by external influences.* Each form of motion of matter—mechanical, physical, chemical, biological— has its specific form of reflection. . . . The development of excitability in the process of evolution led to the occurrence of a new form of reflection—the *sensation* which is already an elementary form of psyche [pp. 64-67].

Soviet authors concerned about philosophical problems in

---

[2] This work will be referred to hereinafter as "the 1966 textbook."

the natural sciences have given much thought to the evolution of reflection (Kedrov, 1959, 1963, 1964a,b, 1965; Ponomarev, 1967; Korshunov, 1969). This has been linked closely to an analysis of the forms of interaction between material bodies. The characteristic feature of the most elementary form of reflection is said to consist of the mechanical effect of the action of one object upon another—changes of mass, force, inertia etc. The interacting bodies reflect each other in an amorphous, undifferentiated form equal to the product of mass and acceleration. Thus the same change can be brought about in an object by the action of different masses as long as the product of mass and acceleration remains the same. Mechanical reflection is also incidental and episodic, being limited to the moment of interaction. Finally, it is a diffuse reflection, since the effect of interaction is global and not expressed in specific changes.

In the case of physical reflection, the objects interact not only as wholes, but also as assemblies of molecules. This means that the external actions are fragmented so that a differentiated reflection is already possible which in turn yields specific, localized changes. Furthermore, irreversible changes can take place and the connections among molecules lead to the chain transmission of the reflected influences. These features are regarded by Soviet scholars as the underlying premises of sensations. The limitation of this form of reflection is seen in its dependence upon the nature of the interacting objects: the more they differ, the less adequate is their reciprocal reflection (e.g., the relation between heat and electricity). Correspondingly, an object properly reflects those features of another object operating on it which it possesses itself (e.g., the interaction between electrostatic fields).

The chemical form of reflection and interaction is regarded as the most advanced existing in inanimate nature, because at this level there are a greater variety of reactions. The chemical substance is adjusted to the nature of the acting agent thereby resulting in a diversity of reactions. In that the nature of the chemical substance can be revealed only in the totality of its interactions, the reflection is discontinuous, since isolated reactions lead to a qualitative change of the substance. The exception of colloids is strongly emphasized by the authors. It is precisely the quality of increasing the stability of their structure in response to external influences that enables the colloids to make the transition from nonsensory to sensory matter. The Russian biologist Oparin (1957) hypothesized that living albumin took shape from the albuminoid material composing coacervates. Although colloids already possess a capacity to increase or decrease their receptivity to external influences, this adjustment is episodic and limited, being contingent on certain physical and chemical properties of the acting agents. Finally, because this capacity does not emerge from the colloid's need to conserve its own structure, the external influences cannot yet be classified as either "useful" or "damaging," as is the case with living organisms.

The major feature of biological reflection is seen in the separation of reflection from the general process of the object's interaction with its environment (Orlov, 1962). This is a specialized reflection, different from the processes of assimilation and disassimilation. The basic and specific function of this kind of reflection consists of the signaling of changes in the environment. The following description by Orlov of stages of reflection in living organisms is typical of Soviet publications.

> The first stage is that of excitability, i.e., the body's capacity to react to external influences is dependent on the state of excitation of the tissue. Then occurs the capacity of sensation and, finally, the highest form of psychical activity—consciousness, which is a quality of man only and occurs under the influence of specifically human, productive activity. Consciousness is a product of social development [p. 124].

Various findings, particularly in biology (Koshtoyants, 1964) are regarded by Soviet psychologists as validating the idea that reflection is a basic property of matter. Hence Soviet psychology postulates that psyche can be studied objectively only within the general framework of material phenomena. For Rubinshtein (1957a) this implies studying the types of interaction between man and his environment, so as to discover their laws and relationship to inferior forms of interaction. Traditional psychology, he argued, failed to disclose the nature of psyche because it approached the subjective world as a primary reality.

It is certainly not surprising that despite the impression produced by textbooks that the theory of reflection is a settled issue, this concept has been the subject of a live and continuing controversy. Ananev (1960), for instance, felt that an understanding of "reflection" involved two components: first, the genetical-historical aspect, sensation being a product of the development of matter; second, the relation between sensory matter and non-sensory matter in the organism. This relation is basic to the functioning of the sensory systems because each sense organ is a complex unit belonging precisely to that kind of matter which corresponds to its stimulus. Thus each sense organ is composed of various kinds of matter and physical and chemical processes similar to those which take place in the reflected object which has stimulated the sense organ. Hence the optical structure of the eye, the chemical reactions in the olfactory glands, the acoustic structure of the ear, the mechanism of the muscles, etc. are all modeling certain phenomena in the nature.

Ponomarev (1960, 1967), who has given much thought to the concept of interaction, has pointed out the difficulties of precise definition. The proposition that the relevant sciences —physics, chemistry, etc.—should be concerned with corresponding forms of interaction has not been generally accepted and thus types of interaction inferior to the object-subject relationship remain inadequately described.

The question has been raised whether reflection at the level of conditioned reflexes is a type of psychical reflection. Shorokhova (1952) for one rejected this suggestion:

> According to Pavlovian psychology, psyche implies the reflection of those stimuli which do not have a meaning of their own for the organism. This is the only scientific concept which avoids an arbitrary, subjective approach to psyche and helps to reveal the stage of evolution when the psychic form of reflection of reality occurs [p. 96].

Mogendovich (1958b), a student of sensory processes, took a different position:

> . . . the study of the physiological mechanisms of man's behavior by the method of conditioned reflexes does not provide a direct indication of the psychical processes as active functions of the brain. The conditioned reflexes reveal the physiological mechanism of associative links, the connective function of the cerebral cortex, but do not give direct information of the physiological nature of sensations, perceptions, representations and other psychical functions. This is an utterly different physiological problem which is just beginning to be approached by physiology. The method of conditioned reflexes is used among other methods with the simultaneous obligatory investigation of the subject's psyche [p. 3].

A related problem is that of the relationship between the formation of temporary bonds in general, with the conditioned reflex as a particular case. Bykov (1944), a coworker of Pavlov known for his studies on the conditioned reflexes of the inner organs, proposed a distinction between these two concepts. The formation of temporary bonds would be regarded as a general principle of physiology which accounts for the interaction between any organism, including vegetable life, and its environment. The conditioned reflex would constitute a specialized form of temporary connection which was linked to the occurrence of the psyche.

For Anokhin (1968) the questions concerning the stage of evolution at which conditioned reflexes appear and whether such reflexes can be produced in simple organisms are meaningless. He assumed a universal principle of adaptation of any organism to its environment, consisting of an anticipated reflection of successive and repetitious conditions together with a sort of "preventive" adaptation to forthcoming events. It is suggested that this process has been active since the initial stages of living matter. Anokhin put his hypothesis in a philosophical framework stating that

> . . . from the point of view of dialectical materialism, the sequence of stimulations of the external world on the first organisms, regardless of the interval between them and of the quality of their energy, is the most important feature of the spatio-temporal structure of the world, determining the temporal relationship of these organisms to the external inorganic world [p. 16].

The distinction made by the elementary organisms between significant and nonsignificant temporal parameters occurred in the next stage. The protoplasm became capable of reflecting its chemical reactions which were taking place in microintervals of time, the sequence of external events which were running at macrointervals. Such a hypothesis implies the development of an *active* reflection of the external world. Hence, the capacity to signal forthcoming events, which underlies the formation of temporary connections, is one of the oldest properties of living matter. It is manifest in higher animals in the functioning of specialized types of nervous apparatus. Thus in Anokhin's view, the proper question is which apparatus is responsible for the anticipated reflection of external events at different stages of evolution.

Leontev (1959b) took a similar stand regarding the capacity to signal as the most relevant feature of the psyche. The psyche has a role in the organism's adaptation, and this consists in the reflection of those objects and phenomena, acting as signals, which help the organism to deal with the vital phenomena, without participating directly in the metabolic process.

PSYCHE AS AN IDEAL AND SUBJECTIVE IMAGE OF REALITY

Soviet psychology takes a straightforward materialistic position regarding the subject matter of this science and the nature of the psyche. Fleischer (1961) and Blakeley (1964) contributed lucid presentations of the basic concepts of Soviet philosophy. Blakeley wrote:

> Dialectical materialists are those who affirm the primacy of matter over the soul, idea, etc., while refuting the mechanicist reduction and recognizing the fundamentally dialectically structured nature of reality in constant evolution. . . . Idealists affirm the primacy of the soul, idea, consciousness, of the subjective. . . . The metaphysician eliminates motion, artificially abstracts from the real relations between real things, and separates the ideal from the real. . . . The dialectician sees that reality is in a constant motion, that its components are all interrelated, and that all bipolar aspects of reality (like real and ideal) are complementary [pp. 12–13].

The following three statements in the 1966 textbook express the same thinking:

> First, psyche is viewed as a secondary phenomenon, derivative from matter; matter is the primary phenomenon, the substratum, the bearer of the psyche; second, psyche is conceived as a property of a particular kind of organized matter, the brain; third, psyche occurs as a property of the brain to reflect the surrounding material world. The primary nature of matter and the secondary nature of psyche is convincingly demonstrated by the very fact that psyche occurs only at a given stage of development of matter [p. 4].

In recent years, Soviet psychologists have strongly emphasized that psychical activity does not consist only of the underlying physiological mechanisms, but also involves a certain content, namely the reflection of the surrounding reality. Idealistic psychology which regards mind as a primary entity, independent of matter, is seen as originating in primitive man's ignorance regarding the material basis of mind. But in

the modern world, idealism is produced out of class antagonism and by the endeavor of the dominant class to perpetuate
its power. Thus it is regarded as the philosophy of any reactionary group. Materialism fundamentally opposes idealism
regardless of whether it is an objective or a subjective idealism. Consequently, the contemporary neopositivist trend in
philosophy is seen by the Soviets as yet another version of
subjective idealism, despite its claim of lying outside the polemic between materialism and idealism. In fact, it does not
go beyond man's subjective experience and thus fails to perceive the link between the material and the ideal sides of reality (Mitin, 1963). A number of works were published to com-
bat the idealistic philosophy from Hegel to Jaspers (Oizerman,
1958, 1966; Georgiev, 1961; Meleshchenko, 1960; Narskii and
Suvorov, 1962; Chalin, 1959; Korneeva, 1962).

There is a marked tendency to minimize the differences
between the non-Marxist conceptions and to stress their common idealist roots. The following passage is typical (Khromov,
1952):

> The Marxist-Leninist theory of reflection does not agree with either
> the identification or the nonidentification of a thing with its image.
> Idealistically minded philosophers, who deny the reflection of objective
> reality in man's consciousness, actually identify thing and image, the
> matter and the idea of it. Hegel, as well as Berkeley, Mach and all other
> objective and subjective idealists perceive thing and idea as identical [p.
> 126].

Rubinshtein (1957a) abstracted two idealist trends in current
Western philosophy: (1) image is divorced from thing and
conceived as existing only in man's consciousness, which
brings psychology into the realm of pure introspection; (2)
the relevance of the image is emphasized at the expense of the
actual thing, which falls in line with Machism, neorealism,
positivism etc.

The Soviet view on the nature of psyche is also proclaimed

to be dialectical. Psyche is not a passive mirroring of the external world, but rather consists of a process during which contradictions occur between objects and their mental images. There is a development from a superficial and inaccurate reflection, to a deeper, abstract knowledge. Finally, mental images control people's activity and this, in its turn, brings about changes in the nature of the objects which are the original source of the mental images. Thus material things and subjective images form a dynamic synthesis.

The opposition of matter to psyche is twofold: material versus ideal and objective versus subjective. It is precisely the nature of these relationships that has been most controversial among Soviet authors. The ontological versus the epistemological planes, the philosophical versus the biological perspectives, the relationship of the psyche to its two material and objective sources—external reality and the brain—have been among the disputed issues. One can hardly make a clear distinction between the various positions, since they are so closely allied. Moreover, many of the arguments are a function of semantics. However, Payne (1968) suggested a certain delineation between extremist positions.

The ideal nature of the psyche from the Marxist perspective was intelligibly discussed by Rubinshtein (1957a). The mental image is both the reflection of a material object and the product of a psychic activity. Thus, the twofold relationship of image-to-object and image-to-subject poses the problem of the interaction between the objective and the subjective aspects of the psyche. This problem must be confronted in order to avoid Platonism, namely the universalization of the ideal nature of psyche. Such an approach is the only way to understand the independence, albeit relative, of the psyche achieved by man through language which allows him to substantiate sensory images, representations and thoughts. The resultant knowledge, in turn, becomes the subject of cognitive activity. The interdependence of images leads to a lesser reliance on the thinking activity itself. Finally, the product of the cognitive activity is no longer perceived as an independent subjective entity, but as an ideal object. For instance, a digit can be composed of an infinite variety of numbers and yet each time it possesses the same identity ($4 = 3 + 1; 4 = 2 + 2; 4 = 2^2$ etc.). In this case, an ideal object which was once the result of a cognitive process, now appears as an objective reality which has to be assimilated. Hence, according to Rubinshtein, any psychological study of the psyche must account for the mental ability to reflect the various aspects of the external reality.

> Ignorance of this basic proposition is the essence of psychologism—the core of subjective realism. The reduction of the objective, ideal knowledge to subjective ideas, viewed as being contingent only on thought processes, implies its separation from the content of the ideas which reflect the laws of the external reality [p. 44].

Some of the arguments put forth regarding the objective-subjective issue are worthy of presentation to show how philosophical problems of psychology are discussed by Soviet authors. Essentially, they have endeavored to argue (a) the existence of a subjective reality which differs from the objective reality but is not entirely separate from it; (b) the unity, but not the identity, between the objective and the subjective. The subjective nature of the mental image is also considered —like its ideal nature—within the contex of a two-fold relationship: to the external reality and to the underlying physiological processes. Some psychologists, Rubinshtein among them (1957a, 1959a), have pointed up the subjective-objective relationship as a relation of the psyche to the external world. Rubinshtein rejected the idea that an objective research of the psychical processes is only possible through physiological investigation.

On the other hand, Pavlov (Orbeli, 1949) himself emphasized the relationship between the physiological and the psychological aspects of mind. He predicted the marriage between physiology and psychology which would allow for the possibility of fitting subjective phenomena into physiological mechanisms. Yet he did not deny the role of psychology and the following statement by him was frequently quoted by psychologists in support of their positions.

> It would be nonsense to deny the existence of the subjective world. . . . Of course, psychology appears to be inadequate in view of its many sterile efforts in studying and analyzing the higher nervous activity. But psychology as a study of the subjective reality is certainly necessary. It is due to psychology that I can imagine the complexity of certain subjective states [pp. 415-416].

Following Pavlov, Petrushevskii (1952) argued that all research on psychical activity should be linked to physiological investigation. Physiology, for him, embraced the study of higher nervous activity in its relationship to subjective states; whereas psychology extends the study of this activity into the sphere of subjective phenomena, i.e., through the process of reflection. Thus a psychologist starting with the findings of physiology goes on to analyze the subjective states produced by stimulation. For instance, a physiologist would be interested in the physiological changes which take place in factory workers upon hearing the whistle for the beginning or end of each shift (change of heart rate, metabolism etc.), but a psychologist would investigate questions such as the possible link between the hearing of the whistle and the worker's wish to discover new methods of production in order to obtain a higher output for the factory. Some workers may feel guilty at the end of the shift if they have not achieved a sufficiently high performance.

A bold, nonconformistic interpretation of some experimental findings was offered by Kupalov (1962), a close collaborator of Pavlov who headed the Physiological Laboratory of the Institute of Experimental Medicine in Leningrad between 1937 and 1964, the year of his death, and was the editor of

Zhurnal Vysshei Nervnoi Deyatelnosti (Journal of Higher Nervous Activity). His split with his teacher was the result of certain important differences to be discussed later. Kupalov spoke freely about the subjective states linked to the formation of conditioned reflexes in animals. In his experiments, dogs were given bowls of water to drink before they were fed. Next, weak solutions of hydrochloric acid and quinine were poured directly into their mouths before they ate, so that stimulation of the oral receptors by these chemicals became a feeding-conditioned stimulus. Subsequently, the dogs willingly drank more concentrated solutions instead of the water. However, when given these solutions several times without food, they rejected the more concentrated solutions. Kupalov speculated that before the gustatory stimulation by hydrochloric acid and quinine became a feeding-conditioned stimulus, it was associated with a certain subjective state of the animal, whereas after the formation of tne conditioned reflex, it was connected to another state. Thus he concluded:

> Hence, when a conditioned reflex is elaborated, it forms an integral new nervous process which also appears as an inner experience. . . . Subjective phenomena enabled the dogs to transform the reality of their environment, some inner activity, and some physical states, into a reality of their inner world. . . . They gave the higher nervous activity its integrity and led man to experience his individuality. . . . All the subjective states represent organized cerebral processes enriched with the quality of feeling. It is not the physiological structure of the processes of excitation and inhibition which is felt to be experienced, but the reflection of the operations which produced the physiological process. . . . On the other hand, we must admit that psychical phenomena . . . are in fact a subjective reflection of the qualitative characteristics of the cerebral processes. . . . The physiological organization of the nervous processes is not given to us as a direct reality. . . . The basic function of a psychical phenomenon to reflect the external reality . . . or the functioning of the inner organs, or the states of the tissues is dominant to such a degree, that it would seem even strange to think about nervous processes as different from what is given in the form of subjective reality [pp. 31–32].

Boiko (1952) hoped to advance the thinking on this issue and speculated about an objective and a subjective side of the cerebral activity. For him,

> . . . an extremely important feature of the normal human brain, is that it is not only the organ of control over the reflex functions of the body, but at the same time, it is the organ of subjective reflection of the objective reality . . . [p. 164].

However, Leontev (1952) felt that the unity between objective and subjective phenomena, as conceived by Boiko, was merely verbal, since subjective phenomena simply appeared as accompaniments to the cerebral processes. He labeled this position as epiphenomenalist, arguing that it prevented the efficient application of psychology to practice.

Leontev (1955, 1959b) himself, consistently developed his earlier views, rooted in Vygotskii's cultural-historical approach, into a conception of the formation of functional systems. Leontev currently takes the position that

> . . . human psyche is a function of the higher cerebral structures which take shape ontogenetically in the process of assimilation of the forms of activity developed historically. . . . The historical development of the psyche precisely consists in that aspect of human development which is expressed physiologically in the reproduction, modification and complication of these cerebral structures from one generation to the next [p. 396].

In Leontev's view, the experimental investigation of the formation of cerebral functional systems and of their disintegration under pathological conditions—he referred to Vygotskii's assumptions on the localization of psychical functions and heavily relied on Luriya's (1962, 1963) work—might solve the apparent contradiction between two postulates. First, in the course of man's social-historical development, *new* psychical functions and abilities took shape. Second,

. . . in the era of dominance of social laws, the phylogenetic development of the human brain no longer brings about essential morphological changes; the achievements of the historical development are consolidated in objective, material and ideal results of human activity and in this form are transmitted from one generation to the next. New psychological structures are not acquired by an individual through heredity, but accumulate during his own life time [p. 384].

Leontev considers this the fundamental problem of psychology, responsible for dividing it into the social and experimental camps. The question is complex since, at first glance, Leontev's formulation appears to imply that new mental capacities may develop without regard for the morphological features of the brain.

Leontev, admitting that the concept of a functional system was not new, credited Wundt with having made two important contributions: first, that relatively simple sensory processes result from the joint functioning of various receptor and effector organs; second, that a combination of these elements occurs during an individual's lifetime. Sechenov (1903) made a further contribution by proposing that the effector link of a reflex action plays an important role in the formation of the physiological mechanisms responsible for mental functioning. Finally, Pavlov disclosed the way in which cerebral functional systems work. In the early years of his work on the conditioned reflexes, Pavlov (1923) proposed that a certain functional integration takes place between various regions of the central nervous system. But while the previous experimental study of the formation of functional systems was concerned primarily with artificial stimuli, under laboratory conditions, Leontev promoted the study of natural systems. These were assumed to possess certain features essentially different from the formation of chains of conditioned reflexes, including the dynamic stereotype described by Pavlov and his school, presumed to underlie the formation of habits. (1) Natural systems are not based on a definite sequence of associations, but represent a combination of reflexes resulting in a new and general-ized function. The peripheral effects of the compounding ele-ments of the system are reduced and manifest as central, cerebral processes. This means they are no longer subject to di-rect reinforcement and that the system works as a whole. (2) The functional systems are very stable (e.g., visual-tactile asso-ciations are not extinguished in a blind man). (3) The positive reinforcement of the final effect of a functional system leads to the gradual inhibition of the compounding reflexes, while the lack of reinforcement leads to disinhibition. This is in clear opposition to what had been shown by laboratory studies of conditioned reflexes. Leontev relied on a variety of experi-mental findings, some of which will be discussed in the next chapter.

As a result of these findings Leontev regarded the develop-ment of the psychical processes as being contingent upon the human activity through which they are linked to external real-ity. Having resulted from a cerebral activity which leads to the formation of physiological systems, their specific features cannot however be expressed in physiological concepts because they have a certain content which is not reproduced in the morphological structure.

At this point it is instructive to mention an extensive po-lemic which was recently prompted by an extreme "socioge-netic" stand taken by Ilenkov (1968), a philosopher. He maintained that the study of thinking and of the process of reflection in general is the exclusive area of philosophy and that neither physiology nor cybernetics can contribute to it. In Ilenkov's view, the human psyche is solely determined by so-cial factors. Thus he wrote (1968):

> None of the specifically human psychical functions can be derived either from innate cerebral structures or from acquired structures. . . . On the contrary, all the specifically human functions of the brain with-out exception, as well as the structures which make them possible are *determined* 100%—and not 90% or even 99%—and thus *explained* exclu-

sively by the manners of activity of man as a social and not a natural being [p. 149].

Certainly, Ilenkov admitted the role of the human brain in mental functioning but concluded that the brain's activity is possible precisely because of its total liberation from the *determining* influences of purely biological factors. Man's psychology is based on his "being" and not on his brain:

> . . . on the system of relationships of man to man, mediated by things created by man for man, that is to say on the system of relations linked to the production of the world of things and to the abilities corresponding to the organization of this world [pp. 59-60].

Ilenkov argued that there is no essential difference between the brain of Aristotle and that of Democritus, or between Raphael's and Goya's organs of perception. He concluded that study of the human capacity to reflect the reality in images is the exclusive prerogative of philosophy.

Voprosy Filosofii published several strongly negative reactions to Ilenkov's statements (Dubrovskii, 1968, 1969; Smirnov, 1969; Yorish, 1969). The critics pointed out that if one takes the position that the human mind is formed only under the influence of social factors, there must be an explanation as to what changes in the brain are produced by these factors. If one says that such an explanation is superfluous—as Ilendov does—then he either denies determinism, or takes a mechanistic approach, since he is implying that mental phenomena are a *copy* of external objects and are independent of the reflecting subject. Furthermore, the critics referred to studies of brain anatomy, in particular to those of Sarkisov and Preobrazhenskaya (1961) which indicated an individual variability in the cytoarchitecture of the brain, supposed to represent the material substratum of the individual characteristics of higher nervous activity. Dubrovskii (1968, 1969) referred to modern neuromorphological, biochemical and cytogenetic studies of the brain which showed that individual structural differences increase as one advances toward the microlevel of cerebral organization. That is, there are proportionally more individual differences at the synaptic and subneuronal level than at the neuronal level. This was said to suggest that there is a transition from the characteristics of the species to individual characteristics and that genetically individual features are subject to ontogenetic transformations.

Reflection, Information, Modeling of Biological and Mental Processes

The development of cybernetics has given rise to an extensive debate in Soviet philosophy, psychology, neurophysiology and related sciences, about the theoretical and methodological foundations of the new trend in the light of the dialectical materialism. The relationship between brain and psyche, the view of the psyche as a subjective reflection of objective reality have become the subject of an argument couched in the new language of cybernetics. Although proposals to express the idea of psyche as a reflection in such terms as a subjective "image," or as a "reproduction" of the external reality have been a steady subject of polemic in Soviet ideology, in recent years the concept of the psyche as a *model* of external reality has assumed an essentially new significance. It implies the substitution of the concept of reflection with that of information processing, and an analogy between brain and electronic devices capable of self-regulation. Thus, it is not surprising that a large number of publications and symposia have been devoted to this topic. A Scientific Board on Cybernetics was set up by the Presidium of the Academy of Sciences of the USSR in 1959. The Scientific Board on the Philosophical Problems of Contemporary Natural Sciences has a special division concerned with the philosophical problems of cybernetics.

Two periods can be distinguished with regard to the Soviet stand toward cybernetics. Initially, there was an extremely negativistic attitude towards this way of theorizing. Cybernetics was viewed as an illustration of the decadence of "imperialistic" science since it equated man and machine. Russian writers pointed at statements like those of Ashby (1950), who maintained in his *Design for a Brain* that it was not necessary to take consciousness into account in the analysis of the brain's functioning. Furthermore, cybernetics was rejected because of its claim that the opposition between materialism and idealism belonged to the past—a statement by Wiener.

The attitude changed by 1955. Sobolev, Kitov and Lyapunov, authorities on the mathematical theory of cybernetics, published that year what was apparently the first paper in favor of the new science. They stated that any science which undertakes a study of objective processes has as its subject matter the material world. Cybernetics must be regarded as a materialist science. It does not identify consciousness with the functioning of a machine. What is actually being investigated is the processing of information by different systems. This requires the abstraction from the physical structure of the systems concerned. The publication of this work and of another one by Kolman, a philosopher, in the same issue of *Voprosy Filosofii*, marked the beginning of a debate which is continuing at the present time.

In the current attitude towards cybernetics, it is generally apparent that philosophers, who had been intransigent opponents of the new trend, are again among the foremost opponents of the belief in the vast possibilities of modeling biological and mental processes. This statement should by no means be interpreted to mean that all Russian philosophers take this position. What is implied is that philosophers represent the most significant group resistant to the application of cybernetics to biology and psychology.

Mathematicians and the electronic engineers tend to advocate the analogy between cybernetic devices and human activity. Sobolev and Lyapunov (1958) wrote:

> Scientists often raise the problem of confronting the possibilities of human brain with those of a computer. . . . It is sometimes stated that a difference of principle must exist between them. But it seems that at present time one cannot answer the question whether such a difference exists or whether it is only the matter about a quantitative difference [p. 212].

A paper in *Kommunist* reacted to this statement (Anisimov and Vislobodkov, 1960) as follows:

> At first glance this seems to be a dialectical view. In fact, this is a perfect illustration of misapplication of dialectics because quality is reduced to quantity. The main difference between human brain and machine does not consist so much in the different amounts of compounding elements, as in the qualitative difference between the nerve cells and the elements of the electronic machine, in the essentially different kinds of connections which they have with the surrounding world. The result of brain's functioning is *consciousness*. The cybernetic machine has never and will never produce consciousness. Although its operation is seemingly "rational" the machine is not mediated by consciousness and, therefore, is not of a rational nature [p. 112].

Neurophysiologists and psychologists may be regarded, somewhat arbitrarily, as holding an intermediary position. They have brought specific arguments against the equation of technological and biological systems. These will be considered shortly. A cautious stand was taken by Leontev and Krinchik (1961) as a rational for their own experimental studies on human behavior in a choice situation. They wrote:

> Nowadays various opinions are voiced concerning the application of the information theory to psychology. Some psychologists see in the concepts and methods of this theory . . . a unique instrument for turning psychology into a genuine science. Others tend to reject the information theory on the ground . . . that it intrudes into the psychological research depriving it of its specific content. It is obvious that this view-

point is not without some foundation. The undisputed successes of the cybernetic theory have led to an irresponsible application of its concepts by some psychologists. The psychological analysis was replaced by a mere phraseology adapted from the information theory. Furthermore, a wrong and arbitrary meaning is often ascribed to these concepts. Such a tendency naturally helps to consolidate the resistance to their application to psychology and encourage a skeptical and even negativistic attitude towards it. On the other hand, a number of serious attempts have been recently made to grasp the actual value of the information theory for psychology and the limits of its application. . . . We believe that the best way to solve these problems and to liberate ourselves from preconceived and unfounded views is to undertake a detailed analysis of the foundations and results of the application of the information theory to some psychological practical problems. The need to tackle such problems imposes a very careful approach . . . [p. 25].

In a recent paper, Leontev (1970) pointed out that by studying the processes of interaction within and between systems using the concepts of information and analogy, cybernetics has made possible the introduction of quantitative methods in the study of the process of reflection, thereby enriching the theory of reflection as a general property of matter. But he emphasized its limits due to the fact that cybernetics necessarily disregards the concrete nature of the processes of self-control.

The following issues have been among those most discussed by Soviet authors: the relationship between dialectical materialism and cybernetics; the relationship between reflection and the processing of information; the modeling of neurological processes; the modeling of psychical processes, particularly of thinking.

Cybernetics has presented Soviet philosophers with a problem similar to the one raised by semiotics or by Bertalanffy's (1968) theory of general systems, notably the relationship between dialectical materialism which considers the general aspects of all natural and social phenomena, and theories which are also concerned with a large spectrum of facts covering an extensive interdisciplinary area. At the methodological level, the major problem facing Marxist theorists is the application of mathematics and the concepts of formal logic to the study of biological and psychological phenomena. Soviet authors have spared no effort to make it plain that any scientific theory, regardless of its scope, cannot reach the perspective offered by the epistemological approach. There are, however, divergent positions (Rozental, 1963, 1966; Vislobokov, 1965; Maizel and Fatkin, 1962; Libenson, 1959; Biryukov and Tyukhtin, 1964; Biryukov et al., 1967; Moiseev, 1965; T. Pavlov, 1966; Bazhenov, Biryukov and Shtoff, 1964b). Rozental (1966), for one, the author of several works on Marxist philosophy, including a popular philosophical dictionary, conceded that cybernetics has made significant strides toward a scientific understanding of the unity of all natural phenomena. The development of cybernetics has run parallel with the development of knowledge on superior forms of matter, including the functioning of the brain. The cybernetic analogy between brain and machine bears a correspondence to the old mechanical approach, Rozental admitted, however, one important distinction between them, namely that cybernetics is based on knowledge concerning the qualitative differences between the various phenomena. Abiding by the basic distinction made by Soviet philosophers between formal and dialectic logic, he nonetheless stressed the need to take into account the new developments in science, in particular the penetration of contemporary logic in many practical fields. Thus the formal methods of mathematical analysis have acquired a special practical and theoretical significance and are to be included in the Marxist epistemologic theory. Rozental rejected the view that mathematical logic has nothing to do with philosophy and that it is an "inferior" epistemological theory.

Following along the same lines, Novik (1963, 1964a,b,c, 1965, 1968, 1969), the author of several works on the philosophical problems of cybernetics, pointed out that this discipline does not take a pure phenomenological approach but rather proposes a functional modeling of the studied object. Its methods make possible not only a description of functions but also an understanding of the structure of objects. What is modeled is the interaction between the object and its milieu. This may be called "the field of functional connections between object and milieu." This "field" has an objective existence and can be approached independently of the structure of the object and of its milieu. The functional connections represent the innermost structure of the "field." Novik called attention to the study of DNA as a transition from the knowledge of function, notably of the sequence of nucleotides in the molecule of DNA, compared with that of amino acids in the molecule of albumin, to the knowledge of structure—the discovery of the inner mechanism of the synthesis of albumin. Another instance of such a transition is represented in the concept of TOTE (Miller, Galanter and Pribram, 1960) which surmounts the limited behavioristic stimulus-response scheme.

Conversely, T. Pavlov (1966), a distinguished Bulgarian Marxist philosopher, took a rather orthodox position in his address to a conference on the current problems of dialectical materialism held in Moscow. He said:

> Mathematics and cybernetics are particular or special sciences not merely and not only because the sphere of their concern is narrower than that of the dialectical materialism, but also because cybernetics does not solve the fundamental problems of philosophy and does not give a philosophical definition of the concept of matter. Information processing taken as an objective process, no matter how close it appears to reflection as a property of matter, is not identical with it and even less with human consciousness . . . which is the highest form of reflection [p. 152].

Another problem discussed by Soviet students of cybernetics concerns the nature of the processing of information (Zhukov,

1963; Korshunov, 1964, 1969; Pekhterev, 1965; Ukraintsev, 1960, 1963, 1967; Ukraintsev and Platonov, 1966; Tyukhtin, 1959, 1963, 1964a,b, 1967; Berg and Novik, 1965; Novinskii, 1961; Vorobev, 1964; Petrushenko, 1967; Tarasenko, 1963; Lyapunov and Yablonskii, 1964c). The main point of controversy is whether the process of transmitting information and, in particular, the use of signals by cybernetic devices is identical with the process of reflection in nature. If not, then are they divergent processes or is one related to the other? Some authors clearly regard information theory as a natural-scientific implementation of the tenet that matter has the quality of reflection. Thus in a joint paper in *Kommunist*, Berg, a highly regarded expert in cybernetics and a member of the Academy of Sciences of the USSR, and Novik (1965) stated that the concept of "objective reality" existing independent of man's consciousness includes along with the processes of transformation of substance and energy the processing of information. "The informational processes studied by cybernetics substantiate Lenin's hypothesis that the whole of the matter possesses the property of reflection which is akin to the capacity of sensation but is not identical with it" (p. 21).

Tyukhtin (1964a), who has given much thought to the problem of reflection, sees the essence of this process in the isomorphic relationship between the structure of one object and the structure of another object, whereby the latter is influenced by the former one due to the universal law of interaction. Essentially, this also occurs in automation, telemechanics and communication devices. The psychical reflection, however, possesses an additional feature which is found neither in cybernetic machines, nor in inorganic matter, to wit, the ability for objectivity. That is, man and animals reflect the very nature of external objects.

Ukraintsev (1963), another writer on philosophical questions of cybernetics, expressed a view which appears to have gained wide support. To him, the transmission of information is a special form of the general interconnection that exists among natural phenomena under the particular conditions of controlled systems. Information of any kind is gathered and processed in a certain material; yet this material cannot be regarded as either a form of matter or of energy. One can speak about information only on the attainment of a level of organization of the material which makes possible a process of control. The process of reflection is transformed into a transmission of information by virtue of modeling the reflected material.

Finally, the concept of model is a controversial issue (Shalyutin, 1961, 1964; Zinovev, 1960a; Zinovev and Revzin, 1960b; Glinskii et al., 1965; Shtoff, 1963a,b, 1966; Glushkov, 1963a; Akchurin, Vedenov and Sakhov, 1968; Bazhenov, 1964a). Some authors interpreted the word "model" to mean the imitation of one object by another. That is, on examination of the first object there is immediate recognition and knowledge of the other one. The condition for modeling should be the analogy between model and original. Shtoff (1963a), for instance, regarded the model as a reproduced image of an object, the word "image" having the same meaning as in the reflection theory. Other writers, however, avoided this identification. Novik (1969), for one, argued that modeling represents an imitation of the reproduced phenomenon and does not actually attain its essence. And Anokhin (1957) cautioned against the danger of misinterpretation of the terms used. He felt that it is necessary to define exactly what is modeled in order to avoid confusion.

The modeling of biological processes in general and of nervous processes in particular is currently a much debated topic (Sobolev, 1963, 1964; Parin, 1961, 1963, 1964, 1966, 1969; Anokhin, 1957, 1963b, 1964, 1966, 1967; Frolov, 1961; I. Galperin, 1957; Abramyan, 1961; Kolmogorov, 1964; Lyapunov, 1964b; Oparin, 1964b; Markov, 1964; Prezent, 1964; Emme, 1964). It has been discussed on many occasions including meetings of the seminars on philosophy at the institutes of the Academy of Sciences of the USSR (Frank and Kuzin, 1964) and a conference dedicated to the problems of the mathematic modeling of biological processes held in Moscow in 1966 (Vedenov et al., 1968).

"Functional" definitions of life were proposed by Kolmogorov and Lyapunov. To Kolmogorov (1964) ". . . the basic properties of life as a particular manner of organization of matter . . . admit a formulation abstracted from the concrete nature of the underlying elementary physical (particularly chemical) processes . . . " (p. 48). And Lyapunov (1964b) defined life as a state of high stability of matter, which makes use of the information coded by certain molecules to elaborate the conservation reactions. Taking a similar approach, Markov (1964), the well-known mathematician, denied the specificity of biological laws. Arguing against Oparin (1964b), he wrote:

> It [the living organism] consists of elementary particles grouped in atoms and molecules. The physical laws which regulate the system are still valid. This is also admitted by A. I. Oparin. But at the same time biological "laws" are "superimposed." Poor molecule! What should it now do? Which laws to observe—the physical or the new, biological laws? This is nonsense. I think that this viewpoint cannot be logically maintained [p. 169].

This position has raised objections. A typical reaction was that of Prezent (1964), a biologist, who rejected Kolmogorov's view that on *principle* it is possible to design a living being on the basis of the mechanisms of information processing and control. He said:

> One must distinguish between whatever complex *imitation* of vital phenomena, and the creation of a living being and of thinking. For the latter, the machine should have the property of excitability, without which the modeling of life will always be an imitation. *The cybernetic machines imitate the higher forms of reflection skipping over the inferior*

forms since they do not have the elementary property of life—excitability which is necessarily linked to all the other functions of vital activity including thinking . . . without the first level of thinking, the second level will always be an imitation created by man [p. 217].

A major problem concerning the modeling of biological processes, and particularly nervous processes, is that of the relationship between the structure, or the material of a system, and its functions. Some authors have drawn a clear distinction between the two, criticizing the view that real biological systems implement abstract functional systems because this implies an identification of structure and function. No mathematical model of the functioning of the nervous system can surmount the phenomenological level, i.e., can penetrate the structure of the studied system. Similarly, Uemov (1964), the head of the philosophy department at the Odessa State University, stated that in order to function like a brain, a machine should be made of the same material, notably of albuminoid elements, and not of physical elements. Thus, a test tube of organic fluid is closer to the brain than is a perfect electronic device.

On the other hand, it was pointed out by Bazhenov and Biryukov that an opposition between three levels, namely the behavior or functioning of a system, its structure, and its material or substratum may exist only in a certain specific research, but on the general epistemological plane differentiation is relative. In their opinion the very concept of functioning depends on the abstraction, idealization, and hypotheses formulated, and the transition from the study of behavior to the analysis of the structure or of the material of the system depends on the chosen kind of model, on the applied theoretical and technical means of knowledge. In Novik's (1965) view, too, the structure of a system should not be regarded as a mere summation of its components. Two systems may differ with respect to their composition and yet have similar features of the process of reflection. Lyapunov

(1967a,b,c, 1968) accepted two possible approaches. First, the macroscopic approach, where the relationship between input and output is studied with the internal structure of the system being disregarded. In cybernetics this is the method of the "black box"; in psychology, the stimulus-response method. Despite its limitations, this method is apt to discover basic rules of functioning of control systems.

With regard to specific questions raised by the analogy between a cybernetic device and the nervous system, Anokhin (1957) objected to the way cybernetics was applied to physiology. In particular, he referred to the proposal of Garner and Hake to take the final correct reaction of the organism as a criterion of the amount of information processed. Anokhin pointed out that a wrong response does not necessarily mean loss of information, since the more automatic a reaction, the more reduced is its afferentation. However, by increasing the number of impulses, there is greater likelihood that the response will be even less appropriate. Unlike the machine, where any discrepancy between stimulation and processed information can be expressed in a mathematical formula, there is such a diversity of factors operating in the organism that the discrepancies resulting therefrom do not lend themselves to expression in terms of formulae. While there is a definite relation between the magnitude of this difference and the correcting operation of the machine, such a relation cannot be established in the organism.

As has been mentioned above, there emerged from the assumption that reflection involves the processing of information received from objects, the idea that the formation of connections in the brain represents a model of external events. Thus the concept of a nervous model appears equivalent to that of a subjective image. Bernshtein stated that it is adequate to name the assembly of central processes which are actively working out the received information, "operators," and the synthesized reflection of the real world in brain— "model." Sokolov (1964), too, wrote:

A possible approach to the process of reflection consists of regarding the nervous system as a device *modeling the external world,* particularly changes of its inner structure. In this sense, a certain group of changes in the nervous system is isomorphic to the reflected external stimulation to which it is similar. The *image* is an internal *model* occurring in the nervous system . . . significantly modifying the behavior making possible the foreseeing of events and the *active adaptation* to environment [pp. 242-243].

The Soviet studies on the modeling of nervous processes have taken two major directions. First, there are authors who base their work on McCulloch and Pitts' theory of neural network functioning according to the *all-or-none* principle (Gutchin, 1967). Models of neurons and of neural networks based on mathematical logic have been designed mainly at the universities of Moscow, Leningrad and Rostov, and at the Institute of Cybernetics at the Ukrainian Academy of Sciences. However, the tendency to regard this approach as having limited perspectives for the analysis of the brain's functioning seems to prevail (Biryukov and Geller, 1968). It became apparent that the reaction produced by a stimulus operating on the dendrites, which is propagated on the axon, is not a direct effect of the stimulation. Rather, the dendrites and the body of the cell act as a kind of system which integrates all the incoming stimulations and encourages the axon to transmit an impulse reaching the threshold. Kogan, from the Chair of Human and Animal Physiology and the Laboratory of Biophysics, Rostov University (1961, 1964, 1965a,b, 1968a,b,c, 1969, 1970, 1971a,b,c), who along with Sokolov took a different approach, objected to the extrapolation allowed by the neural network theory and to the literal application of schemes of formal combinations of neurons to actual interactions between neurons. In his studies, conditioned reflexes were formed where the conditioned stimulus consisted of the direct electrical stimulation of a point in the cortical-visual or auditory areas, using microelectrodes. In this way, the starting point of the path of conditioned stimulation leading to a reflex response was clearly known. Then various sections of the nervous fibers were removed. As it turned out, these operations did not prevent the occurrence of the reflex. It was also observed, with a few exceptions, that even neighboring neurons worked asynchronically. Thus the interaction between firings appeared to be a matter of chance, and the effect of stimulation varied from trial to trial. Kogan concluded that when a conditioned reflex is formed, unlike the structure of an unconditioned reflex, there is no fixed "scheme" of combination of neurons. He hypothesized that at the higher levels of the brain, organization does not occur according to the principle of a fixed path for each stimulation, and a single function for each element, but rather according to the principle of a probabilistic distribution of the nervous paths and of a statistical effect of the interaction between elements. Thus, there is a basic difference between unconditioned and conditioned reflexes. Accidental interaction between neurons disturbs the stereotypic organization of the unconditioned reflexes, the evolution of which has led to a stable neuronal activity. The increasing complexity of these neuronal mechanisms widened the sphere of influence of external as well as internal factors, resulting in a disturbance of the regularity of strictly organized systems. This contradiction could not be solved within the "schematic" organization of the nervous system. The outcome was the appearance of new levels of the brain which are not organized according to a scheme and for which the chance factor became a working mechanism. Kogan emphasized that there is no antagonism between deterministic and probabilistic systems. Moreover, the probabilistic organization is in a certain sense more reliable since it functions regularly under variable conditions.

Kogan described four types of organization of the nervous system which have appeared during evolution: (1) The retina-like type, in coelenterata, consisting of diffuse connections and polivalent nonspecific neuronal elements. This is the organization of the reticular structure in the brain of superior animals. The transmission of signals is similar to propagation in a continuous milieu. The stochastic character of such an organization ensures its high vitality as well as the capacity for generalized reactions. (2) The ganglionic type of organization in arthropoda. (3) The tubular, segmentary organization of the spinal cord in vertebrates. The second and third types of organization imply strictly determined connections and rigid functions of individual neurons. In higher organisms, they accomplish the stereotyped conditioned reflexes. It is precisely the work of these systems which is described by McCulloch and Pitts' (1943) theory. (4) The projective, integral type of organization specific for the cortex.

The modeling of mental processes will be discussed in the following chapters in some detail. To conclude this section on rather general issues, the following illustration of the contemporary approach by Soviet scholars to the matter-psyche issue is offered. An attempt was made by Kobozev (1966), a biochemist, to analyze the biological mechanisms of thinking. He raised the question as to whether the processes underlying thinking are of a molecular or some other nature. Differently stated, the question concerns whether or not psychical activity is produced by mechanisms consisting of atoms and molecules and, as such, if it is subject to the laws of thermodynamics like any other molecular-cynetic system. A basic feature of these systems is the presence of a spontaneous (samoproizvoilnyi) process which leads to an increasingly more stable state. (For instance, a cloud is gradually transformed into drops of water and if the flow of external energy ceases, it becomes a crystal of ice). Each spontaneous process takes place with a reduction of the corresponding potential, or free energy, thereby resulting in a more stable system. Thus, with regard to thinking, the question to ask is whether the initial system of logical premises necessarily becomes a finite system of logical conclusions. Kobozev's analysis led him to the conclusion that there is a difference of principle between thinking and thermodynamic processes. Although logical thinking is indeed a spontaneous process, it lacks a state of entropy, that is its entropy is equal to zero. Thus, if many different people would use the same information to demonstrate a theorem, the result would always be the same. Since at the normal temperature of life, the atoms and molecules are in an intense thermic motion, it is practically impossible to attain the finite state of nonentropy, which should theoretically take place in nature. The changes take a single direction: from a probable one, from a less stable state, to a more stable state. In that the entropy is the measure of stability, it steadily increases. Thinking is the only natural phenomenon in which an absolute nonentropic state is attained. Therefore, the unequivocal solution of problems cannot be accomplished by the usual molecular processes. At best, these would permit of only probabilistic and approximative solutions. Kobozev's final conclusion was that the material basis of thinking, and of the psyche in general, should be looked for at a level lower than the atomic-molecular, of yet unknown elementary particles, or at a higher level of yet unknown properties of animated matter.

THE REFLEX THEORY

In the period following the Pavlovian conference, Soviet psychology officially proclaimed Pavlov's theory as the only scientific approach to the functioning of the brain, the organ of psychical reflection. The reflex theory was regarded as the "natural-scientific" foundation of Lenin's theory of reflection, Rubinshtein (1952) stated that the reflex theory of the psyche and the epistemological theory of reflection, all knit together as a whole, emerging from the principle of determinism. According to Rubinshtein, psychology should first study the relationship between psychical activity and the external world, and then taking as a starting point the final results of the psychical activity, analyze the physiological processes involved. This approach would lead to the discovery of the nature of the connections between brain and psyche. The correlated result of the two series of investigations would make possible a general definition of the psyche.

Again, as in the 1920's, but apparently in a less spontaneous manner, the appreciation of Pavlov's work was expressed in laudatory terms. Petrushevskii (1952) wrote that:

> the Pavlovian teaching, which is grounded on the dialectical materialism, offers the correct solution to the problem of consciousness. It confirms the Marxist-Leninist proposition that matter is the source of sensations, representations, consciousness . . . [p. 70].

The major statement made at the 1950 conference by its leaders, Bykov [3] and Ivanov-Smolenskii, [4] was that the laws of higher nervous activity—irradiation and concentration of the processes of excitation and inhibition, reciprocal inhibition etc.—were the only correct specific assumptions to be made on the basis of Sechenov's reflex principle. This was the official view and any attempt to introduce new concepts was regarded as a deviation from the principle of determinism. Fortunately, the rigid approach imposed by the conference did not persist for long. The general improvement in the scientific atmosphere during the second half of the 1950's was also reflected in the weakening of Pavlov's authority. The proceedings of a conference held in 1962 (Fedoseev, 1963), sponsored by the Academy of Sciences and attended by some 1,000 persons, are most instructive in noting this change of climate. The 13 major addresses expressing different positions, with Anokhin, Bernshtein, Beritov, Kupalov being among the main speakers,

---

[3] Bykov presented the status of Pavlovian physiology at that time and sharply criticized the deviations from Pavlov's theory, in particular the work of Orbeli.

[4] Originally an associate of Bekhterev, Ivanov-Smolenskii became Pavlov's coworker and already manifested in the 1930's a tendency to oversimplify the study of human reactions. Pavlov himself disagreed with him.

resulted in lively free discussion, noticeably lacking in the kind of self-criticism heretofore expected.

It is generally agreed by Soviet authors that the 1950 conference lead to a narrow "corticalism," i.e., an almost exclusive role was ascribed to the cerebral cortex. It also resulted in a restriction of methodology by ignoring the modern techniques of biophysics, biochemistry, etc. The study of man, in particular the second signaling system, was essentially limited to the procedures developed by Ivanov-Smolenskii in the 1930's. Finally, psychology became a second-hand discipline, as was evident in the death of genuine psychological study in the early 1950's. Even Mitin [5] (1963) admitted that

> . . . the 1950 Pavlovian conference had a number of shortcomings. One may not overlook those aspects which, to some extent, were under the influence of the personality cult. This was particularly felt in making a dogma of Pavlov's theory. The purpose of the conference to orient research along the path of Pavlovian ideas was actually suppressed by the endeavor of any trend inspired by Pavlov's ideas to find support in isolated statements by Pavlov, losing sight of the general theory of higher nervous activity. The dogmatic interpretation of Pavlov's theory lead to the claim that the physiology of higher nervous activity substitutes for the entire physiology of the nervous system, and thereby attempted to reduce all the laws of the nervous system to the laws of its highest level—the cerebral cortex [p. 25].

The current evaluation of the 1950 conference, however, ranges from high appreciation of its role for the development of Sechenov-Pavlov's legacy, to the firm belief that it had a negative impact on the development of Soviet neurophysiology and psychology. Shorokhova, a psychologist affiliated with the Institute of Philosophy of the Academy of Sciences and the author of two books concerned with philosophical problems of psychology and with Pavlov's theory, admitted that the conference was dogmatic, intolerant and biased (Shorok-

[5] Mitin is a philosopher and a member of the Central Committee of the Communist Party; he edited the organ of the Cominform (The Informative Bureau of Communist Parties).

hova and Kaganov, 1963a). But she emphasized the contribution of the conference in enforcing

> . . . that Pavlov's theory on higher nervous activity is a cornerstone of the natural-scientific foundation of Lenin's reflection theory and that its further creative development is linked to the conscious application of the epistemological theory of dialectical materialism. This discussion positively revealed and criticized the nihilistic attitude toward Pavlov's theory taken by some physiologists, psychologists and philosophers. The discussion also exposed the lack of a critical attitude of some Soviet scientists toward fashionable Western anti-Pavlovian theories [p. 65].

This is by no means an isolated view in the recent literature. On the other hand, influential authors such as Anokhin and Luriya blamed the conference for preventing the progress in important areas of research, without pointing at "positive" results. One of the participants at the 1962 conference bluntly said that it would have been better if the 1950 conference had never taken place.

Obviously, underlying the divergent positions mentioned above, are divergent positions about Pavlov's theory, in particular about his conception of the reflex mechanism. Three positions are observable: (1) acceptance of the laws of higher nervous activity, formulated by Pavlov, as the only correct deterministic conception of the brain's function as the organ of reflection; (2) acceptance of Pavlov's theory while proposing new concepts which are controversial from a strict Pavlovian position; (3) acceptance of the principle of the reflex, while distinguishing it from Pavlov's specific hypotheses which are regarded as outdated.

Asratyan, the head of the Institute of Higher Nervous Activity and Neurophysiology, for many years a coworker of Pavlov, may be regarded as a typical representative of the first position which includes among others Voronin (1962, 1965, 1969; Dolin, 1962; Dmitriev, 1964; Biryukov, 1962). For these authors, the conditioned reflex is the basic process of adaptation in animals and man. Asratyan (1963) wrote:

It [the conditioned reflex] goes through a lengthy evolution, starting with the primitive reactions . . . of unicellular and simple organisms, and ending with the conditioned reflexes of the second signal system in man, during the course of which it is subject to deep quantitative and qualitative changes. . . . One may say: regardless of the diversity of the conditioned reflexes, no matter how they differ from each other regarding the degree of complexity and perfection, level of development, kind, structure and localization and even principle of signaling—in all cases, the conditioned reflex is essentially an elaborated form of nervous activity, produced by conditions of life, which reflects adequately, truly and actively the objective reality in its diversity and dynamics, which insures the finest, most exact and perfect adaptation of the organism to its ever-changing environment [p. 327].

Asratyan regarded his own studies, in particular his findings about the bilateral connections formed during the elaboration of conditioned reflexes, as meshing well with Pavlov's conception. He admitted, however, that Anokhin and Bernshtein did contribute new facts which enriched the knowledge about reflex activity. Furthermore, he was prepared to acknowledge that the circularity of the process of excitation, emphasized by these authors, should be given more weight than was done by the Pavlovian school. However, he rejected the attack against Pavlov's basic position and felt that such criticism showed only a superficial knowledge of Pavlov's conception.

Kupalov represented the second position, fully accepting Pavlov's conception about the relations between the conditioned and the unconditioned reflexes. He believed the connective function of the cortex, as described by the Pavlovian school, to be a universal mechanism which causes all the functional states and processes of excitation and inhibition elicited by external and internal stimulations to form a unitary system. But in his own studies (started in 1930 in Pavlov's laboratories) Kupalov obtained findings that led him to the formulation of new concepts. In one experiment conducted by Kupalov and Yaroslavtseva, a few seconds after a dog was fed a metronome was set in motion. Upon hearing it, the dog stopped eating for a few seconds and turned its head to the metronome. This procedure was repeated a number of times before feeding-conditioned reflexes to various stimuli were elaborated in the usual manner. Now, each time, a few seconds subsequent to feeding, the dog stopped eating and turned its head to the side where the metronome had been previously placed. This behavior persisted for several months.

In another experiment performed by Fedorov and Yakovlev, coworkers of Kupalov, dogs were given the task of a difficult discrimination requiring a strong inhibitory process. This resulted in a state of tension, which was observed each time when the dog was taken to the laboratory. All experiments carried out in that setting varied from the results obtained before the start of the discrimination experiment (intensity of reactions, effect of inhibition, etc.). This was clearly the effect of the laboratory itself and not of the discrimination experiment, since no changes in the other experiments were noticed if they were done in other rooms.

Kupalov (1962) interpreted these findings as representing two types of a particular kind of reaction which he called "shortened conditioned reflexes." In the first case, a certain cortical excitation may occur which is not the direct effect of external or internal stimulations, " . . . a reflex of an encephalic origin produced by a corticoceptive stimulation" (p. 119). In the second case, stimulations reaching the cortex may result in a cortical process without an external reaction. Thus, regarding the first experiment, Kupalov hypothesized that a certain state of the cortex produced during the dog's eating became connected with the orienting reaction to the hearing of the metronome. This meant that

> . . . the reaction was not elicited by an external or an internal stimulus, but by a functional state of the cortex, formed during the course of nervous processes produced by external stimulations. This state operated as an independent factor which acquired the property of a feeding-conditioned stimulus due to its coincidence with the orienting reac-

tion to the metronome. It is not a direct reflection of the concrete external world, or of an inner state of the organism, but a reflection of the nervous processes taking place in the cortex itself [p. 117].

In defense of this conclusion, Kupalov emphasized that Pavlov admitted that any state of nervous cells can turn into a conditioned stimulus and that the corresponding reaction should be regarded as a conditioned reflex.

> As regards the second experiment, it showed . . . that different agents of the experimental environment can produce not only an external reaction, or a reaction of the inner organs . . . but also a certain nervous state which may even not become manifest in an external reaction [p. 119].

Following the same path of enlarging the meaning of conditioned stimulus and reaction, Kupalov introduced the term "place" conditioned reflexes, which referred to a group of reactions related to a certain location of the freely moving animal in a laboratory. In these cases, the conditioned reaction does not reproduce the unconditioned motor reaction, notably the animal's movement to the food. Rather, it has its own structure and is based on a more complex organization of the cerebral processes. It essentially implies, however, the usual mechanism of a conditioned reflex and is inhibited when the unconditioned reflex is missing.

The third position regarding Pavlov's theory was developed in the 1930's and 1940's, suffered a setback in the aftermath of the 1950 conference, but subsequently gained a new impetus in recent years, and now marks the wave of the future of Soviet neurophysiology. This approach criticizes classical analytic physiology, which includes the Pavlovian conception, and proposes a basic revision of the concept of reflex so as to include the study of the active adaptation of the organism as a whole, both in animal and man. The trend is represented by Anokhin, Bernshtein, Grashchenkov (1963, 1964, 1965a,b),

Napalkov, Krushinskii, among others. Although relevant differences exist among these authors, they share the belief that a new explanation for the physiology of the brain is being discovered, and are opposed to the strict defenders of Pavlov's legacy.

To begin with, Bernshtein (1961, 1962, 1965, 1966, 1968) felt that during the second quarter of this century, the classical approach to the physiology of the nervous system had outlived its usefulness. Its conceptions no longer fit the knowledge acquired in recent years. It was dominated by a mechanical materialism which had an important role in the struggle against idealistic and vitalistic views. Sechenov (1863) and Pavlov (1923, 1927) made leading contributions to this development. This was a reductionistic materialism which considered the organism as a sum of its component parts, as a reactive system oriented toward maintaining an equilibrium with its environment. The study of the functions of organs and systems, primarily in animals under static conditions—decapitation, decerebration, narcosis or confinement to apparatus—followed naturally from this view and resulted in little practical application. Physiology was thought to be the study of reflexes conceived as elements of any act, and not as elementary acts themselves, with a certain complexity and significance. Complex motor acts were treated simply as chains of reflexes. Finally, the model of the brain's functioning was based on two premises: (a) each cell, in any given moment, receives microelements of information from the sense organs; (b) complex perceptions take shape through the combination of elements, according to rules of association.

Bernshtein (1962) provided the following rationale for his research:

> We are witness to an ever-growing number of indications that the principle of activity not only is manifested in the physiological functions of the individual but is an exceedingly general factor which penetrates

all aspects and forms of vital processes and is the basis of various phenomena studied in general biology. In contrast to the assumptions of the classical period, which treated the organism as a reacting and balancing self-regulating system, contemporary biological thought regards it as an organization characterized by two chief determining properties: In the first place, this is an organization which preserves its systematic identity with itself despite a continuous flow of energy and of the material of the substrate itself. Not a single atom is retained for longer than a very short time in a human or animal organism . . . but the organism still maintains its identity. In the second place, in spite of all this, an organism undergoes *directed changes* of all stages of its existence. This directedness is illustrated indisputably in individual development, beginning with embryogenesis, by the fact that a thousand individuals selected at random from one species develop into individuals which have the same basic characteristics in spite of very different external living conditions. It is particularly important to mention that this directed development—the realization of a definite program for morphogenesis which is ensured by this directedness—is based on a clear-cut *activity* [pp. 446-447]. [6]

In Bernshtein's view, two directions of investigation have developed in modern physiology: the physiology of self-control and the physiology of active processes. While they are very closely related to each other, Bernshtein ascribed a particular significance to the second trend. He thought of active processes as those responses of the organism possessing two essential features: first, the whole organism is included in the performance of an individual act, even of the simplest variety; second, the response of the organism to an external stimulation involves more elements than the stimulation itself. Moreover, the activity aims to solve a task and the expected result is represented in the brain in the form of a model. Two closely linked processes were assumed to take place: the probabilistic prognosis of a forthcoming event and the programming of the action resulting in the occurrence of that event. Any response of the organism, starting with tropisms and ending with complex actions, expresses the organism's capacity

[6] Translated in *A Handbook of Contemporary Soviet Psychology.*

for the coding of information and extrapolation to forthcoming events. Therefore, Bernshtein contended, we may speak about the purposefulness of the response of an organism without the risk of falling into teleology. These views will come up again later in this text.

For the last 35 years, Anokhin (1935) has been working toward developing a theory of a functional system. His model consists of a combination of processes formed under certain circumstances which lead to an adaptive action when the organism finds itself in the same situation. As proposed by Anokhin (1968) the functional system possesses a number of features. (1) It is a circular process running from periphery to center and vice versa. (2) It involves an adaptive effect which determines the distribution of stimulations throughout the whole system. (3) It includes an apparatus, the "acceptor of action" (or effect) for the reception of information about the performed action; this apparatus may be innate—e.g., the chemoreceptors of the respiratory system, or the osmoreceptors which control the osmotic processes of the blood—or acquired by experience. (4) The effect of a functional system produces a stream of return afferentation indicating the parameters of the performed action; the returning afferentation indicating an effect which ensures the satisfaction of the need which elicited the action, reinforces this effect and is labeled "sanctioning afferentation." (5) There is a continuous comparison between the results of the various attempts to attain a certain goal which are signaled by the different returning impulses, and the acceptor of effect which is a constant representative of that goal; the discrepancy between the goal and the result of an unsuccessful action provides the stimulus for the next action. (6) The formation of a functional system includes a stage of afferent synthesis of all involved external and internal stimulations. Two categories of stimulations, the triggering stimuli and the subliminal background stimuli, are integrated with the frontal lobes assumed to have a major role in the process. Some experiments done by Shumilina (1949), a coworker of Anokhin, illustrated this final point. A dog was conditioned to respond with two feeding reflexes to different rhythms of a metronome, the food being placed in two different positions. The dog sat in the middle of the room during the intervals between the stimuli and, upon hearing one of the two signals, ran to the corresponding food-rack. Once the response had been learned, the frontal lobes were removed, resulting in a drastic change of behavior. The dog now ran continuously from one food-rack to the other in a pendulumlike motion. Anokhin (1949b) interpreted these findings to illustrate the disintegration of an afferent synthesis of stimuli: the background stimulation had turned into a triggering stimulation. A control experiment was run to show that the results could not be explained in terms of mere "motor agitation." This time only one conditioned reflex was elaborated to one stimulus, and the removal of the frontal lobes had no impact on the dog's behavior. However, when the dog was fed from the second rack, the same disturbance reoccurred. Anokhin (1968) concluded that

> no understanding of the structure of the process of adaptation is possible, nor any attempt to stimulate human phenomena, without taking into account the working of functional systems, the formation of afferent syntheses, the acceptor of effect, the effect itself and the return afferentation with its result. These features of a functional system form a *non-linear* structure, since some of the apparatuses *anticipate* the events, while others *return* the information about the effect of the action to the central nervous system. The functional system is the physiological expression of the concept of self-regulation so brilliantly advanced by Pavlov as early as 1932 [p. 89].

The conflict between the neurocybernetic school and the traditional Pavlovian approach evolves precisely around the concept of a four-linked, loop-shaped reflex developed by Bernshtein and Anokhin. While Bernshtein admitted that the

classical concept of a reflex arc implied a materialistic determinism, he pointed out that it entailed a fundamental misunderstanding of the organism as a whole, oriented toward
coping actively with the tasks of adaptation. He proposed instead the concept of a *reflex loop,* implying a continuous
stream of afferent signals vital for control and correction.
Bernshtein accepted the possibility that elementary processes,
such as the reflex of salivation, or the reflex of withdrawal
produced by a painful stimulus, may not involve the loop
shape characteristic for controlled acts, either because of the
very short time involved or simply because of their very elementary nature. Yet he did not rule out the possibility that
these two reasons make the loop scheme hard to detect just in
these cases. The reflex loop is supposed to be based on the
formation of afferent systems required for a full and objective
evaluation of the object of the action, as well as of each stage
of the action. Bernshtein stressed the prevalent analytic feature of Pavlov's concept of "analyzer" which was intended to
replace that of "sense organ." Ivanov-Smolenskii's (1950,
1965) later proposal of "syntheso-analyzer" meant no more
than a formal acceptance of the process of synthesis. By contrast, the afferent system was conceived of as a synthetic structure by its very formation, including all, or almost all, the
receptors with the proprioceptors having the predominant
role. It is essentially different from the complex of reception
apparatuses labeled "signal system" where there is no need
for any objective information. The system operates if its effect
is reinforced, while the nature of the reinforcing stimulus is
irrelevant. There is an artificial relation between signal and
reaction. But the receptive system which has functions of control and coordination, such as those needed for solving a motor task, provides accurate and objective information about the
parameters of the act, continuously monitored by the resulting
actions. Bernshtein relied on the mathematical works of Gelfand and his associates (1962, 1964).

Braines (1959, 1961), the director of the Institute of Neuro-cybernetics at the Academy of Medical Sciences of the USSR and Napalkov (1961, 1962a,b, 1964a,b,c, 1965, 1969) have made original contributions in animal psychology, including a strong plea for the development of neurocybernetics—the study of informational processes in the nervous system. Napal-kov felt that the development of cybernetics, showing that large systems consisting of many elements such as the brain have properties unavailable in simple groups of elements, made obvious the need for new methods in the study of the brain. The traditional methods of physiology and psychology illuminated some principles of behavior, such as the rule of trial and error, but criteria for evaluating the applicability of a given principle were ignored. The resulting attempt to re-duce all forms of brain functioning to one or more principles of information processing—to which the Gestalt school can be seen as a reaction—did not provide adequate abstraction and the laws of information processing required for an adequate analysis of brain functioning.

Napalkov extended his criticism to a discussion of the rela-tionship between the Pavlovian school and neurocybernetics. He conceded that the principle of the conditioned reflex and the mechanism of temporary connections underlie all forms of brain functioning. He also acknowledged that the method of study developed by Pavlov was a valuable procedure for the study of informational processes. But, he maintained, the model used in this classical procedure represented only a more simple case of information processing, for typically the orga-nism was isolated from the real environment and put in an artificial milieu consisting strictly of signals controlled by the experimenter. This situation, which facilitates the formation of systems of conditioned reflexes, does not exist in reality. Attempts to design learning automata on the basis of the Pavlovian principles revealed two limitations intrinsic to these principles: (1) the elaborated system of conditioned reflexes is not flexible enough to enable complex programs of reaching the goal in indirect ways; (2) they do not ensure the occurrence of *active* search processes.

Napalkov thought that the logical development of Pavlov's experimental methods should have been the gradual extension of the model to approach the complexity of the real environment. Instead, the erroneous tendency that developed in the Pavlovian school was to regard the method of the conditioned reflex solely as a means for the study of the dynamics of the processes of excitation and inhibition. New experimental findings were not evaluated in terms of more complex informational processes, but were simply related to the laws of irradiation and induction. Moreover, the Pavlovian school began speaking about the spreading of the processes of excitation and inhibition over the whole cortical mass, disregarding the organization of neural elements into systems. The following experiments described by Braines and Napalkov illustrate their theoretical and methodological position.

A study was carried out to investigate the sequence of actions performed by different animals in their attempts to satisfy a certain organic need, namely thirst. Dogs in which a system of feeding-conditioned reflexes had been developed were made thirsty, and then fed to complete satiation. In this way, the organism was supposed to be forced to find a solution to satisfy the need for water. The algorithm included the search for some of the previous stimuli stored in the animal's memory as part of the system of feeding-conditioned reflexes. This algorithm was regarded as representing the processing of information underlying the formation of new behavioral patterns. The process was described as follows:

(1) When a new need, e.g., thirst, occurs the search for the previously elaborated chains of reflexes begins. These stimuli are successively compared with those available. If they are coincident, a reflex reaction occurs and the analysis of stimuli is discontinued. If no coincidence is found, the search continues including more and more new con-

ditioned reflexes belonging to the previously elaborated chain. (2) If any conditioned stimulus associated with the chain of drinking-conditioned reflexes is available at the time that the feeding and drinking chains have a joint conditioned stimulus, the analysis of the stimuli of the feeding chain starts from the joint stimulus. The stimuli of the feeding chain are also compared with the available stimuli. Under such conditions, when two stimuli coincide, a reflex reaction results. (3) If two stimuli coincide and the feeding and defense reflex chains possess a joint stimulus, then the analysis of the chain of defense-conditioned reflexes starts. (4) If a system of conditioned reflexes includes a chain of disinhibitory reflexes and, in addition, there is a conditioned inhibitory stimulus available, then the reflexes forming the chain become active [p. 102].

In another study (Napalkov, 1962a) three series of experiments were conducted, each requiring the subject to connect a series of signals, such as lights and sounds, with a system of responses. In the first series, a chain of responses was formed in which the transition from one stimulus to the next was dependent on the reaction to the previous stimulus. The stimuli were operated by the experimenter in such a way as to render the system of relations between stimuli and reactions completely artificial since it did not offer a picture of the actual behavior under usual conditions of life. In the subsequent two series of experiments, the experimenter's role was reduced in that the subjects themselves set the signals into operation. With incidental occurrence and removal of signals excluded, it was found that the formation of a chain of reflexes was just as fast as in the first experiment. In the third series of experiments, the experimenter's intervention was limited to setting the initial signal into operation. The subjects performed various movements at random and if there was no change, i.e., if no new signals appeared, they stopped the movements, but if new signals appeared the movements were repeated. In this way, various reflex chains were formed, until one of them led either to the attainment of the goal, or to the occurrence of one of the signals belonging to the previously elaborated system. The whole system of reflexes was then consolidated through the reinforcement of the new element. These experiments were done with different species of animals as well as with human subjects. All the animals coped with the first type of experiment, i.e., they were able to respond adequately to conditioned stimuli presented in the classical fashion. The second type of experiment proved to be beyond the capacity of lower animals such as mice. A new signal neither elicited a reaction in these animals nor did it lead to the formation of new motor skills. Napalkov and Bobneva (1962b) assumed that such a task required a large volume of operative memory. In the third type of experiment, only human subjects were capable of coping with the task.

Napalkov concluded that the functioning of self-controlled systems under complex conditions of environment is contingent upon the interaction of different principles of information processing. Although the reinforcement principle plays a significant role, it is too simple and efficient only in inferior vertebrates. In superior animals and in man a complex system of reinforcing stimuli is in operation, making possible a better selection of useful information. A system of conditioned reflexes is formed which is not merely representative of their sum, but comprises a certain structure. Certain conditioned stimuli belonging to this structure acquire reinforcing power and play a major role in the establishment of new conditioned reflexes, by taking part in the selection of the external information. There are two kinds of such reinforcing stimuli. The stimuli belonging to the first type have an intermediary and auxiliary role, providing preliminary reinforcement. The system of reflexes does not take shape if it is not reinforced by an unconditioned stimulus (food). This is the principle of a double reinforcement. Only single, new conditioned reflexes forming part of a chain can be elaborated in this way. The reinforcing stimuli of the second type are stimuli which need not be followed by an unconditioned stimulus. They ensure the formation of "independent" chains of reactions.

While it was easy to determine that reinforcers of the first type are all the conditioned stimuli of conditioned reflexes established previously, the question as to what underlies the reinforcing capacity of the second type of stimuli is more complex. Certain factors could, however, be disclosed. Thus, all the component elements of a complex stimulus acquire this reinforcing capacity. It is widely known that Pavlov described the formation of a conditioned reflex to a combination of two or more stimuli which could not yield a reaction when presented individually. Napalkov (1962a) noted that these stimuli acquire a reinforcing capacity: a new stimulus associated with one of the stimuli belonging to a combination was apt to produce a conditioned (feeding) reaction, without being reinforced (by food). Furthermore, a new conditioned reflex could be formed if a new stimulus was included in an already formed combination, preceding one of its components. The inclusion of this stimulus became a reinforcer of the second type.

Napalkov described more complex rules of information processing, particularly in human behavior. Thus, in man, the selection of external information is not based only on the selection of individual signals and reactions, but also on formed combinations of conditioned reflexes without reinforcement. Moreover, the extinction of conditioned motor reflexes appeared to be selective: they occurred under certain conditions and were inhibited under other ones. It was also noted that certain stimuli had an orientational role towards the attainment of the goal of behavior. Thus, if the subject's actions were reinforced by chance, then all the stimuli present at that moment acquired an orientational role, acting as a sort of intermediary goal.

Krushinskii (1958, 1959, 1960, 1965a,b), from Moscow University, a student of animal behavior, is another author who departed from the strict Pavlovian position. He felt that the concept of a conditioned reflex is insufficient to explain complex forms of behavior. Krushinskii had been interested in the physiological process underlying the animals' capacity to extrapolate, that is to predict the future changes of a certain value on the basis of the information about its regular changes in the past. Various experiments were done with doves, hens, birds of the crow family, rabbits, cats and dogs, in which the animals were to find a stimulus (food) in a rectilinear, constant velocity motion. The food was first in the animal's visual field and then hidden behind a screen. Two types of associations had to be formed between the stimulus (A) and the screen (B) in order for the animal to get the food: (1) an association between A and B; the animal does not perceive A any longer and starts responding to B, which was an indifferent stimulus and now acquires a meaning; (2) an association between A and the direction of its motion; this association is formed after the animal has discovered the regular change of A's position. After the formation of the first association, the animals looked for the food around the screen. After the second association was formed, they searched for it in the direction of its motion.

Two groups of animals could be distinguished. The first group consisted of doves, hens and rabbits, which formed rigid conditioned reflexes of going around the screen. The birds of the crow family, cats and dogs made up the second group, which was able to follow the direction of the motion of the food. It appeared that there are two types of relationships between conditioned and unconditioned reflexes. (1) When the conditions under which the extrapolation reflexes are formed remain relatively stable, elements of conditioned reflexes are involved. The amount of individual experience required for the solution of this problem varies. For instance, the birds of the crow family were able to follow the displacement of food behind a screen without any experience. When the experiment became more complex, these birds required some learning. (2) Under certain circumstances, when a task can be solved either way, a conflict may arise between the extrapolation and the conditioned reflexes. The animal would attempt the extrapolation method, but as soon as this proved too difficult it reverted to the simple method of association.

Krushinskii's conclusions are at variance with the views of other Russian students of animal behavior, among whom is Ladygina-Kots (1959, 1965)—as will be seen in the next chapter—that even monkeys are not capable of grasping cause-effect relations. Krushinskii (1965b) wrote:

> The investigation confirmed that animals are able to grasp elementary cause-effect relations among the phenomena of the external world. . . . These relations are apparently realized due to the animals' capacity to establish associations . . . on the basis of brief information. The investigations showed that the brains of various species of animals possess different capacities to use such information for working out a program of certain behavioral acts of various degrees of complexity. . . . The animals' capacity to form express-informational associations underlying these acts enable them to respond not only to a current situation but also to extrapolate the dynamics of changes of relations among phenomena. . . . The specific fulfillment of these acts and the fact that a single brief piece of information (without reinforcement) is sufficient for the realization of elementary cause-effect relations make them different from conditioned reflexes [p. 63].

A variety of arguments have been put forward against the neurocybernetic approach and in particular against Bernshtein's and Anokhin's contentions, ranging from the philosophical issue of determinism in the nervous activity to specific matters such as the mechanism of inhibition. One has the feeling that the basic issue of the relationship between the reflex concept as the principle of functioning of the nervous system and the specific hypotheses about the nature of conditioned reflexes remains quite confused. On the one hand, the proponents of a revised concept of reflex have emphasized their distinction between the two issues and their acceptance of the principle, but this demarcation is far from being clear-cut. On the other hand, those who held the traditional Pavlovian view, agree that Pavlov's specific hypotheses are subject to change with the acquisition of new data, but they have obviously tended to identify any departure from Pavlov's theory as a deviation from the reflex principle. The position posed by Sarkisov et al. [7] (1963) is instructive.

A comparison between the views on the nature of the reflex of scholars with an anti-Pavlovian orientation, and the views of the Pavlovian school well illustrates the fact that the same words may have different meanings. The use of the concept of reflex requires particular caution since in addition to the different interpretations given by schools of physiology, there are differences in the understanding of its philosophical meaning. It is obvious that when the critics of Pavlov's views reject the application of the reflex principle to the analysis of the complex forms of behavior, they do not reject a certain concrete theory of the physiological structure of the reflex act, but rather the most general philosophical idea of the reflex nature of the vital activity. . . . We emphasize that we cannot, in principle, reject the philosophical concept of reflex. . . . Its rejection would mean rejecting the dialectic-materialistic view of adaptive behavior, and the idea of the unity organism-environment, to yield to vitalism. . . . However, we have to point out that our position requires a clear and consistent distinction between the philosophical and the physiological meanings of the concept of reflex. Unlike the clear philosophical meaning, emerging from methodological principles, the physiological meaning is never definite, being dependent on the continuous development of physiology. We have to take into account that in recent years important advances have been made regarding the nature of the reflex activity . . . largely due to the introduction of mathematical concepts in biology. . . . We have to ask whether Pavlov's theory was shaken by this development. . . . It is obvious that a negative answer should be given to such a question, even if the new concepts of the concrete mechanism of the reflex activity would not have a direct, logical connection to the traditional views of the Pavlovian school. In that case, we should have spoken about the progressive changes of the initial concepts of the Pavlovian school under the influence of sciences related to physiology. If the new concepts which are deepening the physiological theory of the reflex are stimulated by such advances, on the one hand, and on the other hand represent a

[7] A lecture given at the postdoctoral institute for physicians.

further logical and experimental development of basic ideas of the Pavlovian school, then the very question about whether the new concepts
are damaging to Pavlov's theory is pointless [pp. 19-20].

Following this line of reasoning, Sarkisov and his colleagues
played down the significance of the new concepts to show that
they are not as original as they claim to be. First, they traced
back to Sechenov the assumption that there would have to
be more than a single connection between the manifestations
of a function and the stimulations eliciting it. He had introduced the concept of a supplementary signaling consisting of
muscular sensations which have an important role for the
coordination and correction of movements. Furthermore, Sechenov was aware of the possibility of such connections between reflexes when the end of one reflex becomes the stimulus
for the next one. He also analyzed the structure of various
receptors and formulated a detailed description of the role of
the central and peripheral links of the reflex process. As a
matter of fact, Sechenov's role as a precursor of the modern
concepts of neurocybernetics was also mentioned by Rosenblith
(1964). Therefore, Sechenov, as well as Pavlov, is said to have
considered the structure of the reflex activity as including those
processes which are now presented as an alternative to the concept of a reflex arc. The new concepts are not opposed to the
classical concepts but are their logical extension. Hence, there
is a methodological fallacy in Anokhin's and Bernshtein's interpretation of the advances in neurocybernetics. Concluding
their criticism, Sarkisov and his associates stated that regardless of advances involving the structure of the reflex act and
the introduction of new and more complex schemes of a reflex
loop

. . . a reflex act, conceived in its most general form as an act of adaptation, appears under the influence of a stimulus, develops as a sort of
"central process" and ends by an "action." It is precisely in this "active" completion of the reflex, i.e., in its completion in an objective pro-

cess leading to certain changes in the external or the internal milieu of
the organism, that there lies the deep biological meaning of the reflex
act as a mechanism of purposeful adaptation . . . [pp. 30–31].

Additional objections (Kupalov, 1962; Alekseev, 1958) referred to the presumed existence of a fourth stage to the
reflex, consisting of a returned stimulation from a performed
act. It was pointed out that the evaluation of an effect of a
reflex act is not based solely on the returned afferent stimulation but also on information processing, as well as on an additional effectory stage since the coincidence between the effect
of the reflex and the expected result does not simply lead to a
passive denervation, but to an active process of reinforcement
of this effect. That means that what Anokhin supposed to be
the fourth link of a reflex act is actually a combination of two
processes at least. As regards the "acceptor of effect," this
term was said to fail to suggest any specific neurological substratum of psychical images. It means little more than that a
comparison is made somewhere in the brain between different
stimulations. Thus, the substitution of the concept of reinforcement is not justified, since it is precisely the acceptance
of a certain effect of an action by the organism which is the
basis of reinforcement. Finally, objections were made against
the possibility that a number of unsuccessful actions followed
by one which is ultimately "sanctioned."

The Localization of Cerebral Functions

The enforcement of Pavlov's views on the cortical-
subcortical relations and on the localization of the cortical
functions was a relevant part of the Pavlovization of Soviet
neurophysiology and psychology after 1950. A conference of
neurologists and psychiatrists held in 1951 (Banshchikov et al.,
1952) was devoted to the criticism of non-Pavlovian views
regarding these issues, in particular the theory of "cerebral

pathology" supported by Gurevich (1948), Shmaryan (1949) and others. The debate of a psychological conference reflected the same spirit (Decision, 1952; Menchinskaya et al., 1952). A few years later, an extensive discussion aimed at clarifying the Pavlovian position was initiated by *Zhurnal Nevropatologii i Psikhiatrii* (Sepp, 1955; Kukuev, 1955; Grinshtein, 1956; Bassin, 1956; Preobrazhenskaya, 1957; Bakhur, 1956; Gertsberg, 1956; Sarkisov, 1957a,b). Predictably, the change of climate also had an impact on the study of neuroanatomy, histology, etc. and on the formulation of new hypotheses in these fields.

Certainly, one cannot help wondering about the fate of the Pavlovian tenets in the light of new findings concerning the role of the reticular formation of the brain stem in maintaining the functional level of the cerebral cortex. Soviet authors have paid much attention to the new developments and as with the studies discussed in the previous section, one may distinguish between strong holders of the traditional Pavlovian view and students who are more inclined to accept those hypotheses advanced in the West. However, the demarcation in this case seems to be less sharp.

The main tenets of the Pavlovian position were summarized by Ivanov-Smolenskii (1950) in the following statements. (1) The whole cortex is a complex of analyzers. (2) Besides analyzers reflecting the external environment, there are analyzers reflecting the inner milieu of the organism. (3) The motor area performs the function of reception, analysis and synthesis of the kinesthetic stimuli which reach the cortex. (4) Each analyzer has a central part, a "nucleus," which effects the highest form of analysis and synthesis of stimulations, and a periphery for a gross analysis and synthesis; there are no definite boundaries between analyzers which interpenetrate at the periphery. (5) The whole cortex has an associative function; there are no special associative centers or areas. (6) There is no so-called mnestic center, but the whole cortex is apt to imprint the vestiges of stimulation. (7) There is no special area or center for an ultimate integration of stimulations.

Pavlov considered the functioning of the brain as made possible through specific pathways and areas. Yet he did not agree to a narrow and very specific localization of complex functions. Soviet authors have consistently challenged the two opposed schools regarding the localization of cerebral functions (Sarkisov, 1964b). They are critical of what they call the "psychomorphological" approach which assumes a direct relation between the anatomical structure of the brain and complex mental processes, as well as of the "equipotentialist" view that the brain works as an indivisible whole. However, it is admitted (Luriya, 1962) that both schools have facilitated a better understanding of the topic.

According to the Pavlovian school, the evolution of the nervous system essentially consisted of a gradual complication of its organization. New and better differentiated afferent, efferent and comissural connections have developed and the evolution of the peripheral apparatus for reception went together with a higher organization of the cortex. In the course of its evolution, the cortex assumed functions which had been carried out at inferior levels of the brain in a more primitive way; i.e., a "corticalization" of functions took place. Along with the morphological and physiological development of the individual analyzers there was a development of the integrative functions of the higher levels of the central nervous system, in particular the cortex. In man there was a prevalent development of the neocortex, i.e., of the frontal, inferiorparietal, temporoparieto-occipital areas. In comparison with the monkey, there was an increase both in the width of the cortex and the dimensions of the cells, as well as a reduction in the density of cortical cells due to the development of dendrites and axons.

Given this perspective, Soviet authors have rejected, first, the conclusion drawn by investigators such as Nauta, Papez,

Bailey and Bonin that the cortex does not play a major role in the functioning of the nervous system, second, Penfield's theory of a centroencephalic system and, third, the hypotheses advanced by Fessard, Gastaut, Jasper and others concerning the subcortical mechanisms of the conditioned reflex. The results of Russian studies, in particular at the Brain Institute of the Academy of Medical Sciences, have frequently been used as arguments against the above conjectures (G. Vasilev, 1956; Zurabashvili, 1957; Glezer and Zvorykin, 1960; Stankevich, 1960; Sarkisov, 1960a,b, 1963a, 1964a,b, 1965). Thus, studies of the evolution of the mammalian cortex showed that important changes occurred not only in the neocortex but also in the intermediate cortex. As the surface of this area became larger its structure became more differentiated. Kononova (1962) found that the frontal lobes constitute 9 per cent of the cortex in lower monkeys, 14 per cent in superior monkeys and 24 per cent in man. Shkolnik-Yarros (1954, 1962, 1965) noticed significant phylogenetic changes in the structure of area 17 of the occipital lobe. Significant human individual differences were discovered by Sarkisov, the director of the Brain Institute, with regard to the width of the cortex, the density of cells, their dimensions, etc. Blinkov and Glezer (1964) showed that there was a significant development of the inferiorparietal lobe and of the temporal lobe in man, to the effect that there are six areas of juncture among the temporal, parietal and occipital lobes as contrasted to only two such areas in monkeys. He also found a considerable complication of the cellular structure of the central part of the auditory analyzer, area 41, which in man presumably relates to speech. Finally, Adrianov and Rabinovich (1960) showed that the relative dimensions of the reticular formation are remarkably reduced in vertebrates.

These, among many other such findings, are said to negate Bailey and Bonin's (1951) conclusion that there are no objective criteria for the distinction of areas and zones. They have also thought to invalidate Penfield and Jasper's (1954) claim that the reticulate formation is responsible for the ultimate integration of cerebral processes. Convergence of stimulations at the upper areas of the brain stem does not prove that this is the highest level of integration.

Soviet authors have also raised a number of methodological objections regarding the role ascribed to subcortical structures. For example, Sarkisov (1964b) took issue with Magoun and Rhines' statement that by destroying the reticular formation of the brain stem, while keeping intact all the specific afferent paths, it was possible to produce a comalike state. He felt that this could not be proven conclusively because there was no histological evidence that the afferent pathways actually remained intact in view of their immediate proximity to the reticular formation. While Sarkisov admitted the possibility that some changes occur in the cortical-electrical potentials when certain subcortical areas are stimulated, he did not admit that these areas make up part of the reticular formation. Actually, the question has been raised by a number of Soviet authors as to whether the method of local electrical stimulation is at all adequate for the study of cortical functions.

Much importance has also been attached to the problem of the level in the central nervous system at which it was possible to obtain conditioned reflexes. Pavlov admitted three possibilities of connections: corticocortical, corticosubcortical and corticosubcortico-cortical, but was more inclined to regard the connection as being exclusively cortical. He wrote that the basic mechanism in the formation of conditioned reflexes consists in the coincidence in time of a stimulation at a certain cortical point, with a stronger stimulation at another point, perhaps also cortical. As a result, a path is trodden and an association occurs. It seems, then, that Pavlov did not take a firm position regarding the place where connections are formed. Yet the belief that conditioned reflexes are a cortical process *par excellence* remains deeply rooted in the Pavlovian school. There is still a strong tendency to reject the hypothesis of the formation of conditioned reflexes, i.e., of temporary connections, in subcortical structures. As a matter of fact, the findings of Gastaut, Fessard, Jasper, Morell, Lissak and Yoshi have been favorably received, yet their interpretations are consistently refuted. For instance Adrianov and Rabinovich (1960) criticized Gastaut's principle of convergence for its failure to account for a number of facts described when the classical procedures were used. In their view, the electroencephalographic findings to which Gastaut and others referred did not provide a direct proof of conditioned reflexes being formed either in the reticular formation or in the thalamus. Such a conclusion based on the similarity between the effect of local stimulation in the reticular formation, and the occurrence of a conditioned reflex—in both cases there is a desynchronization of the alpha rhythm—was not accepted as reliable. Additional objections were raised by Roitbak (1960) and Livanov (1960, 1969), two authorities in electrophysiology, who rejected the proposition that the appearance of evoked potentials in the reticular formation earlier than in the cortex means that the conditioned reflex was elaborated there. Roitbak also disagreed with Gastaut that during the formation of a conditioned reflex only the focus corresponding to the unconditioned stimulus appears in the cortex, while the cortical area of the conditioned stimulus has no part in the formation of a temporary connection. He pointed out that the same peripheral stimulation can elicit different electrical reactions in the corresponding cortical receptive zone as a result of its association with an unconditioned stimulus. Therefore, any change of a conditioned reflex will be expressed in electrographical changes in the cortical focus of the conditioned stimulus.

Another area of disagreement between Russian neuroanatomists and their Western counterparts concerns the neuronal organization of the nervous system. Soviet authors have strongly inclined to assume that the nerve fibers are connected to each other by way of nervous cells and not directly. For

Polyakov (1960, 1962, 1964a,b, 1965) this issue is basic to the search for the material substratum of the process of reflection. In his view, the nervous system consists of neurons which ensure the coordination among various processes. Any theory which regards the nervous system as a diffuse and undifferentiated network would fail to account for its selectivity, its directed transmission of stimulation, and for the formation of patterns of stimulation and inhibition. However, Polyakov did admit that the neuronal theory needed revision since it became clear that the neurons could not be studied in isolation but only in relation to their environment. Single stimulations are transmitted over wide areas precisely because of certain elements of the neuroglia.

Despite these divergent views, there has been an obvious influence of Western findings concerning the role of subcortical structures for the functioning of the cortex, in particular with regard to the role of the reticular formation of the brain stem (Nebylitsyn, 1964; Bekhtereva, 1965; Zurabashvili, 1958, 1961, 1964; Chernigovskii, 1965b). It has been frequently pointed out, in recent years, that Pavlov himself ascribed a significant role to the stimulations emerging from subcortical structures. One is reminded that Pavlov considered the thalamic nuclei as a "blind force," since the emotions linked to them have a strong influence on the functioning of the cortex. Sarkisov (1964a) emphasized that the work of Magoun, Morrison, Dempsey and Jasper on the relations between the cortex, thalamus and hypothalamus have yielded valuable information. A symposium organized by the Georgian Academy of Sciences (Dzidzishvili, 1960) on the formation of temporary connections illustrates the trends of current Soviet neurophysiology. Some of the opinions voiced were definitely not in line with the classical Pavlovian school. Dzidzishvili, a leading physiologist and a coworker of Beritov, favored the general concept of brain functioning instead of that of cortical functioning. He stressed the difficulty of making a clear distinction between superior and subordinate formations in the nervous system:

> If we were able to perform an operation on the subcortical structures, equivalent to that of the removal of the cortex, then the cortical activity once deprived of the subcortex would appear so disturbed as to reveal the predominant role played by the subcortex . . . [p. 346].

The work of Beritov (1959, 1961, 1966, 1969a,b) challenged Pavlov's theory of the localization of cortical functions from a different perspective (Sarkisov, 1963c). In recent years, he has further developed his concept of a "psychoneural" activity which is distinct from a more elementary conditioned-reflex activity and is assumed to represent the functioning of the stellar neurons.

Finally, the concept of analyzer has come under attack, a topic which will be taken up in the next chapter.

Psyche and Consciousness

The definition of consciousness and the description of its role in human behavior currently constitutes a major concern for Soviet psychology which is proclaimed as the study of man guided by his consciousness (Leontev, 1967a; Kuzmin, 1964; Spirkin, 1959; Shorokhova, 1961; Megrabyan, 1959; Protasenya, 1961). There is a great deal of unanimity among Soviet authors in refuting theories which subordinate the conscious life to the unconscious. All Freudian theories and their derivatives are placed in this category because of their insistence on the dominance of unconscious factors in behavior (Logvin, 1959; Bondarenko and Rabinovich, 1959; Morozov, 1961; Vulfzon, 1965; Kositskii, 1961, 1962; Mikhailov and Tsaregorodtsev, 1961, 1962; Bassin, 1960, 1962, 1963). A comprehensive discussion of this issue is available in English (Bassin, 1963).

By and large, the relationship between mind and consciousness is discussed within the framework of the matter-psyche issue so that the conflicting views here parallel those mentioned at the beginning of this chapter. As a matter of fact, the concepts of psyche and consciousness are occasionally used interchangeably in the philosophical publications. The major points of the Soviet description of consciousness can be spelled out briefly.

Consciousness is regarded as the highest form of reflection and is specific to man. Because of language, human reflection is distinctly different from reflection on the animal level and is not limited to mere reception of impressions. Since man is aware of the content of his impressions, his consciousness is a derivative reflection of the primary reflection, i.e., man realizes the process of reflection itself. He develops a logical system of propositions which represent a creative, transformed reflection of reality. Nonhumans, on the other hand, do not relate to external reality in this fashion and therefore cannot assume a position toward it. The presence of consciousness thus implies the individual's detachment from external reality, the object of his knowledge, and the taking of a position towards other people and, through them, achieving self-realization (Georgiev, 1965).

The essence of consciousness lies precisely in the knowledge of reality but is not confined to sensations, perceptions, representations and thought. It is also defined as being involved in the anticipation of events and actions, as having the quality of purposefulness (Spirkin, 1959). The emergence of consciousness is closely linked to the development of man's ability to use tools, that is a collective mastering of objects and implements in an activity oriented towards the satisfaction of the primitive society.

The following passage from the 1966 textbook gives a straightforward presentation of the view of Soviet psychology.

The new psychical qualities of man occurred as a form of adaptation to new social and work conditions in the life of primitive man. . . . The development of a voluntary behavior, of the ability to foresee and plan the results of work, of imagination and of speech represent an important aspect of the new and higher stage of psychical development in man—consciousness. The planned, conscious activity of man had an essential influence on the character of the productive work. The occurrence of consciousness implies the possibility of self-control, of self-evaluation. This possibility appears only when man possesses speech. . . . The capacity of self-reflection in all the aspects of the vital activity is the capacity of self-consciousness. However, the development of work and speech were not enough for the occurrence of consciousness. The reflection in man's head of the social relations and of his position in these relations has been the most important factor of the development of consciousness and self-consciousness. This understanding occurred together with the division of labor and developed together with it. The division of labor led to a differentiated attitude of the collective toward each member. It required the account of the individual features of each man. . . . The individual qualities acquired a social significance and the individual himself became a person. Now, the individual perceives the qualities revealed in him by the society as his own qualities and takes the same position toward them as the society does. Hence, the person appears as a social phenomenon, and the attitude toward himself becomes the basis for self-consciousness and self-control [pp. 91–92].

3

Sensory Cognition

The theoretical and experimental study of sensation, perception and representation currently holds a major position in Soviet psychology. There is considerable interest in the philosophical problems raised by the role of the sensory experience in human knowledge. The recent approach to perceptual processes in terms of information theory has added a new dimension to the concept of reflection. Although this chapter is primarily concerned with recent studies, certain earlier studies which have provided the background for current investigations have also been included.

Historical Outline of Studies on Sensory Processes

Bekhterev, who appears to have been the first Russian to carry out systematic studies on sensory processes, introduced the method of conditioned reflexes into the study of sensorimotor reactions. Ananev (1958) credited Bekhterev with the finding that each sensory apparatus contains both afferent and efferent components and that phenomena of reverse conductibility take place in the visual, auditory, tactile

· 125 ·

and other sensory systems. It was here that sensory reactions were found to be accompanied by changes of tonus in the whole organism and thus inseparable from emotional states. Bekhterev also pointed to the role of the vestibular reflexes for all the sensorimotor responses in man. Finally, the first description was made of the sequential occurrence of the various sensory modalities in early childhood.

Kornilov, as has been mentioned, demonstrated the relationship between sensory and motor reactions, suggesting their common nature. His study (1921) of the relationship between intensity of reactions and reaction time opened the way for later investigation of the signaling functions of sensations.

Soviet authors regard their studies on the origin of sensitivity as a major contribution because of the implication for a clear extension of the field beyond psychophysics. Blonskii, the first to tackle this problem, hypothesized a relation to the biochemical foundations of life. At the beginning of the 1930's, Leontev (1940) initiated the experimental investigation of the origin of sensitivity, and his assumption about the signaling function of sensations as a new form of adaptation became a major issue in Soviet psychology.

The study of visual processes has become a relevant field of study since the 1920's with the investigations initiated by Teplov, Smirnov and Shevarev which were concerned primarily with the practical study of masking. During the years 1930–1950, Kravkov's studies on visual sensation and, more generally, the relations among the various sensory modalities were central to Soviet psychophysiology. During the same period, the investigations of Bykov, which originated in Pavlov's laboratories, demonstrated the relations between external stimulations and the inner milieu of the organism. In so doing, they pioneered an objective approach to subconscious phenomena (Razran, 1961). The study of interoceptive conditioned reflexes is being continued by some of Bykov's co-workers. During the same period, the 1930's and the 1940's, Teplov conducted studies on the formation of musical aptitudes which have developed into a broad investigation of individual differences. This proved to be a fruitful area of research under Teplov, and was continued by Nebylitsyn, upon his death in 1965. In the late 1930's, an extensive study of the relations among the various sensory modalities, and in particular of the role of paired functioning of the cerebral hemispheres, was started at the Leningrad University by Ananev (1907–1970), a prolific writer. Between 1944 and 1954, more than 70 experimental studies were done on the laws of sensitization and the dependence of the dynamics of sensations on brain functioning.

In the 1950's, Sokolov embarked on a study of the conditioned reflexes formed within a single specific analyzer. These studies, carried out first at the Institute of Defectology of the RSFSR Academy of Pedagogical Sciences, and later at the departments of psychology and physiology of the higher nervous activity at Moscow University, have led Sokolov to a modern theory of perception. He is currently concerned with the application of a stochastic model to the study of perception. Of particular interest are the current studies done at the Institute of Biophysics of the Academy of Sciences concerning the modeling of visual processes.

SENSORY COGNITION AND THE ACQUISITION OF KNOWLEDGE

The premise that sensory experience represents the first stage in the formation of knowledge is basic to all Soviet research on sensory processes (Batishchev et al., 1964; Narskii, 1968; Natadze, 1970). Knowledge commences with the contemplation of objects and phenomena. Lenin (1909) has often been quoted as having written: "From live contemplation to abstract thought, and from this to actual practice, this is the dialectical path leading to truth, to the objective reality" (p. 177). The following statement from a textbook of Marxist philosophy (I. Andreev, 1959) is characteristic:

> In order to be acquainted with an object . . . we first have to look at it, to find out its color and shape, to test its solidity, to investigate it, if possible, by taste, smell, hearing, etc. Only by an empirical inquiry can the material obtained serve as a basis for rational cognition and future familiarity with the object concerned. Any process of thinking is based on the information obtained by either direct or indirect communication with material objects. Thought can only be concerned with some previous sensory experience . . . [p. 130].

The sensory and the rational stages of knowledge are assumed to be closely related to each other. The holder of the chair of dialectical materialism at the philosophy department of the Moscow University, stated this plainly (Georgiev et al., 1965):

> A sensation or a representation cannot occur without thinking. Nor does the "atomism" reflect the real state of things. Any sensory knowledge which is not raised to the level of logical thought cannot pretend to be true knowledge. The realization of the sensory content of consciousness, without which no knowledge is possible, is a complex empirical and logical process of analysis and synthesis, of differentiation and integration of the totality of facts included in man's cognitive and practical activity [p. 4].

In Ananev's (1960) view as well, the transformation of matter into consciousness, which is expressed in specific sensations, as well as the translation of sensations into concepts, are of prime significance in the dialectic of knowledge.

Although there seems to be a wide agreement among philosophers and psychologists that elements of abstract knowledge are already inherent in the sensory processes, two viewpoints have been expressed with regard to the level of sensory contact with external reality at which the process of abstraction and generalization occurs. According to Andreev (1959) and to Rutkevich (1959)—the author of another textbook about dialectical materialism—a process of generalization occurs only in representations, which are therefore a higher form of sensory reflection than sensations and perceptions. However, in Georgiev's (1965) view an elementary generalization is already inherent in sensations, consisting of the relationship between general and particular. This means that sensations do not only set apart the properties of objects in contrast to each other, but also connect these properties to each other. For instance, the sensation of red exists not only because it is opposed to other colors, but also because there is a unity between it and the other colors. It is precisely due to these relations that sensations have a *signaling* function: a sensation provides information not only about a given feature of the object, but also about the other features with which it is related. If one does not admit that sensation implies a certain generalization, Georgiev contended, one fails to understand both the transition from perception to representation and from sensory to rational cognition.

THE SPECIFICITY OF SENSE ORGANS

In the Soviet criticism of idealistic theories of sensation, the viewpoint identified as "physiological idealism" has come under the heaviest attack (Petlenko, 1960). This position is based on Mühler's law of the specific energy of sense organs. Stepanov bluntly stated in the 1966 textbook that Mühler "falsified" well-known facts, drawing conclusions unrelated to them. Furthermore, he charged that the idealistic tenet which underlies Mühler's theory, namely, that sensations do not link, but rather separate the organism from the external world, is to this date still advocated by some scientists.

In recent years, American scientists have tried to demonstrate experimentally the unknowability of the world. They have designed a system of lenses, based on optical laws, such that a person looking through it under specially arranged conditions, sees an orderly room. When the device is removed, it turns out that debris is strewn about in a chaotic state. These idealist-scientists intend to suggest that the eye is like this system of lenses, forgetting that they designed it on the basis of the most precise knowledge of optics [p. 105].

The basic position of Soviet authors is that the specific functioning of sense organs is the result of the evolution of the organism's adaptation to its environment. This evolution has required an accurate reflection of stimuli (E. N. Sokolov, 1962). Any specific response results from the adaptation of a sense organ to a certain group of stimuli. This viewpoint was clearly expressed by the neurologist Grashchenkov (1959):

> We do not deny that some specific qualities are inherent in the functioning of the various sense organs. Unlike Johannes Mühler, however, we do not regard this specificity as a rigid, permanent property of the sense organs, but as something emerging from the relationships of each organism to its environment. . . . Only as a result of a constant interaction between members of the animal world, including man, and environment do specific forms of visual, auditory, olfactory, taste and tactile sensations take form in response to multiqualitative stimuli originating from the external world. Particular stimuli led to the formation of particular peripheral receptors, each possessing clear, well-defined physiological characteristics allowing them to react specifically . . . notably different degrees of membrane permeability, different patterns of negatively and positively charged ions and different frequencies and amplitudes of occurrence of ions on the cellular membrane of a particular receptor [p. 342].

Certainly, Soviet psychologists have been concerned with the problem of relationship between the sense organ's general property of reactivity to any stimulus and its specific response. Ananev (1948) distinguished between sensations and sensory responses to nonspecific stimulations. He saw the difference at the level of the cognitive phase: only a subjective state produced by the stimulation of a sense organ which results in an image of external reality can be regarded as a sensation in the proper sense of the world. In Ananev's view, one may be sure of the presence of sensitivity but unsure of the presence of sensation under the following circumstances: (1) a subjective experience as a result of a functional change in a sense organ submitted to inadequate stimulation; (2) a subjective experience as result of a sense organ being submitted to the simultaneous action of accessory stimuli; (3) a complex subjective experience related to the effect of stimuli, i.e., to the dynamics of the consecutive images. In the above instances, the conversion of a subjective state into an image of reality does not take place. Hence, no process of cognition can be assumed to have occurred. Subjective experiences are converted into meaningful knowledge of objects and their properties only when the stimulus has been applied to the corresponding sense organ.

Ananev reported experiments of his coworkers which offered evidence that the subjective states following non-specific stimulation may be converted into cognitive images provided that certain representations are deliberately elaborated. Berkenblit (Ananev, 1960), for example, has shown that a man can learn to establish the intensity of a painful electric stimulation produced by an induction coil, if he is informed from the start of the experiment of the approximate strength of the stimuli. The average error in estimation was 0.7 cm. at an average intensity of the stimulus, falling to 0.5 and even 0.2 cm. on the application of stronger stimuli. When the intensity of the stimulus was very high, approaching the limit of the subject's level of tolerance, the ability to estimate correctly once again diminished, and it ultimately became impossible to make any estimate because a defense reaction set in. Berkenblit's experiments have also indicated that sensations of pain can be discriminated not only with regard to the intensity of the stimulus but also in terms of the particular qualities of the stimulus concerned. For example, subjects were able to discriminate the stimulation produced by a cronaximeter from that produced by an induction coil.

The possibility for a subjective state to be transformed into a cognitive image was also demonstrated in other sensory modalities previously considered inaccessible to the development of distinct sensory images. Thus, Gusev (Ananev, 1960) was able to demonstrate the capacity of the gustatory analyzer to reflect the biochemical processes related to the metabolism of minerals and carbohydrates during the transition from satiation to hunger and vice versa. Observations were made at various intervals. It was observed that initially as the sensation of hunger increased, the sensitivity for sweet and salted food also became heightened. However, the sensitivity for bitter and sharp-tasting food remained unchanged and in some cases a tendency for a lowered sensitivity was noticed. Eventually, however, a lowering of the discriminating sensitivity for sweet substances took place. Thus, the introduction of a small quantity of sugar to milk was noticed by 85 per cent of the satiated subjects whereas only 55 per cent were aware of the addition of a small quantity of salt. Only 56 per cent of the hungry subjects, however, appreciated the sugar, and 60 per cent, the salt.

Ill-defined sensory reactions to vibration were also shown to be capable of conversion into more discriminating sensations. By systematic and repeated training with a special vibrator, it became possible for deaf-mute children to develop a sensitivity to vibration. These children learned to discriminate different frequencies and intensities of speech sounds and subsequently even of words and sentences. The sounds were transmitted in the form of vibrations of the diaphragm of a vibrator connected to a microphone and were perceived by the children through touch. After 10 to 12 trials, the majority of the children could identify 83 per cent of the transmitted sounds and words, some of them even perceiving all the sounds. They were also able to distinguish rhythm, accent etc.

SENSATION AND PERCEPTION

In Russian textbooks, sensation and perception are usually

discussed in separate chapters. Thus, in the 1966 textbook, there is a chapter entitled "Sensation and Sensitivity" and another one on "Perception and the Capacity of Observation." Soviet authors spare no effort to persuade the reader that the perceptual Gestalt is not a primary formation. Ananev (1960) pointed out that

> . . . the Soviet science emphasizes the qualitative difference between sensation and perception and maintains the integral object-oriented character of the perceptual image, while rejecting the idealistic theory of the primary integrity and structure of perception [p. 230].

However, the nature of the difference between sensation and perception is far from being a clear issue. Certain authors regard sensation as the reflection of a particular property of an object as a whole. Rubinshtein (1948) considered sensation and perception as distinct psychical processes in terms of what is reflected. He felt that the difference becomes evident when the interoceptive and exteroceptive spheres of sensitivity are compared: sensations mainly occur in the interoceptive sphere, whereas perceptions are related to external receptors. Furthermore, Rubinshtein classified the sensations into (a) primary sensory impressions—the hereditary, anatomical and functional properties of the specialized receptors making possible a degree of discrimination of stimuli; (b) sensations resulting from the correlation between the discrimination of stimuli and reactions of the organism. Rubinshtein assumed that sensations take shape as more and more conditioned reflexes are formed on the initial background of the unconditioned reflexes which underly the primary sensory impressions. In time, sensations begin to reflect more complex properties either of the same stimulus or of other stimuli. During the course of the individual life experience, the relevant features of objects are reflected by sensations and these become perceptions when they begin to provide information about objects in the form of clear images instead of signals. Thus, sensation implies an analysis and discrimination of stimuli, whereas perception performs the analysis and synthesis of properties of objects.

However, Volkov (1950), the author of a major work on the perception of objects and drawings, disagreed with these concepts, claiming that they made the erroneous assumption that perception is a more complex process than sensation. He wrote:

> The unity of the perceptual image is ensured by the integrity of the object acting upon the sense organ and, as such, by the unity of the sensations. The richness of this image reflects at the same time the richness of the qualities of the object and, hence, of the sensations themselves. Finally, the general nature of the image corresponds, in certain respects, to the sum of the qualities of that particular object in comparison with other objects of the material world and, as such, to the sum of sensations [pp. 366-367].

But there persists the tendency to distinguish between sensation and perception after the manner of Sokolov (1952):

> Sensation implies the organization of a number of reflex responses to single, simple stimuli; it always corresponds to a certain class of physical stimuli which are grasped as being the same and which, therefore, elicit an identical reaction. Perception involves an organization of reflex responses to complex stimuli and includes a generalization of relations between stimuli [pp. 54-55].

Later, Sokolov (1959) offered somewhat clearer definitions.

> In speaking of perception, we have in mind the reception and organization of the sensory image; this is dependent on the functioning of the analyzers whose task it is to process stimuli of various complexities. In this way, we include in the concept of "perception" both sensation and "perceiving" in the more precise sense of the word. The perception of a stimulus is usually regarded as the transformation of a physical stimulus into a meaningful response. The stimulus originates in the receptor end-organ and terminates in the central portion of the nervous system. In this way, the functioning of the analyzers is mainly considered from the aspect of the centripetal conduction of the stimuli. A careful exami-

nation of the whole process, however, results in the rejection of a possible simple schema as being the basis of perception. The perception of a stimulus should be regarded as the end result of a continuous reflex activity of the analyzers [p. 57].

From a physiological perspective, Beritov (1959) stated that if cortical area 18 is damaged, while 17 remains intact, a patient will be able to see but unable to identify objects, which is to say that he has visual sensations but not perceptions. And Poletaev (1958) wrote in a book about signals, that the eye simultaneously receives a multitude of single signals which, by their being connected to each other, combine into a complex signal—the image.

While agreeing with this view, Georgiev and his coworkers (1965) have made a rather sophisticated attempt to clarify the difference between sensation and perception using the concepts of structure and isomorphism, the latter being a mathematical concept. Thus, the notion of structure is ascribed a broad connotation, including spatial and temporal connections, and is defined as in symbolic logic, notably by the presence of an isomorphic relation. Ashby's (1950) definition of isomorphism is accepted.

Following a similar line of reasoning, Vekker (1961, 1964, 1968), an associate of Ananev, suggested an analysis of the various levels of organization of psychical processes in terms of levels of the signaling process. Furthermore, he proposed basing the concept of signaling on an isomorphism expressing the relation between signals and their source or, more generally, between structure and function. Empirically, Vekker sees three lines of demarcation among levels of complexity of psychical processes. The first and most important boundary is between sensation and perception on the one hand, and the underlying nervous processes on the other. The second line separates the sensory and perceptive processes from thinking. Finally, there is a distinction between pictorial and conceptual thinking.

The organization of signals related to the first line of demarcation assumes different forms which represent a hierarchy from the general principle of spatiotemporal isomorphism, through topological isomorphism, to metric isomorphism, where the relation between signal and its source becomes a direct one. The signals of nervous arousal and the signal-image, which are the two sides of the boundary between the neural and the neuropsychical processes, represent the extreme levels of this continuum. The characteristics of both nervous-signal and signal-image can be inferred from the corresponding forms or organization. Thus the transmission of nervous impulses according to the "all-or-none" principle and the characteristics of nervous regulation of homeostatic reactions are directly related to spatiotemporal isomorphism, while metric invariance underlies the features of perception. The formation of perceptual images as well as the loss of the perception of constancy follow in reverse order the sequence of levels of isomorphism. The perception of constancy of position in space is the least stable or, in other words, the metric of the ground on which the objects appear is the most fragile. Size constancy related to the object itself is next in order, while shape constancy is the most stable. Thus, in Vekker's (1968) own words,

> . . . the empirical characteristics of the phases of formation and disintegration of an image coincide with the levels of its constancy, generalization and extensibility. In turn, these levels, their sequence and structure, emerge from the hierarchy of the forms or organization of signals. . . . This hierarchy . . . makes possible—so far in first approximation—a theoretical account of the dynamics and structure of the different phases of organization of an image within and beyond the limits of constancy. Hence . . . the principle of organization of informational processes includes the empirical features of the whole sphere of *primary images,* or *perceptual images* [p. 61].

Similarly, the secondary images, or representations, express various levels of generalization. While the characteristics of the primary images derive from the metric invariance, those of the secondary images are related to more general forms of invariance representing the transition to the levels of isomorphism underlying the processes of thinking. The latter consist of abstracting the various signal-images from their integral structure, which corresponds to the reflected object, and their *transformation* for a certain purpose. In other words, unlike the formation of signal-images, which is linked to actions of matching, the organization of the informational processes in the course of thinking implies a transformation of the relationships between objects (e.g., their different classification). Vekker (1968) listed several pairs of characteristics of cognitive processes on two sides of the boundary between pictorial and conceptual thinking. These are largely based on the work of Piaget and Stern. For instance, he mentioned the centripetal nature of preconceptual thinking versus the centrifugal nature of logical thinking; the transductive character of preconceptual thinking versus the inductive-deductive character of conceptual thinking; the synthetical structure of pictorial thinking versus the hierarchical structure of concepts.

It appears that the experimental and clinical material provided by Soviet authors is more convincing than are their philosophical and theoretical arguments that perception is not a primary process but rather an end result of a number of complex processes. Thus Zinchenko (1958) and his colleagues (1962a) recorded the eye movements involved in perception and recognition. He distinguished between the two operationally on the basis of predetermined definitions. Perception was defined as the process of building an image; recognition was seen as a process whereby a current stimulus combines with an already existing model which has been stored in the memory. Experiments carried out with children of different ages revealed the presence of two processes which operated sequentially. The first process consists of the isolation of all sensory content appropriate to the task. This sensory content is brought into evidence only during the initial stages of the perceptual process until the object becomes known to the subject. With an increase in age, there is an increased ability to fixate the object visually. Furthermore, it appears that the level of development of this perceptual operation is not entirely dependent on age but also on the nature of the object, whether it is a geometric figure, a map, etc. The second process, which consists of an appraisal of the sensory content, is the operation which leads to the formation of the image. In the course of this process, various generalized schema are elaborated. In other words, this constitutes a process whereby the visual information is coded.

Ananev (1968a) reported on three cases of visual disturbances resulting from brain injury, one of which concerning visual agnosia is relevant here. The patient was under Ananev's care during his rehabilitation. He was properly oriented in space. Though with limitations, he could distinguish the presence of undifferentiated objects and had pupillary reactions to light. However, space had the appearance of a continuous stream of light, or of rays of light as they appear through fog. Objects were discriminated only on the basis of auditory and tactile information. The beginning of recuperation was marked by the appearance of amorphous and meaningless "blobs" distinguished only by their brightness and size. The blobs subsequently became increasingly chromatic and were discerned in relief. At this stage, however, the patient was still unable to reproduce any object as such, either verbally or in drawings. He made many errors in reading and writing. His dreams were nonvisual. In no way was he guided by visual sensations, having to depend almost exclusively on tactile stimuli and verbal cues. It was only after three months of treatment that the patient had improved to such a degree that he began to perceive objects. Ananev concluded that normal vision is not based on an abstract visual function.

INTEROCEPTIVE SENSITIVITY

One of the main contributions of Soviet psychophysiology is the work which has been done on the capacity of the internal organs—the thorax, abdomen, lymphatic system, etc.—to transmit differentiated impulses. A great deal of effort, above all by physiologists, has been exerted to produce the evidence that there exists a so-called visceral analyzer as well as a close connection between external and internal stimulations. Even if doubts have arisen regarding some of the methods used and the validity of the statistical analysis, the amount of the findings and the logic underlying the investigations are sufficient to attach major importance to this work.

The presence of afferent nerves as an anatomical entity was first advocated in Russian literature by Sechenov (1866) in his *Physiology of the Nervous System.* He also wrote about the vague feeling which constitutes either the good mood of the healthy man or the slack, dull mood of the ill man. Sechenov supposed that this is the background of the feelings of hunger, thirst, fatigue etc. He was of the view that these states consisted of the summation of impulses arising from all organs of the body which possess sensitive nerves. The pain arising from either inflammation, experimental strangulation, or mechanical or electrical stimulation of the intestine was to Sechenov an indication of the presence of afferent nerves in the walls of the intestine. The concept of visceral sensitivity was also supported by Russian clinicians. Botkin (1899), one of the outstanding Russian clinicians of the second half of the 19th century, was very much intrigued with the problem of visceral afferent impulses. Pirogov, in 1910, advanced the view that each organ makes its presence felt in the general structure of the organism by the sensations arising from it.

The systematic study of visceral sensitivity began in Pavlov's laboratories. In his initial works on the physiology of the circulatory system and of the digestive glands, Pavlov expressed his firm belief in the presence of afferent nerves in the internal organs. This subject concerned Pavlov well before he undertook his studies on conditioned reflexes. As early as 1897 he published a work which showed that the mucous membrane of the stomach possesses tactile sensitivity. He was also able to demonstrate the ability of the pancreas and other digestive glands to differentiate between the chemical compositions of food and other physicochemical processes. Pavlov felt that in addition to the external analyzers that are in the cerebral cortex there are analyzers which are able to differentiate the impulses arising from the internal organs. Nikiforovskii, in 1910, embarked upon a study of the conditioned reflex regulation of vegetative functions. He was followed by Tonchikh, in 1912, Podkopaev in 1914, Tsitovich, in 1917 and others. In 1924, Leibson, working in Orbeli's laboratory, was the first to be able to obtain a conditioned reflex originating from the kidney in animals. A year later, Krasnogorskii obtained the same reflex in children. Bykov commenced in 1936 a series of extensive studies, the results of which were summarized in his monograph *The Cerebral Cortex and the Internal Organs* (1944). Another group of studies initiated by Mogendovich (1957) in 1930 was concerned with the relationships between the motor and the visceral systems.

One of the topics of the above studies was the action of external stimuli on the internal receptors. Airapetyants and Balashkina, Bykov's coworkers, irrigated the mucous membrane of the stomach of a dog using a fistula with water at different temperatures. Water at 38°C was associated with feeding, while the irrigation with water at 26°C was not reinforced. After 16 irrigations, the dog was able to differentiate between the two temperatures: water at 38°C provoked an intense salivation, whereas there was no effect following the irrigation with water at 26°C. This was interpreted as a discriminative inhibition, a supposition which was tested by applying the classical method of the Pavlovian school. A new stimulus, a loud sound, was introduced in the middle of the experiment in order to produce a disinhibition. The irrigation of water at 26° associated with the sound produced a salivary reaction so intense as to equal that following a positive stimulus. Conversely, irrigation of water at 38° had a reduced effect because of the inhibition of the positive conditioned reflex. Similar experiments were performed by Vasilevskaya, another coworker of Bykov, in which irrigation of water was differentiated from irrigation of a 0.2 per cent solution of hydrochloric acid.

Another major object of study was the relationship between exteroceptive and interoceptive conditioned reflexes. Olyanskyaya succeeded in effecting changes in respiration in man through conditioning. A number of subjects were requested to perform a certain muscular activity at a rate which was indicated by the beats of a metronome, e.g., 80 beats per minute. Respiration was recorded before the start of the work, during its performance and after its completion. The instruction "be ready for the experiment" was given five minutes before the work was to start and the metronome began beating two minutes before commencement. The actual work commenced only when the actual instruction to do so was given. An increase in respiration was recorded from the first days of the experiment.

Interesting findings regarding the reflex relationships between different internal receptors have been reported by Mogendovich and his coworkers, Haidukova and Chlaev. They studied the influence of thermal stimulation of the stomach on plethysmograph recording in the hand. The subjects were requested to drink 250 ml. of water, which was regulated at a different temperature for each occasion. Water at a temperature of 22°-30°C produced a constriction of the vessels of the hand which lasted for one and a half minutes, at a temperature of 8°-15°—a vasoconstriction lasting for three minutes and even longer. The changes resulting from the drinking of water at 50°-52° had two distinct phases: an initial constriction was followed by a rise beyond the original

level for a period of approximately three minutes. Mogendovich felt that the initial .constriction was a result of the reflex
influence of deglutition on the tonus of the vessels of the
hand. This hypothesis was validated by carrying out similar
experiments on patients suffering from stenosis of the oesophagus who were nourished through a gastrostomy. The water
was introduced directly into the stomach through the gastrostomy. In these cases, the warm water did not produce any
vasoconstriction whatsoever and the plethysmographic recording became dependent only on the temperature of the water:
warm water resulted in vasodilatation and cold water in vasoconstriction.

The study of interoceptive sensitivity gave rise to several
questions. Among them were the anatomical and physiological
classification of receptors, the location in the brain of the "internal analyzer" and the features of internal sensitivity in
comparison with those of external sensitivity. With regard to
the classification of receptors there is a tendency to consider
the stimulus and not the receptor as the main criterion of
classification. Ananev, who is of the opinion that the
classification of receptors by organs, i.e., stomach, heart, urinary bladder receptors, is entirely meaningless, referred to the
fact that the various receptors are to be found in the same
organ. This problem was also discussed by students in the
Bykov school, particularly by Chernigovskii (1962, 1965a,b).

Chernigovskii identified four different groups of receptors
which are common to all the internal organs: chemoreceptors,
thermoreceptors, baroreceptors and pain receptors. Slonim
suggested a general classification of unconditioned and conditioned reflexes which also included the interoceptive reflexes.
Reflexes were grouped in accordance with their role of determining specific biological processes and three major classes
were defined. In the first group are the homeostatic reflexes
which maintain the internal milieu, and the feeding reflexes
which maintain the constant composition of the organism.

The second group comprises those reflexes which result from changes in the external environment, first of all the defense reflexes. Reflexes related to the conservation of the species, notably the sexual and the parental reflexes, constitute the third group. The interoceptive reflexes are of paramount importance in the first group of reflexes. They are also involved in the second group of reflexes but their role is reduced. The role of interoceptive signaling is once again important in the third group of reflexes. The unconditioned and conditioned reflexes include a number of reactions arising out of the heterosexual contact as well as reactions linked to certain functional states of the sexual system, e.g., pregnancy.

Mogendovich provided experimental evidence to show that the internal or "visceral" analyzer functions as an entirely independent entity. In one of these studies, total gastrostomy and oesophagoduodenostomy were performed in a dog but the cardial sphincter (the sphincter between the oesophagus and the stomach) was maintained intact. Dilatation of the duodenum followed the operation and the latter acted in place of the stomach as a sort of food reservoir. This reorganization of the digestive system had an effect on the development of what Mogendovich called the "sense of proportion" regarding food. The dog resumed eating gradually after the operation and on each occasion ingested only a little food. These reduced portions of food corresponded to the volume of the duodenal reservoir and was regarded as a result of interoceptive signaling. The resection of the cardial sphincter resulted in the dog's losing its "sense of proportion"; that is, the dog ate until it vomited.

The research on the so-called kinesthetic analyzer has held a particularly important place in the study of interoception. In 1911, Krasnogorskii, one of Pavlov's first coworkers, hypothesized that the analysis and synthesis of movements is under the control of a particular cortical area. In the experiment aimed to confirm this—this is one of the classical experiments of the Pavlovian school—one of the paws of a dog was flexed and at the same time the animal was fed. Another paw was then flexed but this action was not reinforced. A conditioned salivary response was obtained on flexion of the first paw, while flexion of the second paw had an inhibitory effect. The subsequent extirpation of the cortical area related with tactile sensitivity appeared to prevent the elaboration of the conditioned reflex which did not occur when the experiment was repeated. On the other hand, the extirpation of the motor area did not have any effect, since the tactile stimuli still elicited the conditioned response. These experiments led Pavlov to the conclusion that the role of the motor cortical area was not an exclusively efferent one. It is able to discriminate stimulations from muscles and joints which can form temporary bonds with other kinds of stimulation.

Although the view that the analysis and synthesis of kinesthetic stimuli is performed in the cortex very much prevails, some authors questioned whether these stimuli are indeed related to the corresponding movements through conditioned and unconditioned pathways. Mogendovich took it for granted that the stimulation of certain cortical cells initiates a particular movement and, conversely, that the performance of certain movements initiates the transmission of afferent impulses to the cortex. He was, however, unsure whether the connection is conditioned or unconditioned; in other words, strictly following a Pavlovian line of reasoning, whether the connection is innate or acquired.

The subject of the cerebral localization of interoceptive conditioned reflexes together with that of the specific characteristics of the interoceptive sensitivity are regarded as highly significant by Russian authors. It is their belief that this study is one of the ways of a scientific and objective approach to the subconscious phenomena. Three major questions have been raised regarding (a) the role played by the subcortical formations; (b) the localization of the cortical end of the "visceral" analyzer; (c) the role played by the cortical premotor area.

Much evidence has been advanced in order to prove that the interoceptive impulses reach the central nervous system at various levels, including the cortical level. According to Bykov, the brain stem ensures the vital functioning of the organism, whereas the cortex, on the basis of the signals received from the internal organs, enables the organism to adapt to whatever conditions prevail in the external and the internal environment, particularly with regard to metabolism, circulation and nutrition. Smirnov (cited by Mogendovich, 1958a) studied the effects of the removal in dogs of either the whole cortex or certain parts of it, on the functioning of the salivary, respiratory, vagal cardioinhibitory and gastrosecretory centers of the brain stem. The removal of the parspraecuciatum gyri sigmoidei resulted in a long lasting depression of the cardiac rhythm. This effect was reproduced, but only temporarily, by an injection of 0.01 g. of morphine. The elimination of the cortical influence, particularly of the motor area, on the subcortical centers resulted in an increase in the excitability of the latter. On the other hand, any stimulation of the subcortical centers was demonstrated to bring about a change in the functional state of the cortex. Uritskaya, a colleague of Mogendovich, noted that stimulation of the receptors in the stomach, either naturally, by the ingestion of food, or artificially, by the introduction of a balloon, resulted in the changes in the excitability of the motor area: the excitability increased following either a strong or real stimulation, and decreased after a moderate stimulation. On the other hand, experiments by Cherkasova, another associate of Mogendovich, on dogs, rabbits and rats succeeded in demonstrating that the metabolic reactions to the stimulation of the mechanoreceptors of the stomach are not under the influence of the cortical motor area.

Investigations have apparently invalidated the assumption that the premotor area constitutes the cortical center of the vegetative sensitivity. Experiments initiated by Bykov in which this area was bilaterally extirpated in dogs indicated that this operation had no visible effect on the conditioned control of the biliary secretion or of any other vegetative function. In Bykov's view, the premotor area is not related to vegetative functions, in the way that, say, the occipital lobe is related to vision. Nevertheless the possibility was considered that the premotor area partially represents the "nucleus" of the interoceptive analyzer since, unlike the exteroceptive analyzers, there is no concentration of cells constituting the interoceptive analyzer. Interoceptive stimulations are generally diffuse involving the whole cortex.

Ananev (1960), very much in agreement with Bykov's school, described the following features of the sensations originating in the organism. (1) They indicate changes in the internal milieu with particular regard to changes in tension or tone (e.g., the sensations of hunger and thirst), or to excess or lack of certain substances in the organism (salts, acids, etc.). (2) They have a certain intensity which corresponds to either an increase or decrease in the need of the organism for certain substances. (3) Their onset is insidious and they persist for longer periods of time than sensations produced by external stimulations. The latent period of reaction for the external analyzers is measured in seconds, whereas that of the internal analyzer is measured in minutes. This is an indication of the inertia of the nervous processes which have a role in the formation of temporary bonds with the internal receptors. (4) They are not as precisely demarcated and defined as the external sensations. Accordingly, it appears that the cortex is not stimulated by isolated impulses but rather by groups of impulses reaching it at the same time, and that the interaction between the internal organs does not allow for an accurate subjective localization of the interoceptive sensations. (5) The internal sensations are accompanied by emotions, the intensity of which is contingent on the summation of the impulses occasioned by changes in the organism as a whole. Thus, the role of the subcortical structures must be taken into account since they are implicated in the mechanism of emotions.

In recent years, two major lines of research on the comparative physiology of interoceptive and exteroceptive reflexes have developed. Bulygin and his coworkers (1960a,b, 1961, 1962, 1963, 1967, 1970) of the Institute of Physiology of the Belorussian Academy of Sciences is responsible for one line of research, and Airapetyants *et al.* (1952, 1960a,b,c, 1963, 1966a,b, 1967a,b) of the Pavlov Institute of Physiology of the Leningrad University is directing the other approach.

Bulygin studied the formation of conditioned reflexes in response to visual and auditory stimuli reinforced by various extero- and interoceptive unconditioned reflexes. Three types of reflex reactions were described, the differences between them consisting in the anatomical area involved and in the role played by the cortex and the subcortical structures. The first type of reactions is that of the sympathetic nervous system whose task is to regulate the physiological and physicochemical processes involved in vegetative and somatic functioning. These reactions are at the subsensorial level and produce a state of diffuse excitation of the central nervous system. Such reactions, for example, are related to the functional changes in the stomach, intestine, liver and kidney which result from the chemical stimulation of the mucous membrane of the small bowel with a five per cent–40 per cent glucose solution. This kind of stimulation produces neither respiratory changes, nor has it any visceromotor or viscerosalivary effect. As a matter of fact, the elaboration of a conditioned inhibition of the stomach contractions on the basis of this unconditioned reaction was found to be practically impossible.

In the second group of reactions, the vegetative changes mentioned above are accompanied by respiratory changes, salivary and motor reactions, restlessness and the adoption of peculiar postures usually following contractions of the smooth musculature. Such reactions were produced by the stimulation of the stomach and the small bowel with concentrated solutions (10 per cent–20 per cent) of potassium chloride and sodium chloride. These can be described as general defense reactions which are accompanied by an excitation of the central nervous system. They can serve as a basis for the elaboration of conditioned reflexes. It was noted, however, that the various components of the conditioned reaction were formed after a different number of associations: the respiratory and motor reactions took place after seven associations, the salivary reaction, after 21 associations and the inhibition of contractions of the stomach, only after 130 associations.

The third type of reactions is the most specific and differentiated and involves organs having both somatic and vegetative functions. Unlike the two other types of reactions, the cerebrospinal components of the vegetative response predominate. These reactions are accompanied by distinct sensations. Conditioned reactions can easily be elaborated on the basis of all the components of these reactions.

The studies conducted by Airapetyants and his colleagues have taken two directions: the visceral conditioned-reflex activity and the cortical mechanisms of spatial orientation—a topic which will concern us later in this text. It is the position of this school that the formation of interoceptive conditioned reflexes, that is conditioned reactions to the stimulation of internal organs, requires the participation of the highest level of the nervous system of a given species. In dogs, this is a cortical function. Lobanova, a coworker of Airapetyants, failed to associate a visceral stimulation with the electrical stimulation of the skin after the total removal of the cortex.

Contrary to the earlier findings mentioned above, extensive studies in Airapetyants' laboratory have demonstrated the role of the cortical motor and premotor areas in the formation of interoceptive conditioned reflexes. The bilateral removal of these areas in dogs resulted in a protracted extinction, and even total abolition, of previously formed conditioned reflexes to the stimulation of the kidney, stomach, urinary bladder and uterus. The histological analysis showed degeneration of the thalamic nuclei, the extent of which was related to the size of the cortical damage. However, during the course of a period lasting from two to seven months, these reflexes gradually reappeared. Although the differentiation of stimuli was considerably disturbed after the operation, this process was also gradually restored. The formation of new conditioned reflexes was possible. A significant difference was found between the paired internal organs—e.g., kidney—and the single organs, like the stomach, regarding the role of the two cerebral hemispheres in the visceral conditioned-reflex activity. The paired organs were found to have counterlateral connections to the cerebral hemispheres, while the unilateral removal of the cortex did not produce any remarkable disturbance of the conditioned reactions to the stimulation of the stomach.

Airapetyants and his associates have also studied the role of the limbic system in the formation and stability of visceral conditioned reflexes. It was shown that the extensive bilateral removal of the anterior limbic areas resulted in a drastic and prolonged extinction of conditioned reactions to mechanical and chemical stimulations of internal organs. Interestingly enough, in connection with the evidence about the role of the limbic system in emotional reactions, the exteroceptive conditioned reflexes remained unaffected.

Airapetyants' conclusion regarding the functioning of the "internal analyzer" is particularly instructive. He stated that Pavlov's distinction between a nucleus of the analyzer responsible for the complex analysis and synthesis of stimuli, and disseminated elements capable only of an elementary analysis and synthesis of stimuli, cannot fully explain the effect of the removal of the cortical motor and premotor areas on the interoceptive conditioned reflexes.

Sensory Interaction

Russian scholars have provided an impressive amount of experimental evidence to indicate that the specific action of a stimulus on a particular receptor is very likely to produce changes in the functional state of other receptors. These investigations also have had a practical application. For example during World War II a number of procedures were elaborated by the Psychophysiological Department of the Institute of Psychology of the RSFSR Academy of Pedagogical Sciences, designed to improve dark adaptation of the eye. These included the sponging of the face and neck, when warm, with cold water, the chewing of sweet or sour tablets, physical exercises, increasing the rate and depth of breathing. Experimentation in this field was instigated by Kekcheev (1946), Dolin (1962), who taught until his death in 1969 at the chair of higher nervous activity at the Moscow University, and others under Kravkov (1948). The latter had actually started his studies in the field of vision previous to 1930, at the Institute of Biophysics. In the early years of his work, Kravkov attempted to apply Lazarev's (1923) ionic theory to the study of visual phenomena. It was supposed that since ionic sodium and potassium favor the concentration of acetylcholine in tissues, whereas ionic calcium and magnesium lead to its reduction, various concentrations of acetylcholine may produce optimal effects for the various color-sensing apparatuses of the eye. The study of chromatic sensitivity became Kravkov's chief concern over the years. He summarized his work in two important monographs in 1950 and 1951. The following is an outline of some of the more relevant experiments performed by the Kravkov school. The interested reader is referred to a survey of this topic by London (1954).

Semenovskaya (1959) studied the conditions influencing the dark adaptation of the eye. They demonstrated that hyperventilation (eight–10 respirations per minute) reduces the time required for dark adaptation from 40″–45″ to 5″–6″. By contrast, both the beats of a metronome and the noise produced by a small electric motor had the effect of increasing the time required for dark adaptation. On removing the auditory stimulus, the sensitivity of the peripheral vision quickly returned to its normal value and on occasion temporarily exceeded this value. It was found that if the subject hyperventilated for 2′ during the period of auditory stimulation, the negative effect on the visual sensitivity was nullified. Kravkov (1950) reported that auditory stimulation tended to increase the sensitivity of the dark-adapted eye to blue-green light; at the same time, it reduced the sensitivity to orange-red light. The sensitivity to the extremities of the spectrum remained unchanged. It was also demonstrated that the introduction of adrenalin into the dark-adapted eye has similar effects. Furthermore, the application of an anelectrotonic current and of a catelectrotonic current had opposed effects. The introduction of ionic calcium into the eye increased the sensitivity to green light and lowered it to orange-red light. Ionic potassium had the opposite effect. Olfactory stimuli also had an effect on color sensitivity. Thus, the smell of indol decreased the sensitivity for red, increasing it for green: the smell of rosemary had the opposite effect. Finally, variations in posture were found to influence color sensitivity. Hyperextension of the head resulted in a significant reduction of the sensitivity to green, increasing the sensitivity to orange-red.

Kravkov's school also investigated the reflex relationships between the various component parts of any one sensory organ. The eye was in particular extensively studied. Orbeli (1945, 1949, 1962) had already described an antagonistic relationship between the rods and the cones of the retina, so that the stimulation of an area which consists predominantly of cones results in an increased dark-adaptation time, while the stimulation of the periphery of the retina, where rods predominate, lowers the sensitivity of the cones, reducing the dark-adaptation time. Kravkov provided experimental and clinical evidence which validated Orbeli's assumption. For instance, it was shown that the just described observations were absent in persons with color blindness.

Various hypotheses have been proposed to explain the interaction between sense organs. The application of the ionic theory was already mentioned. Orbeli's theory of the trophic-adaptive influence of the vegetative nervous system was also considered as a possible explanation. Semenovskaya (1959) believed that there is a particular group of stimuli, for instance certain sounds, the smell of geraniol, etc., that have a stimulating effect on the sympathetic nervous system, similar to the effect of adrenalin, cardiamin, etc. Another group of stimuli may affect the parasympathetic system in the same way as parasympathomimetic drugs such as pilocarpine, carbocholin, the berries of Schizandra chinensis, etc. Works of Western authors on this topic were mentioned.

The frequent observation that weak accessory stimulation increases the visual sensitivity, that stimuli of average intensity have no effect, whereas strong stimuli decrease visual sensitivity, as well as the fact that the visual sensitivity increased at the termination of the accessory stimulation, led to the assumption, in line with Pavlov's reasoning, that an induction relationship between processes of excitation and inhibition may be involved. Ananev suggested an integration of Pavlov's hypothesis with that of Ukhtomskii (1925) about the effect of dominant foci of stimulation. Under conditions of simultaneous stimulation of several receptors, the sensitivity of one is dominant and stimuli impinging on the other receptors have the effect of strengthening this major focus of excitation.

A new direction of investigation of the reflex processes taking place during the perception of objects was initiated by Sokolov (1951, 1955) who embarked on his work in Kravkov's laboratories. Originally, Sokolov was interested in the perception of brightness and color. He held the view that the perception of objects and their discrimination on the basis of their surface properties is a function of the various connections formed between the specialized parts of the visual analyzer. As a result, the object is reconstructed into an assembly of indicators which corresponds to the property of the object surface to reflect a beam of light in a specific and constant manner. In order to discriminate objects by the brightness of their surface, it becomes necessary to perceive both the luminosity of the environment and that of the object. The beam of light reflected by the object is perceived by the receptors situated in the center of the retina, and it is here that the image of the object takes shape. Light from the optical field as a whole stimulates the receptors situated at the periphery of the retina. This gives rise to rather vague, indistinct sensations. The fusion of these two sets of sensory impressions allows for the discrimination of objects. Sokolov believed that this might be the explanation of the phenomenon of object identification which, in his opinion, neither Helmholz's theory of unconscious reasoning, nor Wundt's theory of apperception, nor the Gestalt theory had succeeded in clarifying.

Subsequently, Sokolov embarked on an extensive study of the three types of reflexes which he maintained could be formed in any one analyzer: orienting, adaptive and defense reflexes. The orienting reflex, or "activity," has become a major subject of study for Russian physiologists and psychologists since the time of Pavlov's work. Initially, at the very inception of the study of conditioning, the orienting reflex was regarded as having a disinhibiting and thus disturbing effect on the conditioning process. But very soon it became recognized as a major factor underlying all forms of behavior. Pavlov considered this reflex to have considerable biological significance: it suspends any other unconditioned or conditioned reaction under circumstances of stress. Consequently, the orienting reflex was ascribed a central role in conditioning, particularly with regard to the process of differentiation.

The first studies regarded the orienting reflex as a motor reaction aimed at the orientation of a receptor toward a stimulus; this could take the form of alerting of the body, head and eyes to the source of stimulation, the pricking up of one's ears, the alerting of one's sense of smell, etc. (Vinogradova, 1961). Later the study of the orienting activity was extended to its various vegetative components. These included respiratory, cardiac, vascular, muscular, pupillary and electrographic (the depression of the alpha rhythm) reactions. It was found that all these reactions have certain properties in common: they are elicited only by a new stimulus; they are not confined to a particular area, which means that they are not related to the specific quality of the stimulus, but are unspecific reactions to most stimuli; they terminate on the repetition of a stimulus and reappear on the application of a different stimulus or of an additional stimulus; they appear to be sympathomimetic reactions (with the exception of bradycardia).

These studies significantly broadened the concept of an "orienting reflex" and, as such, paved the way for Sokolov's investigations. He was particularly impressed by some ideas proposed by Anokhin as early as 1935 and further elaborated in 1949. Anokhin felt that the receptor component of the unconditioned reflex was capable of integrative function. Experiments done in his laboratory by Laptev (1949) showed that an alimentary stimulus initiated rapid travelling action potentials on the lingual nerve of dogs, first elicited by touch, then by temperature and finally by chemical stimulation. Since each wave has its specific period of latency, it is possible that each wave could serve as a signal for the impulses immediately following. Regarding this complex nature of the unconditioned reflex, Sokolov considered as a possibility the development of intra-analyzer conditioned connections which would play a major role in the process of perception.

Sokolov described two forms of orienting reflexes: a generalized and a localized, specific reflex. The method of a testing stimulus was used to study the sensitization effect of the orienting reflex. For this purpose, a visual stimulus of 80 per cent of threshold intensity was applied before and after the application of a sound which elicited the orienting reflex. On observing the light, the subject was requested to clench his fist. If the sound failed to elicit an orienting reaction, expressed in the depression of the alpha rhythm of the occipital lobe, the intensity of the test stimulus remained at a level below that of the threshold. Conversely, on occasions when the sound did elicit an orienting reaction, a sensitization of the visual analyzer, the visual stimulus increases the depression of the alpha rhythm and a motor conditioned reflex in the form of muscular contraction occurs. Subsequently, the sensitization effect is weakened and accompanied by a weakening of the orienting reaction.

Sokolov and Paramonova (1961b) emphasized the selective termination of an orienting reflex. Thus, when the reaction elicited by a visual stimulus acting at a 40° distance from the central fixation point comes to an end, no reaction is produced upon changing the stimulation point to 35°. But a reaction does occur at the angle of 50° and increases at the angles of 60° and 70°. Similarly, a sound which no longer produces an orienting reaction can be reactivated by changing its pitch. Sokolov hypothesized about the formation of a "neural model of the stimulus." This is conceived as a particular group of cells which retains the information concerning the properties of a stimulus which had been applied many times previously. The model has a function somewhat similar to that of a filter in which there is a selective blocking of the impulses arising from the afferent systems. If the characteristics of a stimulus operating on the sense organ at a given moment are similar to and coincide with the features of its model, no orienting reaction takes place. On the other hand, when a stimulus differs from the model with regard to any of its parameters, the orienting reaction does appear. The orienting reaction is sensitive to any prolongation or shortening of stimulation time to changes in the frequency of stimulation, and to changes due to the application of various combinations of stimuli.

Additional experiments were done by Sokolov (1961b,c) to prove that the depression of alpha rhythm is a function of an increase of stimulation and not an expression of an external inhibition. (As is generally known, Pavlov had described this type of inhibition of a conditioned reflex as being produced by a new "indifferent" stimulus). The effect of an intermittent light on the occipital biocurrents, both before and after the application of a sound eliciting an orienting reflex was explored. It was shown that the alpha rhythm depression occurs at a time when the cortical neurones are in a state of accentuated readiness. In other words, the depression of the alpha rhythm was accompanied by an increase in the sensitivity to light and an accentuation of the lability of the cortical neurones. Danilova (1961) observed that the interaction of visual and auditory stimulations depends on the character of the orienting reflex. If the reaction to a sound takes a generalized form, there will be a sensitization effect on the visual analyzer which manifests itself in changes in the biocurrents. Alternatively, if the reaction to the sound has a local, specific orientation, the effect is one of inhibition.

Furthermore, Sokolov has extended the meaning of the orienting reflex including reactions at the single neuron level. Thus, a stimulus is supposed to operate at a number of levels: (1) the conduction on specific pathways of the information used for the formation of the model; (2) the confrontation between the received information and the formed model resulting in the appearance of impulses of discrepancy when the stimulus does not coincide with the model, and the concomitant activation of the reticular formation through the cortico-reticular connections. With regard to the structure of the orienting reflex at the level of the neuron, Sokolov presumed that each component of the orienting reflex has a particular type of neuronal counterpart. First, there are specific afferent neurons and their reactions manifested with each repeated stimulation. (These neurons were discovered by the German neurophysiologist Jung [1962] in the visual cortex of the cat and are known to react to light and dark). There is a second group of neurons responsible for the temporal extrapolation of signals. These neurons do not react to initial stimulation but to subsequent repeated stimulation. Sokolov referred to observations made by the American neurophysiologist Morell). Finally, a third group of neurons has the task of comparing the different impulses with the stored extrapolated impulses. Findings of Hubel and Wiesel (Hubel, 1960) at Harvard University, as well as joint experimental studies by Vinogradova (1961), a former coworker of Sokolov, and Lindsley (Vinogradova and Lindsley, 1963), supported Sokolov's viewpoint.

In highlighting the formation of conditioned reflexes, Sokolov emphasized the relationship between orienting and conditioned reflexes. Thus, as long as the conditioned reflex is neither firmly established, nor automatized, it is accompanied by orienting reactions elicited by both the conditioned and unconditioned stimuli. Stabilization of the conditioned connection coincides with the disappearance of the orienting reaction. The repeated application of the conditioned stimulus results in the formation of its model. The reinforcement of a new stimulus in a way similar to that in which previous stimuli were reinforced results in the formation of a single generalized model. The new stimulus, however, may also be reinforced negatively, and this results in a complex situation when two different models are formed, one corresponding to the positive stimulus and another one, to the negative stimulus.

The adaptive reflexes are reflexes which help accommodate the analyzer to the quality and intensity of the stimuli; e.g., the reflexes of contraction and dilatation of the pupil. The following features were ascribed to this type of reaction: it is proportional to the strength and to the quality of the adequate stimulus; the sign differs according to whether the stimulus is applied or withdrawn; it is maintained during the whole of the period of application of the stimulus; it occurs only in response to an adequate stimulus; it is not extinguished by repetition; it may be inhibited by extraneous stimuli, being temporarily replaced by an orienting reaction.

The stimulus, on attaining a certain intensity, causes a painful sensation, and a defense reaction is set up. This is expressed in respiratory, vascular and humoural changes and results in a modification of the action of the stimulus on the receptor. Sokolov maintained that it is the interaction of the orienting and adaptive mechanisms at the cortical level that constitutes the reflex basis of perception. He considered the relationship between the orienting and defense reflexes to be similar to the relationship between the epicritical and protopatic kinds of sensitivity, as described by Head. A defense reflex may stimulate an orienting reflex owing to a change in the action of the stimulus; in its turn, it may be inhibited by the orienting reflex. Thus, for example, guinea pigs in Danilova's experiments were not affected by an electrical stimulus during their orienting activity. Sokolov's major work as well as a comprehensive summary of his theory—with an emphasis on the cybernetic orientation—are available in English.

The Functional Relationships Within Analyzers With Paired Receptors

The relationships between paired receptors had already concerned Pavlov in connection with the symmetrical functioning of the two hemispheres of the cerebral cortex. The first observations on this subject were made by Krasnogorskii in 1911. He obtained the transfer—which he called "static irradiation"—of a tactile conditioned reflex from one side of the body to the symmetrical receptors. In 1924, at Pavlov's suggestion, Bykov and Speranskii (according to Maiorov, 1954) started a series of experiments to test the tactile symmetry in dogs. They showed that a differentiation between symmetrical tactile responses is possible only by splitting the corpus callosum. In this way, the body is divided somewhat into two parts and conditioned reflexes can be elaborated for each of them separately. It was also shown that after sectioning the commissural connections between the two hemispheres of the brain, dogs were unable to localize the direction from which a sound was coming. Similar experiments were subsequently performed by Abuladze (1961), and in recent years, Bianki and coworkers (1959a,b, 1960, 1967, 1969, 1970a,b,c, 1971 a,b), at the Laboratory of Comparative Physiology of the Paired Function of the Brain, at the Institute of Biology of Leningrad University, and Batuev (1966, 1970a,b, 1971) have been prominent in this field. Bianki's experiments in dogs after sectioning the calossal body showed the possibility of elaborating a defense motor reaction consisting of lifting the right forepaw in response to electrical stimulation of the right posterior paw. As in normal dogs, the initial generalized reaction gradually turned into a local reaction. Thus, the formation of a complex defense movement which involved the homolateral limbs did not require the joint functioning of the two motor cortical areas.

Ananev and his coworkers have been concerned with the relationships between paired receptors in man. Studies have been done regarding seeing, hearing and smelling. Particular attention was given to tactile perception and its relation to vision. In Ananev's (1960) view, binocular vision in most cases approximates monocular vision. There are individual differences. The information received from the two eyes for spatial orientation is unequal. The leading or dominant eye provides the same information as binocular vision. This functional asymmetry could be the result of temporary connections formed during the course of the individual's life experience. The relative dominance of one eye over the other is due to the reciprocal induction between the cortical nervous processes. Thus a positive induction operates in the case of monocular vision. Vision through only one eye, the other being closed, produces a process of inhibition in the cortical cells connected to the closed eye through the optic nerve. This has the effect of intensifying the process of excitation in the cells connected to the open eye. As a result, the sensitivity of the open eye increases. It is well-known that inexperienced marksmen as well as individuals who look through microscopes, usually close one eye in order to see better. On the contrary, both the experienced marksman and microscopist use both eyes: the weak stimuli, originating from the eye that does not directly participate in the observation, have the effect of increasing the sensitivity of the other eye. Ananev supposed that this mechanism of induction is a result of the learning experience. Experimental studies of Ananev's coworkers seemed to confirm this hypothesis. Miroshina-Tonkonogaya showed that it is possible to transfer a conditioned increased sensitivity from one eye to the other. The increase of illumination was associated with the beat of a metronome, thus obtaining the increased sensitivity of one eye, the other being closed. This was then transferred to the other eye, both from the dominant to the nondominant and in the reverse direction. Neimark studied the induction relations between auditory stimuli. He observed that the relations between the left and right ears, whether symmetrical or asymmetrical, are contingent on the source of the auditory stimulation. Thus, on using an audiometer, the hearing was symmetrical in 43 per cent of the cases, while only 14 per cent of the subjects had a symmetrical hearing when a diapazon was used.

Leiberg studied the relations between the olfactory receptors. He found a similar dependence of the symmetrical and asymmetrical relations on the nature of the stimulus. Thus, the same subjects, on smelling acetone, showed a dominant response of the right nostril, while on smelling alcohol the left nostril was predominantly involved.

Ananev's school paid a great deal of attention to the asymmetrical relations between the two hands as a source of tactile information. These studies started in 1937 with the particular purpose of investigating the relationship between tactile and kinesthetic sensations in the process of handling an object. It was demonstrated that this relationship differs from the right and left hands. The difference was explained by the fact that man deals with two different kinds of objects: the objects on which the labor is performed and the tools by which the operation is implemented. The right hand has historically handled the tool, while the left hand manipulates the object being worked upon. This is why the right hand is said to deal mainly with the kinesthetic impulses originating from the tools, whereas the left hand predominantly receives the tactile impulses coming from the surface of the object.

Following on the same line of reasoning, Shifman (1948) suggested that the tactile sensations arising from the hands have far more in common with visual sensations, in relation to the manipulation of objects, than with tactile sensations arising from other parts of the skin. The latter merely indicate the locus of contact with the external environment, or the temperature of the object, etc. The tactile sensations of the hands allow for the determination of the spatial coordinates of the perceived object and the establishment of a relation between it and another object serving as a frame of reference. The tactile image is fragmentary and successive, but it becomes simultaneous with the help of visual representations. It can also be continuous when the object is small and enters completely into the "tactile field" of the hand. As a matter of fact, visual perception may also be fragmentary and successive when the object is not situated within the observer's visual field.

A relevant question about the tactile perception of objects

has been raised by Vekker (1961), who later wrote a monograph about the modeling of perception, and Lomov, who is currently the head of the laboratory of engineering psychology at Leningrad University: to what extent does the displacement of the object touched by a motionless hand play a role in the ultimate tactile perception of the object? Various geometric figures were applied to the palmar surface of the first phalanx of the subject's index finger, in such a way that contact was successively made with all points on this particular surface, the finger being held quite motionless. Most subjects did not recognize the object, but when informed that the displacement of the touching object ends at the point of onset, the tactile identification considerably improved. This remained, however, a partial perception. A correct tactile image of the object was only gained by the displacement of both object and hand. This allows for a dynamic system of coordinates to be brought into action in order to account for the changes in the direction of motion.

The Leningrad students of the hand as a source of sensory information speak about an "active touch" (Parachev, 1963) and distinguish between macro- and micromovements of the hand in the course of the tactile perception of objects. Macro-movements, which are movements of the hand as a whole, have a twofold function: to scan the object, i.e., to analyze the information concerning the impinging object; to supply information about the basic features of the object such as integrity, objectivity, continuity, etc. Micromovements are defined as movements of the fingers with high frequency and low amplitude. They serve to make the muscular reactions more accurate and to obtain information about the surface of the object. The processing of the tactile information follows a certain sequence of acts depending on both the structure of the object and subjective factors such as experience and skill. The process of scanning is supposed to be controlled by a cerebral center of active touch which operates in two directions in order to attain a state of equilibrium between the speed of the information reaching the cortex and speed of its processing. The equilibrium obtained could be regarded as optimal for the purpose of solving the perceptual task. Parachev was particularly concerned with the latter problem, with the objective of finding the algorithms of active touch.

CONSTANCY OF PERCEPTION

Soviet authors have consistently expressed their belief that the constancy of perception of shape, size, brightness and movement of objects is achieved through systems of connections formed either between the component parts of one analyzer, or between different analyzers. Volkov (1948, 1950) objected to the classical experimental approach to perception on the following points: (a) no study was made concerning the meaningful perception in everyday practice; (b) the perception of the three dimensional object as well as the relationship between the visual image and the visual angle were overlooked; (c) the study of perception was limited to a study of surfaces and of sizes; when three dimensional objects were studied, the research was again restricted to a study of the perception of size; (d) the study of perception of size ignored the concrete processes involved, the oscillations, errors, corrections. In Volkov's view, the terms of "apparent size" and "apparent form" were superficial.

Shevarev (1948, 1959a, 1962) is another student of perception who criticized classical theories on the constancy of perception, particularly regarding the brightness of achromatic surfaces, promoted by Helmholtz, Hering, Katz and Koffka. He contended that these theories had a common erroneous starting point: they regarded the single, unrelated sensation as being inconsistent, whereas a combination of a number of sensations was thought to show a considerable constancy.

Finally, Ananev (1968b) considered the limitation of many

studies on the relation between the constancy of perception and the volume of the visual field, to the investigation of the informational side of perception, as an essential shortcoming. Not enough attention was paid to whether monocular perception was performed by the dominant or the nondominant eye for a certain visual function. The following are some of the experiments done regarding the constancy of size and shape.

Bein (1948) supposed that the constancy of size is due to the fact that people commonly deal with certain colors, sizes, forms and other characteristic properties of objects. Her purpose was to study the perception of size independently of the nature of the perceived object itself. She found that the perception of the size of objects which were familiar to the subjects was more constant than the perception of either geometric figures or meaningless irregular blots. A comparison regarding the constancy of size perception in normal children, feeble-minded children and in adults revealed that the constancy of perception in normal children of 10–11 years old was similar to that of adults, constancy in the mentally retarded children being somewhat lower.

Shevarev (1962) suggested comparing two perceptual situations: the perception of a certain surface at a limited distance and under natural conditions, and the perception of the same surface through a small orifice. This situations were said to differ in two respects. First, in the case of perception under natural conditions, an accommodation of the vision to the perceived surface must have taken place. Each area of the retina is reached by radiations emanating from a specific area of the perceived surface. In the case of perception through an orifice, the accommodation of the eye is confined to the limits of the hole and each element of the retina is stimulated by radiations emanating from a restricted area. Second, the angles of a surface perceived under usual conditions are far larger than those of the perception through an orifice. These findings prompted Shevarev to conclude that the different intensities of light transmitted to the eye by various areas are responsible for the constancy of the luminosity. Shevarev referred to an "elementary" area, admittedly an arbitrary concept, by which he meant the area whose size approximately corresponds to a single cone. Rubinshtein (1952) disagreed with him, since he did not believe that the physical properties of visual stimulation can explain color constancy. He maintained that a central factor is responsible, notably the cortical processes which connect the stimulation from the surface of the perceived object with the overall stimulation.

Bzhalava's (1958, 1962) investigations into the figural aftereffect, based on Uznadze's (1949) theory, deserve particular mention. A major aim of these studies was to refute Köhler-Wallach's hypothesis of a saturated field. After subjects were given time to adapt to darkness, two circles, 17 and 25 mm. in diameter, were simultaneously placed in front of them for a period of two seconds. It was noted that after the light was switched on, the afterimage of the two circles occurred at the same time as during the actual exposure. The experiment was repeated 15 times with identical results. As a control experiment, two circles of equal size, 18 mm., were placed before the subject. On this occasion, too, the figural aftereffect was obtained. However, the two circles appeared to be of different sizes: the circle which held the position of the larger one in the previous experiments now appeared as the smaller of the two circles. In 64.2 per cent of the experiments, this contrasting asymmetric illusion was manifest, whereas the symmetric illusion, i.e., one in which the circle which held the position of the larger circle in the previous experiments, now appears the larger of the two, was observed only in 15.8 per cent of the experiments. In 20 per cent of the experiments, no difference of size was obtained. Bzhalava concluded that the occurrence of an illusion in the control experiment was caused by the establishment of a fixed set due to the repeated perception of objects of unequal size. The effect of a stimulus usually has a dynamic nature dependent on the subject's orientation and expressed in the way he perceives objects.

Further experiments were done to confirm this assumption. The set pattern of perception was established for the left eye only (the right eye being closed), and control experiments in which the left eye was closed gave results which were very similar to those described above. Similar illusory aftereffects were obtained. The same illusion resulted when the tactile sense was put to the test. Spheres of unequal size were touched and, in the control experiment, spheres of equal size were perceived visually. It was also noted that the illusion occurred with other geometric figures, such as ellipses, triangles, quadrangles, pentagons, parallelograms and circles. Bzhalava interpreted these findings as evidence that the illusion is not a result of some local changes and cannot be explained by the trace theory. He disagreed with Köhler's theory that the figural aftereffect appears only in the presence of an electrically saturated field, limited to the volume of the perceived object. Furthermore, he regarded Köhler's subsequent amendment, that the field does not have to be circumscribed to the outline of the object perceived, as an unsatisfactory compromise. As a matter of fact, in Bzhalava's view, Köhler's experiments did not contribute anything essentially new to this subject. The phenomenon described by him was similar to the contrast illusion described by Uznadze in 1931.

A systematic study of the ontogenetic development of the constancy of perception has been done by Ananev and his coworkers, who approached the growth of sensory cognition in close relation with the intellectual and social development of the individual.

Several questions were raised by Dvoryashina (1964). How do the monocular and binocular mechanisms interact? What role does monocular vision play in the binocular perception of space? Is there a discrepancy between the monocular systems in young children, and if this exists, what is its nature and role in various stages of development? Following is an illustration of an experiment with 21 three to seven year olds. Two white rectangles were presented simultaneously, 15–20 times in an experiment, each time for three-seven seconds, at a distance of 15 cm. from each other, and of 200 cm. from the subject. A conditioned reflex reinforced by food (candy) was formed to the perception of a pair of unequal rectangles: they had the same breadth, but different heights, 5 and 12 cm. This pair was differentiated from another pair of rectangles of the same size. The experiment itself was preceded by a preparatory stage. First, only the positive stimulus was presented. A subject was regarded as having learned the discrimination if he did not fail more than once out of 10 trials. Then the negative stimulus was introduced and the discrimination was considered learned if there was only one error in 20 trials. After preliminary stage, the differential threshold was established for each subject in a series of trials where the difference in size between the two rectangles of the positive pair was gradually reduced to the critical discrimination points. The size of the rectangles of the negative stimulus was also varied. The constancy of shape was measured for two positions of a standard object (a white square of 10 × 10 cm.): the angles of inclination of .95 and .65. This was measured for both monocular and binocular vision. The standard stimulus was presented together with another test-stimulus in a variety of combinations: first with the largest object and then with those of average size. If a subject had a stable negative reaction (at least six times) to a particular combination, the size of that test-stimulus was taken as being equivalent to the size of the standard stimulus.

The results led to the distinction of three periods in the development of constancy. The first stage which included the three youngest subjects (between three years, one month and three years, five months) is that of the initial occurrence of constancy. The cases of lack of constancy prevailed. The second period, which included 10 subjects between four and five years, eight months, was described as that of a considerable fluctuation of constancy, when instances of its reduction, in comparison with the younger children, alternated with its acute increase. In the third period, including children between five years, eight months and six years, 11 months, the constancy of shape was relatively stable. The development from the relative predominance of the binocular vision over the monocular constancy in the first two periods, to its absolute dominance in the third period was noted. The asymmetric functioning of the monocular vision also played a role. Finally, a difference between the constancy attained with the left and right eyes was also observed in all subjects. In the youngest children, the indicators of constancy with one eye coincided with binocular constancy. In the older children, binocular constancy prevailed over the constancy of the dominant eye. Ananev interpreted these findings as showing the role of the joint functioning of the two cerebral hemispheres in producing the metric invariance of the psychical reflection. The binary effects, particularly in binocular vision, and the lateralization of functions, ensure the stereoscopic nature of visual perception as well as the visual-motor coordination.

Ananev also interpreted the findings of Tolman and Postman, regarding an age factor in the formation of size and shape constancy, against the background of his own views. These authors, following Brunswik's (1956) assumption, explained this fact by assuming that size constancy depends on depth signals, whereas shape and color constancy are contingent on finer proximal mediators. According to Ananev, size constancy is linked to a general property of space notably its extent (protyazhennost) and to its division into segments. Shape constancy is linked to spatial orientation which depends on the formation of a system of reference including the body image. This is further related to the child's motor experience in handling objects and even to reading and writing. It is for this reason that shape constancy is achieved later than size constancy.

Ananev and his coworkers also came to the conclusion that the influence of the volume of the perceptual field on the constancy of perception has a developmental variation. Their findings indicated that in preschool children and in elderly people, not only was the monocular vision more accurate than the binocular vision, but it even further improved when the visual field was reduced. As far as elderly subjects are concerned, the reduction of the visual field was supposed to provide better conditions for the analyzer's work. It is felt that the contradiction between these findings and the reduction of constancy produced by the restriction of the visual field, commonly described in the literature, is due to different experimental procedures. In the studies done by Ananev's group, a minimal number of elements was maintained in the visual field.

The dominance of the visual system is explained by Ananev's school not simply in terms of the prevalence of optical information. The visual system is regarded as an internal channel between all the analyzers, much the same as the kinesthetic analyzer, and as a transformer of signals. In man, this later function, namely the ability to visualize any sensory signals, is supposedly due to four factors: (1) the integral, object-oriented *(predmetnyi)* nature of the perceptual image; (2) the object-oriented actions which are regulated by perception; (3) the significance of the perceived object which enables perceptual knowledge to be abstracted and maintained in the form of constants; (4) the spatial organization of the simultaneous images. The visual system is assumed to operate on three levels: sensory, perceptual and apperceptive (representations). While the auditory system functions on the same three levels, the apperceptive level is manifest only in specialized forms of verbal and musical representations. Tactile sensitivity is not a unimodal system since pain, thermic and kinesthetic sensations are also involved. Finally, the development of visual constancy precedes the kinesthetic constancy which is also lower and is further reduced in the absence of visual control.

PERCEPTION AND ACTIVITY

Soviet psychologists have emphasized strongly the relation between the process of perception and the person's needs and activity. However, the stress has been placed exclusively on the positive effects of this relation, whereas the "projective" distortions have been totally disregarded. It is postulated that perception is formed and verified in the course of the person's activity. At the same time, Soviet authors pointed to the contingency of actions themselves on perceptive processes. In this, they followed Sechenov's lead that the sensory image is a regulator of actions.

Ananev (1968a) maintained that no matter how relevant the study of perception may be as an informational process—he labeled the connections investigated in these studies "perception-object"—they are insufficient for the understanding of the role of perception in man's life. For this, it is necessary also to study the "perception-subject" connections. The experimental findings on the relationship between sensitivity and needs certainly should be regarded as further convincing evidence of the dependence of sensation on the nature of the stimulus. However, the Soviet interest in this matter is not directed only by a wish to demonstrate a philosophical tenet, but by a number of practical considerations as well. Soviet authors have confirmed the role of training in the achievement of sensitization and have offered valuable practical guidelines on certain training procedures.

Shvarts (1954), a researcher in Ananev's laboratories, studied the improvement in visual recognition of objects which had been weakly illuminated. Before the experiment, the subjects were informed that they would have to learn to recognize "letters" presented in a weak light. The experiment itself began after each of the subjects had been given the opportunity to adapt to darkness. The subjects were instructed to recognize and locate the position of each dimly illuminated figure, consisting of the letters T, Sh (Ш), and E of the Russian alphabet. The minimal brightness at which the subjects recognized the letter as established with the aid of a device invented by Kravkov. Four series of experiments were carried out. In the first, the subjects were not informed as to the accuracy of their responses. After 400 tests, average recognition had improved by 40 per cent. In the second series, where the results were communicated to the subjects, there was an improvement of 310 per cent. In the next series, all faulty responses were punished by the administration of a weak electric shock. In this instance the average improvement attained was 470 per cent. In the final series, the subjects were shown the results of the test on the indicator of the device; the result of the test was shown as well as the level they had to attain in the next trial. This procedure followed each test, and at the end of the series the sensitivity had increased by 845 per cent. The experiments were repeated after five months and it was found that the previous improvement was maintained at the level of about 830 per cent. There was also a positive effect on the recognition of other letters of the Russian alphabet (i.e., a transference of training).

Shvarts attempted to define the factors responsible for the obtained improvement. For this purpose, the same experiment was repeated with another group of subjects. On this occasion, only the first and fourth series were carried out. It was found that sensitivity improved from 150 per cent after the first experiment, to 820 per cent after the second experiment. It thus appeared that the methods of reinforcement used in the second and third series of the previous experiment had, in effect, no influence on ultimate improvement. Shvarts felt that the increase in sensitivity resulting from training under conditions of reduced illumination was due to the fact that as the light became weaker the cues for recognition of forms underwent change. This involved the attainment of a new threshold based on a reflex mechanism whereby newly conditioned connections between the form of the figure and its recognition were established. The results obtained in the final series of experiments were explained by the development of a high tonus in the cortical-visual area. This was supposed to be secondary to the content of the task itself. In order to determine the role of cortical and peripheral processes in the retina, Shvarts performed a further experiment in which the subjects were instructed to recognize similar forms, utilizing only one eye. She then demonstrated that the improvement obtained as a result of training in a single eye was transferred to the other eye. This was regarded as an illustration of the role of cortical processes.

Kaufman, another coworker of Ananev, observed that the absolute and differential auditory sensitivity is higher in persons whose profession requires the ability to distinguish changes in sound intensity. Thus, automobile and aeroplane mechanics have a high sensitivity for the sounds of their engines. Physicians are usually highly sensitive to the sounds of percussion and auscultation. The sensitivity to minor difference in pitch is better developed among violinists and cellists than among pianists. Similarly, Teplov (1961) showed that this kind of discrimination can be considerably improved by training.

Elucidation of the characteristics of auditory sensitivity has been one of the primary objectives of the studies by Leontev and his coworkers (Leontev and Ovchinnikova, 1958, Leontev and Gippenreiter, 1959a; Ovchinnikova, 1959a,b). These researches were aimed at testing Leontev's basic assumption that the development of the psyche implies the formation of functional systems. Two additional specific assumptions were made. First, that the ability to discriminate the quality of sounds has developed in man as a special faculty to perceive music. Second, that for all intents and purposes, the discrimination of tones is dependent primarily on the intonation of sounds, or vocal activity, by the subjects themselves. Sounds of different pitches or different frequencies are discriminated if subjects are requested to vocalize the tones heard. Ovchinnikova observed that following exercises of tonal differentiation, initially in a loud voice and then softly, subjects demonstrated a better ability to differentiate sounds of the same tone quality. But only to a very small extent was an improvement achieved in recognition of sounds of different tone qualities. Even if the subjects underwent training in the differentiation of different tone qualities, or timbres, the results obtained were not significantly better. Subjects learned to discriminate one combination of pitch-tone from another, but were quite unable to evaluate the pitch as an independent feature (i.e., they had relative but not absolute pitch discrimination). This was obtained only after special exercises of vocalization.

Leontev and Gippenreiter tested the hypothesis that the aptitude for pitch differentiation develops only in people with a certain degree of musical ability. A sort of tone deafness takes place without this, partially compensated by a highly developed capacity to hear verbal sounds. Insofar as most modern languages are atonal, they do not require the differentiation of the pitch parameter, and consequently pitch discrimination has no semantic value. In tonal languages, however, the tonal element has a sense-discriminating function. Thus it was assumed that people speaking such languages (e.g., Vietnamese) must have developed tonal hearing. Accordingly, experiments were done on Vietnamese students at Moscow University. Of the 50 students, only five showed a lesser capacity for pitch differentiation. But four of these five were natives of Central Vietnam where the spoken language is less dependent on tonalities.

An additional experiment was done by Ovchinnikova (1959b), who established a certain degree of pitch differentiation by exploiting an artificially elaborated auditory-manual system, so that a conditioned connection was formed between perception of sound and tonic contraction of the muscles of the hand. On hearing a sound the subject was requested to press a button with an intensity corresponding to that of the sound. After the test, the subject was informed about its result. In this way, a conditioned reaction was formed: the stronger the sound, the stronger the contraction. It was noticed that intoning also became more and more accurate. Furthermore, if the hand was occupied in some other action at the same time—e.g., the subject was asked to draw lines with a pencil—the pitch differentiation became markedly disturbed.

In the light of what has been discussed in this section, one would anticipate criticism by Russian psychologists of the Weber-Fechner law. Ananev, in fact, considered the Weber law to be valid only with regard to average intensities, offering the observation of the considerable reduction in discriminative sensitivity for very weak as well as very strong stimuli as evidence for this viewpoint. Fechner's law, which implies that the discrimination threshold is constant regardless of the intensity of the initial stimulus, was also regarded as being valid only for average intensities of the stimuli. Ananev admitted the possibility of making a determination as to the average value of the discrimination threshold for color sensations. He considered, however, that such a finding was likely to confuse the essential difference between thresholds of specific sensations such as red or blue. Furthermore, differences between high and low tones, between different smells and different temperatures might also become obscure.

Thus the general feeling is that the study of sensations should in no way be restricted to the quantitative relationship between the intensity of stimulation and the sensory response.

SPATIAL PERCEPTION

Sechenov's work has again influenced considerably the investigations into perceptual orientation in space. His suggestions have inspired much of the study on the relationships between the various sensory modalities that underlie spatial orientation. The question as to which of the analyzers play a leading role in spatial orientation represents a major point of controversy.

Sechenov (1866) maintained that muscular sensitivity plays a dominant role in spatial orientation. He believed that the perception of distance, height, and speed of displacement is a function of muscular activity. This proposition prompted many investigations including the extensive series of experiments done at Leningrad University (Airapetyants, 1966a; Airapetyants and Bianki, 1960a; Airapetyants et al., 1960b,c; Airapetyants and Batuev, 1963, 1966b; Batuev, 1966; Bianki, 1960). These authors admitted that all analyzers have a role in spatial analysis, each providing a specific amount of information about the spatial relations between objects. The visual, vestibular and cutaneous analyzers were thought to be of particular importance. They maintained, however, that spatial relations become meaningful to the organism only during muscular activity. For the purpose of determining the role played by each of the analyzers, Airapetyants and Batuev carried a series of experiments on animals using the following procedures: the simultaneous removal of all the distal receptors connected with the vestibular apparatus; the successive removal of these receptors at intervals of between one and nine months between operations; the stitching together of the eyelids or the application of an opaque bandage on the eyes;

the extirpation of the cortical-motor area. Various conditioned feeding, respiratory and defense reflexes were then elaborated. In one of these experiments, the effect of the elimination of the visual, auditory and vestibular receptors on the spatial orientation of cats was investigated. It was noted that whereas the cat was unable to jump over a horizontal bar, conditioned running, as a response to a tactile stimulation was maintained. Subsequent anesthesia of the paws led to chaotic movements. The conditioned reactions gradually recovered. At this stage, the sygmoid convolutions were extirpated. Their total ablation was followed by an absolute lack of movement coordination, the ability to orient spatially being completely lost. Batuev (1970a) concluded that the conditioned running observed after the removal of the visual, auditory and vestibular receptors was an effect of the joint functioning of the tactile and motor analyzers. The general conclusion arising out of these experiments was that subsequent to the removal of the mentioned receptors, new compensatory functional relations take place. The motor analyzer together with the visceral sensitivity are mainly responsible for this functional reorganization.

A further series of experiments was performed which aimed at determining the effect of extirpation of the sygmoid convolutions on various sensory modalities. Batuev observed that the visual discrimination of geometrical figures was lost in cats after unilateral extirpation. The auditory spatial orientation was also markedly disturbed. Airapetyants noted that dogs were no longer able to discriminate the direction, frequency and intensity of sounds after the total ablation of the motor area. In addition, disturbances in the discrimination of thermal stimuli and in the field of the vestibular sensitivity were observed.

Beritov (1959, 1961, 1969a) stressed the role of the visual and labyrinthine receptors in spatial orientation. Experimenting on cats and dogs, he observed that after removal of the visual and labyrinthine receptors, the spatial orientation was almost impossible. Beritov went so far as to suggest that spatial orientation is achieved solely through the labyrinthine receptors. The olfactory and tactile, as well as the visual and auditory stimulations which occur during movements, were supposed to be projected through labyrinthine sensations to definite points in the environment. On destruction of the labyrinths, and on covering the eyes, movements aimed at orientation toward the stimulating object were completely lost. The animal was even unable to proceed in the same pathway it had already traversed several times.

In addition, Beritov performed several series of experiments with different groups of children. The groups were comprised of normal children of kindergarten age, of pupils of 12–14 years of age, and of blind and deaf-mute children of all age groups. Normal children were transported blindfolded from one place to another within the room or building and then returned to the starting point. These children were subsequently quite able to repeat independently the path they had just traversed, thus illustrating the role of proprioceptive stimulations, originating from their feet, in spatial orientation. In the next experiment, where the children were transported from place to place while seated on a chair, they were just as capable of repeating, quite accurately, the path they had just traversed. There were no significant differences between the results of these two experiments. Another experiment was then conducted to investigate the role of vision in spatial orientation. On this occasion, the subjects were requested to walk blindfolded along a path drawn in the form of a Z on the floor, which they had been allowed to perceive just prior to the covering of their eyes. Under these circumstances, the orientation was somewhat better than when the subjects were transported around. This finding led Beritov to conclude that visual projection of space is more precise than labyrinthine projection.

The role of labyrinthine receptors was reasonably well

demonstrated by experiments on the deaf-mute children. Two groups of subjects were tested: a group with nonfunctioning labyrinths and a group with intact labyrinthine receptors. The first group of subjects was unable to traverse blindfolded the same path over which they had been led one or more times. They were, in addition, unable to retrace this same path after having been transported around in a chair. Many repetitions were required before this group learned to maintain the correct direction of the path. These children were able to distinguish left from right turning when twisted around while seated on a chair. This seemed to Beritov to be a function of the receptors situated in the skin, skeletal muscles and internal organs. Yet these stimuli are not sufficient to allow for complete orientation. Proprioceptive stimuli are only able to provide the basis for relatively simple types of spatial orientation and this only by virtue of the fact that proprioceptive stimulations can be converted into conditioned signals for certain movements.

The second group of deaf-mute children achieved complete spatial orientation and were able to follow blindfolded the original path after having been led over this path or transported around it on a chair. The spatial orientation of congenitally blind children, or those who became blind before the age of two years, was found to be far superior to that of normal children. This fact was also advanced by Beritov to prove the important role played by the vestibular apparatus in spatial orientation.

PERCEPTION OF TIME

Perception of time is regarded by Soviet authors as a reflection in the brain of objective duration, speed and sequence of the phenomena of reality (V. Pavlov, 1966). Time, like space, is one of the basic objective properties of matter.

This proposition is opposed to the idealistic views. Both James' nativistic and Munsterberger's genetic theory have an idealistic and metaphysical basis; Bergson and Minkovsky adopted a machist viewpoint, and Janet's sociologic terminology does not mask his idealistic standpoint (Elkin, 1962). The behaviorist position is also rejected.

For Sechenov, the perception of time is an expression of the duration of both auditory and muscular sensations. During daytime hours, man either moves around himself, thus experiencing protracted sensations, or he observes the movements of objects and hears and appreciates sounds of varying durations. Hence, days endure like sounds. The distinction between duration and the more static and concrete notions of movement of both the day and the year lead to the concept of time. Pavlov noted that the effect of time is like that of any other stimulus. A particular kind of inhibition was described as occasioned by the delay of the reinforcement.

Elkin, who over a period of years has carried out extensive studies on the role of the different sense organs in the perception of time, believed that the motor analyzer plays a major part in the perception of time. This, he maintained, is the result of rhythmic and fractional character of movements and of the periodic alternation of the processes of excitation and inhibition. The following represent some of the characteristics of the kinesthetic reflection of time: the underestimation of long-lasting movements; the overestimation of brief movements; the more accurate perception of the duration of completed rather than of uncompleted movements; the accurate perception of the sequence of movements. Elkin reported severe disturbances in the perception of time in hemiplegic patients, in encephalitis and in cerebellar dysfunctions.

The perception of time also appeared to include tactile perceptions. Thus the duration of brief, short-lasting tactile contacts tended to be overestimated. The estimation of the time interval between tactile contacts took the same direction but seemed to be more accurate. Perception of time improved when rhythmic tactile contacts were applied.

Auditory sensitivity also seemed to play a role in the perception of time. The estimation of time intervals on the basis of auditory stimulation was found to be comparable with the results obtained for proprioceptive sensitivity. The auditory perception of time could be improved by training. The characteristics of the motor, tactile and auditory perception of time were explained by Elkin on the basis of the interacting cerebral processes of excitation and inhibition. The overestimation of the duration of short intervals was interpreted as a result of the prevalence of a state of excitation over an inhibitory process. Conversely, the underestimation of duration was said to be a manifestation of the predominance of inhibition over excitation, the inhibition being an adaptation to the prolonged action of the stimulus. Elkin mentioned the illusion of the simultaneous perception of two stimuli operating successively, one strong and one weak, as further evidence for his hypothesis. In this instance, the strong stimulus was assumed to give rise to an aftereffect and, as such, its duration is perceived as longer.

Elkin has also indicated the role of the visceral sensitivity in the perception of time. Among the rhythmic visceral functions, both respiration and cardiac activity were ascribed a particularly important role in the estimation of time. Reduction of visceral sensitivity in certain neurological disturbances, for example, in the case of a thalamic tumor, was shown to be accompanied by distortion of the perception of time. Experimental increase of the body temperature altered visceral sensitivity and also resulted in a less accurate orientation in time.

Finally, Elkin was able to find a relationship between the perception of space and the perception of time. He showed that the correlation between them decreases from muscular and tactile sensitivity to visual and auditory sensitivity. He further observed that the more accurate the spatial discrimination of two points of tactile stimulation, the better the perception of the duration of the stimulation.

REPRESENTATION AS A SENSORY PROCESS

The concept of representation has been used extensively in Soviet psychology. However, its meaning is far from clear and one can distinguish at least three different interpretations. First, there is a philosophical concept, as used in the texts of Marxist epistemological theory, following Marx, Engels and Lenin. In this context, representation has a very broad connotation of the sum total of our knowledge about objects, the subjective *image* of the objective world. There is a second, more specific concept of representation, linked to memory (Stempovskaya, 1958). It refers to the "primary image of memory" (Teplov, 1961), which appears after the perception of an object. In the 1966 textbook, there is a chapter entitled: "Representations and Memory." Leontev (1970) was critical of this meaning, since it implies a superposition of sensory images associated with the name of the object. Although such a concept of representation concedes the possibility of transformation of the representations of an object, Leontev felt that the meaning is actually that of a fixed structure conserved in memory. Finally, there is the most widely used concept of representation as the highest form of sensory cognition (Georgiev et al., 1965). It is this usage that concerns us here.

Representation is said to be a stage in the process of abstracting the general features of objects from their individual appearance. Representation differs from perception in at least two relevant aspects. It is not related directly to the impingement of the object on the sensory organs. It is the result of repeated subject-object interactions, as a result of which it is independent of certain irrelevant features. As has been mentioned, Soviet authors emphasize the degree of generalization already inherent in sensation and perception. However, with sensation similar and dissimilar aspects of objects are confounded, whereas in perception, although the similarity between objects is more relevant, the generalization is expressed only in terms of concrete sensory features.

On the other hand, representations are more dependent than perception on the individual's orientation and attitudes. Georgiev assumed that the development from perception to representation takes place in the following way. Initially, the identification of an object requires the perception of its whole contour. Eventually, through a number of manual and eye movements only partial perception becomes sufficient. The relations established between part and whole are based on the corresponding relations in the object itself. This implies that there is already a certain elaboration of the image of the object separated from the object itself. Georgiev (1965) wrote:

> With the development of representations and the transition to thought, representations can further depart from perception in the sense that they no longer require a stimulus in the form of the perception of a certain object. Representation may be produced by another representation or by a thought. . . . However, the detachment of the representation from perception does not mean its divorce from perception. This does not refer only to perceivable objects but also to the representation of unperceivable objects. Such representations are, for instance, the intuitive model of microphenomena studied by contemporary physics. Thought plays a remarkable role in the creation of such representations. . . . A certain similarity between qualitatively different phenomena, including macro- and microphenomena, is uncovered through thought. This allows the transfer of concrete features (shape, volume, continuity and discontinuity) to unperceivable phenomena. This transfer can be achieved only from properties which have been perceived by the subject. In this case, too, representations are based on perception [pp. 157–158].

Whether animals have representations has been the subject of sustained polemic in Soviet psychology. Students of animal behavior, particularly of monkeys, such as Roginskii, Vatsuro, and Voitonis (1949) showed the presence of elementary representations in animals. Ladygina-Kots (1959), was most explicit when she wrote that in the chimpanzee

> . . . generalized visual images are formed as a result of summation of trials which were successful in the past. . . . But even if the chimpanzee does obtain generalized visual images, the general representation . . . is efficient only in the presence of *stable relationships* between things. When these relationships are disturbed and a new situation occurs, the chimpanzee resorts again to new effortful searches for solution . . . in order to detect the essential features of objects [pp. 308–309].

Ladygina-Kots described the limitations of the representations and thinking in monkeys. These representations are strictly confined to the immediate environment. (She wrote about the "situational constraint" of the monkeys' representations.) Monkeys are incapable of establishing a mental *(myslennaya)* connection between representations, and to combine them into a complex image. The connections between objects established by monkeys are of two forms. First, there are connections achieved with the participation of generalized representations on the direct basis of the perception of objects which are selected by the chimpanzee according to certain attributes that enable him to attain his goal. Second, there are connections achieved with the participation of generalized representations. The monkey is guided by the visual image of the tool which is appropriate for the attainment of the biological meaningful goal. This *practical synthesis* is the limit of the chimpanzee's representation and thinking. The elaboration of connections on the mental plane, on the basis of correlations between vestigial stimulations is of an insurmountable difficulty for monkeys. Therefore, the complex temporospatial connections which monkeys are capable of forming do not become cause-effect relationships.

Beritov (1961), it will be recalled, has consistently maintained that animals have representations. It is his view that there are two types of animal behavior. In the first kind, each behavioral act is dependent on previous external and internal excitations. In the second kind, the animal's behavior is not solely contingent upon these stimulations, but is also influenced by the concrete image of objects of vital importance. The animal is guided by the representations of these objects as though the latter were actually present.

PERCEPTION AND INFORMATION PROCESSING

One of the major links between psychology and cybernetics has been provided by studies of the processing of information involved in perception, particularly in visual perception. These studies are conducted in several institutions, among which are the departments of psychology at Moscow and Leningrad universities and the Institute of Biophysics of the Academy of Sciences. The following is a brief survey of some of the major directions of study.

Leontev and Krinchik (1961, 1964a) and Krinchik (1961, 1962a,b, 1966, 1968, 1969, 1970) claimed to have prepared the groundwork for a quantitative study of psychological functions, especially sensory processes. They took as their starting point a comparison between human perception and the processing of information by machines designed to discriminate between stimuli. They emphasized that the analogy between man and machine can be made only on an abstract level permitting a quantitative evaluation. Leontev and Krinchik regard such an analogy as having practical importance in view of the fact that the automation of production is based on information processing, hence man becomes a vital link in the system. Furthermore, the quantitative expression of the processing of information by man enables a deeper insight into the nature of perception.

Leontev and Krinchik carried out experiments designed to study the dependence of reaction time on individual and average information. These dependencies were expressed by the formula $I_i = \log_2 pi$, and by the formula $H = -\sum_{i=1}^{k} pi$ respectively. They turned out to be basically different. Two experiments were performed, each of them consisting of two parallel parts. In the first experiment, one of two lights went on and the subject had to respond by closing the switch with which it was paired. The probability of occurrence of the two stimuli was varied so that each had either a low probability ($p < \frac{1}{2}$), or a high probability ($p > \frac{1}{2}$). A light went on every 10 seconds. It was preceded by an auditory signal at the sound of which the subject was to watch the light. When this went on, he had to react as quickly as possible. In the second part of the experiment, the amount of average information was varied by changing the number of signals of equal probability. The response latencies for conditions of two, four and eight signals were studied. The experiments demonstrated a linear dependence between reaction time and amount of information.

In the second experiment, one of a series of signals was given a special meaning: the subjects were warned that if they exceeded a certain reaction time, the device would be destroyed and the experiment would be discontinued. The introduction of the factor of significance resulted in a reduction of the reaction time under both conditions of processing individual and average information. An additional experiment was then performed to determine the relationship between reaction time and various degrees of significance of the stimulus. Three degrees of meaningfulness were used: (1) an informative reinforcement, namely the subjects were made aware of their delayed reactions; (2) a negative reinforcement, consisting of a light shock which followed a delayed reaction; (3) a warning reinforcement as used in the previous experiments. All other signals were neutral. The effects of the negative and warning reinforcements were stronger than that of the informative reinforcement. That is, the significance of the stimuli manifested itself in a corresponding reduction of the reaction time and parallel increase in the rate of gain of information. Leontev and Krinchik presumed that these two parameters could be taken as criteria in assessing man's attitude towards impinging stimuli. They contended that this paradigm of the way man obtains information and deals with complexity of choice could be extrapolated to the problem of man's general relationship to his environment. In other words, the two factors on which reaction time is dependent—the individual and average amount of information—have psychological correlates. These are the degree to which the signal is unexpected and the degree of complexity of the choice. Hence, human processing of information is not a passive reflection of the statistical structure of signals, but rather an active operation. The subject optimizes the perception of information: while the perception of frequent signals takes more time, the perception of infrequent signals is faster.

The probabilistic and informational structure of perception has also been studied by another group of psychologists under Sokolov, at Leningrad. E. N. Sokolov's (1958a) concept of a neural model of the stimulus has already been dealt with. Some of his studies on the tactile processing of information are now briefly reported. The use of tactile sensations of a hand or finger in recognizing an object has proved to be a convenient way of studying the orienting reflex as a mechanism of informational control. It was assumed that while this operation was of the same nature as the orienting reactions of the eye, it had the twofold advantage of providing both a receptor system with a single channel, and a longer time in which to study the reactions. In experiments carried out by E. N. Sokolov (1960b) and Arana (1961), Chinese letters were represented by checkers on a checkerboard divided into squares. The size of the checkers and the distance between them were equivalent to that of the first segment of the index finger. The subject was allowed to touch the checkers with the tip of the index finger only. The path made by the movements of the finger expressed a system of orienting reactions necessary to recognize the letters. The subject made a series of hypotheses. A hypothesis was changed depending on the presence or absence of a checker in a particular square. The number of hypotheses was gradually reduced. While the subjects started with a number of hypotheses larger than the number of presented letters, at a certain point in time the number of probes corresponded to the number of letters being shown. When one hypothesis was more significant than others, it resulted in a letter being identified with a fewer number of squares probed. The results of this experiment were interpreted as showing that a connection exists between the neural model and the process of extrapolation. Recognition involves a series of "neural models."

Sokolov extended his findings about the tactile constituent of the orienting reaction to all situations of a spatial or temporal sequence in human behavior. He hypothesized that a detailed recording of complex signals in the nervous system underlies the probabilistic nature of perception, and that the process of recognition implies a relating of unknown stimuli to memory traces. This is brought about by the following factors: the impinging stimuli, a system of signals stored in memory, the probability of occurrence of each of these signals in the course of the experiment, and the probability of occurrence of an elementary cue of a given stimulus.

A different contribution to the study of the processing of information in perception has been made by Vekker (1964), one of the first students and later one of the first research fellows of the Department of Psychology at Leningrad University. His monograph *Perception and the Fundamentals of Modeling It* was characterized by Ananev in his foreword as being the first work to unite psychology, neurophysiology and cybernetics. Vekker attempted to deal with the modeling of perception on the plane of psychological theory. He pointed out that his approach differed from the modeling of the end-result of the process of recognition of objects. In the former, one gains insight into the organization of sensory images, while the latter was said to be more concerned with the mathematical and technical problems raised by the design of machines capable of identifying a given stimulus. Vekker also pointed out the necessity of knowing the characteristics of sensory images when considering the design of such devices. To him, "the structural and functional features of the sensory image should be described in a scientific language which would include both the *model* and the *simulated* processes" (p. 9). Vekker emphasized the control aspect of cybernetic systems. Thus, of the two trends advanced in the theory of information processing, the first being linked to the theory of communication, and the second to the theory of control, Vekker felt closer to the latter. Insofar as he stressed information more as a factor of control and as a definite organization of processes, Vekker is more in accord with Wiener's point of view than with that of Frick.

Vekker's primary interest has been in tactile perception which was a major trend of Ananev's school. A collective monograph on *Touch in the Processes of Cognition and Work* published in 1959 summarized this research. The emphasis on the perceptual control of manual activity was largely responsible for Vekker's bias towards the informational-control of the hand in the process of manipulating objects. While his specific study differed from that of Leontev's, both shared the idea that the sensory image has a signaling function. The close connection between signaling and control was stressed by Vekker (1964) as follows: "The circulation of information relays the instruction from the source of information to the signal system and then to the response" (p. 62). These result in certain features of the response: (1) the spatial-kinetic structure of an action reproduces the structure of the handled object, notably its shape, size, outline, etc: (2) integrality, i.e., the overall correspondence between object and action; (3) variability, where postures and trajectories replace each other; (4) stimulus and response generalization; (5) transfer from one organ to another, that is the same instruction can be carried out by different organs; (6) universality of control; (7) reliability and redundancy of control; this is not so much a matter of accuracy of each aspect of the action—as is the case in a machine—but it is rather referred to the correct orientation of the entire responding system to the structure of the object. It is in the nature of the control that Vekker distinguished between the functioning of the nervous system and that of the machine.

A significant portion of Soviet studies on the processing of visual information was devoted to the investigation of eye movements (Luriya, 1961; Khomskaya, 1962; Gurevich, 1957, 1959,a,b, 1961, 1962; Yarbus,[1] 1965). The following is an illustration of these studies.

Khomskaya (1962) studied the effect of various factors on the regulation of eye movements. She conducted a series of four experiments in which the horizontal movements of the right eye were recorded. In the first experiment, the subjects were requested to look as quickly as possible from one bright point to another. In the second experiment, the subjects followed a bright point moving at an increasing speed. The purpose of the third experiment, which studied the effect of fatigue, used the same procedure employed in the first experiment. In the fourth experiment, the shape, amplitude and frequency of the eye movements were recorded, and after an interval of 25-30 seconds, the subjects had to reproduce the movements from memory.

The experiments revealed differences between eye movements controlled by a visual stimulus and those performed

[1] Yarbus' important monograph which summarizes his work based on an original technique is available in English.

without visual control. The change in afferentation had an effect on two parameters of the eye movements: shape and frequency. In the case of spontaneous changing of the fixation point—the first and third experiments—the eye movements were saccadic, whereas in the second experiment, the stimulus in motion produced a sinusoidal curve. The role of visual control was particularly evident in the last experiment. On terminating visual control, the eye movements lapsed from their sinusoidal form and turned into saccades, despite an unchanged frequency. Khomskaya noticed a close relationship between the shape of eye movements and their frequency. Thus, the sinusoidal curve was maintained up to a frequency of 0.8–0.9 movements per second, at which stage the movements reverted to saccades. The transition from the sinusoidal form to the saccadic was gradual and to a large extent depended on the given frequencies. Khomskaya concluded that the two levels of control which operate are related to different forms of afferentation.

Gurevich, from the I. P. Pavlov Institute of Physiology at the Academy of Sciences of the USSR, extensively investigated the oculomotor fixation reflex as an instance of an elementary conditioned reflex. Based on Pavlov's theory, Gurevich (1959b) stated:

> The external stimuli having formerly coincided with reactions fulfilled reinforced, on eliciting a reaction by way of its effectory centre, simultaneously produce in the higher proprioceptive centres, changes similar to those which, beforehand, became reinforced at the fulfilment of the reactions. During the course of the reaction, the impulses ascending to the higher proprioceptive centres from the sensitive endings in the effectory organs are constantly recodified according to the functional state of these centres and, being thus transformed into signals of correction, take part in the control of the reaction until its fulfilment and repeated reinforcement. Thus, it appears that behaviour acts remain on the whole adequately directed, because of the regulation during their course of the efferent nerve supply by the higher proprioceptive centres, according to the changes brought to these centers by conditioning stimuli [p. 1220].

Gurevich chose the conditioned oculomotor fixation reflex as the object of his studies, due to the simplicity of the oculomotor apparatus, its nervous connections, as well as the feasibility of recording eye movements. The subjects were requested to turn their eyes in the dark from one direction to the other in response to a sound and to keep doing so after the stimulus was no longer presented. These experiments revealed the possibility of fixating a point in response to a signal in the absence of a controlling visual stimulus due to the "muscular sense." Gurevich hypothesized that during the formative stage of a conditioned reflex, a temporary connection between the conditioned and the kinesthetic stimulations was established, as well as a controlling temporary connection between the conditioned stimulation and the sensory centers of the reaction. According to Gurevich, the analysis of the oculomotor reflex at a stage when the fixation points are varied demonstrates that purposeful behavior has similar characteristics to systems with automatic control. During the process of perception, specific double reverse pathways become operative and, at the same time, the initial discrepancy between the exteroceptive and the proprioceptive centers is eliminated. The reverse stimulations and sensory events of external and internal origin become reciprocally controlled. Gurevich's position is opposed to that of Bernshtein as well as to that of MacKay who think of the organism as a system controlled by effector programs which originate in events in the environment. Gurevich regards the brain functioning as independent of current events; each act is based on mechanisms already learned by the organism. These mechanisms are organized and generalized due to the innate systems possessed by the organism. It is his belief that his model is apt to combine several major concepts proposed in the psychophysiology of sense organs and the physiology of the higher nervous activity. These include Helmholz's "unconscious reasoning" Sechenov's "muscular sense," Beritov's "psychonervous representation," and Anokhin's "acceptor of effect."

A diversity of Soviet studies on the modeling of sensory systems could be included in bionics to which Russian scholars have paid an increasing attention (Linkovskii and Smuglyi, 1964; Braines et al., 1967). Braines and a group of authors defined this new science as being concerned ". . . with the utilization of the principles of organization and functioning of living organisms and their elements, for the improvement of the existing technological systems and the creation of essentially new ones" (p. 197). The First All-Unional Conference on Bionics was held in 1963, and in 1965 the Second All-Unional Conference on Bionics had already taken place to conclude the results of two years of extensive study. The investigations were conducted on the olfactory system (Bronshtein, 1960), on the auditory system, particularly in mammals (Gershuni, 1965, 1967), and on the visual system. Eventually the most significant studies have been done on the visual recognition of objects. Glezer (1959, 1960, 1961, 1962a,b, 1966 a,b,), from the Laboratory of the Physiology of Vision at the I. P. Pavlov Institute of Physiology has probably given the most lucid account of the problems involved in the study of the visual recognition of objects and his work will be presented now at some length.

Glezer held the position that the mechanisms responsible for various aspects of functioning of the visual system, such as photosensitivity, visual acuity, and color vision are ultimately oriented towards the recognition of objects, and that this should be the major topic of the physiology of vision. The first question to be asked concerns the nature of the visual image of the object which results from the process of recognition Glezer accepted the cybernetic definition of an image as an assembly of stimuli which yield one reaction, in this instance of the visual system, including the retina, the subcortical and cortical projections, as well as the associative areas neighboring the 17th area, whose functions are related to processing visual information. In the higher regions of the brain, a neuronal structure is supposed to exist which reacts in the same way to the sight of an object regardless to its spatial position. Thus, an important characteristic of a visual image is its invariance. This is defined by Glezer as a "generalization at the level of differentiation accomplished by the visual system" (p. 5). While innate mechanisms do have a role in this process, it is assumed to be largely a result of learning.

Glezer rejected the hypothesis that the neuronal structure responsible for the formation of the visual images is organized in the form of models the coincidence with which produces their arousal. He admitted this possibility only for a small number of the most frequently encountered objects. But the representation of any object in the form of its model would not be economical for the nervous system. The alternative is the dichotomy principle, that is, the operation of a set of opposites. In the case of n objects, $\log_2 n$ operators would be sufficient for the recognition of each object. These operators cannot be innate. Their number and structure are defined by the alphabet or assortment of visual images learned by each individual. There are a number of stages of processing the visual information. The primary transformation of the visual information is carried out by the receptive fields of the retina. The next stage, which consists of the identification of the simplest configurations is performed by the cortical receptive fields.

According to Glezer, the visual system possesses several channels, or systems, each of which describes a certain property of an object. Each such system consists of neurons which react selectively to certain characteristics of the object. This results in an object being modeled in the form of a selection of signals, or simple features which build up the complex features. Thus, unlike a perceptron, the complex features are not formed of signals originating in the receptors, but of signals produced by a system with a complex organization. This makes possible a more economic transmission of the information about the individual features, each of which can be used for the description of different objects. The generalization attained in the process of recognition is paralleled by a detailed information about the object. Hence, Glezer conceived the activity of the nervous system as consisting of two mechanisms. In the first place, there is a parallel transmission of information about the size, position, color, etc. of an object on independent channels. This mechanism makes possible the transition from a generalized symbol to the reflection of a concrete object. In the second place, there is a description of an object, element by element, accomplished by the system of primary processing of information, notably the receptive fields.

A further question discussed by Glezer is that of the specificity of the visual image: is sensory image a general category, so that one cannot distinguish between, say, the visual and tactile images of an object? His answer is that as a result of the process of evolution, several specialized mechanisms have developed in the inferior as well as in the superior regions of the visual system.

Finally, there is the problem of the classification of visual images, or, stated differently, the question of the relationship between the formation of concepts and the categorization of visual images. Glezer contended that the dictionary of visual images is limited and can be compared, but not identified, with the selection of words which constitute the vocabulary of an individual. He clearly distinguished between recognition as a visual task, and the formation of a concept as a logical task. To him, the relationships between objects in visual space are evaluated in the visual apparatus by a system which localizes the objects and measures the distances and angles between them according to the horizontal and vertical coordinates of the visual space. It is said of the distance between different images in the visual space that it is not to be determined by the conceptual categories to which they belong. For instance, it is unlikely that an airplane and a ship occupy neighboring areas merely because they are both means of transportation.

Neither can two images of the same object viewed from different angles be expected to form a unitary image. Thus, the selection of visual images coincides only partially with verbal concepts. There is an essential difference between the criteria used for the visual discrimination of objects and the criteria which one mentions when asked about the differences between the same objects.

An experiment by Prazdnikova, an associate of Glezer, showed the difference. The subjects, four-year-olds, had to turn off a light by pressing a right or left key, depending on whether they were presented with an acute or an obtuse angle, respectively. After the consolidation of the reflex and the stabilization of the latency period, the angles were presented in different positions. Some subjects coped with the task and were aware of the similarity and difference between the two situations. Others also responded correctly but could offer no explanation. Glezer interpreted this finding as showing the lack of reflection of the visual image, which became a conditioned stimulus, in the logical conceptual system. Thus the elements in which the image can be decomposed do not coincide with the description given by the visual system. This is also supposed to happen to the adult under usual conditions. For instance, one finds it difficult to describe at once the differences between the male and female face. The visual system can make decisions without abstracting all the details and, hence, these are not included in a logical description.

Glezer also relied on neurological findings to show the difference between visual and logical functions. Thus, agnostic patients who have lost the capacity to recognize objects are able to establish logical connections between objects. In cases of left temporal lesions, when the agnostic disturbance is accompanied by a disturbance of the process of generalization and of the memory of the names of objects, these disturbances are selective and do not show a general disturbance of thinking (Kozh, 1964).

Comparative studies done by Prazdnikova showed that the

invariance of the visual image is a result of evolution. The experiments were done on fish and monkeys (baboons). A differentiation between reinforced lighted geometrical figures, and unreinforced unlighted geometrical figures was elaborated in all the animals. The invariance was studied with regard to the following features of the stimuli: (1) Position of presentation. During the formation of the (motor) reflex, the stimuli were presented in the same place. After the consolidation of the conditioned reflex and the stabilization of latency, the fish as well as the monkeys reacted to the lights regardless of the place of presentation (for the fish, in one of three or six places). (2) The size of the objects. Change of size did not have any effect on the learned response. In fish, the differentiation was maintained when the size of either the positive or negative stimuli was either enlarged or reduced, and when the stimuli were again made equal (both were either larger or smaller than originally). It was also maintained when a small positive object was replaced by a larger one, and a large negative stimulus was replaced by a smaller one. But it was disturbed in the reverse situation. (3) Rotation of the geometric figures. Change in inclination abolished the differentiation in fish, but had no effect in monkeys. When simpler stimuli were used, consisting of one or two lines in different angles, the fish reacted to one vertical line which had the same direction as the positive geometric figure. The monkeys, while failing to react to one line, reacted to two lines regardless of their rotation. To Glezer, these findings indicate that the monkeys reacted to the geometric figure as a whole. The fish did not possess the image of the angle as such. This was demonstrated by an additional experiment in which a reinforced obtuse angle was differentiated from an acute angle which was applied at once in three rotations. The differentiation between the positive stimulus and the three negative stimuli was not obtained at the same time but at different rates. Thus, the three differentiations were elaborated independently. (4) The elimination of details. A differentiation between a square and a triangle was obtained in fish. When the two geometric figures were replaced by their outlines, the square did not elicit the reaction and was no longer differentiated from the triangle. Additional similar trials clearly showed that the fish distinguished only the direction of lines and reacted neither to angles nor to the number of sides and angles. (5) The change of the color of the geometric figures disturbed the differentiation in fish. Neither this experiment nor the previous one were done with monkeys because it had been already shown by other authors that these two factors did not affect a learned discrimination in these animals. (6) The substitution of continuous drawings by their outlines and vice versa disturbed the differentiation in fish but not in monkeys. (7) In fish, the reversal of the white and black colors of the figure and ground, respectively, resulted in both stimuli becoming positive. This had no effect on the monkeys' responses.

Glezer drew an analogy between the process of visual recognition in fish, and the operations of a perceptron. The perceptron is presented with several versions of an object and this results in the formation of an area in the multidimensional space of the receptors corresponding to that object. This area is made up only of the points which were presented in the course of teaching the machine. The visual system of fish has the same limitations. On the contrary, monkeys can be taught to identify an object by using a single version of it. When different versions are presented they are recognized.

Glezer disagreed with Hebb (1949), who proposed the hypothesis of a conceptual activity which is not elicited directly by a sensory stimulation but occurs as a result of the stimulation of a sector of the cell assembly. (Hebb referred to errors in drawings which show that the observer sees in an object more than there is in it.) Glezer pointed out that an object may be wrongly identified in a picture even if this has no common elements with that object. Thus, when a tea pot was exposed for 70 msec., an observer perceived (clearly, he claimed) a pair of scissors. This means that the recognition was not made by elements, since there were no common elements between these two objects. However they may have in common at least one of the separating functions. Under a limited exposure, a part of the code-meaning is reproduced by guesswork. A certain object can be visualized even if the wrong code was reproduced. The occurrence of a conceptual activity, which is identical with making a decision about the nature of the object, is not related to elements or parts of the picture, but to complex features. The same process is supposed to take place in patients with right temporal lesions who see only a part of a picture. They are unable to operate with the whole selection of discriminatory functions. Their fragmentary vision means that they stick to a single operation. Glezer contended that the mechanisms of constancy may have innate components, although he did emphasize the role of learning. For instance, size constancy in man may be innate. (Hebb showed that this phenomenon is innate in mice.) Thus, Nevskaya, an associate of Glezer, was able to train subjects to recognize in a mirror reflection the geometric figures which had been presented previously.

A position similar to that of Glezer has been held by Aizerman (1962a,b) and Braverman (1962) from the Institute of Automation and Remote Control. Their work is concerned with the simulation of the visual recognition of objects. Specifically, they have searched for the algorithms of inference from the recognition of certain variations of a given object to any variations of it. Aizerman raised the following question: what process of learning is involved when pupils who have been presented with several variations of the letters a and b are later able to recognize all the other variations of these letters? He thought of two principles on which the program of a machine able to solve such a problem should be based. In the first place, the program should include as many different characteristics of an object to be sufficient for the recognition of all its different versions. In the second place, the program has to include one or a few universal characteristics which underlie the very concept of image but are not important for the recognition of concrete objects. Aizerman (1962a) defined the concept of visual image as follows:

> By visual image we mean an infinite plurality of visual sensations, e.g., the result of the observations of different plane figures which have the following characteristic: people who have seen a few elements of this plurality confidently relate to it other elements which they have never seen before. Thus, for instance, the portraits of all the participants to a meeting is not an image because if some of them are shown to a person who was not there, he will not be able to say about another portrait if that individual attended the meeting or not. But the concept of a 'man's portrait' is an image . . . [p. 175].

According to this concept of visual image, Aizerman assumed that universal characteristics of all images do exist. Thus he formulated the hypothesis of "compactness."

> . . . the smooth transition from one element of an object to another is always possible so that all the intermediary variations will also be perceived as elements of the same object; on the contrary, there is no smooth transition from the elements of one object to the elements of another without the occurrence "on the way" of variations regarding which there is no unanimous opinion as to which of the objects they belong. . . . The hypothesis of compactness states that there is a certain portion of the receptive surface which corresponds to all the variations of an object, and that different portions correspond to different objects without common points between them [p. 177].

The process of teaching a machine to discriminate between two visual images consists of presenting it with a number of random elements of the two objects, that is with different points of the two receptive areas. Its task is to discover the surface separating the two areas. Two algorithms were employed. First, the algorithm of "random surfaces": the machine is presented with two points belonging to two different images (i.e., the digits 0 and 1) and it selects a random separating surface. New points are then presented, and other separating surfaces are randomly selected by the machine, until the end of the teaching process when a large number of surfaces are stored in the machine's memory.

The second algorithm is that of the construction of "potential surfaces": the machine, which is presented with a point, constructs the function of a point in space that reaches its maximum in that point, and, while being positive everywhere, is diminished on moving away from it in any direction. When several points belonging to that surface are presented, the machine constructs functions for each of them and then combines them. As a result of the teaching process, a separating surface is obtained, serving as a projection of the line which separates the constructed potential surfaces.

Two experiments were done to test the two algorithms. For the first experiment, 160 variations of each of five digits—0, 1, 2, 3, 5—were prepared; 40 variations were used in the teaching experiment, the remainder, in the control trials. Up to 89 per cent of correct responses were obtained for each variation. The second experiment consisted of two parts in which the same five digits and all the 10 digits were used respectively. Only 10 variations of each digit were used in this experiment. In the first part, all 750 responses were correct; in the second—85 per cent of the 1400 responses. In Aizerman's view, the operations of perceptrons can be explained by his hypothesis of formation of compact areas in the receptive surface.

Bongard (1961, 1962, 1965, 1967, 1970) from the Institute of Problems of Information Transmission, at the Academy of Sciences of the USSR, has taken a different approach. He pointed out (Bongard, 1962) that

. . . one of the difficulties of modeling the animal's behavior is that there is no continuous correspondence between the stimulus presented, the milieu in which the animal lives, and his purposeful actions in that milieu. Very often we encounter cases when minor changes in the environment require considerable changes in behavior and vice versa; apparently sharply different signals require the same response. The study of the recognition problem faces an identical situation. For instance, different variations of the letter "a" can differ more from each other, than "A" differs from "YA." Thus, there is no continuous correspondence between the receptive space about which M. A. Aizerman speaks, and purposeful reactions. The most difficult situation is that which occurs when Braverman's hypothesis of "compactness" of images of objects in the receptive field is not applicable [p. 189].

Bongard assumed that the recognition of an object in a new variation is possible due to the abstract concept of that object. The concept is formed as a result of the object having been seen in different variations, but it includes a broader class of variations than those which served as its basis. A new variation of a certain object can be recognized as such only on the basis of characteristics which do not vary under different conditions of observation of that object. Bongard (1961) made a distinction between traits and characteristics of objects. A trait is ". . . a degenerate reflection of the image of the object . . . an algorithm which is a degenerate transformation of the appearance of an object. The result of the transformation we shall call *a characteristic of the object according to a given trait*" (p. 2). Not all traits are useful for recognition. Useful traits are those which satisfy the following two conditions:

(1) they must divide up the group of objects subject to the difference (there must exist, at the minimum, two objects having different characteristics with respect to this trait; (2) the characteristics of each object should be constant, and not dependent on "conditions of observation" [p. 2].

These considerations underlay Bongard's program for a

computer able to recognize images of objects. The program included the following operations: (1) observation of different variations of objects, selection of the useful traits and recall of the characteristics of the object on the basis of those traits; (2) observation of new and unfamiliar variations of the same objects and establishment of the similarity of their characteristics with those stored in the memory of the device.

An initial experiment was done in which the machine was presented with a set of arithmetic matrices, each of which corresponded to a different rule. The machine was not programmed with these rules. Its task was to reveal and subsequently recognize them in any set of matrices. Bongard felt that this program suggested a method of determining universal characteristics. It consisted of the construction of several logical functions from the incoming data. The computer, although able to construct many logical functions, selected those which provided the useful traits. However, the application of this program for the recognition of geometric figures turned out to be complex. For this purpose, Bongard used another program based on physiological findings of the Institute of Information Transmission Problems (Nyuberg, 1962; Byzov, 1962; Maksimov, Zenkin, and Byzov, 1965), which showed the role of the different layers of the retina in processing the visual information. Bongard's program simulated four stages of the coding of visual information. The first stage modeled the functions of the bipolar cells of the retina, among which were the distinction of the outline of an image and the tuning up to the general illumination. The second stage represented the function of the ganglionic cells which react to changes in the intensity of light. The connections between the bipolar and ganglionic cells were formed through learning; once a connection was established, it was extended to the whole layer of bipolar cells. At this point, there was a recoding of the data by the subcortical centers. (Bongard mentioned that this was a weak part of this program.) Finally, the role of the cortex in determining the logical function of the 10,000 variations of connections between the previous three stages was included in the program. In one of the experiments, the computer was presented with four letters of different sizes, print, etc., its task being to produce abstract representations of the letters. The machine coped with this task—although it made some errors—thereby indicating an ability for deep generalization, beyond the capacity for either a perceptron or Aizerman's program.

To conclude this chapter, the current challenge of the traditional Pavlovian concept of analyzer should be mentioned. Snyakin (1961a,b, 1963) and Esakov (1961), from the Laboratory of Physiology and Pathology of Sense Organs of the Institute of Normal and Pathological Physiology, the USSR Academy of Medical Sciences in Moscow, and Demirchoglyan (1961, 1968, 1969) from the Laboratory of Visual Reception of the Armenian Academy of Sciences, at Erevan, have been most prominent among the Soviet writers who pleaded for the need to review the concept of analyzer which implies an activity taking place within the limits of a one-sided three-membered chain. Demirchoglyan mentioned that the term, analyzer, had the merit of stressing the organic and functional connections between peripheral receptors and sensory centers in the brain. The following are some of the arguments which he put forward, based on both earlier and new findings of Western and Russian investigators, to show that this concept is limited. (1) Histological studies discovered centrifugal pathways leading from the central nervous system to the receptors. These fibers innervate the eye, in particular the retina, the ear, the cutaneous receptors and the organs of taste and smell. (2) Following Orbeli's lead about the sympathetic origin of the efferent innervation of the sense organs. Mkrtycheva (1962) established the effect of the sympathetic nerve on the content of visual purple in the retina, and Demirchoglyan and Sverdlov showed changes in the electroretinogram (ERG) after the destruction of the sympathetic innervation of the eye. (3) It was clearly shown that there is a cortical control of sensations. Various names were suggested such as a conditioned photochemical reflex, conditioned sensory reflex, and conditioned adjustment reflex, for the finding that a conditioned reflex excitation can produce shifts in the light, color and electrical sensitivity of the eye similar to the effect of an adequate light stimulus. Studies in Demirchoglyan's laboratory showed that many stimuli which are inadequate for the eye, such as smells, sounds, tastes and electric shocks to the skin have an effect on visual functions and become more active when they produce conditioned reflex stimulation and involve cortical feedback mechanisms. Experiments on rabbits using the contact lens-electrode showed the possibility of conditioned reflex changes in the ERG.

On the basis of these and other findings, Demirchoglyan proposed the concept of a system of circular nervous processes in the analyzer, which can be divided into three groups, clearly manifest in the visual system: (1) the peripheral level of regulation of receptor processes in the retina; (2) the feedback pathways from the subcortical formations to the retina, reflecting the influence of other analyzers; (3) the cortical centrifugal influences on the retina which play a major role in the analysis of visual information.

4

Thought and Language

Soviet psychologists have devoted a great deal of their work to the study of thought, as the long bibliographical list appended to the publications on this subject will attest. As a matter of fact, the development of Soviet psychology as a distinct school owes much to the study of thought with some of the major characteristically Soviet concepts growing out of precisely this area of inquiry.

Three factors appear to have contributed to this development. First, the aim of the theoretical and experimental study of thought—like the study of sensory processes—was to provide arguments for the dialectical-materialistic epistemology (Markova, Matyushkin and Mukhina, 1970). In this respect, the study of thought, with its relation to sensory cognition, on the one hand, and with language and speech, on the other, was more relevant than, for example, the study of emotions. Second, it is apparent that Soviet authors were more confident when dealing with intellectual processes than with other areas in psychology. While they readily found support in the "classics of Marxism" for their arguments concerning the objective nature of thoughts and of language, the application of the theory of reflection to the sphere of emotions and to a psychology of personality in general required a sophistication which they were late in acquiring. It goes without saying that the theories of emotional life which developed in the West, and above all psychoanalysis, were a main target of their criticism; however Soviet psychologists themselves lagged far behind in developing their own theory of personality.

In the final analysis, concentration on the study of thought was prompted by pragmatic educational purposes. The development of conceptual thinking in the school child in the various fields of study such as arithmetic, biology and geography has been a major concern for the Soviet students of thought and a great proportion of their publications deal with these topics. The experimental study tended, at least in some cases, to take the form of a rather narrow functionalistic study of teaching methods. Rubinshtein (1959b) was critical of this tendency, claiming that this was not a genuine study of the thinking process. He wrote:

> In our Soviet research the emphasis is laid on the final result of a thinking process. This is due to a practical orientation towards assisting school teaching methods, the main purpose of which is to help the pupil to handle already elaborated, or firmly assimilated generalizations. Unlike the majority of studies, our own research is oriented towards the processes underlying the manifest result of thinking. Our investigations of thinking are not only concerned with the automatic application of previously elaborated generalizations, but with the earlier stage when specific relations are analyzed for the first time and then become generalizations. In this way we can penetrate the inner mechanism of thinking . . . [p. 319].

Rubinshtein admitted that no study of thinking can be complete without the consideration of the categories to which its results belong. Thinking is always concerned with a specific content, such as geometry or grammar. However, this should not be the subject matter of a psychological research, since it cannot lead to a general psychological theory of thinking.

Thinking should not be identified with the operations involved in any particular field of study, for these should be regarded only as specific expressions of the basic thinking processes. If these specific operations are separated from the basic process and their content overemphasized, such a study becomes extrinsic to the framework of psychology and belongs rather to the actual study of logic, geometry, grammar, etc.

In the last 20 years, the Soviet study of thinking has undergone a substantial evolution. Two events occurring in 1950 had a considerable impact on developments in the years to follow. First, the Pavlovian conference led to a severe limiting of researches to study the interaction of the two signal systems, and its development in children, with strict adherence to Ivanov-Smolenskii's position. Second, in the same year, Stalin's answers to a number of questions regarding Marxism and linguistics literally brought an upsurge in the Soviet views about the relation between language and thinking. At this point, there is a remarkable change for the better in the late 1950's, which continued unabated in the 1960's, resulting in powerful advances in the study of language and its relations to signs, signals and symbols, in the investigation of the psychology of problem solving, particularly in the field of information processing and heuristics.

Soviet views about the relationships among thinking, sensory cognition, language and speech will be discussed first, followed by a review of some of the main theories of problem solving.

THINKING AS A SECOND STAGE OF COGNITION

Abstract versus Concrete Cognition

Soviet psychology regards abstract cognition and logical reasoning as the second and highest stage of knowledge about objective reality. Thinking is said to lead to an acquaintance with the essential features of things, as typically stated by Lyublinskaya in the 1966 textbook:

Thinking is the highest and the most complex among the cognitive processes which represent forms of reflection of the surrounding world by man. While involved in the process of perception man gets acquainted with individual and concrete objects which are acting directly on his sense organs, due to thinking he knows such qualities of objects which cannot be realized directly. The characteristic feature of thinking consists of the reflection of objects and phenomena in their essential features, casual connections and relations between the properties of each object as well as between different objects and phenomena [p. 225].

Thus, while being in close contact with external reality, thinking surmounts the boundaries of sensory cognition. Leontev (1964a) strongly emphasized the Marxist rejection of both the idealistic view that thinking is a pure act of consciousness superimposed on the perception of things, and the metaphysical reduction of thinking to mere associations of sensations. Soviet philosophers have been very concerned in recent years with criticizing the concept of abstraction proposed by the theory of general semantics of Korzybski, Hayakawa, Rapoport and Johnson (Brutyan, 1961a,b, 1963, 1965; Reznikov, 1961, 1963a,b, 1964; Narskii, 1963; Zvegintsev, 1961, 1963; Korneeva, 1962; Rapoport, 1963). They objected to the view that abstract thinking is not a process whereby the essential properties of objects are separated from the nonessential, but rather one through which some aspects are isolated from others; that there is no qualitative difference between the sensory and the verbal modes of abstraction; that sensory abstraction, in fact, produces better apprehension of objects than the verbal abstraction and that thinking is of a personal and subjective character.

Thinking and Language

The proposition that thoughts exist only in the form of language remains basic to Soviet psychology. In the words of the 1962 textbook:

Man's thinking is expressed in words which in turn are conveyed in speech. To some people, words and speech appear necessary only to make their ideas accessible to others, while they claim that there would be no need for words to form ideas. This view is erroneous. For just as a painting owes its existence to the colors the artist puts on the canvas, so an idea exists only as a result of speech. One is impossible without the other. According to Marx, speech is the immediate reality of consciousness. It is the natural stuff of thinking. . . . The fact that thinking and language are inseparable does not mean that they are identical. Thinking is the reflection of the objective reality, while speech is a means of expressing and consolidating thought and, at the same time, a tool for transmitting it to others [pp. 140-141].

It is accepted that Engels was the first to propose the proposition that work and speech are the two main stimuli in the development of the human brain, and Soviet writers (Protasenya, 1961; Zhdanov, 1969) contended that man's use of tools was the first step in the direction away from the purely sensory world. The use of tools broadened the knowledge about relations between objects. For example, when striking an object with a stone hammer, the toughness of that object had to be considered in relation to that of the hammer. Progressing from this stage, man learned to identify the properties of objects before actually making use of them; moreover his knowledge could be communicated. A distinction was thus drawn between a cognitive aim and a practical result.

The relation between thinking, language and speech has been one of the most controversial in Soviet psychology since 1950. A lively polemic arose in linguistics that year and soon extended to psychology. The issue was whether articulated speech is the only tool of abstract thinking. Until 1950 the theory of the Georgian linguist Marr was considered the only Marxist theory of language. According to Marr (1925) there was a stage in the development of man when he used a language of gestures which served not only as a means of communication but as an instrument of thought as well. Abstract ideas associated with speech appeared at a later stage, to be followed by thought in terms of formal logic, the appearance of which coincided with that of social classes. The most recent stage is one of dialectical-materialistic thought, which leads to pure thought independent of speech.

In June 1950, Stalin in *Marxism and Questions of Linguistics,* proclaimed Marr's theory to be anti-Marxist. He claimed that sonic language, the language of words, had always been the only language of mankind and served as the only means of communication. According to Stalin, no means of communication can replace sonic language. Thinking is inconceivable without language,

> . . . no matter what thoughts occur in one's mind, or when they occur, they appear and exist only on the basis of linguistic material, on the basis of concepts and sentences. . . . The reality of thought is manifest in language [p. 39].

Needless to say, Stalin's propositions gave rise to numerous publications which followed this line in linguistics and psychology.

It is apparent that despite the fact that Stalin is no longer quoted, his proposition about the unity of language and thinking is still influential. However, the debate continues and it seems that his intervention in the 1950 polemic in linguistics contributed little to the clarification of the issue from the Marxist point of view. To illustrate this point, consider some statements made by different authors in the period following Stalin's work. Shemyakin (1952) wrote that,

> . . . one of the ways in which Soviet psychology still maintains that language is a phenomenon of individual consciousness is the attempt to separate language from speech. With this as a basic tenet, it is sometimes argued that language is a social phenomenon, while speech is an individual one. It is also asserted that speech is a process of communication via language. But both these assumptions are erroneous. Language cannot exist only within the individual and independent of the society as a whole. Attempts to separate language from speech are misleading and are rooted in the idealistic concept of language as a "system of ideal

values" and of speech as an "individual act of speaking." It is wrongly assumed that individual speech is the basis of language, so that the individual appears distinct from the society as a whole, as if one human being alone could produce language [p. 295].

Rubinshtein (1957b) also contended that basic terms were not clearly defined; "language" and "speech" were used interchangeably; the relations between thinking, language and speech were examined either on the functional level or on the genetic level; and thinking was described as an activity in itself rather than the result of an activity. But Rubinshtein differed from Shemyakin when he stated that speech is ". . . the utilization of a language by an individual according to circumstances; this is a vocal activity, expressed in verbal utterances, by means of which the communication is made; language is the totality of the means of speech" (p. 43).

Finally, the unity between thinking and language was understood by Shchedrovitskii (1957), a logician, in the following manner:

. . . thinking is not a direct and independent object of research; it appears to us above all in language, or, more exactly, we are given a language in which thinking is manifest. But, on the other hand, language too exists only in an inalienable connection with thinking; we cannot approach them separately but we have to deal with a whole . . . language and thinking being facets of it. We name this whole "linguistic thought," underscoring in this way its internal inseparability [p. 31].

In the opinion of the linguist Kert (1967), this statement amounts to an erroneous identification of thought and language, while A. A. Leontev (1968), another linguist, regarded Shchedrovitskii's work as an important contribution.

In recent years, the discussion of the above topic has continued with an obvious deepening of the arguments on both the theoretical and empirical levels. As before, the linguists contributed the major share of the publications. There is in addition, however, an important psychological contribution to the issue. Several orientations are discernible. First, there are authors who follow the classic distinction made by Saussure and thus regard speech as the implementation of language as a social means of communication within the context of an individual act. This view was clearly expressed by Chikobava (1967), a leading Gruzinian linguist. For him,

> . . . language is a system of signs functioning as a means of communication and as an instrument of thought. Hence, language has two functions: an *interindividual*—it is a means of communication—and an *intraindividual*—it is an expression of thought. The first function is the leading one: a language which ceases to be a means of communication . . . cannot maintain the intraindividual function. Nobody can think for very long in a language which he cannot possibly use as a means of communication . . . [p. 18].

From this, Chikobava went on to state that an analysis of the relations between thinking and speech should follow the path from the intent to its expression. That is, thought is the initial fact which is implemented in acts of speech. "The intraindividual function is first, and is followed by the interindividual function" (p. 29). But ontogenetically, there is a reverse process: from expression to intent. That is to say, words and their meaning represent an independent variable, but, once assimilated, speech becomes the bearer of both the interindividual and intraindividual functions.

> Language, a dependent variable, is the result of the storage of speech in memory, and is accomplished by speech acts. Through their manifestation, speech acts are of a psychophysiological nature. Language as a potential factor exists in memory. The existence of language is physiological phenomenon [pp. 29-30].

However, Chikobava pointed out that, by its destination and use, language is a social phenomenon. Thus,

> . . . language is a system of signs, physical by their material, social by

their destination. If the linguistic signs were not physical by their material, they could not become a means of communication. If the elements of language, which are physical by their nature, were not signs, they would be studied by natural sciences. But since signs have meaning, they cannot be studied via the natural sciences: the problem of meaning is alien to natural sciences [p. 30].

A similar view was expressed by two other linguists, Andreev and Zinder (1963), who proposed the use of four terms: language, speech, speech act and speech material. The speech material is the concrete realization of the system of language; the speech act is a process which results in speech material; speech is a combination of linguistic elements within a context.

A second direction, which is ultimately the most relevant from the perspective of physiology and psychology, has already resulted in an impressive body of findings (Kozhevnikov and Chistovich, 1965). Speech is treated as a complex structure in itself, involved in the process of thinking in various ways and degrees, and not as a mere implementation of language. This position was made explicit by Zhinkin (1963), a major representative of this trend. According to him, speech is a complex phenomenon and has to be studied by linguistics, psychology, physiology, logic and physics (acoustics in particular), leading to a general theory of speech activity. Zhinkin pointed out that there is a need not only for a basic philosophical proposition accepted by all Marxists, but also for a specific theory based on the facts described by all the sciences concerned. The studies which follow this line of reasoning are concentrated, by and large, on the investigation of "silent" internal speech.

Russian interest in the role played by internal speech in the thinking process has its starting point in Sechenov's idea that thinking is accompanied by a silent speech consisting of contractions of the muscles of the tongue. Subsequently Pavlov assumed that it is precisely those stimulations originated in the speech organs and transmitted to the cerebral cortex, which form the basis of the second signal system. Blonskii, and in particular Vygotskii, were among the early Soviet psychologists who paid much attention to this subject. Later, instructive clinical and experimental investigations were carried out at the Leningrad University. Thus Ananev (1946) concluded that the disturbances of the logical-syntactic structure of language are of a different nature in "sensory" and "motor" aphasia. Sensory aphasia does not consist of a complete disintegration of internal speech; rather there are "zones" of disintegration along with zones which remain intact. The predicative forms of language in sensory aphasia are not disturbed, although they are impaired in motor aphasia, where the substantive forms exist intact. Ananev hypothesized that a close relationship exists between the predicative forms of language and the motor functions.

Studies were done which revealed the role played by internal speech during the process of problem-solving. In these studies the investigation of inner speech was rather indirect, they did, however, open a path for further research. Baev (1958) asked subjects to solve three problems, one consisting of comprehending a scheme, the second relating to the visual reproduction of a particular situation ("You go out of the house, walk straight for 50 m., then you come back and walk 50 m. left," etc. At what distance will you then be from the house?"), and the third being purely abstract, namely the explanation of a proverb. Concomitantly the subjects had to repeatedly count loudly up to four. Baev noticed that the average time taken to solve the three problems were 3.27 seconds, 3.46 seconds and 3.61 seconds, respectively. He concluded that the more abstract a problem, the greater the participation of the silent speech.

A similar conclusion was reached by Novikova (1957). She measured the biocurrents of the speech organs in normal as well as deaf-mute children. Some of the latter used their fingers, together with writing and articulation of some kind. An electromyogram recorded muscular contractions which motivated the finger movements. The experiments revealed intensified electrical impulses from the speech organs in all subjects who were capable of verbal articulation, when engaged in an intellectual activity. The same effect was obtained in the hand muscles of subjects who used gestures as a speech aid. But electrical impulses during the experiments became gradually weaker when intellectual activity was reduced.

The works of A. N. Sokolov (1956, 1960, 1963, 1967, 1969) and Zhinkin (1956a,b, 1959, 1963, 1964) are particularly illustrative for the specific study of the psychophysiological aspects of internal speech. Sokolov considered the following processes as a starting point in his hypothesis. Speech, he contended, starts with stimulation of the cortical-motor neurons of the vocal centers by visual, auditory, tactile, etc. impulses. In turn, these neurons stimulate the muscles of the speech organs which are responsible for the phonation and articulation of verbal sounds. At the same time, contractions of these muscles produce the cortical stimulation which was regarded by Pavlov as the basic element of the second signal system. The same process is involved in the latent articulation of speech during an intellectual activity. These contractions also give rise to an increased excitation in the cortex, which orients thought on certain objects and the consequent process of their comprehension. Although motor stimulation is inhibited during the course of thinking, nevertheless there are still auditory and visual stimulations. These impulses from the speech organs maintain the functional tonus of the second signal system, contribute to the fixation and recall of the verbal material as well as to the formation of thought before their actual communication. A reverberating circuit which underlies the relationship between thought and speech is thus assumed to be operating here. The muscular contractions involved in the speech organs do not represent a passive verbal reproduction of thoughts, but play an active role in controlling the process of thinking. Sokolov was aware of the dangers in assuming that thought is possible without the participation of speech, motor impulses and thus put forward the following arguments. (1) In the articulation of words, there is not only a speech motor activity, but also an auditory process involved. There is a stable connection between these two such that all speech motor impulses are linked to the verbal-auditory ones and, conversely, the auditory and visual perception of words is linked to the speech motor impulses. Despite their weakness, the residual motor impulses are able to elicit verbal connections in the auditory sphere and in fact compensate for the inhibited movements. (2) The work of certain muscles in the vocal cords can be substituted by other muscles which do not participate directly in speech. These are, however, effective only for stereotyped thinking processes and are based on well-formed speech connections. (3) Vestigial, motor, auditory and verbal stimulations all play their roles in thinking processes.

Sokolov attributed a three-fold function to verbal stimulation during the course of thinking: (a) the maintenance of the functional tonus of the second signal system, necessary for the normal thinking process; (b) the consolidation and reproduction of verbal material, i.e., memory; (c) the analysis and synthesis of verbal material, since the formation of these processes and the intellectual activity involved precede the communication itself. Thus, Sokolov's presumption was that the precise quantitative evaluation of the electromyogram of the muscles of the speech organs recorded during internal speech, constitutes a valid method for the psychophysiological study of thinking.

A detailed presentation of Sokolov's (1969) experimental studies is available in English. The speech motor reactions were recorded during various intellectual activities, such as solving mathematical problems, reading texts and reading in foreign languages. The hypothesis was that there should be a direct relationship between the intellectual effort and the intensity in the stimulation of speech organs. The experiments actually seemed to have shown that the speech motor impulses of latent articulation emerge discontinuously and with varying intensities. Strong impulses arose during the course of the verbal fixation of solutions to problems and the mental formulation of responses. Conversely, the impulses originating in the speech organs are reduced when (a) stereotyped acts are performed, particularly those which do not require the mental retention of partial solutions; (b) the subject answers questions on material with which he is familiar; (c) reading in the mother tongue.

A number of cases were noted where subjects who were presented with complex problems unexpectedly showed a considerable reduction of the speech motor impulses, even to the point of complete elimination. This finding gave rise to a rather different direction of investigations by Zhinkin who employed new experimental procedures. Dissatisfied with the explanation that this was due to individual differences between types of verbal representations, Zhinkin saw no solution in the notion that some people are not subject to the effect of motor impulses in problem solving, specifically, and in thinking, generally. He claimed that the methods utilized in this sort of experiment were unsatisfactory. They neither allowed for the complete recording of rudimentary movements of the vocal cords, nor for the recording of nerve impulses which might appear in the various peripheral regions of the speech motor analyzer, i.e., the throat, larynx, diaphragm and bronchia. In Zhinkin's view, the methods used are efficient only when the movements of the vocal cords are evident, but one cannot draw any conclusion when they are not.

Zhinkin looked for a stimulus which was able to inhibit the cortical areas of the speech motor analyzer while leaving the peripheral areas free. He assumed that under such conditions, all the reverse impulses emerging from the peripheral regions would also be inhibited, that they would not reach the cortical projection and therefore not be under control. He likened this situation to the condition of motor aphasia. That is to say, if a person's tongue is immobilized and the reverse impulses are not intensified, he will be unable to articulate words. Zhinkin mentioned such an experiment which had been carried out by Luriya. He felt that in this way, it would be possible to clarify the role of the reverse connections in the internal speech, with respect to which part of the speech process is involved, and to how much analytic and synthetic activity is still possible within the stream of peripheral impulses.

Zhinkin utilized two types of stimuli as the basis of his experimental research. The first type consisted of a group of sounds that formed a spectrum in which there was random interference of frequencies. The sounds produced were stronger than verbal sounds and more overpowering. The second stimulus was made up of movements of the subject's hand in rhythm with the movements of his speech organs. Zhinkin's aim was to study the nonspeech rhythmic interference. The two disturbing actions were supposed to be only partly coincident with the movements of the speech organs, so that the second stimulus would be equal to the first. Zhinkin took for granted the fact that the variation of difficult tasks, while keeping under control the intensity of disturbing stimuli, at the same time permits a rigorous analysis of the speech mechanism. Thus it is possible to establish the extent to which the peripheral impulses from the speech organs are necessary for the internal speech.

Zhinkin's line of reasoning in his experimental work represents an attempt to interpret speech and nonspeech interference in the light of information theory. In his view, speech has a self-control mechanism which seems to maintain a certain equilibrium between two pairs of processes. The first pair is represented by the reception and transmission of signals; the auditory stimulation is transmitted through the receptory link to the speech motor analyzer. Without auditory reception one is deaf and, conversely, hearing accomplishes its control function only if the speech sound is received. Learning to speak involves a relationship between the sequence of speech movements and the series of speech sounds. The second pair of processes consists of phonemic composition of the word and the composition of the verbal communication. In both cases a process of selection is involved. The selection of phonemes which make up a specific word is limited, while the selection of words in a sentence is unlimited. The choice of words for communication cannot be determined accurately, although some rules of this selection do exist. The selected words form a sentence which can be analyzed only after the entire communication has taken place. In other words, the selection of phonemes accords with strictly defined algorithms, while the selection of words is only partially in accord with them. There are logical, grammatical and semantic algorithms, but no algorithms exist for the selection of specific words. While the syllables of a word are not interchangeable, the words of a sentence can be so manipulated up to a point. Thus, words, which form the line of contact between the two links of speech mechanism, can be regarded first as representing a synthesis of analyzed phonemes, and second as merely undifferentiated signaling elements. The transition from the first stage to the second is made in two directions. When the decoding takes place, e.g., when reading occurs, one turns isolated words into a meaningful passage. Similarly, when one is required to write, the meaning must be codified into words. Further, while the transition from phoneme to morpheme is firmly consolidated in memory, the coding of a communication is not recorded in memory. The grammatical scheme adopted in this process is instantaneous and therefore lacks a rhythmic structure. It is for this reason that after the phonetic and morphological analysis has been accomplished, the selection of words may still proceed unhindered by the inhibiting stimuli. The actual process of verbal communication is free of the return stimulations from the voice-producing organs. The movements of the speech organs which might be disturbed by the inhibiting stimuli play a controlling role only in the analytical stage of word formation. It is during this stage that a balance is established between the phonemes and the impulses emitted by these organs.

Zhinkin's comparative research of the respiratory system of man and baboon (with the aid of roentgenographic recording) appears to have proved his assumption that the respiratory system in man is adjusted to the speech mechanism. Thus, any similarity between the vocal sounds produced by monkeys and the articulation of humans is limited to single syllables. There is a clear-cut distinction between the signals produced by animals and the phonemes of human speech. Both the respiratory systems and the vocal cords in monkeys are without the controlling ability necessary for the selection of sounds and the formation of words and sentences. Monkeys are only able to produce eight syllables, which are separated from each other. Thus when the monkey is pronouncing one syllable, his vocal cords are not prepared for the next one. This means that monkeys do not have a respiratory system adjusted to communication and consequently, a single produced syllable consumes the uncontrolled energy of the entire respiratory system.

A third direction can be discerned in recent years, one in which the concept of a "speech activity" is given a prominent status in the analysis of the relation between thinking, language and speech. The linguist A. A. Leontev (1963, 1967a,b, 1968) has been the main proponent of this trend. His conjectures are based on the Vygotskii-Leontev concept of activity according to which all human activity is said to be structured and purposeful. Hence, speech activity implies that speech acts are strictly organized and subordinated to a goal. It is not an activity per se, not a goal in itself, but it forms part of a certain activity, either purely theoretical or partly practical. It is precisely the system of speech acts which is the subject of linguistics. In Leontev's view, linguistics is concerned with that which is specific for speech activity, while psychology addresses itself to those aspects which are found in any human activity. The relation between language and society is an instance where there is a need to take a broader approach than that of pure linguistics, for the social functions of language are closely linked to its structure. Social factors influence language as an assembly of concrete speech situations.

Thus, for Leontev, psycholinguistics is the theory of speech activity. It is part and parcel of a general theory of activity. An independent study of speech processes is possible only on a more basic level, for instance, in phonetic studies. But in studies of grammar, particularly of semantics, the intent of the speech activity cannot be reduced to an assembly of sounds. A speech act always implies establishing a correspondence between two activities. Leontev (1963) felt that

> . . . therefore the possibilities and limitations in the use of American psycholinguistics for the construction of a general theory of speech activity is an extremely complex problem, since this starts from contradictory methodological principles [p. 110].

Furthermore, Leontev regards verbal activity as representing a unity between communication and generalization. This unity is expressed in several functions of language manifested simultaneously in a given speech activity. However he disagreed with Roman Jakobson's presentation along a continuum of six functions of language, including communication and the poetic functions. Leontev preferred Kainz's distinction in *Psychologie der Sprache* between functions of language which are necessarily manifest in any speech act and facultative functions. Communication belongs to the first group. It is manifest in three ways: it influences the behavior of one or more individuals; it influences mass behavior through the media; and, it controls one's own behavior. The function of language as a generalized reflection of reality consists of the assimilation of the social-historical experience of mankind. Furthermore, language has a national-cultural aspect since it reflects concepts linked with the experience of a certain people. However, Leontev pointed out that the presence of some national characteristics of naming or some specific semantic features is not to be identified with the national character of a language and even less with a specific way of thinking of a particular nation, as was assumed by Whorf.

Language is also a tool of knowledge: mankind gains acquaintance with reality through theoretical activity. This is to be distinguished from its function as a tool of the intellectual activity of a certain individual, since no result of such an activity is new for the group. Finally, speech has three roles: the nominative function, the so-called diacritical function—a system of verbal signs used in certain specific situations—and the expressive and esthetic function.

The meaning of Leontev's concept of "speech activity" may become clearer in light of his critical remarks of other views. Thus while he highly regarded Zhinkin's work, in which speech was approached as an activity, Leontev disagreed with the hypothesis of a "selection of sounds" from the "stock of phonemes," and a "selection of words" from the "word stock for the construction of a communication," since a word appears as a unit of communication and the communication itself as a self-contained entity. A speech act is not approached as having a certain place in the system of activity as a whole.

Leontev was particularly critical of the views of Andreev and Zinder because of the implication that the analysis of the verbal material, i.e., of a text, should be the first step. To him, a text does not exist without its construction or perception—reading—so that to start a psycholinguistic study with the text would mean, metaphorically, to start the construction of a building with the first floor. Furthermore, a speech act is conceived as a process and not as an activity: it only transforms the features of the verbal material from their potential into their actual form. This conception of speech—Leontev mentioned that it is generally accepted in linguistics and by most schools of psychology—implies that a certain linguistic code is in operation in the human brain. Roman Jakobson is said to have taken this simplified approach when he identified two pairs of categories: language-speech and code-communication. This means that speech simply cannot contain any essential features not available in language, except for those related to the rules of combination of linguistic elements.

A similar standpoint—which Leontev regarded as also based on Vygotskii's views—has been taken by Shchedrovitskii (1957, 1964a,b,). He has endeavored to construct a logical apparatus which takes into account not only already formulated statements, but also the forms of thought. Thought is conceived as an activity of elaboration of new knowledge. The major process consists of the detachment of a certain intent from the general "stock" which makes up the objective reality. The system of signs and the ways in which thought operates depend on the nature of the intent reflected in the system. This "linguistic thought" is the result of a development.

Verbal Conditioning

Pavlov's theory of the two signal systems stimulated a considerable number of investigations which primarily attempted to solve the following problems: the relationship of the stimulus of the first signal system to the corresponding word; how the organizing role of the second signal system has developed in human behavior; how conditioned reflexes are formed during the learning of a language; what relationships exist between the meaning of the word and the component parts of the word, in particular the phonemic aspect; the nature of the role played by conditioning when the grammatical structure of a language is being learned by children.

The first systematic research into the interaction between words and related stimuli was made by Ivanov-Smolenskii (1930). He initiated a series of experiments in Pavlov's laboratories on the complex motor conditioned reflexes in animals. Subsequently, his interest in the development of motor conditioned reflexes in children brought him to study the relationship between stimuli in the two signal systems. His resultant hypothesis was that conditioned bonds between the cortical projections of direct stimuli and the corresponding projections of spoken and written words develop in the course of the child's growth. These conditioned bonds were said to form a "dynamic structure." Thus the elaboration of a conditioned connection with one of the stimuli which compounds such a structure will result in other stimuli in the structure becoming effective.

The investigations which began in the early 1930's continued for several years, the last report issued on this work apparently being published in 1940. At the Pavlovian conference in 1950, a landmark was reached in the history of the study of the second signal system. One of the major aspects of bringing Soviet psychology into line with Pavlov's theory consisted of taking the interaction between the two signal systems as a basic physiological mechanism of the human psyche. The selective spreading of stimulation from the first signal system and back again was assumed to account for the relationship between sensory and rational behavior. This hypothesis led Ivanov-Smolenskii to a large number of experimental studies. Two major methods were used which greatly influenced subsequent research. (1) The elaboration of a motor conditioned reflex by *prior* instruction. Children were told that at a given signal—the sound of a bell—they were to press a button. It was observed that children between the ages of five and six pressed the button spontaneously at the hearing of the bell, after a few trials. It was considered that a conditioned link was formed between the experimenter's instruction and the child's reaction. The stimulation spreads selectively from the cortical-auditory area where the word "bell" is projected to the cortical-motor area where the movement elicited by the word "press" is projected. (2) The elaboration of a motor conditioned reflex by instruction given to the subject *after* the application of a signal to press a button. Fadeeva (1960), one of Ivanov-Smolenskii's coworkers, thought that this method revealed some aspects of the processes of excitation and inhibition connected with the development of speech and voluntary movements in children.

The impetus of the work conducted under Ivanov-Smolenskii slackened in the late 1950's when the studies tended to be evaluated according to their own merits. These were seen as only one of the possible approaches to the understanding of the human psyche; besides they failed to develop Pavlov's theory of the second signal system. Doubtless, this was due to the change in the prevailing climate of Soviet psychology. However, this criticism was also occasioned by the inability of Ivanov-Smolenskii and his colleagues to account for the complexities of the linguistic processes, since this group tended to be guilty of oversimplification. Bearing in mind the role played by Ivanov-Smolenskii's work in Soviet psychology in the 1950's, it is worthwhile to dwell at some length on the criticism of Russian writers themselves.

It was noted that the attempt to apply to adult behavior those methods originally designed for use on children revealed the inefficiency of the methodology and in particular of the procedure of elaborating conditioned reactions by preliminary instruction. Many "disciplined" adult subjects did not react to the signal unless the instruction was given each time, yet it is hard to believe that such a subject failed to grasp the experiment. The reply given by Ivanov-Smolenskii and his school to this criticism was that this was a "technical" problem. Fadeeva claimed that there is a clear distinction between these instances and those experiments where the elaboration of conditioned reflexes failed because of a disturbance of the cortical-connecting function: (a) the reaction can be obtained either by the application of supplementary stimuli, or by the way of a positive induction; (b) the experimenter's instruction has an initial positive effect; (c) the subjects themselves can furnish information about the stimuli and their reactions; (d) anamnestic data can be used to clarify, at least partially, the cause of the lack of reaction. Some critics, however, saw these problems as springing from a more fundamental source.

In Myasishchev's (1960) view, the method of using only a verbal instruction is inadequate in the study of human reactions which are usually motivated by more generalized instructions. The application of this method is likely to prompt the subject to infer a general instruction from various particular ones, in which case he is acting according to a *supposed* instruction, but only after each direct instruction. Also, under this method, one cannot determine how the reactions are formed when the subject is given an instruction. As to the lack of a motor reaction to a signal, this cannot be seen as symptomatic of the lack of connection between conditioned and unconditioned stimuli, since this connection often manifests itself in the subject's verbal report. Myasishchev, however, saw some validity in the use of the method as a way of possibly gauging levels of mental development. For instance, it is easy to arrive at a conditioned reflex in demented or retarded subjects owing to the absence of more complex connections which would act as an inhibitory factor. On the other hand, the motor reactions in normal subjects may not become obvious despite the formation of the conditioned connection. In Myasishchev's opinion, this proves that the mechanism involved in this conditioning is not part of the conditioned reflex mechanism found in animals; it is only possible as a result of the verbal factor which exists in the experimenter's instruction and the latent inference by the subject himself. Out of this there arises the need for a different interpretation of the motor conditioned reflex in both man and animals. Myasishchev argued that by describing the motor reaction in man as resulting from the received instruction, Ivanov-Smolenskii has thereby emphasized that the conditioned reflex in animals is based on unconditioned reinforcement, while in man it is based on conditioned reinforcement. Yet, the difference between these mechanisms is not only confined to a difference in reinforcement. Besides a complex verbal formation, the instruction also represents a complex interaction between the experimenter and the subject. Furthermore, the instruction must be understood by the subject.

> *"Comprehension"* is not a physiological concept but needs a further physiological explanation. Finally, the instruction may be understood in various ways, either as an order referring to a single action, or as a general instruction [p. 132].

Myasishchev further objected to Ivanov-Smolenskii's concept of "selective irradiation," which means that the stimulation spreads selectively from one cortical area to another. It is, rather than a radiation, a temporary bond between the stimulus and the designated word. Furthermore, he continued, there is a more complex connection between the word and the action than Ivanov-Smolenskii implied. The word not only means a verbal designation of a signal, or of a reaction, but also implies ". . . a process of planning, reorganization, schematization, generalization and abstraction, stemming from external stimuli and movements" (p. 133).

While Luriya (1959) admitted that Ivanov-Smolenskii had made a significant contribution to the study of man's higher nervous activity, he objected to his simplified approach to the psyche which overlooked the complex structure of human activity. Furthermore, he objected to some of Ivanov-Smolenskii's methodological conjectures, in which criticism he agreed with Myasishchev. Luriya noted that under normal conditions the method of formation of motor reactions by way of prior instruction is only apparently different from that of their formation by constant verbal reinforcement. The result is very similar and the difference only consists in the fact that in the first case, the subject receives a general instruction from the experimenter, whereas in the second case the subject instructs himself; he receives cues from the signals and formulates a general rule of procedure. In Luriya's view, the essential feature of the interaction between the two signal systems is the production of a generalized connection between the previous experience and the experimenter's instruction. He pointed out that the participation of the second signal system in the formation of new experiences may account for the specific characteristics of the new connection, namely, their quick formation, their stability and simultaneous flexibility, and their independence from external reinforcement. Possibly, it is just these characteristics which may be disturbed in pathological brain conditions. Luriya felt that it would prove worthwhile to examine changes in the structure of elementary psychical reactions resulting from brain disturbances. Here, it would be necessary to compare the characteristics of the connecting function and the interaction of the two signal systems in pathological states, and to examine the formation of psychical reactions by both verbal instruction and verbal reinforcement.

The major part of Krasnogorskii's (1952, 1954, 1958) work has been the study of the development of the word as a generalized conditioned stimulus which represents classes of nonverbal stimuli. Krasnogorskii, who was one of Pavlov's co-workers, participated in the research on this subject when it first began in the 1930's. He was interested in the way words with broader meanings incorporate words of a more specific meaning. In Pavlovian terminology, this would mean the capacity of a word as a signal of a class of stimuli belonging to the first signal system, to represent other words which are signals of a more limited class of nonverbal conditioned stimuli. Thus, language was seen as a system of integrated hierarchical signals. Following from this premise, it could be argued that the development of speech in children is directly linked with the level of integration of words and may be taken as an indication of the child's capacity for abstract thought.

Fedorov, a coworker of Krasnogorskii (1954), associated six names of birds by means of many associations. A conditioned reaction was then formed in a 12-year-old child to one of these words. He noted that the other five words also produced that conditioned reaction, whereas words designating other animals or even other birds were ineffective. But the word "bird" had the same effect. Krasnogorskii assumed that although the words designating various birds are incorporated in the general word "bird," they are not connected among themselves, unless this connection is elaborated by reinforcement. The reaction produced by "bird" shows the capacity of this word to integrate words of a less generalized meaning.

Volkova (1953), another colleague of Krasnogorskii, continued on the same line as Fedorov. An association between five names of birds was formed by means of many repetitions reinforced by giving sweets to children. The result was a conditioned salivary reaction produced by either each of the five words, or by their combination. But the name of another kind of bird did not produce any reaction. When this name was also reinforced, the result was that all the names of birds became conditioned stimuli. It was concluded that the word "bird" in this experiment produced a generalization of the verbal stimuli. Names of birds not included in the reinforced association of words became conditioned stimuli when the word "bird" was introduced. The reinforcement of the association between "sparrow" and "bird" was said to increase the excitability of the cortical cells related with "bird" and conditioned reactions were formed for all the names of birds. Other experiments revealed the discrimination made by subjects between "integrators" of both different and opposed meanings. Thus, a conditioned reaction was elaborated for "crow," which was differentiated from "sunflower." The subjects were then presented with other names of birds and flowers. All the names of birds produced the conditioned effect, whereas the names of flowers did not. Similar results were obtained when the words "good" and "bad" were used as conditioned stimuli. When the word "good" was substituted by synonyms or sentences containing a positive implication, such as "the pupil answers well," or "the pupil helps his friend," the same conditioned reaction was obtained. Conversely, when words and sentences which expressed something negative were presented, they produced no reaction.

As previously mentioned, many attempts have been made to prove the existence of the same basic processes in the two signal systems. Some of the arguments pointed to the manner in which children perceive words, reminding one of the behavior of animals when presented with complex stimuli. Thus, Voronin (1952) showed that the beginning and ending stimuli of a chain were more effective than the middle ones. Similarly, Krasnogorskii noticed that the position held by syllables in a given word play an important role in the child's grasp of this particular word. Initially, the child would remember either the first or the last syllable, or the syllable which is stressed. Near the end of the child's first year, when he can recognize words, he usually hears only the stressed syllable of a word.

Furthermore, Pavlov extended his assumption about the formation of "dynamic structures" in the cortex to processes in the second signal systems. Subsequently, this was supposed to explain why a word which a child just learned to use is grammatically correct. Sokhin (1951) studied the manner in which children use the instrumental case in the Russian language. He showed that up to about two and a half years of age they employ only the masculine suffix. Then a period follows in which the feminine suffix is used, even for words which had previously been pronounced correctly. It is only later that the child begins to differentiate between the two and use them correctly for masculine and feminine nouns. That is, a child uses the correct word but applies the wrong suffix since he is not aware of the grammatical relationship involved. It is only when he becomes aware of this relationship and can discriminate between the two "static verbal stereotypes" that he can use the correct instrumental case.

In similar fashion Sokhin approached some other situations where children learn to use grammatical rules. One example is the child's use of the past tense in Russian. He noted that up to the end of the second year, a child adds the suffix for the feminine gender, when referring to a past action, and after that age he begins to use the masculine gender. For Sokhin, a conflict takes place between the two stereotypes. At the beginning, the feminine gender is more frequently used than the masculine gender, and then gradually there is a discrimination between them.

Some of Sokhin's experiments concerning the developing ability of children to grasp the meaning of words are worth mentioning. The understanding of prepositions was taken as an appropriate subject for study. One experiment was aimed at finding out what children of two to three years, five months understood by the word "on." They were presented with a cube and a disc, both of the same size and were asked to "put the cube on the disc," and "put the disc on the cube." Children between the ages of one year, 11 months and two years, four months did not grasp the meaning of "on" and displaced the two objects at random. Yet in another experiment when they were told to "put the ball on the couch," they acted correctly. From these observations, Sokhin inferred that this was not a function of understanding the preposition "on," but rather the action was suggested by the situation. Children between the ages of two to two years, three months acted according to the meaning of the proposition, yet they did not grasp the relationship in which one object should stand to the other one, thus often reversing the position. The task of putting an object "under" another one was even more difficult. However, the task of putting the ball "under" the table proved to be easy. Since in this instance the difference in size was supposed to have accounted for the correct action, the children were asked to put a small disc on a large cube. A large number of correct responses was then obtained: 92 per cent. But when the children had to put the larger object on the smaller one, only 30 per cent of them understood the task. Furthermore, the difference in size did not result in a significant improvement in the children's understanding of the preposition "under." When two objects of the same kind and size were given either cubes or discs, the results were poor: a correct response was obtained only in 12 per cent of the trials.

Children between the ages of three and three years, five months were much more capable of disregarding the nature of the objects and their different sizes. In 71 per cent of the trials, the instruction to place the cube on the disc when the cube was larger than the disc was understood correctly. When the objects were of the same size, the instruction was carried out correctly in 90 per cent of the trials, and when the smaller object had to be placed on the larger, all the children responded correctly. Sokhin concluded that in preschool children, the influence of the concrete situation is lessened with the understanding of language. These children grow to realize the generalized meaning of words and the grammatical structure of sentences and increasingly tend to be guided by the verbal context as distinct from the concrete situation.

This study leads us to other investigations which have attempted to discover the processes which bring about the meaning of a word which itself acts as a stimulus. Research has been carried out on the development of the relationship between the meaning of words, intonation and their phonic strength. Shvarts (1960) elaborated a conditioned reflex to a certain word in order to see if this effect is transferred to synonyms, and to words of different meanings, but with similar sounds. The word "doktor," when associated with flashes of light, resulted in a decrease of peripheral sensitivity. When "doktor" was replaced by "vrach" (a synonym of doctor) and "diktor" (which means dispatcher) conditioned effects were obtained in both cases. Similarly, when "dom" (house) was changed with "dym" (smoke) conditioned effects were obtained. But when the initial words were associated with the light from 14 times to 28 times, the effect produced by words which sounded similar was reduced. But the synonyms remained effective. Similar results were obtained when vascular reactions were recorded plethismographically. The words mentioned above were associated with cold water, a vasoconstriction appearing in instances analogous to those described. Shvarts also investigated the effect of certain factors which she assumed changed the functional state of the cortex. She administered chloral-hydrate, which is a sleep-inducing drug, to a number of subjects. The conditioned effect of the "active" words decreased significantly, the reaction to synonyms was also absent, while the words with similar sounds became effective. It appeared that the verbal conditioned stimulus temporarily lost its effect as a generalized signal.

The above procedure was used in Luriya's (1961) laboratory to obtain a differential diagnosis between normal and oligophrenic children. Motor and vegetative vascular conditioned reflexes were elaborated on various words. Results showed that in normal children between the ages of 11 and 14 years in whom a motor reaction had been elaborated in the word "cat," vascular reactions also showed up on words with related meanings, such as "mouse," "dog," "tomcat." Mentally retarded children showed vascular reactions to any presented word. Motor and vascular reactions were exhibited by mentally retarded children when presented with words of similar sound, while words with similar meanings produced weak reactions.

We shall turn now to the work of Koltsova and Boiko who have been prominent in recent years among those who have studied the interaction between the first and the second signal systems. They have been critical of Ivanov-Smolenskii's conjectures, advancing different hypotheses.

Koltsova (1958, 1967), the head of the Laboratory of the Physiology of Higher Nervous Activity of Children at the I. P. Pavlov Institute of Physiology, has been particularly interested in the relationships between abstraction and generalization. She pointed out that while philosophers and psychologists, on the one hand, and physiologists, on the other, use these terms interchangeably, there is a difference in orientation: the first group regards them as logical categories, while the second is interested in their underlying mechanisms. Furthermore, philosophers and psychologists regard abstraction as a primary process consisting of the separation between essential and nonessential features of objects, and generalization as a secondary process, whereas physiologists speak about the decomposition of the assembly of features of an object in its compounding elements and are concerned with their different strengths, expressed in the intensity of the orienting reaction. This analysis is not equivalent to abstraction. The generalization based on it—the similarity established between two or more objects regarding a certain feature—does not necessarily reflect the essential properties of the objects concerned. The steady association of the name of an object with that object results in the name becoming the equivalent of a property common to all the objects named in the same way. For instance, if five dolls of different colors and sizes are given to a child on 20 occasions for purposes of play, the shape will be reinforced all 100 times, while a certain color or size, will only be reinforced about 20 times. That is, the shape becomes a stronger stimulus than either the color or the size and the word "doll" is associated with it. The approximately identical shape serves as a basis for generalization. This is a *reinforced generalization* to be distinguished from the generalization described by Pavlov which precedes the differentiation between conditioned stimuli. According to Koltsova (1967), ". . . generalization is a real process which has a definite functional substratum. If this functional substratum changes, then both the sphere and level of generalization changes" (p. 308). But in her view, there is no physiological reason to speak about abstraction as a real process. The level of generalization is a sufficient basis for the description of a psychical image as concrete or abstract. "Concrete" and "abstract" only describe the form of reflection of reality which is determined by the functional level of the process of generalization.

Furthermore, Koltsova raised the problem of the nature of the process of generalization elaborated with the participation of words: is it identical with the generalization attained at the level of the first signal system or is it essentially different? She pointed up two common aspects of the underlying physiological mechanisms. First, in all instances of the formation of conditioned reflexes of the second and third degrees (when a new stimulus becomes a conditioned stimulus by its association with an already active conditioned stimulus) and the elaboration of a dynamic stereotype, on the one hand, and the formation of concepts, on the other, it is a matter about the formation of systems of reactions. Second, in both signal systems there is a reduction of the signaling role of a complex of stimuli to a single stimulus. One word substitutes for many nonverbal stimuli. The study of the development of generalization in children showed that the more developed the process of integration, the more economical is the form in which it is manifest.

The development of generalization in both signal systems is contingent upon the formation of systems and the presence of flexible relations between the elements of a system. The first factor represents the functional substratum of the process of formation of images, whereas the second factor is responsible for the recognition of images. Hence ". . . *the development of generalization at all levels of activity of the cerebral hemispheres represents a unitary physiological process*" (p. 165).

Following Krasnogorskii, Koltsova distinguished four stages of integration. At the first stage, which occurs by the end of the first year of life, the word begins to substitute for the sensory image of a certain single object (e.g., "doll" means one definite doll). It is the equivalent of that object, more exactly of its shape which is physiologically a stronger stimulus than others. The word is connected precisely to this stimulus and produces the same effect. In the second stage, the word substitutes several sensory images of homogeneous objects (e.g., "doll" means different dolls); the signal meaning of the word is broader and less concrete. The word which substituted for a strong property of a single object is now generalized for similar objects, thereby becoming the equivalent of that property of these objects as well. Such a generalization is *reinforced* by the surrounding people who handle the objects and who name them in the same way. This stage is attained by the end of the second year of life. In the third stage, which is reached by three to three and a half years of age, the word substitutes for several sensory images from different objects ("toy" means dolls, balls, etc.). This inclusion of different objects in one word cannot be based on the generalization of an identical behavior, or of an elaborated system of connections. Playing with a ball is different from playing with a doll. Different systems are reduced to a single general system, while each of them maintains its functional integrity. Koltsova admits that this is a general statement which requires further study. In the fourth stage of integration—five-year-olds—the word expresses a series of generalizations of the previous level (the word "thing") and its sensory roots are hard to trace.

Koltsova suggested the following steps to this process of generalization. (1) The word (e) substitutes a complex of sensations $(a + b + c + d)$. This means that an adequate reaction requires the information included in all the elements of the complex. (2) One property of the object is detached as the strongest, e.g., the sensation (a), while the others yield weaker reactions. This means that $a = e$; (a) has all the information necessary to differentiate between objects. The information included in (b), (c), and (d) is superfluous. (3) The child becomes familiar with objects which are alike in some way, $(a_1 + b_1 + c_1 + d_1)$, $(a_2 + b_2 + c_2 + d_2)$, etc. The components a, a_1, a_2, etc., are abstracted as physiologically the strongest and are linked to each other by generalization. This generalization is further reinforced without the realization of the fine differences between a, and a_1, or a_2. Thus the relation $a = e$ is again obtained but it covers the relation $e = (a + b + c + d) + (a_1 + b_1 + c_1 + d_1) + (a_2 + b_2 + c_2 + d_2)$, etc. Thus, as the integrative function of the word becomes ever larger, the form in which the generalization is expressed is increasingly reduced.

To Koltsova, the following are the most relevant questions: what is the nature of the extrasensory image elicited by a word? Which aspect of the word is connected to the images obtained from real objects? To answer these questions, Koltsova analyzed the similarities and differences between the connections formed with and without the participation of the word. The sensory image is, first of all, a kinesthetic image and the strong component of the complex of sensations is precisely the kinesthetic one. Accordingly, a_1, a_2, a_3, etc. are kinesthetic components. On the other hand, underlying the formation of a generalized image, through a word, is the establishment of conditioned connections between the articulation of the word, and the kinesthetic impulses from the handling of objects. In addition, there are auditory and visual stimulations. This means that the image formed by the mediation of a word also has a sensory basis which is broader than that formed without the participation of a word, because of the inclusion of more than one complex of sensations. Hence, the image formed by the mediation of a word is extrasensory not in the sense that it is formed outside the sensory sphere, but in the sense that it does not reproduce the concrete features of the reflected objects, that it does not belong to the category of signal-images but rather to that of signal-codes.

As to the differences between the generalization of stimuli in the two signal systems, the generalization of nonverbal stimuli is possible only on the basis of systems of temporary connections and connections obtained by the participation of conditioned and unconditioned stimuli. The integrative capacity of a word which has not yet become a generalizing signal has the same limitation, whereas a word which is already a "signal of signals" can include a large number of nonverbal stimuli in a system where sensory connections predominate. The unconditioned-reflex basis is no longer manifest. Koltsova described eight types of sensory-conditioned connections which represent a sort of continuum with respect to the number of associations required for their formation and stability. (1) An association between "indifferent" stimuli without reinforcement. For instance, after 12–15 associations between a light and a sound, when the light goes on, a child turns his head in the direction of the expected sound. (2) An association is formed between an indifferent stimulus and a conditioned stimulus which is no longer reinforced. Thus turning on a light, which was associated with a sound that had previously been made the conditioned stimulus of a blink reflex, produces the same effect. Centers of unconditioned reflexes are clearly involved in this type of sensory connection since both orienting and defense reactions are involved. (3) An association between an indifferent stimulus and a continuously reinforced conditioned stimulus. (4) An association between two stimuli presented each time in the same order, which have an identical signaling meaning, e.g., a light and a sound which were made the conditioned stimuli of a blink reflex but are not reinforced any longer. (5) An association between a stimulus which was made a conditioned stimulus but is not reinforced any longer, and a continuously reinforced conditioned stimulus. (6) An association between the same stimuli where both are continuously reinforced. (7) An association between two conditioned stimuli of different reflexes, e.g., feeding and defense, which are not reinforced any longer. (8) An association between the same stimuli which are continuously reinforced. The last two types of connections have the strongest reinforcement due to the interaction between three unconditioned reflexes: orienting, feeding and defense. Words acting simply as conditioned stimuli have the same effect as nonverbal conditioned stimuli involved in the sensory connections of types 1 and 2 which extinguish easily and become constant connections only gradually. Words acting as concepts, at the higher levels of integration, lead to the quick formation of stable and at the same time flexible connections of types 6 and 8.

Koltsova disagreed with Ivanov-Smolenskii that the specific feature of generalization at the human level is the selective irradiation of the excitation from one signal system to the other. In her view, the spread of excitation along previously established paths is characteristic for any elaborated form of generalization, not only in man but in other species as well. To prove this, however, Koltsova referred to findings of animal studies where the analogy with the selective circulation of the excitation produced by a nonverbal stimulus to its verbal counterpart is not quite persuasive. Thus, Schastnyi (1957) elaborated in dogs a defense reaction to a chain of stimuli, the sequence of which was reinforced, so that they formed a stereotype, in the Pavlovian sense. If one of the stimuli belonging to this combination was presented, followed by a chain of stimuli to the sequence of which a conditioned feeding reflex had previously been elaborated, then all the stimuli were transformed from the "feeding stereotype" to a "defense stereotype." This would appear to be an utterly different situation.

Boiko (1958, 1959, 1961, 1964, 1967a,b) initiated in 1953 an extensive study at his Laboratory of Higher Neurodynamics, at the Institute of Psychology of the Academy of pedagogical Sciences. His investigations have been focused on the orienting-positioning (ustanovochnye) reactions which constitute part of complex acts, the performance of which required certain intellectual operations.

Boiko distinguished between two approaches to the second signal system. The first is that of Ivanov-Smolenskii, which he simply called the conditioned-reflex theory. The second is his own theory, which he labelled "dynamic." Boiko admitted that various kinds of temporary connections underlie all forms of mentation, yet he emphasized that the physiological mechanisms of man's reactions to words cannot be reduced to the general laws of conditioned reflexes common to animals and man. There are also psychophysiological laws specific to man only. Boiko objected to Koltsova, claiming that she had simply added to the general mechanisms of higher nervous activity the strengthening of words as conditioned stimuli, due to the variation of the corresponding objects and to the frequency of associations between different features of objects and their reinforcement. As a matter of fact, Boiko regarded the work of both Ivanov-Smolenskii and Koltsova as based on a narrow-reflex (uzkoreflektornaya) theory.

Boiko summarized his theory under three points. (1) The physiological mechanism of abstraction is manifest in the sensory sphere in the form of positioning reactions to various aspects of objects, and is mediated by words. Boiko made a distinction between orienting reactions and positioning reactions. When the child turns his head and looks in the direction of the ball in response to the question "where is the ball?" his reaction is independent of the location of the ball itself. This is a typical reaction for the second signal system. (2) The first signal system is not limited to the physiological mechanism of sensations but also includes the mechanism of representations which play a major role in positioning reactions. The generalizing function of words cannot be accomplished without the intermediary mechanism of the first signal system which prevents a negative induction between the stable meaning of words and the variable complexes of sensations with which they are connected. (3) The physiological mechanism of the specifically human form of generalization can be understood only if one takes into account the interaction between at least several words and their generalized conditioned effects. Boiko emphasized that the process of generalization in man cannot be analyzed by studying the relation between isolated words and the corresponding objects.

In Boiko's experiments, subjects were presented with a panel of lamps with corresponding reaction keys. Two pairs of lamps were flashed successively, with one lamp being common to the two pairs. The subjects had to determine this lamp and to press the key. Boiko contended that this reaction was not a motor conditioned reflex since it was equally determined by visual and verbal stimuli, notably the experimenter's instruction. This type of reaction and similar types led him to the following hypothesis about the physiological processes involved. A special kind of intracentral controlling impulses, originating in the speech area of the cortex and forming the functional system referred to by Pavlov as the second signal system, reaches the cortical visual area. This results in a change of the functional readiness of the visual analyzer. On the other hand, impulses emerging from the first signal system reach the second system through temporary connections already established. The two streams of excitation interact in the multiple systems of neurons lying between the speech area and the central part (nucleus) of the analyzers of the first signal system. In this process there is a regrouping and transformation of the connections between the speech area and the cells of the visual area representing the projection of the common lamp. Solving a problem, in this case discovering which is the common lamp, is precisely the result of this process. Boiko (1969) wrote:

> The process of solving problems presented verbally is based on the formation of special temporary connections which differ from the reflex-conditioned (connective) links and are called *dynamic* because they are built up anew every time, in the course of the interaction of previously established connections, i.e., they are the product of neurodynamics [pp. 151–152].

Additional experiments were done to validate this hypothesis. Thus during the experiment just described, single lamps were flashed occasionally, and the subject had to press a reaction key with the right hand as quickly as he could. The corresponding to the common lamp was pressed with the left hand. This was a "testing" or control reaction which was elicited either at the start of the basic experiment, in its middle, or at the end, that is, at various stages of the process of comparison between pairs of lamps. The single lamp could be either the common lamp, or another lamp of the set, or even an "indifferent" lamp, i.e., a lamp which was not on the panel. The measurement of the latency period of the control reaction—measured to one thousandth of a second—indicated the functional readiness of different points of the visual analyzer during the experiment. It was noted that the cortical projection of the common lamp had a higher reactivity, expressed in a shorter latency of the control reaction, than the projections of lamps unrelated to the experimenter's instruction. In Boiko's interpretation, the entire process of problem solving is regulated by inhibitory impulses emerging from the speech areas to the visual analyzer. Each word of the instruction produces, in the speech area, a number of stimulations which interfere and are reciprocally intensified, while the noncoincident stimulations inhibit each other according to the rule of a negative induction. These stimulations reach the visual analyzer on pathways already formed. Meeting with the impulses originating in the visual area results in the formation of the pattern of connections mentioned above. According to Boiko, this is the mechanism not only of the visual-motor reactions taking place in the second signal system, but of all the processes of this system. In his view, we understand different phrases because from each word there emerge neural impulses which go to different analyzers. These connections change according to the composition of the verbal communication and a new *content* occurs in consciousness.

The experimental studies of verbal conditioning mentioned in this section, as well as the argument regarding Ivanov-Smolenskii's theoretical and methodological positions, have essentially been confined to the framework provided by Pavlov's thesis of two signal systems in man. However, some basic questions should be asked concerning the way Pavlov extrapolated from the notion of a signaling-conditioning function of the nervous system in animals to the explanation of human behavior, in particular, language. Pavlov's explanation of animal behavior implies two ideas: (1) the animal has a finite number of needs; (2) there is an infinity of stimuli in the animal's environment to which it is basically "indifferent." These neutral stimuli acquire a significance for the animal when they signal the restricted number of stimuli which have an intrinsic value for the organism.

To explain human adaptive behavior by assuming the development of a second category of signals, namely words, implies the transference of the two theses mentioned above. It is difficult to accept this for the following reasons. Man's needs are virtually unlimited, as are the number of satisfying stimuli. Any object may, theoretically, satisfy a need at a given moment. That is, there is no category of nonverbal stimuli whose value for human beings is only that of a signal. So that, while we may speak about a system, which includes all possible signals, in relation to animal behavior, we cannot define the "first system of signals" in man. What are the "first signals of reality?" What are the signals and what is signaled? Words might readily be seen as signals whose value consists in the "representation" of categories of stimuli. Indeed, they form a system. But nonverbal stimuli do not represent the "first" signal system in the Pavlovian sense. This is by no means a matter of mere semantics. These questions are conducive to specific research issues (Rahmani, 1963).

Signs, Signals, Symbols, Words

Soviet philosophers who have engaged in a campaign against neopositivism have extended their opposition to semiotics—the science of signs. They have regarded the works on the artificial means of communications as a product of the idealistic views on language. Opposing the positivistic ideas on the relationship between reality, thinking and language, Soviet philosophers have pointed out that the dialectical development of phenomena in nature was distorted, since the moment of stability of real events was overlooked the relative nature of all phenomena was exclusively taken into account. Consequently, language was regarded as the determining factor and not as a reflection of an objective reality.

There is currently a decided tendency to admit that the artificial language of science has to be studied by a specific science and that semiotics must be distinguished from the positivistic philosophy (Reznikov, 1961, 1963b, 1964; Abramyan, 1966; Maltsev, 1965; Revzin, 1964; Vetrov, 1965). Soviet philosophers, logicians and linguists speak about the need to develop a Marxist semiotics which constitutes part of the Marxist epistemology. This is necessary because of the impingement of cybernetics on information theory in many areas of study to the extent that scientific language becomes more and more abstract. A Marxist semiotics is expected to analyze the ways of development of artificial languages and their relationship to natural languages. Certainly, the major problem is that of revealing the objective content of the various means of communication, notably, signs, symbols, signals and words. The following is a summary of some basic propositions advanced by Soviet authors.

Signs *(znaki)* can operate on the brain and produce sensory images. Since signs stand for actual objects, they can appear both as actual objects and imagined objects. Therefore, signs are an instrument of the process of knowledge. They can represent the essential properties of classes of objects. The connection between an actual object and its image—the sign—is real. Although there is an element of arbitrariness, it plays only a secondary role. Signs also function as a means of communication, which brings them into the realm of social relations.

The process of signaling requires the presence of two systems, one which emits information and one which receives it. The first system acts upon the second. There is an element of isomorphism between a signal and some of the properties of the signaling object or event. A signal produces a reaction in the receiving system which is controlled.

Reznikov (1964) defined a symbol as ". . . an objective mark, or thing used arbitrarily yet in close connection with the image which it implies and which expresses a certain content that is frequently abstract and very important" (p. 149). A symbol is different from a signal in the following respects: (a) it does not lead to definite and direct actions; (b) it is itself a limited and concrete, thus standing in contrast to its symbolized content; (c) there is a relation, even if a remote one, between its own insignificant meaning and the symbolized content.

Primitive Thinking

The position of Soviet authors on this subject has already been touched upon. It seems worthwhile, however, to expound it at further length. Both Protasenya (1961), who wrote a monograph on this subject, and Zhdanov (1969) who also devoted a monograph to this topic and made a thorough analysis of the kinds of activity of primitive people, have been critical of classical approaches to primitive thinking. Essentially, they objected to the view of Spencer, Taylor and Thorndyke, among others, that there is no difference between primitive thinking and the thinking of modern man. Protasenya contended that this has been contradicted by the history of knowledge. While he agreed that the laws of logic are of a universal character, he pointed out that they are not invariable.

On the other hand, the views of Levy-Bruhl, Cassirer, Blondel, and others who overemphasized the difference between primitive and modern thinking have also been rejected. It is claimed that the theory of a prelogical nature of primitive thinking was encouraged by bourgeois ideologists who emphasized the anthropological and cultural-historical differences in order to justify imperialistic enslavement of natives and racism. To Protasenya, this theory is entirely inconsistent with the creation of myths which presupposes the ability for abstract thinking. Primitive man could not have made a satisfactory adjustment to his milieu, let alone change it according to his needs, if his thoughts were entirely involved with magic. Totemism, animism and fetishism are the ideological products of man's struggle with the forces of nature.

Some further critical remarks were made by Panfilov (1957), who disagreed with the assumption that figures in primitive languages (Hindu, Melanesian, Polynesian) actually express quantities of concrete objects, Shemyakin (1956), who disagreed with Levy-Bruhl that memory takes the place of thinking in primitive people, and Ramishvili (1956), who thought that the above-mentioned Western writers had over-emphasized the role of gestures in primitive communication in relation to concrete thinking.

CONCEPT FORMATION AND PROBLEM SOLVING

Soviet studies on concept formation and problem solving can be discussed under one heading since the theories overlap to a large extent. In linking these two subjects, the reader may arrive at a clearer picture of the Soviet approach to thinking. We shall first examine some of the major problems of concern in this area and then turn to a description of some of the main theories.

Thinking and Associations

The role played by associations in thinking is still a highly controversial point in Soviet psychology. Some writers definitely favor a theory of associationism, and there is some tendency to reinterpret the concept on the basis of hypotheses of Sechenov and Pavlov. On the other hand, strong arguments against this premise were put forward, paralleling those propounded in the Western literature. Primarily, the objection was that the process of association did not account for the purposefulness of thinking. In the 1930's and the 1940's, such criticism was generally accompanied by an opposition to the explanation of thinking processes in terms of conditioning. So, for instance, we find severe criticism of the Pavlovian theory of association in the earlier works of Rubinshtein (1946) and Teplov (1947). However, their later works revealed a marked change of attitude. One may even detect contradictions in their statements. Thus, in 1946, Rubinshtein wrote that the process of association is fortuitous and does not present an objective picture of the initial stimulus, which is external to it. The process of association cannot, therefore, explain the process of problem-solving in which an objective assessment of the factors involved must be included, For Rubinshtein, elementary associations and complex thinking were two entirely different things. Teplov took a similar stand.

> In psychological terminology the concept of association corresponds to that of the conditioned reflex. The theory of association was the greatest contribution of bourgeois psychology of the 19th century. The theory of the conditioned reflex provided a physiological account of the laws of association. . . . Yet an explanation of all psychical phenomena by the formation of associative or conditioned reflex bases is absolutely wrong. [p. 35].

However, in 1957, Rubinshtein wrote:

> The concept of association must be maintained in psychology, but it must be transformed in order to work out a psychological theory of association on the basis of the physiological theory of conditioned reflexes. This is one of the most important immediate tasks of psychology . . . [p. 125].

Yet in his own theory of thinking, as Samarin (1962) correctly observed, Rubinshtein did not leave much room for the concept of association.

Leontev (1964) pointed out that the idea of thinking as an associate process is fraught with insoluble difficulties. Associations cannot account for the selective and purposeful character of thinking. That is why there has been a need to introduce concepts drawn from philosophy such as creative synthesis, active apperception, etc.

In recent years, however, a number of works have been published which defended the association theory. Some writers clearly accept this line of reasoning, while others attempt to adapt the approach to bring it closer to the opposing camp. There is disagreement as to the type of associations underlying the thinking processes. Soviet associationists regard association as the most general concept of the psychology and physiology of the higher cortical functions. Association should be the basis for any study of the psyche, in particular of the intellectual processes. The organization of knowledge about objects and phenomena, without which no intellectual activity is possible, presupposes the formation of associations between them. Any syllogism would bring to the fore a corresponding generalized association. A main argument shared by all associationists is that their critics only point to elementary, constant associations.

The associationists contend that the classic theory of associations failed to realize the relationship between association as a unit of mental activity and the integral character of this activity. This failure is said to result from their idealistic philosophical attitude. Yet they tend to be more indulgent toward the failures of this school than toward those of other "bourgeois" views, notably the Gestalt theory. Thus Samarin (1962) wrote:

> Associationism was not able to realize the dialectic relationship between simple and complex, because of its erroneous philosophical position. But neither was the problem solved by the opponents of associationism who hold idealistic and clearly reactionary views concerning the nature of the higher psychical processes, particularly thinking. Those who criticized associationism correctly emphasized the active quality of the psyche, which was not considered in the associationist theory. Althought the associationists (for example Bain) did study this problem, they were unable to fathom the contradictory and extremely complex process of the reflection of objective reality and to explain . . . the source of the active nature of the psyche and its role in purposeful behavior. . . . However, the opponents of associationism also failed to offer a scientific explanation for the active and voluntary quality of the psyche . . . and their own attempts at a solution are based on idealism and agnosticism. If the emphasis on the singularity of the higher psychical processes and on the active role of the psyche marked a progressive step in the development of psychology, calling attention to aspects of mental life overlooked by associationists, other critical remarks were definitely of a regressive nature. Among these was the tendency to separate the higher intellectual processes from their sensory basis and to consider them in principle opposed to each other. The metaphysical view of the

integrity of the psyche as an *a priori* datum was also reactionary [pp. 55–56].

Thinking and Structure

The criticism of the Gestalt theory was already mentioned. With regard to the process of problem-solving, the main targets of criticism were the concept of "insight" and the assumption that this process consists of a sequence of reorganizations of the problem-situation (Antsyferova, 1963). According to Rubinshtein (1959b), the Gestalt theory restricted the process of thinking to the correlation of transitory phenomenal situations. The interaction between object and subject during the course of the process of solving a problem was reduced to the interaction of phenomenal situations. In addition, while Selz, of the Würzburg school, separated the internal conditions of thinking from the external conditions, the Gestalt theory made an attempt to transfer the whole determination of thinking to a subjective dialectic of its content.

The reordering, or reorganization of the structure of the problem to be solved, and the sudden finding of the solution, are essentially seen by Soviet authors as the result of an analysis and synthesis of the elements of the problem. Their basic position is that the logical operations consist of the reflection of objective reality by processes of analysis and synthesis (Sviderskii, 1962; Babosov, 1963). But, along with philosophical considerations, there is the more specifically psychological argument supportable by experimental evidence. Voronin (1952, 1962, 1965, 1969), whose field of research is the study of animal reactions to complex stimuli, touched on this subject and claimed to trace a phylogenetic development of the processes of analysis and synthesis.

Hence, it is understandable that those Soviet students concerned with complex intelligent behavior in monkeys strongly emphasized that the phenomenon of sudden problem-solving, as described by Köhler, implies the generalization of conditioned reflexes acquired by these animals as a result of the processes of analysis and synthesis under various conditions. This proposition was clearly expressed by Antsyferova (1961) who described two forms of generalization contingent on the formation of conditioned reflexes. The first form consists of transposing various conditioned reactions—digestive, manipulative and defensive—elaborated to certain objects and their properties, to similar objects and properties associated to these reactions. The second form consists of transposing conditioned reactions having to do with the ability to orient and investigate from the circumstances in response to which they were initially established to similar circumstances. Thus, for Antsyferova, animals have the capacity to distinguish the essential elements of certain situations, even though they may differ from those encountered in earlier experiences.

The following passage by Ladygina-Kots (1959), who studied the behavior of chimpanzees for a period of 40 years, is illustrative for this point.

> The *multilateral practical analysis* performed by the chimpanzee when he distinguishes the properties and various parts of whole objects is closely linked to the *practical synthesis* he performs when using the properties of objects in order to construct its dwelling-place, or to establish a connection between various objects in order to solve experimental tasks requiring the use of tools. . . . We recognize as *thinking* the practical analysis-synthesis of the chimpanzee when he identifies the properties of objects and, in particular, their use as tools in reaching food [p. 300].

The experiments of Rubinshtein and his coworkers, which will be mentioned later, on the processes of analysis and synthesis in problem-solving in man, as one would anticipate, follow along much the same line of reasoning.

In concluding this section, mention should be made of the increasing Soviet interest in Piaget's work which is regarded as a development of the theory of structure (Nepomnyashchaya, 1965; Antsyferova, 1965).

Following is a survey of some of the theories of thinking. The order of presentation progresses from associationistic theories to nonassociationistic.

Associations by Contiguity

The role of contiguous associations during problem-solving has been emphasized by Shevarev (1892-). A deputy member of the Academy of Pedagogical Sciences, Shevarev (1948) first studied the constancy of perception before exploring the processes of association formed in school children during their learning (1959a,b, 1966). He has also been interested in the relation between perception and thinking (1962).

While Shevarev admitted that thinking implies one's attempt to solve a certain problem, he argued that not every intellectual process involved in the realization and solution of a problem is necessarily part of the thinking process. Nor does the concept of mediation express the essence of the thinking process. Shevarev felt such models to be too vague. One must differentiate between those problems solved by syllogisms, the conclusion of which is precisely the solution of the problem, and those problems, the solution of which is also based on an inference, but not coincident with the conclusion of the syllogism. To determine, for instance, the mantissa of a logarithm, one has to make an inference, but the number found does not depend on the conclusion. Only the first case represents the actual thinking process. The syllogisms whose premises are known, however, represent only an elementary case of thinking. Most thinking requires a search for the premises, and this necessitates the processes of analysis, synthesis, abstraction and generalization. Only those processes which lead to the discovery of the premises of a syllogism are genuine processes of thought. The abstraction involved in the perception of objects is not thinking.

According to Shevarev, thinking involves essentially the formation of an association by contiguity between two psychical processes and its retrieval. The latent existence of an association as a relatively stable cortical structure is distinguished from its manifestation for short periods. In other words, one has to distinguish between the functional readiness of an association and its actual occurrence which is contingent upon the individual's task. An adult, for instance, will always say six after five when he is asked to count. The first member of an association can be any psychical process, including a conscious external action, while its second member can also be any psychical process with the exception of sensations which imply a current stimulation. Following the classical associationists, in particular Ebbinghaus, Shevarev pointed out that the mere contiguity of events is insufficient for the formation of an association. It is also necessary that the events be unified as a whole, this unification being most efficient when the members of the association are related to each other by their very nature.

Much of Shevarev's theory is concerned with classifying the associations by contiguity formed during the thinking process. He proposed two criteria of classification: (1) the subject's realization of the two components of the association; (2) the degree of generalization, or variability of the formed associations. Thus in the associations formed in the course of problem-solving in algebra, subjects are aware of the first number of the association because the task is conscious. There are cases in problem-solving when one must first solve an auxiliary problem. This secondary problem is frequently solved before one is aware of it, awareness only resulting later during the realization of the major problem. Thus, there is a retrieval of an association between the awareness of the first and the second problem. The reduction to the same denominator, for instance, of fractions with different denominators, is supposed by Shevarev to be done frequently without one being aware of its meaning.

A different type of association is formed when an unfamiliar problem is to be solved for the first time. The data are analyzed in order to perform familiar transformations which may lead toward a solution. Discovering these elements in the problem which relate to a specific transformation triggers an immediate awareness of the task "to perform a certain transformation." Two associations are retrieved in this situation: (1) between the perception of the main problem and the perception of a derivative task, namely the transformation; (2) between the discovery of certain elements of the problem and the performance of a transformation. The first member of the second association, however, does not imply the awareness of the main problem, and this is the difference between these types of associations. In the former case, furthermore, the subject is convinced that the secondary task is appropriate, while in the latter case he is aware that the secondary task may be inappropriate and even misleading. Hence the analysis of a complex problem consists of the detection of those elements which constitute the first member of an association of the type mentioned above. If such an association is not formed, one will remain oblivious to the task of performing a transformation which will lead to a final solution. Shevarev raised the question as to whether associations can be formed when one is unaware of any task.

The second classification of associations made by Shevarev concerns constant and variable associations. It was his belief that in almost every field of human activity, various actions are performed in accordance with certain rules. The rules may be divided into two groups: (1) explicit rules indicating definitely what one has to do in a certain situation (e.g., the rules of multiplication of polynomials); (2) implicit rules which do not give an exact indication (e.g., the rules of chess). The actions performed according to rules have the following characteristics: they are learned; they are deliberate; they involve the analysis of concrete situation as a first stage, and the carrying out of a certain operation, as a second stage.

In many instances, the perception of the concrete situation and the performance of the operation are simultaneous. These actions are generally known as skills or habits, but the terms taken either separately or in combination do not accurately convey the necessary concept.

All actions according to rules may be divided into two groups: natural actions, such as those involved in performing school tasks, work, etc.; artificial actions, such as those performed with the tachistoscope, the learning and reproduction of nonsense syllables, etc. Study of artificial actions does not clarify the structure of natural actions, and only by investigating natural actions themselves can the structure of work, play and learning processes be discovered. Algebra and arithmetic were regarded by Shevarev as an appropriate subject for study. In his study, he raised the following questions: (1) What rules govern the succession of processes in the transition from the first stage to the second stage? (2) What is the structure of an action when it is performed automatically, and while it is learned? (3) How are these actions to be classified? For Shevarev, the answer to the first question is a prerequisite for understanding the processes of thinking. He considered two possibilities. First, each action is solely the result of a preceding association, or series of associations. Second, in some, if not all instances, the processes involved in actions are essentially different from the process of association. In Shevarev's view, both the Würzburg and Gestalt schools failed to invalidate the basic proposition of the associationist psychology. Even if the hypothesis of "determining tendencies" or of other factors differing from association processes holds true, the associationist hypothesis is not ruled out.

Yet Shevarev contended that the association hypothesis has to provide answers to certain questions. Can a problem be solved once the rules are known and understood? If this is not the case, one has to see under what conditions and with what frequency students successfully solve problems without understanding the rules involved, when they already have some experience of the problem being solved. Then there is the question of what kinds of associations underlie the development of specific skills or habits. What psychological principles should be applied in elaborating the most economical teaching methods based on the use of appropriate associations?

Shevarev assumed that the answers to these questions are contingent upon a solution to the problem of classification of associations. Five different meanings may be applied to the term association. First, an association is defined as an acquired connection between two psychical processes, one of which is the cause, or one of the causes of the other. The established association manifests itself as a "trace" in the cerebral cortex. However, so far it has not been possible to determine a "trace" physiologically. Therefore, Shevarev contended, if one accepts this interpretation, he must be clear about the way in which the association is expressed, about the stimuli involved and their effects. Second, the concept of association refers to the combination between two psychical processes resulting in the connection mentioned above. Third, association implies two phenomena: a potential association and its recall at a definite moment. In this sense, one must speak about evoked associations, since in order to refer to an actual association, the process in which it is manifest has to be described. Fourth, association refers only to the fact that one concrete psychical process is followed by another, without any consideration of the nature of this connection. In this instance, the concept of association is used without either reference to the recall of previous associations or to the formation of new connections. Occasionally, the term association is even used as a description of the sequence of processes resulting from unconditioned connections. This wide range of meanings for one concept is undesirable. Finally, Wundt's concept of association expressed the characteristic tendency of idealistic psychology which does not recognize the difference between sensation and representation.

In Shevarev's view, each association is to be seen as being connected contiguously. Facts which are related to each other by their similarity are not actually associations, but consist of the transfer of the acquaintance with a certain object to a similar object. One kind of contiguity described in the literature is that of constant associations. However, the various factors revealed in the study of the connections involved in intellectual processes cannot be reduced to constant associations. Generalized, variable associations play a particular role. Shevarev initiated the study of these associations with an analysis of the structure of objects. He regarded all the properties of an object as belonging to two categories: constant and variable. An association may be constant when it involves only constant properties. Yet, at other times, an association may also include variable elements, although only the constant properties belong to its content. In still other cases, constant and variable properties are associated. In the first category, a process of abstraction takes place of all known associations, while in the second category there is a process of concretization. These are abstract-variable associations. A final group of associations is made up of the concrete-variable properties. By classifying the associations in this way, four groups are obtained: (1) constant associations, where both terms are constant; (2) semi-variable associations, where one term is abstract-variable and the other is constant; (3) abstract-variable associations; (4) concrete-variable associations.

Shevarev's experiments sprang from the hypothesis that people usually solve problems in arithmetic, algebra and geometry without being aware of the rules which they are applying. Thus, instead of working through each logical step of the problem, a method of concise reasoning based on generalized associations is used. The first term of the association is coincident with the minor premise of the syllogism, while the second term can be regarded as the conclusion of the syllogism. The subject is not aware of the major premise. This was supposed to happen when a child had to solve the following problem. One buys 2.8 kg of biscuits at x rubles a kg. How much does he pay? The following deductive reasoning was supposed to be involved. Given the amount of the merchandise and the price of one unit, the cost of the whole amount is determined by multiplication of the two known figures. The major premise presents the general principle, the minor premise is the general formulation of the problem and the conclusion identifies the required operation. The subject was not aware of the major premise. When asked, "What did you think of the problem?" he said "Nothing; it was clear from the moment I read the problem, I knew what I had to do." This means that two processes took place. First, the subject realized that the problem was concerned with a certain amount of merchandise and its price per unit, and second, that these two figures had to be multiplied. The first process could not possibly serve as a logical basis for the second process. Only the major premise, of which the subject was unaware, could be seen as such a basis. The first process could lead to the second only through a generalized association.

Associations by Similarity

Samarin (1962) regarded intellectual activity as consisting of some sort of architecture of associations and he saw the evolution of the intellect as consisting of a transition from elementary associations to complex ones. He gave the term association a very broad connotation. It is

> . . . a connection between psychical processes from the simplest to the most complex. However, as psychical processes are necessary links of reflex actions, the very nature of the reflex action implies connections between movements (in the motor and speech areas), as well as connections between psychical processes which reflect the impinging stimuli (perception of the stimulus, its representation and the corresponding concept) and the response (performance of reflex movements, the visual control of such movements) [p. 383].

Associations are the psychological equivalent of temporary

connections, Pavlov's theory providing the general laws of their formation.

Samarin classified associations into four groups which would parallel the stages of the child's intellectual growth: local; partial-systemic; intrasystemic; and intersystemic. A local association is the basic unit of the intellectual activity. It is relatively isolated and it is not yet connected to the system of knowledge or, for some reason, has been cut off after having been connected. The initial intellectual activity of infants consists, by and large, of local associations. It is also the first stage in the acquisition of words in a foreign language, as well as in the acquisition of any more or less isolated piece of knowledge. However, local associations do not in themselves initiate an intellectual activity. For this, two conditions are necessary prerequisites: (1) the assimilation of relevant local associations; (2) their inclusion into a system of connections.

Some clinical observations were interpreted by Samarin as showing evidence of local associations. Thus, it was noticed that in patients with frontal disturbances, the system of higher intellectual activity had disintegrated, while the ability to perform isolated actions remained intact. For instance an engineer who was no longer able to solve simple arithmetic problems, had no difficulty in adding and subtracting; a carpenter was unable to plan a model, although his technical skills were unimpaired. For Samarin, these are instances of local associations, which are the first group of associations to become evident and the last to suffer impairment.

Partial-systemic associations imply a partial knowledge of a subject matter provided, for example, by a passage of an article or a chapter of a book. These associations hold a central position in the intellectual activity, since new facts can be selected and evaluated in accordance with a system of associations; they also represent a step forward to associations for a higher level. At this stage, processes of abstraction and generalization are possible, although these are limited regarding the amount of knowledge included and the ability to make use of it.

The third group, intrasystemic associations, consists of the reorganization of newly acquired information and its inclusion in the relevant available system of knowledge. At this level, a methodical intellectual activity is possible. These associations form a system of skills and habits, and presuppose the ability to apply acquired knowledge.

Finally, there are the intersystemic associations which cover the various systems of knowledge, skills and abilities leading to broad generalizations. They integrate intellectual activities, such as ideas and principles, and as a whole form the basis for one's attitudes. Intersystemic associations facilitate the dialectical thinking by absorbing analyzed facts in multiple systems of associations. The development of the four classes of associations starts around the time the child begins school, takes shape during the course of the formation of the partial-systemic associations, continues throughout the individual's life and is linked to the widening of experience, interests, views and beliefs. The reorganization of the intersystemic associations expresses the deepest changes in the human intellect.

Samarin did not share Shevarev's view that all associations are contiguous. He pointed out that the classification proposed by Shevarev himself showed that the eliciting of generalized associations is also contingent upon the establishment of similarities. Samarin went on to argue that to admit only the possibility of contiguity as a means of establishing associations is to fail to understand how generalization occurs. For example, when a subject reacts to the sound "la," he first reacted to all musical sounds. If associations were formed by contiguity only, each reaction would have to be elaborated separately. Samarin even claimed that the establishment of similarities between phenomena is the basis of all rules of psychology. For instance, all digit series have the characteristic that each preceding digit in the series represents a smaller number than the next one, and the concept "larger-smaller" characterizes the numerical relationship between digits through the formation of associations by similarity.

In Samarin's view, one cannot speak about reasoning without taking into account the associations of similarity and contrast. Contiguous associations only represent single, isolated judgments. They do not reflect the content of these judgments, but merely a sequence of their component parts. On the other hand, associations of similarity are based on the content of judgments and require a series of other associations to form a specific system. Thus, for instance, in order to understand the sentence "Chapaev and Schiors are heroes of the Civil War," and to make clear the concept "hero," several additional judgments are needed to establish the relation between the two names and the Civil War.

Samarin (1962) went on to draw a general conclusion:

> The most important prerequisite for any thinking process is the choice of relevant judgments which must correspond to all the details of the problem and be correct as to their content. This choice is dependent on the level and extent of knowledge and its degree of organization to form the necessary associations. It also involves the law of contiguous associations, as well as the laws of similarity and contrast. It is precisely the function of the associations of similarity that makes possible the choice of judgments from contiguous associations. Contrasting associations, on the other hand, inhibit those associations which do not fit the particular situation. One would expect, therefore, that the chosen judgments are intercorrelated according to the logical construction of thinking, in other words in accordance with: (1) contiguity (the manner in which it is constructed); (2) similarity (the establishment of an identity between the subject and the predicate of the chosen judgments) [p. 245].

Thinking as Analysis and Synthesis

An extensive study of the process of problem-solving was initiated by Rubinshtein in 1953 at the Department of Psychology of Moscow University and at the Division of Psychology of the Institute of Philosophy at the Academy of Sciences. The main points which emerged from Rubinshtein's philosophical position are summarized in the following lines, based on his own works (1957a, 1958, 1959a,b, 1960a,b), as well as on the works of some of his coworkers (Slavskaya, 1966, 1968; Matyushkin, 1965, 1970; Brushlinskii, 1967, 1969a,b).

(1) The dialectical-materialistic principle of determinism postulates that external causes act on any body, phenomenon and process through their internal conditions. The external causes imply assemblies of factors, not incidental single situations. Internal conditions here mean the specific nature and logic of development of that body, phenomenon or process.

(2) Determinism applies to thinking, a process of continuous interaction between the thinking individual and the object to be known. This interaction involves the inclusion of the result of each act in the subsequent course of process. Thus the object of knowledge does not act as the sole trigger, rather each step of the thinking process leads to a change in the object and this in turn determines the next step until the problem is solved.

(3) Thinking is above all a theoretical activity and its study should make use of the study of the personality. This means that one has to consider the motive behind thinking and the significance of the problems to be solved. (As a matter of fact, this tenet has not been implemented in Rubinshtein's experimental work).

(4) The process of thinking is expressed in specific operations related to definite areas of study such as physics, history, etc. The psychological study of thinking, however, is expected to disclose the processes of analysis, synthesis and generalization manifest in the course of solving any problem. While the specific thinking operations are the result of the cognitive activity of mankind, the psychological theory of thinking aims to discover the individual process. The psychologist, for instance, is interested in the basic thinking process underlying the con-

struction of a geometric figure. Slavskaya emphasized that the concepts of analysis, etc. are not mere substitutes of notions previously proposed in the theory of thinking; rather they express the objective regularities of the thinking process to be discovered by experimental study and in this way they are expected to become explanatory concepts.

(5) Rubinshtein's school proposed two major methods for the study of problem-solving. First, the subject's reformulation of the problem during its solving is analyzed. Underlying this method is the idea that thinking is a verbal process: the verbal expression of thought is the development of the thought itself. The result of each step in solving a problem is formulated verbally, and by that very fact, it becomes an objective starting point for the further analysis of the problem. Thus, the reformulation of the problem implies establishing new connections among the various features of the object or the phenomenon which raised the problem.

The second method involves presentation of the subject with cues or an auxiliary problem at different stages of solving the original problem. It was assumed that variations of the external conditions would help to discover the role of the internal conditions. This transfer, which Thorndyke explained in terms of his hypothesis of identical elements, was widely used by the Gestalt psychologists. In Soviet psychology this method was also used by Leontev. Contrary to Leontev's studies which showed that the auxiliary problem is helpful only if it is presented after the subject has made several attempts to solve the main problem, Rubinshtein's school first concluded that the auxiliary problem should be introduced before the main one. Later studies showed, however, that there was no clear time relation between the presentation of the auxiliary problem and the efficiency of the transfer. While the first method more closely approaches the subject's behavior under natural conditions, the second method allows for better control procedures.

(6) The solving of a problem consists in analyzing its elements through a process of synthesis. Slavskaya (1966) felt that the Gestalt approach to thinking led to the discovery of a new quality in the studied object, and the concept of structure as coming closer to the concept of analysis-through-synthesis than any other concept in the psychology of thinking. But the positivistic methodology did not allow the Gestalt theory ". . . to define the nature of this new quality, to discover the dialectic of its occurrence, the mechanism of transition from unknown to known" (p. 205). Furthermore, Slavskaya pointed out that the Gestalt interpretation of the occurrence of a new structure as a change of the functional meaning ascribed to the object concerned, implies that this is a purely subjective act and not a new objective feature discovered by analysis. The experiments done by the Gestalt school dealt with the simplest form of qualitative change. This was illustrated by Szekely's (1950) study. Different functional meanings of a given objective were included in the same structure in order to follow its qualitative change. Yet this procedure does not always require the subject to discover any essential properties of the object. The solution of a problem may also consist of the discovery of relations on a lower level.

Rubinshtein's premise was that thinking consists of analysis and synthesis, abstraction and generalization, where analysis and synthesis hold interdependent positions in one and the same process. Analysis is usually achieved by synthesis, i.e., separation of the parts is dependent upon the characteristics of the whole. A valid analysis of the whole must include not only an analysis of its parts but also of the relationships between them, thus arriving at a reorganization of the whole. It is precisely this reorganization which constitutes the synthesis whereby new connections between the parts are established. Analysis and synthesis then are the common denominators of the whole cognitive process and represent the unity between the sensory and logical aspects of cognition.

There are two levels of analysis and synthesis: the first is related to the sensory image of objects, and the second to the verbal image. On the first level, analysis consists of isolating the sensory qualities. On the level of theoretical knowledge, analysis and synthesis take on new forms. Here analysis consists of abstraction, while synthesis is accomplished by two processes: (1) correlation between the facts obtained by the analysis of the factors involved; (2) the application of these facts to new circumstances. Thus, synthesis involves the construction of new and progressively more complex systems.

(7) Abstraction takes place in both the sensory and rational spheres, but has a different form in each instance. The simplest form consists of the partial isolation of some properties of the perceived object. Underlying this kind of abstraction is the physiological process of inhibition of weaker stimuli by stronger ones. Strong stimuli would be those properties of the object which bear a close relationship to biological and social needs. This elementary form of abstraction does not reveal any new characteristics of the object, being merely the perception of the object. As such, sensory cognition is confined to practical needs, whereas abstraction on higher levels is not limited by these boundaries.

(8) Generalization also takes place on two levels. Simple generalizations fall within the framework of the first signal system and are expressions of the physiological process of irradiation of stimulations. This type of generalization (obobshchenie) is found when children name various similar objects with a word they have learned previously. There is also a higher level of generalization (generalizatsiya) which manifests itself both in the empirical and theoretical spheres and consists of comparing the common properties relevant in different phenomena. An empirical generalization does not necessarily lead to new knowledge. The theoretical generalization results in the discovery of the essential relationships between objects.

The following passage by Rubinshtein (1959a) summarizes these points:

> In transferring the solution of a problem from the plane of practical action to the visual or the mental plane, the prerequisite condition is an analysis of the content of the problem and, through synthesis, their correlation to the question asked. This analysis leads to the detachment of the essential aspects of the problem . . . Generalization occurs as a result of the analysis. . . . The common essential properties of objects then become apparent. The generalization which follows analysis determines the progress from the cognitive to the practical activity. . . . Only when the generalization is accomplished, is it possible to solve problems theoretically [p. 64].

The processes of analysis and synthesis, generalization and abstraction require the investigation of their formation. These processes develop throughout the course of a lifetime, their development being contingent upon the subject matter dealt with. Therefore, any research on thinking along these lines should not be limited to the period of early childhood, but should include all the stages of development. If this is not done, there is likely to be a failure in understanding the connection between the content and form of the thinking process. Thinking develops when the individual assimilates knowledge elaborated by society. Each act of assimilation requires a previous corresponding development of the thinking capacity, and this in turn creates the possibility for the further assimilation of knowledge. During the process of mastering an elementary system of knowledge, which is associated with a specific logic of the subject matter concerned, there develops a logical system of thinking that serves as a necessary condition for mastering a more complex system of knowledge. Knowledge elaborated in the course of social-historical development, and assimilated by an individual, is incorporated into his ability to think and functions within this framework. Hence, not only the growth of individual thinking but also its content, as well as the ways of its functioning are socially determined. Thinking, however, should not be identified with knowledge.

The approach of Rubinshtein's school to the study of thinking can be illustrated with examples of experiments conducted by some of his coworkers. Zhudava studied the transition from the trial and error method to visual or mental evaluation of the problem. Children between the ages of three and six were asked to remove a candy from a vase. They were to do this with the aid of an implement which they could chose among several made available to them. Three experiments were done. In the first, the children were supplied with objects of various shapes and colors. Thus a usual situation was simulated in which relevant and irrelevant conditions were present. In the second experiment, objects of various shapes were again given but they were all of the same color. Each of the two experiments was divided into four stages. In the first stage, the implements were of both appropriate and inappropriate shapes. In the second and third stages, only inadequate shapes were presented. The last stage repeated the first stage. It was noted that the children did not reach a solution without the negative reinforcement of the intermediary stages.

In the third experiment, consisting of two stages, the children were again presented with objects of various shapes and colors. In the first stage, the adequate shapes were indicated by a light signal, in contrast with the next stage in which a light signaled the inadequate shapes. It was observed that this procedure helped the children to solve the problem "empirically," without the perception of the useful features of the objects. The children first tackled the task in all three experiments on a practical level; at first they had to make actual attempts, but later merely the visual evaluation of the situation was sufficient. In some cases, even the visual analysis was superfluous, since the children immediately ruled out any inadequate shapes. All in all, the experiments showed that regardless of their age, the children's way of tackling the problem was the same; they progressed from the practical level to a solution on the mental level.

The process of analysis through synthesis was also investigated by Antsyferova. She used a method practiced by Szekely but interpreted the results in her own way. Subjects were asked to balance objects of various weights in such a manner that the balance itself would be disturbed without outside intervention. One of the objects was a candle. The difficulty in this problem resided in the fact that the subjects had a predetermined conception of a definite function of the candle, i.e., that it gives light. Hence they overlooked the property which was pertinent to this experiment, namely, that the candle loses weight when it burns. In their first attempt, the subjects analyzed the effect they had to obtain in order to set-off the imbalance. By relating this effect to the conditions of the problem, they arrived at a reformulation of the desired result, which was that the disturbance of balance bore no relationship to a change of position in space, but rather that it was related to a change of weight. The first solution proposed the use of quickly melting substances. Only later did the subjects arrive at the correct solution.

Finally, another experiment worth mentioning is one by Matyushkin (1960). He chose the unit system of counting as the topic of his research. In a preliminary experiment, students were asked to express several numbers in the usual system of 10, and in the system of base 5. Students who had no knowledge of number systems were unable to solve the problem spontaneously. According to Rubinshtein, a subject ignorant of the relationships involved in the decimal system is likely to fail at coping with such a task. It is understandable that these students were not able to transfer the numbers to the system of 5.

Several auxiliary experiments were done in which the subjects had to find the formula for expressing any number in the decimal system. That is, they had to determine the relationship between the number of digits and the value of each digit in the decimal system. However, even after they had found the formula, the subjects were still unable to transfer it to the system of 5, because they had approached the problem in its totality, without an analysis of its basis and theory. Consequently, they were unable to make a generalization at a higher level, namely to discover the formula of number systems. Now, they were asked to find the formula for expressing any number of the system of 5. After having arranged a series of digits in the system of 5, they were able to express any digit in this system. By comparing this formula with that of the decimal system, the students grasped the general relationships between digits. They were then able to find the formula for any system.

Both Rubinshtein's theoretical and methodological approach were subjected to criticism by Samarin, who disagreed with the analysis-synthesis explanation of the process of problem-solving. Samarin (1962) pointed out that Rubinshtein had approached analysis and synthesis on a purely logical level and that these were not seen as psychological activities. And, further,

. . . what in fact determines analysis and synthesis, what is the basis of their depth or superficiality, what are the factors which make them move in the appropriate direction? Analysis means taking apart, and synthesis means putting together, and one can separate things and put them together arbitrarily. If both a baby and a scientist employ analysis and synthesis how is it that their results are incomparably different? In other words, to say that analysis and synthesis play an ultimate role in thinking means nothing in itself and does not explain anything. The questions to be asked are how, in what direction and on what level is the analysis-synthesis activity performed. Thus, what ultimately counts is not the brain's capacity to analyze or synthesize but rather what determines these functions. . . . [Analysis and synthesis] are determined by *the systems of knowledge and skills* assimilated by man, by his life experience, his convictions. . . . The system of knowledge . . . determines the bringing to the fore of the necessary knowledge, the elimination of facts deemed inadequate for the solution of a given problem, and the reinforcement of those elements which lead to the solution. Many errors are possible; they are not incidental, but are determined by errors in the system of knowledge itself [pp. 182-184].

The Internalization Hypothesis

The hypothesis that thinking essentially consists of an internalization of external acts of behavior was developed by Galperin (1953, 1957, 1958, 1959, 1960, 1966, 1969a,b). A member of Vygotskii's school, his work, like Leontev's, represents a development of the cultural-historical approach. In that a number of Galperin's works are available in English, [1] the following presentation is limited to some of the main points of his theory with an emphasis on its critical discussion in Soviet psychology.

Galperin drew a distinction between his own psychological account of the development of the child's thinking, and other theories including those of Bühler, Vygotskii and Piaget. He regarded these authors as either using physiological concepts, or as being concerned with the stages of the child's assimilation of the logical rules. Galperin took issue with Piaget's statement that any psychological explanation of thinking necessarily leads either to physiology or to logic. Furthermore, he disagreed with the behavioristic denial of conscious phenomena, as well as with the Gestaltist concept of isomorphism between physical, physiological and psychological structures. Galperin contended that because of the failure to develop a psychological theory of thinking, psychologists avoid speaking about psychological processes proper. His objective has been to separate the specific psychological processes from the physiological, logical, pedagogical ones. Galperin, whose emphasis has been on the concept of image, has assumed that the child's thinking—as described by Stern, Vygotskii and Piaget

[1] He recently contributed an extensive presentation of his views to the volume edited by Maltzman and Cole (1969).

—represents the result of his orienting activity based on the image of the objects concerned.

As if to anticipate the criticism that he was following the traditional idealistic concept of image, Galperin argued that he was not referring to a nonmaterial structure, since the structure itself is formed in the course of an orienting activity. His concept of image, however, is not altogether clear as is apparent in the following passage (Galperin, 1966):

> It [the image] occurs because during phylogenesis a stage unavoidably appears when the organism's reactions cannot be successful any longer if they are not oriented towards an object which is not the direct target of behavior but will be encountered in the next moment. Such an orientation towards an absent object is possible because the organism possesses the physical reflection of that object. However, the stimulus of these reactions is the reflected object itself and not its physical reflection. It is precisely the orientation towards the original object based on its physical reflection which leads to the construction of the image. The orienting activity is building up the image and also makes use of it [pp. 246–247].

Galperin's work has been concerned with the problem of how concrete, external actions are transformed into intellectual operations. This transformation is supposed to pass through several stages during which the external actions are changed along four parameters: (1) the level on which the action is fulfilled; e.g., a child may perform an action either by the aid of objects, by talking aloud without the use of objects, or by talking to himself; (2) the degree of generalization, i.e., the extent to which relevant properties are distinguished from irrelevant ones; (3) the completeness of the action in that it can be performed by means of a set of operations, or in a reduced form; (4) the degree of familiarity with the action; for instance, a child carries out an action using an appropriate procedure which he has been taught, but is capable of using it only under supervision because of insufficient mastery of it. These parameters are relatively independent of each other, so that the same actions can be performed in various ways. However, Galperin ascribed the most important role to the first parameter, namely the level of mastery of an action, and his studies have been concerned primarily with the changes occurring along this parameter.

Galperin described four stages in the process of internalization of an external act into a mental act. The first stage is that in which the orientational basis of the action is formed. There are three types of orientation. The first type consists of the teacher giving a practical demonstration of the action to be performed. No verbal indication is given. It was observed that with this procedure, the correct action is performed only after much trial and error. The performance of the action is at the mercy of circumstances. In the second type of orientation, the practical demonstration is accompanied by a comprehensive verbal instruction. The action is now learned more easily and the acquired experience can be used to solve other similar problems. However, the transfer is limited to problems which include elements identical with those appearing in the original situation. The third type of orientation consists of a systematic analysis of the action to be performed, so that the necessary conditions for its carrying out can be fully understood. This time the learner's mistakes are few and limited to the initial steps. The acquired experience is very stable and the possibilities of transfer to situations of the same category are increased. Galperin compared his description of these types of orientation with the usual description of the learning process. He concluded that learning by trial and error corresponds to the first type of orientation, while the sudden discovery of solutions corresponds to the second type of orientation. As to the third type, Galperin claimed to have been the first to describe it.

The second stage of internalization of an external action consists in its mastery. The action is "materialized," i.e., the student deals with representations of the object, such as diagrams, schemes, etc. In this way, he becomes acquainted with the essential features of the object, which can be compared, measured, etc. Galperin pointed to the difficulty of discovering the "materialized" form of a mental action because it frequently does not correspond to the concept of that action. He felt that it is the psychologist's task to discover the materialized forms of the thinking process involved in learning. These are not revealed in the current teaching methods. In the second stage of learning, the assimilated action can be abbreviated, i.e., some of its links can be omitted. But this should be done when the student understands why he can skip over a certain operation, so that he is able to go back from the abbreviated action to reconstruct the entire mental operation when this is necessary.

The third stage of internalization consists of the instruction given by the teacher without using any external support. In Galperin's (1959) own words,

> . . . [the third stage] seems to be not only a system of denominations relevant to the essence of the concrete action, but also a particular reality, the reality of language. . . Not only the action itself but also its reflection in social consciousness and the newly learned formulations are brought into the child's consciousness [p. 455].

The fourth stage is subdivided into two phases. In the first phase, the external action is transferred to the verbal sphere, the subject instructing himself aloud (external speech to oneself.) In the second phase, it is only the internal speech which participates in the performance of the action. The action is now a pure mental act, assuming, as Galperin (1953) put it, the appearance of ". . . introspection, but which so often has been taken to be its real nature" (p. 223). [2] Galperin expressed his belief that only by analyzing the formation of a mental activity is one able to understand why this gives the impression of being as if divided into a concrete and a concep-

[2] Translated in *Psychology in the Soviet Union*, ed. B. Simon.

tual part, and why the concrete content takes on an "extra-sensory" form, while the conceptual content takes the form of introspection. He wrote (Galperin, 1959):

> We must bear in mind not only the objective sequence of the acquisition of knowledge but also the *psychological sequence of the forms of thinking*, the sequence of stages from the material reality to the higher levels of thinking and from the mental activity to the grasping of generalized concepts. For the time being, we do not have any specific data to demonstrate a sudden formation of a new mental activity. By contrast, a careful analysis leads us to the conclusion that a *mental activity* does not appear in this way, but through an external, material or materialized action [p. 450].

The above propositions form the basis of a set of teaching procedures. It is understood, however, that students should not be presented with tasks which require them to discover something new, but with tasks which have to be realized and performed. Therefore, the first learning process is to perceive the external and material forms of the object or problem. If the objects and the means for carrying out the action in its original form are not available, then its materialized form should be used. The teacher or the investigator who organizes the learning experiment should select the relevant characteristics of the concept and explain them. Then, they have to be presented in a concrete way, written on pieces of cardboard. The problem to which the newly learned concepts will be applied are to be presented on another set of cardboard pieces. After the students have thoroughly assimilated the information on the cardboard pieces, these are removed. The students are asked to repeat aloud the definition of the concept and to find out if it corresponds to the problem. In those instances where students have failed to recall the definition of the concept, the pieces of cardboard are presented again. The experiment is not to proceed to the next stage until the concept has been learned. When it can be applied to the problem, the action becomes generalized, abbreviated and is mastered.

Galperin's hypotheses have given rise to a great deal of controversy among Soviet psychologists (Kabanova-Meller, 1959a,b; Menchinskaya, 1960; Rubinshtein, 1959b; Samarin, 1959; Lyublinskaya, 1960). Several objects were put forward on the theoretical as well as the methodological level, revealing a certain amount of confusion as to the terms used. Rubinshtein disagreed with the assumption that mental acts are formed by a process of internalization of external actions. In his view, this is a misinterpretation of the historical nature of human thinking and implies a mechanistic approach to its social determination. Rubinshtein could accept the term "internalization" if it meant the intellectual, theoretical activity which occurs during mental development, but he felt that the restricted meaning of this concept represents the effect of the process of intellectual growth itself.

Kabanova-Meller emphasized three points of disagreement with Galperin. First, she underscored the difference between the concept of a "mental" *(myslennoe)* act, which means an action made up "in the head," and an "intellectual" *(umstvennoe)* action which may be supported by external elements, e.g., a drawing. The latter concept is a more general one and includes the "external" action as well as the "mental" one. Thus, a distinction is to be made between these two concepts and not between "mental" and "external." Second, Kabanova-Meller felt that the transition to a mental activity did not represent a general law in the development of knowledge, but rather a particular situation. Intellectual abilities can be formed without any transition from external actions. Finally, she raised the question as to the precise role of the internalization of an external action—when it does occur—for the assimilation of knowledge. According to Kabanova-Meller, a process of internalization occurs in both cases of problem-solving behavior, notably the reproduction of knowledge and of previously learned methods of work, as well as the performance of new actions, but in different ways. Galperin overlooked this difference and therefore misinterpreted the results of his experiments.

Kabanova-Meller illustrated her position by an experiment in which students learned to establish spatial relations. Dull fifth-grade students were asked to find out which were the right and left banks of a river. They had previously learned the rule that if one stands in a position looking down a river, the right bank is on the right-hand side and the left is on the left-hand side. Thus they were aware of having an observation position and of seeing which way the river flowed. It was required that they establish these relations mentally, i.e., without changing their position or turning the head, a task which they solved quite easily. Next, they were presented with a map and were instructed as to which were the right and left banks. In this instance, too, they were able to indicate the direction of the river, that is, they had established a reverse relation: riverbank-observation point-direction of river. However, at first they were inclined to change their position and only afterwards were they able to cope with the task on the mental plane.

Menchinskaya claimed that Galperin's endeavor to guide the subjects toward the solution of the problems given to them, rather than regard them as independent researchers, ultimately leads to a limitation of their ability to perform such mental activities as analysis and synthesis, thereby resulting in a hindrance in the development of productive thinking. That is, the students have not been given the opportunity to look for independent, original solutions.

Productive Thinking

Ponomarev (1960, 1967, 1971), who belongs to Leontev's school but whose research has been more along the lines of his own interests, has endeavored to clarify the processes involved in the creative solution of problems. In his view, many concepts used by psychologists who study thinking are lacking in clarity. There has been a tendency to equate thinking with problem-solving and to misinterpret the concept of task. Ponomarev felt that Woodworth's distinction between thinking problems whose solutions are attained indirectly and tasks which are solved directly did not clarify the issue.

Ponomarev put forward the view that the methods of assimilating new knowledge should be taken as the criterion for differentiating between these two types of problem-solving. One wonders, however, if he is in a better position to provide a meaningful answer to the problem he raised. Let us consider the following passage (Ponomarev, 1967):

> We differentiate between thinking-tasks and non-thinking tasks. . . . While taking the attainment of new knowledge as the criterion for defining a thinking problem, we see that all intellectual problems which are not thinking tasks are solved on the basis of knowledge previously acquired; this is to say, on the reproduction of previous thinking. Hence, the terms "productive" and "reproductive" thinking. Strictly speaking, therefore, the process of solving problems which are not thinking problems may be called reproductive thinking. It follows from this that reproductive thinking can be understood when productive thinking is understood, since it is an outcome of the latter. This would only be correct, however, in principle, as in most cases, reproductive thinking anticipates the productive thinking, mediating and preparing the ground for it [pp. 116–117].

Furthermore, Ponomarev pointed out that the study of thinking has been primarily concerned with the ways in which already acquired knowledge is used in the process of problem solving. The study of deductive thinking has indeed advanced to the point where aspects of the intellectual activity can be delegated to computers. By contrast, the process of acquisition of new knowledge which cannot be obtained directly through logical deduction has been neglected. Finally, in his discussion of the approach to thinking in contemporary psychology, Ponomarev emphasized that the studies have essentially taken one direction: the investigation of the development of thinking. The investigators have overlooked another basic area of interest, namely the interaction of subject-object in the process of solving a problem. By that he was referring to the interaction between the changes occurring in the material which presents the problem and the solver of the problem. During the process of solving a problem, the subject manipulates the object and discovers new properties of it; that is, he obtains new sensations and perceptions. These become an additional factor determining the further manipulation of the object and the disclosure of other properties, etc. In Ponomarev's view, the developmental study is at least incomplete if this interaction of subject-object is not analyzed. The understanding of the subject's development requires an analysis of the causes of transformation of one subjective state in another one. This transformation is precisely related to the interaction subject-object.

According to Ponomarev, the crux of the matter is that the act of thinking, as any other kind of action, can be divided into two parts: (1) an elementary form of interaction between subject and object, which is unconscious; (2) a higher form of interaction, which is relevant to the purpose of the act and is a conscious and active adaptation to a stiuation. These types of interaction are amalgamated, manifesting themselves in the heterogeneous character of a mental act. A thinking act modifies an object either intentionally or unintentionally. Unconscious products of the process of thinking may be essential to productive thinking.

The aim of Ponomarev's experimental research was to reveal the characteristics of mental acts by analyzing the two parts of the interaction mentioned above. He surmised that this method would shed some light on perception, memory and attention.

Thinking and Teaching

Following are some theories on thinking proposed by authors who have been concerned with the process of problem-solving in the classroom in the most direct way. Kabanova-Meller (1956a,b, 1959a,b, 1962, 1968), a student of thinking, has conducted all her experiments in a school situation. Her theoretical position can hardly be ascribed to a given category. Criticizing that school of thought which reduced mental activities to associations, she maintains that the psychological concept of association should not be confused with the physiological concepts of conditioned reflex and temporary connection. As a matter of fact, she has attempted to reconcile various points of view, to the extent of linking associationism with Galperin's hypothesis, which she did not reject altogether.

Kabanova-Meller considered the process of problem-solving as consisting of the formation of various associations between verbal and visual stimuli. The solutions were assumed to contain two parts: (1) the reproduction of previously acquired knowledge; (2) the processes dealing with visual aids, such as the perception of the objects involved and the abstraction of certain features. Three groups of associations were described.

One group consists of the (1) connections between perceived objects or groups of objects. These are the primary associations which are consolidated in memory in the form of representations, concepts, theories, etc. The associations described by Samarin were regarded as primary associations. In the same group are included the associations which Spence and Bugelsky referred to as sensosensory.

(2) Connections between representations, concepts, etc., previously formed independently of each other, are classified as secondary associations. The recalled elements in these associations play the same role as the external stimuli for the primary associations. Whether an association is of a primary or secondary order can be determined by analyzing the way in which it has been elaborated. For instance, students were asked to look at a perspective picture of a certain area and

then figure out where that region was presented on a topographical map. The spatial relationship established was considered to be a primary connection because the children had previously seen the picture. But when they were asked to imagine a geographical area seeing solely on the basis of a topographical map, the response was regarded as a secondary association.

(3) The connections between perceived objects and previously elaborated representations or concepts, as well as between various elements of previously acquired knowledge are intermediate associations. This category includes connections between old and new associations, but with the proviso that external stimuli provide new knowledge, while the already acquired knowledge is reproduced from memory.

The formation of associations in all three groups involves a mental activity. Connections, which are established between either directly perceived or evoked elements, i.e., between psychological structures, share the common characteristic of being consolidated in memory in the form of isolated or eventually linked representations or concepts. Each of the three categories of associations is composed of several types of connections in accordance with certain criteria: connections between perceived or represented objects can be established either by contiguity or similarity; the connected elements may belong either to the same or to different areas of knowledge; they can be either verbal or visual; they may differ among themselves according to their direction and mobility (e.g., a child who memorizes a poem may connect the lines in a single direction, but in learning to count he establishes connections in both directions); connections may be formed between isolated elements, small groups or broad systems of knowledge.

The work of Bogoyavlenskii (1951, 1957, 1959a,b, 1962, 1969) and Menchinskaya (1955, 1966, 1967), at the Laboratory of Psychology of Learning, the Institute of Psychology of the Academy of Pedagogical Sciences, is apparently the most characteristic example of approaching theoretical problems of thinking and learning in terms of the practical pedagogical aims of school training. Bogoyavlenskii was concerned with the teaching of grammar and spelling, while Menchinskaya's interest has been primarily in the teaching of arithmetic.

Bogoyavlenskii claimed that there are two main problems in the psychology of learning: to determine those factors involved in the child's intellectual development, and how his cognitive capacity can be advanced in a rational way. He agreed with the common viewpoint that any development of thinking depends on the amount of knowledge assimilated, pointing out, however, that not all accumulated knowledge necessarily leads to such a development. In that thinking only develops out of a process of specific training, it is necessary to develop a system of intellectual operations, or a general set of methods, to prompt the thinking activity.

Bogoyavlenskii stressed the role of the child's motives in learning. He made a speculative attempt to employ one of the principles of dialectical materialism, namely the struggle between contradictions, for the understanding of the relationship between motivation and learning. In the sphere of thinking, opposites were assumed to be present in the relationship between previous experience and acquisition of new knowledge, between the social value of a certain piece of knowledge and the individual's personal needs and inclinations, between the concrete aspects of phenomena and their abstract, essential features. The intellect develops in the course of thinking and is directed towards a reconciliation of these contrasts. It is the task of the school to help children become aware of these opposites and to offer guidance in resolving them with the awareness that such contradictions present an intellectual problem. A positive motivation must be created so that the child's cognitive interest in solving the problems he must face is aroused. The teacher has to see that the child is aware of the classroom problem as being relevant to his life demands.

In Bogoyavlenskii's (1962) own words: "The child should realize the conflict between old and new knowledge and should wonder how he can surmount this conflict. An important factor is the reinforcement of the inner response to the understanding of the problem" (p. 76). Bogoyavlenskii distinguished between direct reinforcement—the teacher's positive or negative attitude—and indirect reinforcement, by establishing a relationship between the problem to be solved and the child's past experience. Indirect reinforcement was assigned a particular role, since the child's attitude was assumed to be contingent upon his concern for his acquired experiences.

Bogoyavlenskii has been primarily concerned with the methods for developing the child's intellectual activity. He found that these methods are well developed with respect to relatively elementary skills, such as basic algebra, or the spelling rules, but where the learning of more complex concepts is concerned, the pedagogical literature deals somewhat exclusively with methods of transfer and consolidation of knowledge. School children are not taught how to assimilate material and much of the teaching is concerned only with the results of thinking. Children's mistakes are corrected but little attention is paid to the guidance of their thinking.

Menchinskaya closely followed Bogoyavlenskii's line of thought. She, too, emphasized the need for developing methods concerned with intellectual procedures, flexible enough to be applied under changing conditions. Once such intellectual operations are learned, the capacity for theoretical problems is broadened, whether it is the matter about school problems or problems of practical life. Menchinskaya criticized the distinction between concrete and abstract thinking as well as the assumption that there is a transition from one type of thinking to the other, contingent upon the age of the child. Her contention is that these two types of thinking are mutually related by a sequence of fine transitions. What was previously abstract can become concrete and in turn can contribute to the solution of further abstract problems. Thus, the transition to a new stage of thinking is not only supported by concrete operations but also by abstract ones. Gurova (1964, 1968) also supported the idea that the acquisition of knowledge and skills does not necessarily produce a parallel development in logical thinking. While children are able to reach a certain level of generalization without any special training, they are not aware of the thinking process involved. If one is aware of this process, each step can be compared with the expected result and the course of solving a problem is better controlled.

The experimental studies of Menchinskaya and her coworkers provide an illustration of the theoretical position just outlined. Some of them are now reviewed. Kalmykova (1955) studied the development of thinking during the study of physics. Tests were given to sixth grade students, aimed at the formation of the concept of "pressure." The subjects were dived into three groups, A, B and C, and the experiments were conducted in three stages. The purpose of the first, preparatory stage, was to see if the subjects possessed the necessary knowledge to understand the concept of pressure and to make them familiar with the concepts "power of pressure" and "surface of pressure." This preparatory stage applied to all the three groups. During the second, or "teaching" stage, which occupied the major part of the experiment, the children were taught the concept of pressure itself. The effect of pressure, its force on a given surface, was demonstrated for each group. This teaching stage was performed in three ways. Group A was given pieces of cardboard containing the characteristics of pressure. Group B was not given any written indications to assist them in solving the problems. Group C was also given the meaning of pressure in written form and was asked to solve practical problems before being faced with theoretical ones. Groups A and B were asked to solve theoretical problems from the textbook. While group A was given assistance throughout, the other groups received help only when it was required. The third stage, a control experiment, was identical for the three groups. All subjects were asked to solve theoretical as well as practical problems, some of them being familiar to the children while others required the application of acquired knowledge to new conditions.

The results of the experiment showed that group A easily solved those problems where the children had been told the necessary operations, i.e., simple problems in the first stage of learning the concept of pressure. At the beginning, group B was faced with some difficulties, but later coped with these tasks as adequately as group A. The control experiment showed that the more intelligent children of both these groups were able to work independently in formulating the relationship between the force of pressure and its effect. The least bright of the children worked in a less rational manner but the differences between the two groups themselves was insignificant. The advantage obtained by the procedure applied to group B became noticeable when the children were asked to solve more complex problems. Group C—contrary to what one might have expected—was poorer than the other subjects in solving concrete problems unfamiliar to them. Kalmykova concluded that the thinking capacity of a child can be developed only when he is allowed to solve a task independently. This method is more likely to develop his analytic faculties.

Menchinskaya (1966) discussed this study and felt that the process of abstraction involved in applying acquired knowledge to solving problems is different from the abstraction taking place in concept formation. She proposed the terms "secondary" and "primary" abstraction. In the latter case, the process of abstraction takes place together with that of generalization, while in the former case abstraction and generalization have already been accomplished, but are as though masked by new concrete instances. Hence the subject is faced with the problem of recognizing a notion or a principle which he has become familiar with in new circumstances. The concrete material which has supported the assimilation of that notion or principle now prevents their application to solving problems related to a different concrete material. Instead, the process of problem solving is facilitated by drawings or diagrams which have concrete and abstract characteristics as well.

Studies done by Kudryavtsev (1961, 1964) are also relevant for the topic under discussion. He was interested in developing procedures to advance the child's capacity to solve theoretical and practical problems as well. The subjects of Kudryavtsev and Yakimanskaya's research were students of experimental schools within the "500 schools plan" which at that time operated the program for the introduction of polytechnic education in schools. The experiments were aimed at the application of knowledge acquired about electricity and mechanics in physics classes. A preliminary experiment showed that 30 eighth-grade students had difficulty in managing variations of a basic electrical circuit. Many students failed to distinguish between the relevant and the irrelevant elements of the various circuits. This result prompted Kudryavtsev to perform a "teaching experiment," conducted in three stages, with six average and weak seventh-grade students.

The first experiment consisted of four tasks. (1) The students were asked to draw a circuit of an electric light system that connected with two light bulbs (which they copied from the textbook). (2) They were to draw a circuit of an electric light system for three bulbs. (3) They were asked to recognize various circuits for parallel and serial systems (for this aspect the experimenter gave some assistance by pointing out the essential features). (4) They were asked to recognize a number of various already printed circuits.

The second experiment which consisted of tasks aimed at developing the students' ability to draw circuits independently, utilized the following four tasks: (1) drawing a circuit of an electric light system for four bulbs (two students were able to draw more than one variation); (2) identifying unusual electrical circuits: the serial circuit resembled the parallel circuit in the textbook, while the parallel circuit was lengthened (five students did not cope with this task); (3) the students were presented with pieces of paper on which nine signs were drawn representing light bulbs for which they were asked to draw a parallel circuit operating them. (This task was given because of the observed difficulty in drawing parallel circuits and precisely because it required the student to be aware that neither the number of lights nor the particular electrical circuits were relevant. All students were able to identify any variation with the experimenter's assistance.) (4) The independent setting up of serial and parallel circuits, with five light bulbs, with as many variations as possible. Although only four students did more than two variations, this was a significant improvement. The experiment ended with a third control series. Kudryavtseva concluded that the combination of theoretical study with practical application resulted in a far better understanding of the theory itself. Thus her objection was that the usual practice in Russian schools was to separate theoretical study from practical learning.

Problem-Solving and Information Processing

We now consider approaches to the study of thinking processes in terms of probability and information theory. Soviet authors have recently become very much interested in the application of cybernetic concepts to the study of problem-solving. Along with the interest in Western works—those of Polya and Miller-Galanter-Pribram were translated into Russian and Bruner's (1956) *A Study of Thinking* is frequently quoted—there has been criticism of Western approaches, in particular those regarding heuristic thinking.

Shemyakin (1960, 1963, 1969), of the Laboratory of Thinking and Speech at the Institute of Psychology in Moscow, has studied the process of problem-solving in relation to the information provided to the subjects. In an experiment done by Zakharov (1959), an associate of Shemyakin, students from various faculties were given three tasks. (1) They were presented with eight letters and a sheet of paper divided into two parts, which were called "cells." They were told that the experimenter had a definite arrangement of the letters in mind, i.e., four in each cell, and that after each trial of setting up all the letters they would be told how many letters were correctly placed in each cell. Finally, they were informed that after eight trials the experiment would be discontinued. (2) The subjects were told that the four letters which had to be put in a cell formed a Russian noun in the nominative case. The subjects were divided into two groups. Group "A" was given the two tasks in the sequence mentioned above, and group "B" started with the second task. This procedure was supposed to reveal the effect of training. (3) The subjects had to arrange the letters in the two cells according to a principle which was not revealed. The experiment was expected to provide answers for two questions: whether limitation of the number of possible hypotheses at the onset of the second experiment (the indication of the principle reduced the number of initial hypotheses from 70 to four) made the task easier; how hypothesis making is influenced by the difference between the instructions given in experiments 2 and 3. The results were checked against the "ideal" solver of these problems of information processing—the electronic computer. The experiments showed that the curves obtained in all three experiments, while showing the gradation of difficulty, differed from the curves obtained from the computer. Of the three experiments, the second came nearest to that given by the machine. Yet, even in this case, the result differed greatly from the anticipated one, i.e., only a small proportion of the supplementary information supplied in this instance was used. Thus, only one-seventh of the subjects found the solution after the first two trials, despite the fact that the problem might have been solved after two trials. About 75 per cent reached the solution after the fifth and subsequent trials. The negative effect of the first experiment on the second was noted as was the fact that group B did better than group A. Finally, the curves of experiments 1 and 3 were quite similar. Shemyakin's (1963) interpretation of these findings reveals his position. He accepted Zakharov's distinction between a theoretical and a psychological difficulty in solving problems of this type.

The theoretical difficulty has a formal character and is a function of the number of trials necessary for solving the problem in each stage without loss of information. The psychological difficulty is the result of a partial or even a total loss of the information needed for solving the problem. For the machine there is only a theoretical difficulty; for man there is also a psychological one. The experiments showed that . . . the psychological difficulty does not coincide with the theoretical. This is dependent on the ways of supplying the information: the psychological difficulty was closer to the theoretical when the information was given fully at once, and increased when this was given gradually. In psychological terms, this means that the psychological difficulty is less when man is only required to remember the information but it increased when he also has to draw logical conclusions in relation with its use. . . .

How to explain that in Zakharov's experiments the subjects lost information? Each trial in this experiment, except for the last one, consisted of two stages. In the first stage, the information was received, while in the second stage one of the possible arrangements was chosen. A full account of the information can indicate which of the attempted arrangements are to be avoided, but does not allow any conclusion as to which possibility should be given priority. In other words, the selection of a possible solution after each trial, except for the last one, is a matter of random choice. This means, objectively, "to throw the dice" and as regards "success," man and machine are in the same situation. There is a difference between them, only in the first stage of trials. The machine takes into account the information by simply recalling it and acts in strict accordance with the instruction given. Man disobeys the instruction and attempts to classify the objects. . . . For instance, he arranges the consonants in such a way that by mentally adding vowels certain

words are formed. Man, unlike the machine, is searching for a meaningful solution for each problem. The "search for a principle" represents the third stage of each trial. This is precisely the stage when the
information is lost. Man sacrifices information for the sake of his principle [pp. 23–24].

Shemyakin's own research was concerned, among other
things, with the classification of colors. He noticed a considerable lack of agreement among people with regard to the
naming of colors. Thus, he noted that while "cherry-colored"
is defined in one dictionary as approximating the dark-blue,
another one describes it as being nearer red. Experiments were
done with 150 adults who were presented with 112 pieces of
cardboard each containing the name of a color. The subjects
were asked to divide them into groups, in such a way that each
group would include various shades of the same basic color.
As was expected, the first series of experiments showed that to
a large extent the classifications were uniform. The smallest
number of groups consisted of basic colors: white, black, red,
yellow, green and dark blue. Two tendencies were manifest in
the classifications: to distribute the cards in accordance with the
verbal connections and according to the represented colors.

The second experiment consisted of two stages. In the first
stage, the subjects were asked to classify the names of the
shades of a number of colors into the six basic colors mentioned above. This seemed to be a rather easy task but the
majority of names were those referring to a two-toned color.
In the second stage, the classifications were left to the subjects'
own judgment. Except for nine subjects who preferred the
previous classification, all the others proposed classifications
slightly different from those made in the first experiment.

The last experiment was also divided into two parts. In the
first part, the subjects were asked to classify the pieces of cardboard but this time the 11 pieces of cardboard which had the
general names of the colors (white, black, grey, red, brown,

orange, yellow, green, sky-blue, dark-blue, violet) were put away. This resulted in an increase of the number of groups. Groups of colors were formed which previously had either been used infrequently or not at all such as "milky" and "grassy." At the same time, there was more grouping around the colors white, black, red, green, brown, yellow and dark-blue, despite the absence of the names of these colors. Then the 11 pieces of cardboard were introduced again and the subjects told that they might change the previous classification. Here, 90 per cent of the subjects changed the classification with a result very close to that obtained in the first two experiments.

Shemyakin concluded that a group of names of basic colors exists around which all other colors are ranged but that this "nucleus" is not constant. Hence, variable associations are established between the names of the basic colors. Shemyakin pointed out this lack of any definite rule, such that the naming of colors followed neither a rigid nor an arbitrary system, but was rather of a probabilistic nature.

MODELING OF THINKING, HEURISTICS, PROGRAMMED LEARNING

The position that a machine is capable of thinking and as such can replace—and, on occasion, even outdo—the human brain has always been a major objection levelled by philosophers against cybernetics. This proposition, once an explicitly untenable facet of Marxist ideology, remains a central concern in the Soviet opposition to cybernetics, but one notices in recent Russian publications that it has become a subject of lively debate. Points similar to those voiced by Western authors are now raised quite independently from the standard arguments deriving from Marxist theory.

The premise that thinking processes are linked to the organic matter from which they arise is of prime importance. The human brain is the product of a long twofold evolution:

natural development and social development. Its further development outside of human society is inconceivable. The concept of machine is related to inorganic matter, and as such is only an imitation of genuine thinking. The machine cannot set tasks for itself. The operation of "generalization," as carried out by the machine, is limited and not comparable with similar operations performed by the human brain. Gurevich stated that the current automata approximate the nervous system of insects. An electronic device, e.g., MacKay's automaton, is only capable of using acquired experience when called upon to repeat similar tasks. When faced with new situations, the machine uses the trial-and-error method. And whereas man can learn the right approach from a negative result, the machine would only register a negative result. The machine makes only a statistical record of successes and failures. It processes all data in strict succession in order to arrive at a given result, unlike human thinking which is apt to skip over intermediary stages to achieve the identical result.

On the other hand, there are arguments which stress the significance and the possibility of modeling human thinking. Glushkov (1963a,b, 1964a,b, 1966), the director of the Institute of Cybernetics of the Ukrainian Academy of Sciences and a deputy member of the Academy of Sciences of the USSR, is a leading advocate of the thesis that any form of human thinking can be modeled. In his view, a technological system designed on the basis of already known programming principles could succeed in this direction. A machine can be more intelligent than man; a computer designed to plan the national economy may surpass the ability of the constructor himself. Glushkov did concede the impossibility that the machine could move through all stages of evolution at the informational level and ultimately attain consciousness. For this to be possible it is necessary to provide the machine with a vast amount of data including information on heredity, mutations and natural selection, in addition to the various physical processes that occur on Earth. But it is possible to achieve a model of thinking by technological systems due to the finite number of neurons and their discrete nature. At the informational level, then, the functioning of the brain is governed by a finite number of rules. Glushkov, however, also expressed certain reservations. He believes that the *essence* of thinking will forever remain an expression of man's inherent ability: a machine can be more intelligent than an individual or a group, but never more intelligent than mankind.

In approaching the problem of formal languages, Glushkov (1964a) raised two questions: (a) to what extent can actual languages be formalized?; (b) what aspect of human thinking can be modeled by means of formal languages? It is his belief that there is a solution to the first question, but he emphasizes that any formalization of a language has only a limited value, as any reproduction loses its validity with the passage of time and the development of the natural language. With regard to the second question, Glushkov maintains that neither thinking as an entity nor thinking in terms of its logical components can be adequately expressed in a formal language. The relationship between thinking and experience extends beyond the limits of formal linguistic systems and, implicitly, beyond the limits of mathematical logic.

A rather lucid description of the characteristics of learning in man and machine was offered by Feldbaum (1964), a computer designer. He conceived the process of learning as ". . . a process of interaction between teacher, student and academic subject taking place in a closed circuit; it is not reduced to an open chain of transmitting information from teacher to student" (p. 427). Only isolated moments of learning are fulfilled in an open circuit. The latter can function only if the transmitted signals have meaning for both transmitter and receiver. This requires a previously established connection between teacher, student and material through their interaction in a closed circuit. Thus, the processes of learning in a child, in particular the formation of the second signal system, take place within a closed circuit. Once the language and its relations to the world of objects have been formed, the transmission of information is possible within an open circuit. When an essentially new piece of information is to be transmitted which requires a new language and a new alphabet, a new closed circuit must be formed. Hence the interaction between the three components of a closed circuit is the "unit" or the "cell" of transmitting information.

The learning or teaching automata are of three types: (1) open systems; (2) systems with a circuit closed within the automaton itself; (3) systems which include the object of learning. The latter type is the most important. *"The process of teaching an automaton is a process of purposeful modification of its algorithm; the algorithm elaborated in the course of teaching is not incorporated in the automaton* (previously or in the process of teaching the automaton) *by its designer"* (Feldbaum, 1964, p. 436). This bears an important similarity to the nervous system of the newborn infant who possesses reflexes and instincts but has not yet acquired knowledge. There is an additional analogy between man and machine: both obtain as a result of learning certain skills and are able either to do things which they could not do before, or to improve their previous performance.

There are, however, essential differences. First, whereas man is taught in order to develop a broad variety of abilities and skills, a machine is taught simply for the purpose of fulfilling definite tasks. Second, whereas the influence of other people plays an important role in human learning, there is no "collective" of automata. Third, the current mathematical methods are appropriate only for the discovery of algorithms of deductive thinking: the application of a certain method to the data of a problem necessarily leads to a definite solution.

Creative thinking is, doubtless, linked to the power, logic and consistency of the deductive method. It is due precisely to the discovery of the general methods of approach to problems, to the possibility of inferring partial rules from general laws, that certain sciences have made rapid progress. But the inference accomplished with the help of ready-made formulae cannot be regarded as the main aspect of creative thinking. On the contrary, this process can rather easily be automatized and assigned to a machine. If the thinking capacity were to be evaluated on the basis of the strength of deduction . . . one should not only conclude that automata think, but that they can think much better than man and that people are poor thinkers. Certainly, this is not true, first of all because the process of deduction plays only an auxiliary role in creative thinking. As a matter of fact, the main point in making an inference is the discovery of deductive rules, and this is not done in a deductive way. In creative thinking, the major role is held by the inductive, heuristic method . . . [pp. 457–458].

Feldbaum conceded that certain types of automata, notably the self-teaching systems, do have an inductive, heuristic character. But this way of thinking has been formalized to a very limited extent. The mathematical methods currently used are too precise and detailed. There is a need to develop more flexible methods which can operate with analogies rather than with identities. Feldbaum concluded that the current possibilities of teaching automata can be compared only with the simple methods of training and coaching. But the modeling of the functions of the second signal system will be possible.

This brings us to a consideration of the views held by Soviet students of the process of problem-solving on the subject of heuristic theory. It seems instructive to present an evaluation of the pioneering work of Newell, Shaw, and Simon by different Russian writers.

Brushlinskii (1967, 1969a,b) emphasized the limitations of Newell, Shaw, and Simon's heuristic program for the "General Problem Solver" which is regarded by these authors as a model of the process of problem-solving in man. In his view, this program consists only in the preparation of the machine to solve problems formulated in advance, using known methods. Although intermediary "new" results may be obtained in the course of solving a certain problem, all the possible alternatives have to be considered in advance. If an alternative unforeseen by the programmer occurs, the machine needs new instructions, that is, the program has to be broadened. Brushlinskii (1969a) wrote:

> If there is thinking involved here, it does not belong to the machine, but to the man, the programmer. Thinking is necessary, in particular, precisely because all or some ways of solving the problem are unknown and have to be revealed. If, according to the "heuristic" program, these are known in advance (teleologically) then the major difficulty of the problem either falls away or is greatly diminished. The unknown quantity which will be discovered in the course of the thinking process appears as something which had been known at the beginning. Thus there is teleology in the modeling of thinking. The cognitive process is "modeled" or inferred primarily from its final product, i.e., what is not known yet and will appear as a result of the investigated process, is mistaken for the basic cause. As a matter of fact, the objective necessity of the process, or activity, emerges precisely from the fact that the unknown quantity which is gradually discovered is not known at the beginning [p. 261].

Thus, in Brushlinskii's view there is a masked teleology in the psychology of thinking, pedagogy, heuristic theory and cybernetics consisting of the identification of the requirement of the problem, with the unknown quantity. This is pointed out in the works of Polya and Miller, Galanter, and Pribram. Whereas the requirement of the problem is known and formulated from the very beginning, the unknown quantity is determined step by step in the course of the solving process. Brushlinskii also noted that in the heuristic approach, thinking appears as a blind choice of alternatives and not as an oriented and selective course. In this respect, it is a step backward in comparison with Wertheimer's analysis of productive thinking.

Brushlinskii objected to the tendency to emphasize the identity of the *results* obtained by man and machine in solving the same problem but to admit that there is a difference between the processes involved in the two instances. First, this is a matter of principle: the separation of result from process is metaphysics. This, he contended, amounts to a negation of the process itself. Second, the identification of the product of the machine with that of human thinking implies the reduction of the result of a psychic process to its external, formal-symbolic aspect. The development of the thinking ability, the role of the individual's needs and of the type of personality are ignored.

Finally, Brushlinskii raised the question of the relation between the general theory of problem-solving, or heuristics (the term was introduced by Dunker in 1935) and the psychology of thinking. He is opposed to both the idea that heuristics is an independent field, and even more, that it replaces the psychology of thinking, as well as to the suggestion that it comprises part of the latter, dealing specifically with productive thinking. As to the first possibility, Brushlinskii rejected it on the ground that heuristics is little more than a set of methods and procedures for problem-solving, which are not essentially different from those used in previous studies. As a matter of fact, its definition as any method or procedure which helps to heighten the efficiency of a problem-solving system, or as a method of transforming a problem to bring it closer to the solution are purely pragmatic. With regard to the second possibility, Brushlinskii disagreed with the separation of productive and reproductive thinking, by the early associationists and the Würzburg school. To him, any process of thinking results in something new, no matter whether this is a "discovery" for oneself. Furthermore, any thinking process is based on acquired knowledge. The pure reproduction of knowledge or of previously used methods is not yet thinking.

A different stand was taken by Tikhomirov and his colleagues (1964, 1965a,b, 1966a,b, 1967, 1969a,b, 1970). These authors, too, pointed at the limitations of Newell, Shaw and Simon's analysis of thinking at the level of elementary processes of manipulation of symbols. They disagreed with the thesis that the complex processes of thinking can be reduced to manipulation of symbols. In their view, only the solving of problems by the machine can be reduced to relations between symbols or signs which are the "units" of this process. The major factor in problem-solving in man is the meaning which physical objects assume in a concrete situation. *"The operations on meanings are the most important characteristic of human thinking"* (1967, p. 39). "Meaning" is a variable which can be controlled experimentally, giving the direction of man's searching activity.

Tikhomirov and Terekhov admitted, however, that human thinking *can* be described as a manipulation of symbols. Thus, the term "heuristics" defined by Newell, Shaw, and Simon as any principle or device which contributes to the reduction of the number of trials in solving a problem can be applied to both machine and man. But to analyze thinking only in these terms is to omit its specifically human nature. They concluded that ". . . in analyzing the relation between man's thinking and the work of a computer, *it is necessary to distinguish between heuristics common to man and machine, and specifically human heuristics"* (p. 40). With specific reference to chess, this statement implies that Newell and his associates' definition of a plan as a group of problems in which the main problem is broken down in order to shorten the search of the solution is applicable to man, but this is by far not enough. Man's plan in a game situation includes the prognostication of the partner's moves. The very structure of the plan depends on the evaluation of the possible outcomes. The purpose of future studies should be to reveal specifically human heuristics and the possibility of their use in programming, instead of describing thinking in terms of the computer's work. This is also maintained regarding the control systems studied in engineering psychology which tend to substitute the psychological analysis of thinking by a description of the ways in which a certain problem would be solved by a computer.

Finally, in the view of Pushkin (1965a,b, 1967, 1969a,b), from the Psychological Institute of the Academy of Pedagogy of the USSR, the programming principles formulated by Newell represent only a partial understanding of the psychology of thinking. To him, the mathematical procedures, or heuristics, used for the reduction of the number of trials do not represent a theory of the *process* of human problem-solving. Pushkin pointed out the lack of difference on principle between heuristic and logarithmic programs and considered that the term "heuristics" was inappropriate for the procedures used to reduce the number of alternatives. He acknowledged, however, that the heuristic programming tackled certain relevant problems of the psychology of thinking and that the further development of the psychology of productive thinking as well as an adequate description of human intellectual activity are contingent upon the advance of these studies.

A few final words about programmed teaching, which is one of the most controversial issues regarding the practical applications of cybernetics (Kalmykova and Lipkina, 1965; Leontev and Galperin, 1964; Landa, 1962, 1966, 1969; Alekseev, 1963; Rozenberg, 1965; Shapiro, 1965; Sidelkovskii, 1964; Ladanov, 1964; Moskaeva, 1965; Itelson, 1963, 1965; Matyushkin, 1971). Objections have been raised to the introduction of the algorithm method in school in that it is likely to lead to a mechanistic form of thinking. It has been said that mathematical formulae are not suitable for pedagogical purposes. The advocates of programmed teaching argue that creative, imaginative thinking is not the opposite of "mechanical" thinking. The algorithm method does not reduce the student's initiative and does not inhibit the creative search for the solution of problems. On the contrary, they argue, when students are well trained in using algorithmic procedures, their attention is freed to look for original solutions. With regard to the application of formal logic, these authors say that as a matter of fact, one cannot speak about any such method as "pure" formal logic since the formalization of logic is only a means of explaining specific topics in a concise way. The degree of formalization depends on the nature of the material. Teaching requires rather an elementary formal logic. These writers, especially Landa, caution about the unlimited use of the algorithmic method. Landa admitted that there is no clear-cut answer to the question as to whether programmed teaching is better than conventional teaching methods. The choice of teaching methods is contingent upon the aims of teaching, on the programmer's attitude toward the process of acquiring knowledge and skills and the theoretical issues underlying the programming.

5

Memory

The processes of memory have been intensively investigated
by Soviet psychologists. When one considers the tremendous
emphasis placed on intellectual mental ability, it is not surprising that this subject holds so important a place in Russian
psychology. The main concern of most work in this field involves the dynamics representing the subject's activity during
the process of remembering, which has become a favorite
theme of Russian students. One of the major and often repeated objections leveled at the Western investigators of
memory has been precisely the fact that memory was not
approached from the perspective of the subject's activity, in
particular, practical activity. Western students, according to
the Russians, thus tended to isolate the objects which have to
be memorized from the actual activity which is directed towards a certain goal.

What follows is a brief survey of some of the propositions
and experimental studies, since Smirnov and Zinchenko's
(1969) comprehensive account in English covers most of the
relevant work. Attention is given to those studies which have
attempted to understand the physiological foundations of

memory, a topic not included in the above-mentioned presentation.

Blonskii is regarded as the first Russian author to advance a more or less comprehensive theory of memory. He raised a problem which has been the concern of all Russian students of memory: the relationship between associative-mechanical and logical memory. Blonskii was said to have failed in his attempt to solve the problem of transition from inferior to higher forms of memory. This was attributed to the fact that Blonskii reduced motor memory to automatic movements which were detached from mental images. He considered that only motor memory can be explained by the theory of the conditioned reflex.

The researches of the Vygotskii-Leontev school are currently regarded as having contributed much to advance the knowledge about the relationship between memory and activity. Vygotskii (1926) defined memory as an activity consisting of the retrieval of past experience in current behavior. Leontev developed this concept further in his 1931 monograph. Despite its being criticized (Zinchenko, 1961), Leontev's theory is regarded as an important step towards a better understanding of the structure of memory, in particular of the relations between involuntary and voluntary recall. Its impact is felt in the work of Smirnov, the Director of the Moscow Institute of Psychology, and Zinchenko, who was until his death in 1969 the Chairman of the Department of Psychology at Kharkov University, both of whom became the most authoritative writers in this field.

CRITICISM OF CLASSICAL THEORY

Zinchenko has critically reviewed most of the major theories on memory. In his view, Ribot, Ebbinghaus, Hartley, Priestley and Baine oversimplified the mechanism of association and distorted the psychological aspects of memory.

Memory was not regarded as an activity of the subject oriented toward objects or their images, but as a mechanical
product of associations. The impingement of objects on the
sense organs was considered sufficient for an imprint on the
memory to be formed. On the other hand, Zinchenko recognized that the association school brought many new important
facts to the subject. Valuable concepts regarding the general
role played by different associations in mental processing have
been formulated. The plasticity of the brain has been greatly
emphasized, a property which has been viewed as basic in
order to allow for the formation, storage, and activation of the
traces of previous stimulations.

Familiar with the criticism of the Gestalt theory by Western authors such as Postman, for example, Zinchenko felt that
the proponents of Gestalt theory have criticized the associationists only in one aspect, namely the limitation of the study
of memory to the formation of peripheral connections. Gestalt
theory maintained that the formation of connections between
objects could not be explained on the basis of their contiguity
alone. By emphasizing, however, the universality of the whole,
regarding it as an explanatory principle, Gestalt theory
really clarified nothing, and in fact introduced a somewhat
mystical point of view. Synthesis was divorced from analysis,
the role of the latter being very much underestimated. In addition, overlooking the role of the subject's activity in memory
was regarded by Zinchenko as a further shortcoming of Gestalt theory. The structure and form of the material to be
memorized plays an important part in the memory process
and it is to the credit of the Gestalt school to have pointed
this out. However, this is not the determining factor but only
one of the properties of memory. While maintaining that the
efficiency of memory is dependent upon the organization of
the material, the Gestalt theory somewhat confused memory
with perception, and in so doing disregarded the specific laws
of the mnemonic processes. Furthermore, Gestalt theory did

not attempt to explain the differences between voluntary and involuntary memory.

Zinchenko also criticized other Western trends in the study of memory. On the one hand, he objected to the behaviorist school for ignoring the role of consciousness in memory and for reducing the study of memory solely to that of involuntary memory. On the other hand, propositions emerging from a phenomenological position were lauded for emphasizing the synthesizing role of consciousness in memory but attacked for failing to raise the specific problem of memory because of their idealistic approach to the active nature of consciousness. The role of the subject's "intention" is said to have been correctly stressed; this was not, however, regarded as a factor which regulated the process of memory, as compared to a situation in which intention is lacking. This inconsistent characterization of the factor "intention" prevented a lucid description of the distinctive features of voluntary and involuntary memory. While the concept of association was maintained, its application was restricted and, as a result, two concepts of memory were arrived at: an associative and a meaningful memory, this dichotomy having a negative role in the subsequent history of the study of memory.

Investigations into Involuntary Memory

The objectives of Russian research into both involuntary and voluntary memory have been three-fold: (1) an analysis of the process of memory when the material involved in a certain activity is remembered; (2) an investigation of the relationship between memory and the tools used in a certain activity; (3) the study of the relationship between memory and the subject's motivation. In most of these researches, certainly the major ones, both involuntary and voluntary memory have been regarded as being dependent mainly on the above factors. Whereas voluntary memory implies that the ultimate goal of the subject is to understand the material concerned, involuntary memory is directly linked to the remembering of the material. This variation in emphasis brings about significant differences between the two kinds of memory particularly with regard to the tasks to be performed, the subject's motivation, and the mechanisms of the recall.

Soviet students of memory hold the view that the relationship between the subject and the material to be memorized is paramount in conditioning the final involuntary imprint of the image of the object concerned. Involuntary memory is linked to the place held by the object in the subject's activity; i.e., whether it is linked to the main purpose of the action or whether it is linked to the conditions determining the ultimate performance. Furthermore, the influence of the subject's motivation on the involuntary memory has been pointed out. Zinchenko carried out an experiment aimed at observing the manner in which the same material is memorized under two different sets of circumstances: when memory is the ultimate objective of the action undertaken, and when memory is the result of the incidental impingement of the object upon the sense organs. Illustrations of various objects were depicted on 15 pieces of cardboard; in the right-hand corner of each piece of cardboard a two-digit number was recorded. One group of subjects was asked to classify the picture objects according to the numbers of the cardboard pieces. The second group of subjects was requested to arrange in sequence the cardboard pieces on the basis of their numbers. In neither instance were the subjects asked to memorize the pictured objects, but upon completion of the test, they were requested to describe and list the items. It was observed that those subjects who classified the material recalled 13.2 per cent of the pictured objects but only 7 percent of the numbers. The second group recalled 10.2 per cent of the numbers and .3 per cent of the pictures. Zinchenko concluded that the mere impingement of an object on the sense organ is not sufficient for its memorization. Even the simpler forms of memory are contingent upon the subject's activity.

Similar experiments were done by Rozanova (1959), an associate of Leontev. She suggested that under certain conditions, memorization can occur at an elementary level, that is to say, without any form of activity of the subject oriented toward a certain goal. This was put to the test in the following experiment. Various differently colored pieces of cardboard depicting several objects were presented to the subjects who were requested to name the objects and to classify them in terms of their distribution on the pieces of cardboard. It was found that the subjects remembered not only the objects and their properties, but also the position of the pieces of cardboard on the board. They also remembered the colors of the objects. Rozanova interpreted these findings as showing an elementary level of subject-object interaction in memory. She performed additional experiments which showed that unlike the relevant features of an object that were memorized, secondary details could not be reproduced. These were retrieved once the name of the object and its major features were recalled. Rozanova considered that the remembering of these secondary features could be attributed to the formation of connections at the level of the first signal system.

An instructive experiment on the functioning of latent memory was done by Idashkin (1959). He described four stages in the subject's orientation toward the material he is to memorize. The purpose of this orientation is to select the elements necessary for the action to be undertaken. This is achieved in two phases: (1) a preliminary orientation phase whereby the essential elements of the objects concerned are distinguished from the nonessential; (2) exclusive orientation towards these essential elements. Thus the irrelevant features of the object are analyzed superficially and only during the initial phase of orientation. This is why the memorization of these features is deficient.

The difference in memorization of the different features of objects involved in an activity has convincingly been illustrated by A. A. Smirnov (1948) and Leontev and Rozanova (1951). Smirnov presented several sentences to the subjects. They were requested to name the grammatical rule to one or several words of a sentence (e.g., the tense of the verbs). The subjects were then requested to apply these rules to an equal number of sentences composed by themselves. It was observed that they remembered three times as many sentences from the latter group. The explanation for this expected result was, according to Smirnov, that the sentences proposed by the experimenter served only as a means for the attainment of the goal, in this case establishing the grammatical rule, whereas the composition of the other sentences by the subjects themselves constituted the major purpose of the action itself.

Finally, Leontev and Rozanova examined the processes underlying the formation and the elicitation of associative connections which, in their view, determine involuntary memory. Subjects were presented with 16 circles of cardboard, each containing a number of words. Three experiments were performed. In the first, the subjects were to remove from the group of cards, certain cards chosen by the experimenter. In the second, they had to remove all the cards containing words beginning with the letter S. In the final experiment, the subjects had to determine which letter of the alphabet most words on the cards began with. After 15 minutes had elapsed, at the end of each experiment, the subjects were asked the following questions: what were the initial letters of all the words?; which words were written on the removed cards?; which words began with the letter S?; which words began with other letters? The subjects participating in the first experiment were unable to answer any of these questions, while the subjects in the second experiment were only able to indicate the former position of the cards they had removed. In the third experiment, which was to clarify the different results obtained in the first two experiments, all the subjects recalled the initial letters of the words. The authors' conclusion, based also on results obtained from other experiments, was that depending on the content of the performed action, the elements of the situation are recalled selectively. The subjects remember not only those elements that are directly linked to the result of their action but also other elements which have a bearing on the result. Four types were described as being elaborated during such experiments: (1) connections concerned with stimuli arising as the result of the action; (2) connections concerned with stimuli which orient the action towards attaining the result; (3) connections concerned with stimuli constituting the conditions of attaining the goal; (4) connections concerned with the basic stimuli leading towards an orientation on the subject matter and not towards the actual content of the subject's action.

Zinchenko critically reviewed the work done by Western investigators on involuntary memory. His discussion was mainly concerned with the theories about latent learning, particular attention being given to two conflicting theories: the theory of reinforcement and the theory of sign learning. In Zinchenko's view, whereas the former theory entirely neglected the role of cognitive orientation, the latter, while emphasizing the mental state of the subject, completely overlooked the role played by the process of reinforcement. He contended, furthermore, that both theories tended to neglect the dynamics of the nervous processes. The proponents of reinforcement theory have limited the role of this factor to reward and punishment. The cognitive theory, on the other hand, correctly stressed the importance of the subject's orientation, but because of its concept of a purposeful behavior which is adequate from its very inception, this theory oversimplified the problem of memory.

Zinchenko further criticized the tendency to identify incidental memory with latent learning. To him, latent memory

constitutes a particular type of involuntary memory characterized by difficulties in reproduction and occurring under circumstances where unfavorable conditions underlie the motivation and perception. Latent memory occurs more frequently
under conditions of incidental memorization; the memorized
material does not enter the content of the subject's activity.
Zinchenko pointed out, however, that not all incidental memorization is latent, since the recall of auxiliary material can
often result from a motivated act instigated by some other
cause. On the other hand, he took it for granted that the mo-
tivating conditions could be so unfavorable that all the material belonging to the content of the action is only latently
remembered. For the same reason, Zinchenko assumed that
latent memory is possible even within the framework of voluntary memory. These instances, however, are by far the less
frequent.

Zinchenko concluded his review of Western works on involuntary memory by admitting that these studies have contributed a great deal of valuable factual knowledge to the
understanding of the dependence of the efficiency of involuntary memory upon various kinds of orientation, motivation, so-
called instrumental reactions, etc. He felt that this was of
considerable empirical value; all factors involved appear as an
independent entities present in varying number of combinations. The concept of involuntary memory was not defined
because it was always identified with either voluntary
memory—both being functions of orientation—or with latent
memory. Finally, Zinchenko was critical of the lack of genetic
research in the field of memory, for he regarded such an
investigation as a prerequisite to a better understanding of the
nature of involuntary memory.

RESEARCHES ON VOLUNTARY MEMORY

As has been previously stated, Soviet psychologists regard

voluntary memory as a particular type of activity with specific aims, motives and methods. Investigations have been performed which sought to examine the processes whereby various aims interfere with this activity. The role played by the subject's motivation as well as the effect of different methods have also been investigated. To begin with, Smirnov studied the influence of various mnemonic aims on the process of remembering. He observed that an individual who was required to reproduce a text as accurately as possible was oriented towards understanding the content of various parts of the text. Words and even whole sentences were pronounced either aloud, softly, or in silent speech representing different stages of assimilation of the text. When a subject was required to reproduce a text as completely as possible, he was concentrated on the meaning of the whole text and in particular on the relationship between its separate parts. Unlike the first instance, less attention was paid to the content of the different parts. A reduction in the speed at which the text was read facilitated the attainment of the latter objective. Finally, when subjects were requested to reproduce the complete text and at the same time pay attention to the sequence of the constituent parts, the tendency was to subdivide the text into its parts giving each a title, in order to keep their sequence in mind. It thus appeared that the goal of the mnemonic activity interfered not only with its results but also with the nature of the activity itself.

Research on the influence of mnemonic activity on its actual performance constitutes a major topic for the Russian students of memory, much of this work being linked to the basic genetic approach of this school. Seeking to understand how different intellectual procedures are utilized for the purpose of remembering various types of material, Smirnov performed the following experiment on children of the second, third and fourth grades. The children were requested to memorize two texts which differed significantly: one was logically and clearly constructed and enabled the content to be subdivided into different themes, while the other had very little logical organization, the subject matter being presented in a rather haphazard manner. Smirnov noted that pupils of the second grade were entirely unable to organize logically the content of either text. Only some of the older pupils were able to do this. Generally speaking, the subjects did not make any effort to organize the text logically. While aware of the difference between them, they had no appreciation of the greater degree of difficulty required by the second text. Although the subjects were able to logically divide the text into sections when required to do so, they did not make use of this procedure as a mnemonic method.

Others experiments on adults allowed Smirnov to conclude that thinking plays a three-fold role in memory. First, thinking is manifest in the division of the material according to the meaning of its parts. Two forms of organization were described: involuntary-pictorial and logical-descriptive. The former indicates an organization which is not an independent and conscious activity. This approximates the behavior of the pupils just described. The voluntary-descriptive organization is systematic. Relevant headlines and questions are formulated. On most occasions this method is not utilized when the text is reproduced and its details are frequently forgotten. Smirnov explains this by indicating that the choice of supportive factors is associated with an understanding of the content of the text. The subject has to reproduce the latter and as such the text is memorized better than the various points of the prepared plan.

The second aspect of the thinking-memory relationship refers to the association made by the subject between the material to be reproduced and his previous knowledge. This occurs particularly for difficult material which must be reproduced completely, accurately and thoroughly.

The relationship between cognitive activity and memory

was one of Zinchenko's main interests. It was his contention that tasks which involve the classification of objects, the organization of the material to be memorized according to a plan, and the selection of points of reference necessary for recall, could be grouped together under the heading of cognitive activity. Zinchenko was firmly convinced that without the full development of these intellectual activities, mnemonic processes cannot take place. Three stages of the relationship between these activities and memory were described. In the first stage, the intellectual activity is not employed as a means of attaining the mnemonic goal. This fact became apparent in experiments with five-year-olds. The children were given 15 pieces of cardboard on which different objects were drawn. They were asked to classify the objects into four groups: kitchen, garden, nursery, yard. The pieces of cardboard had to be arranged on four places on a table. Twelve of the 15 pieces could readily be classified in the four groups. It was noted that at this age, the classification had to be organized in detail by the experimenter. The children were unable to skip over intermediary stages. Six-year-olds exhibited characteristics of the second stage. The classification of objects already appeared as an independent action; they were arranged in the four groups and clear relations were established between them. However, much time was spent over the selection and classification of each piece of cardboard. This indicated that the subjects' activity was still somewhat divided and uncertain.

The final stage of the relationship between the intellectual activity and memory manifests at a time when the principle of classification can also be applied to other objects and when the action becomes more and more concentrated. The use of the cognitive activity for memory begins at the second stage only. The formation of mnemonic actions thus lags behind that of the cognitive activity by one stage. This is explained by the subject's intense concentration on the assimilation of the cognitive action. The latter may be employed to further the mnemonic goal only at the stage when it is no longer dependent on the manipulation of external objects. Mnemonic actions may be regarded as more complex than the cognitive ones. This is attributed to their structure which requires that a cognitive orientation be subordinate to the mnemonic orientation so that the cognitive action attains a certain level of development. When he is oriented towards knowing the objects, he attempts to reveal their properties and the relationships among them. This differs from the mnemonic action. The cognitive orientation can coincide with the mnemonic orientation when it is brief, somewhat automatized. It then becomes subordinate to the mnemonic goal.

Zinchenko further illustrated his distinction between the cognitive and mnemonic stages in experiments on ninth grade pupils. These subjects were requested to present two plans, one based on a cognitive approach and the second based on a mnemonic approach. The first plan was of a general nature, the objective being to grasp the logical structure of the text; the formulations were relatively free from the actual wording of the text. The mnemonic approach entailed the formulation of a detailed plan whose wording approximated the given very closely. Zinchenko advised that in order to put across new knowledge, the cognitive approach should be encouraged, since it leads to a better understanding of the academic subject. On the other hand, the mnemonic approach directs the pupils' effort towards memorizing the material instead of gaining an appreciation of its actual meaning. This is only recommended as part of the teaching process when the material to be presented is simple, and as such, the mnemonic act can take place simultaneously with that of the cognitive action.

Experiments carried out by Istomina (1953) under the guidance of Leontev provided a good illustration of how the Russian authors view the association between the cognitive and mnemonic approaches. The experiments were to examine the role played by motivation in the process of memory. The subjects were preschool children between three and seven years of age. In one of the experiments, which was performed under usual laboratory conditions, the children were required to memorize five words read to them. In another experiment carried out in a play situation the children were required to buy from a shop five objects which previously had been indicated to them during the course of their play in the kindergarten. It was noted that memory was far better in the play situation than under laboratory conditions. Istomina maintained that this was due to the different motivation operating in each case. When the children were simply requested to memorize several words, they accepted the task since they wished to communicate with the experimenter. In the play situation, a good memorization signified the possibility of performing the subsequent activity. This circumstance favored the transformation of the involuntary memory into voluntary memory which was an expression of the need that the children felt in order to memorize. Three levels of memory achievement became apparent during the play situation. The first level was found to predominate in the youngest children between three and four years of age. It was not the objective of these children, who enjoyed the play situation, to memorize; thus they made little effort to remember the experimenter's instruction. At the second level, the four to five year olds, while already wanting to memorize, were unable to attain this objective since they lacked the mnemonic means. The five to seven year olds, particularly the children of six and older, attained the highest level of memory. They endeavored to remember the content of the instruction and frequently requested that the experimenter repeat the directions.

In summary, it appears that Soviet writers, for the purposes of emphasizing the genetic sequence of inferior and superior forms of memory, generally advocate the division of memory into involuntary and voluntary. Involuntary memory is postulated as representing a genetic stage in the evolution of the mnemonic process. The development of involuntary memory is an absolute prerequisite for the formation and functioning of a voluntary memory. The developmental transition from one form of memory to the other and the relationships between them, are dependent upon the subject's specific activity being associated with its objectives and the means by which it is carried out. For this reason, Soviet authors do not regard involuntary memory as a process opposed to voluntary memory. It is not purely passive and lacking any logical character. Involuntary memory can be logical provided it is based on some form of cognitive activity.

THE PHYSIOLOGICAL MECHANISMS OF MEMORY

Expectedly, the neuronal basis of memory has in Soviet publications most frequently been attributed to the conditioned-reflex processes. Studies of the processes of remembering and forgetting have been particularly concerned with the application of Pavlovian theory. At least on certain occasions there was a tendency toward oversimplification. Zankov (1951a,b), for instance, made a distinction between two aspects of memory, closely related to each other; the psychical imprint of the object itself, and the imprint of the connection between two objects, or between an object and an activity. As an illustration of his position, Zankov referred to the pupil who learns the name of an island and studies its outline on a map. In this way, the child establishes a connection between a name and a representation. Three queries are raised by Zankov in this regard. (1) In what way is the outline of the island impressed on the child's psyche? (2) What is the mechanism by which the name of the island is impressed on the child's psyche? (3) What allows the child's memory to retain the connection between the image and the name of the island?

Zankov regarded the last question as relatively simple: a

contiguous connection is established between the image and its name. The irradiation of the process of excitation occurring in the corresponding groups of cortical cells and its subsequent concentration by a process of inhibition was thought to be the general mechanism underlying such a connection. With regard to the impression of the object itself, Zankov considered the retention of the trace of the excitation, after the cessation of the stimulation, as the responsible factor. This trace is maintained only when the state of excitation is coincident with the presence of an active state in a group of cells, thereby forming a temporary connection. If this does not take place, the excitation spreads over the entire cortex. Zankov, in conforming to the practice of most Russian authors at that time, repeatedly made references to the theory of localization of psychical processes, particularly to Pavlov's proposition that there is no mnestic center, to the concept of a dynamic stereotype and, of course, to the interaction between the two signal systems.

Pavlov's theory of inhibition was given as an explanation for the frequently observed fact that immediate reproduction of learned material is far less complete than subsequent and latter reproductions. Krasilshchikova (1956) studied this aspect of memory, asking a number of subjects to memorize 12 pairs of words; each pair contained one Russian and one German word. She noticed that the reproduction of the words in the middle of the series was far less accurate than the reproduction of the pairs at the extremities. This frequently observed fact was more obvious upon the immediate reproduction of the words. Krasilshchikova regarded the series of words as a complex of successive stimuli, explaining her findings on the basis of the different forms of inhibition described by Pavlov. She assumed that each cortical point corresponding to an element of the verbal series was subjected to a negative induction from the other elements. The words situated at the middle of the series were subjected to a two-fold influence from both ends of the series. It was also thought that a so-called trace inhibition was in operation here since each word was not reproduced immediately upon being heard but only after the whole series had been presented. These inhibitory processes are stronger at the middle of the series and are more manifest at the immediate recall. At a later stage, the middle components are freed from inhibition. This effect was also partially ascribed to the dominant role played by the second signal system during the later recall of the series, the latter being less dependent on the "pictorial" aspect of the material. The ability to persistently retain the learned material subsequent to its initial reproduction has been explained on the basis of a process of negative induction. Krasilshchikova saw this as resulting from a conflict between superimposed "functional structures." The first structure which corresponds to the initial reproduction of the material, with its errors, is inhibited by the subsequent, more thorough understanding of the material. But the effect of this negative induction gradually weakens, particularly if there are no repetitions of the material, and the original formulations recur.

Soviet authors naturally have discussed Ebbinghaus' forgetting curve. Their criticism of this concept stems from the view that memory is basically a physiological process embedded in and dependent on the individual's activity. They maintain that the process of forgetting is not primarily a function of the time elapsed subsequent to the period of learning, but rather is dependent on the nature and the amount of the learned material. Sokolov (1954) felt that Ebbinghaus' curve expresses only one of the many possible ways of forgetting and thus is applicable only to a certain amount of the learned material. The main fault of Ebbinghaus' work was said to lie not so much in the artificiality of the experimental conditions, as in his attempt to generalize his results as if they constituted universal laws of memory. His results appeared to be contradictory especially in the case of meaningless material. Both the nature of the material and its amount were overlooked and consequently, despite the appropriate control of laboratory conditions, Ebbinghaus failed to establish an association between the recall of the material and the time that had elapsed since its learning.

Sokolov studied the effect of increasing the amount of learned material on its recall. In one experiment subjects were asked to memorize series of 13, 13 × 4, and 13 × 8 meaningless syllables, whereas in another experiment, series of 10, 20, and 40 paired words were memorized. The material was presented at intervals of 20 minutes, one hour, eight hours, one day and eight days subsequent to the initial occasion. Of course, it was observed that the meaningful material was retained to a far greater extent than the meaningless material. When the amount was increased, however, the forgetting curve of the meaningful material approximated that of the meaningless material. Sokolov concluded that any increase in the amount of meaningful material, above a certain limit, tends to inhibit the formation of connections within the material and thus reduces the capacity to recall it. Conversely, a reduction of the quantity of meaningless material resulted in a forgetting curve which approximated that for the meaningful material. The retroactive inhibition was regarded by Sokolov as a particular case of the negative influence that the quantity of learned material has on memory.

The role of the amount of learned material on memory was also studied by Shardakov. School children from the first to ninth grades were instructed to memorize various passages made up of descriptions, definitions, explanations, etc., from the school texts in biology, geography, literature, history, mathematics and physics. The children were interrogated on the material they had learned after various intervals of time, ranging from one day to six months. It was observed—in accordance with Ebbinghaus' results—that forgetting was greater during the initial days after learning than for the later periods. Significant differences, however, were observed for the different parts of the material. Thus, after six months, 60 per cent of the main points in the passages memorized were remembered, whereas the complete reproduction of the text was possible only in 21.55 per cent of the cases. Shardakov reported, however, on an increased recall of logical entities with the passage of time. Thus, 27 per cent of these were remembered on the first day, whereas about 52 per cent were remembered after two months.

Finally, Elkin (1956) attempted to explain the process of forgetting in terms of Pavlovian theory and equated forgetting with inhibition. He assumed that there are two forms of forgetting, unconditioned and conditioned, the latter being a result of the nonreinforcement of the learned material. Elkin performed an experiment in which the subjects were requested to memorize 10 words presented in a certain sequence. The second word was more difficult than the others and its recall proved, indeed, to be more difficult. Subsequently another series of words was presented. On this occasion, all the words were of equal difficulty. The recall of the second word, however, was more difficult than of the others.

We shall turn now to utterly different attempts to account for the biological foundations of memory, in line with the recent findings in both neurophysiology and biochemistry. It will be noted that in this field, too, there are Soviet authors who departed from the traditional Pavlovian position.

Beritov (Beritashvili, 1968, 1969a; Beritov, 1969) has extensively studied the physiological bases of memory. This study represents a significant part of his theory of a psychonervous activity of animals. As a matter of fact, one notices a certain redundancy in Beritov's prolific writings, and much of his argument regarding this topic is similar to his discussion of the physiological foundations of the animal behavior guided by representations.

Beritov distinguished three types of memory in vertebrates:

image, emotional and conditioned-reflex memory. Image memory, which seems to have held the most significant place in Beritov's studies, consists of the recall of perceived objects, notably food objects, thereby reproducing its image and its location. This kind of memory is based on the perception of a part of the object, or of the situation in which it was fully perceived in the past. It is regarded as a short-term memory if it lasts only several hours. This happens when food is perceived only visually without being tasted and smelled. The olfactory memory is longer, while the auditory memory is much shorter than the visual memory; the vestibular memory is the shortest. Long-term memory implies that the image of the food and its location has been maintained several days. This is possible when the visual perception of the food is accompanied by its taste and smell.

The image memory of mammals is exclusively a neocortical function which is lost after the removal of the cortex. Short-term visual memory is related to the secondary visual area. Similarly, the auditory memory is related to the secondary auditory area. The prefrontal proreal gyri and the inferior temporal zones play a major role in short-term memory unrelated to any specific sensory modality. The bilateral removal of the proreal gyri lead to a temporary disturbance of the mnestic function of both associative and inferior temporal zones, because of their connections with the premotor and motor-cortical areas, as well as with the subcortical somato-vegetative structures. The subcortical structures—nucleus caudatus, the reticular formation, the lemniscal system and the cerebellum—are also ascribed a role in memory. Beritov concluded that the image of perceived objects is not coded in any particular area of the whole system of structures responsible for memory, since the removal of none of them results in a total loss of memory. This effect is obtained only after the removal of all the associative pyramidal neurons of the neocortex.

Beritov assumed that the retention in memory of the image of food and of its location is dependent upon molecular and submolecular changes of the protein in the activated postsynaptic regions. A special active protein is supposedly formed with participation of a ribonucleic acid, that is, intermediary and ribosomal RNA. This protein facilitates the transmission of excitation in the postsynaptic membrane. When the food is perceived only visually, the action of this protein may last only several hours. When taste and smell are also involved, the perception of food is accompanied by an emotional excitation. In this instance, a stable protein is formed in the postsynaptic regions of the nervous circuits involved in memory, which remains active for days and weeks. Hence, Beritov hypothesized that in each activated pyramidal associative cell there appears an RNA-intermediary and active protein which are not specific for each new object. He thus took issue with Hydén's (1965) theory that on the perception of each new object there are specific changes in the ionic equilibrium in the cytoplasm leading to a specific ribosomal RNA in the nucleus of the nerve cells. Beritov assumed that the repeated excitation of the nervous circuits cannot be merely the result of the activation of a specific protein formed upon the first stimulation of the neural circuits. Furthermore, he disagreed with the assumption that only a given modulation of frequencies of electrical discharges, produced by the perception of a certain object, results in the activation of this specific protein. Beritov referred to the current view in neurophysiology that the excitation of a nerve cell and its axon is an effect of electrical currents evoked by localized postsynaptic potentials. If the first stimulation of pyramidal cells takes place without participation of the specific RNA and the specific protein produced by it, we may expect that repeated stimulations take place in the same way. Finally, Beritov pointed out that insofar as the neural circuit linked to a certain image of an object can be activated even by the perception of a part of that object, or merely of its surroundings, the modulation of electrical discharges in the associative neurons must be quite different.

Emotional memory is defined by Beritov as the reproduction of a certain emotional state on the recurrence of the circumstances in which that state appeared originally. This kind of memory was studied particularly with regard to fear. According to Beritov, the mechanism of fear memory consists of the temporary connections between the sensory elements of the neocortex responsible for the preception of objects, and the "mechanism of sensory integration of fear" localized in the archipaleocortex. Both the objective and subjective manifestations of these connections are controlled by the "psychoneuronal complex" underlying the image of the location of the damaging agent. Animals deprived of the neocortex also possess the memory of fear but here it is produced in the archipaleocortex by means of the connections between its elements, which perceive the situation in which the painful stimulation occurred, and the mechanism of fear. Such connections are also formed in intact animals but they are controlled by the cortical image of the object.

The conditioned-reflex memory depends on the development of synaptic mechanisms in relation to the reverberation of excitation in the associative neurons. The growth of available synapses and the appearance of new ones prolong the reverberation and the period of increased excitability thus facilitating the creation of a stable and active protein in the postsynaptic regions. The extent of these changes is contingent upon the frequency of reinforcement.

Sokolov's (1964, 1969a) theory of perception also has important implications for the explanation of the process of memory in a different way than the traditional Pavlovian position. He (1964) assumed that two types of memory are involved in the mechanism of the orienting reflex:

(a) an operative memory which retains the confirmed hypotheses; (b) a long-term memory consisting of the stable record of images. If the probability of occurrence of a given image is below a certain value, it is eliminated from the operative memory. Therefore, the account of the frequency of occurrence of different images is most important for the regulation of the structure of applied hypotheses. Moreover, new hypotheses, extracted from the long-term memory, can be introduced into the system of operatively verified hypotheses. The process of recognition also implies the retention of the probabilities of occurrence of the characteristics of each image [p. 265].

The reader is reminded that Sokolov hypothesized the presence of a special group of neurons whose function is to extrapolate, that is to predict the future values of signals on the basis of past experience. He assumed that it is precisely these neurons which have the capacity to retain the traces of stimulations. Sokolov felt that the task of afferent neurons to transmit current information could hardly have been carried out, were these neurons also to have had a mnestic function. Thus, Sokolov agreed with Hyden's molecular theory of memory, according to which the information reaching the brain is simultaneously retained in a series of neurons. This is why memory is basically undisturbed after the removal of large areas of the cortex. Sokolov, however, pointed out that Hyden's theory does not account for the mechanism of extrapolation which includes the active reproduction of stored information. It faces the problem of explaining the transfer of information retained at the molecular level, to specifically organized sequences of nervous impulses.

Soviet authors basically agree in their definition of operative memory as the momentary information necessary for the solution of current problems (Lomov, 1966). However, Lyapunov (1968), who has taken a different approach, offers a concept of operative memory which is worth citing at some length for its broad implications. He wrote:

By "operative memory" we mean that part of memory where the information is recorded in the course of life. Everything connected with man's learning and perception has to deal with the long-term conservation of the received information in the nervous system, i.e., with its operative memory. This memory has different sections. Thus, processes of memory were discovered (in the temporal lobe) which serve for the memory of vocabulary; other processes serve for the formation of words and sentences, while others are related to information about the external world, etc. . . . For us, the fact that operative memory is utilized by different areas of the central nervous system is of particular significance. A part of memory is used by "consciousness"; other parts are used by various regions of the central nervous system which regulate the physical functions of the organism necessary for maintaining its vital activity, or for fulfilling its biological functions within the limits of a population. Man's behavior under normal conditions is controlled primarily by consciousness. This fact often leads to a considerable underevaluation of the instances where many other functions of the nervous system, unrelated to consciousness, are also based on the information of the operative memory. In these cases, the operative memory is included in the functioning of the higher systems of control. Man's highly developed consciousness, and his being accustomed to behaving according to certain social demands, in many cases block this "direct" influence of the higher systems of control of his behavior.

These circumstances are expressed, on the one hand, in Freud's views, and, on the other, have led to the popular and, in our opinion, by far unjustified and extremely skeptical, one-sided evaluation of these views in our country. From the cybernetic point of view, man's sexual activity is controlled by the higher layers of the nervous system. The functioning of these layers is not immediately manifest in man's behavior. It can be blocked by consciousness. At the same time, if consciousness is eliminated, the manifestations of the levels of control, including the purely biological functions of the organism, becomes more direct. This is precisely the cybernetic interpretation of Freud's basic view underlying psychoanalysis. It must be added that in Freud's times, the current information theory was not elaborated yet and there was no precise language for the description of informational processes. Therefore, Freud presented his views in a language which now makes difficult the understanding of their essence. This is why there is frequently a negative attitude toward his work and even idle talk. It is also understandable why Freud paid particular attention to sleep and to states close to delusions. . . Hence, it seems to us that the basic ideas of psychoanalysis can reasonably be interpreted from the cybernetic position. It is very desirable to restate Freud's views in the contemporary scientific language [pp. 82–83].

MEMORY AND SLEEP-LEARNING

In recent years, some Soviet authors have embarked on the controversial study of "hypnopedia" or sleep-learning (Kulikov, 1964; Zukhar, 1965). In the view of Bliznichenko (1966), the head of the Laboratory of Experimental Phonetics at the A. A. Potebnya Institute of Linguistics of the Ukrainian Academy of Sciences, and a student of memory phenomena during sleep, the possibility of transmitting information during sleep and of consolidating it in memory has both theoretical and practical significance. He traced the history of these studies in Russia back to the 1930's, where several research institutes and clinics carried out investigations in this area. Studies are currently being conducted at the Laboratory of Experimental Phonetics and Psychology of Speech at the M. Torez State Pedagogical Institute for Foreign Languages #1 in Moscow, by Artemov, at the University of Leningrad, and other institutions.

In the contemporary studies, the information is transmitted during natural sleep. (It has been suggested that the term "hypnopedia" may be misleading since it suggests the use of hypnosis). Bliznichenko stated that the information is well retained and reproduced like that relayed to an awake subject. Moreover, he claimed that a larger amount of material, notably words in a foreign language, can be memorized. Thus, students who were usually able to learn 15–20 words a day, memorized in one night session of sleep-learning 35-50 words, and in some cases as many as 135 words. Bliznichenko felt that even this figure is not the limit of the mnemonic capacity under the given circumstances. The sleep-learning procedure was also applied to the teaching of mathematics, physics, geography, economics and radiotelegraphy. Soviet authors, however, strongly emphasized that this kind of learning is not meant to substitute for the didactic methods of teaching but rather to supplement them.

The procedures of teaching during sleep have been worked out in joint phonetic, acoustic, psychological and pedagogical studies. It was concluded that the intonation of the transmitted information plays the most significant role. The intonation has to be different from that of usual speech. Unlike the latter, which is closely linked to the logical structure of the communication and to its emotional side, the intonation of the hypnopedic speech has to be monotonous. The fundamental frequency is minimally varied. The secondary melodic (prosodic) characteristics of speech are also kept at a minimum. The following is an illustration of hypnopedic studies.

Zavalova and her colleagues (1964) experimented on subjects between the ages of 19 and 37, who possessed either an average or a heightened suggestibility. Before going to sleep, the subjects were told that they would hear certain words during their sleep and that they should not be disturbed by this. In addition, the more suggestible subjects were told that they should attempt to remember what they heard. Then, during their natural sleep, a series of 10 simple words, 10 more difficult and unfamiliar words—names of drugs—and a complex text were presented to them over a tape-recording. The electroencephalogram, electrocardiogram, GSR, respiration and articulogram were recorded throughout the experiment. The reading commenced one hour after the subjects had fallen asleep and lasted for two hours. After a four-hour interval the material was repeated, on this occasion lasting from 30 minutes to two hours before the subjects awakened. On awakening they were presented with the series of words that had been relayed to them during their sleep, together with two similar series of new words and were requested to recall all the words. A control group was presented with the same series of words. It was noticed that the subjects of the hypnopedic experiment remembered the words presented during their sleep at a rate far better than the other series of words. For the control group, there was no difference among the series of words. The recall of some of the experimental subjects was as much as twice as good as that of the control subjects. The same group of investigators (Zukhar, 1964) also conducted an experiment of collective hypnopedia.

Similar experiments were performed by Kulikov on young school children and mathematics students, and the reported results were even more impressive. While asleep, the children were read a story whereas the students were read a text about the typology of nervous activity. In this case, all the subjects, not only the more suggestible ones, were requested to perceive and memorize the texts read to them while asleep. The experiment showed that on awakening the subjects were able to reproduce the texts without the slightest awareness of the source of their knowledge. A number of subjects were under the impression that they had dreamt the content of the text. It was also observed that subjects who reported on dream images related to the content of the text had a distinctly superior recall of the text. Kulikov believes that the preparation of the subjects for the experiment with regard to the perception and memorization of the material is paramount. In this way, the subconscious processes operating during the course of sleep are oriented towards a specific activity. At the physiological level, these phenomena are explained on the basis of the Pavlovian concept of a "watching point," through which the subject is supposed to be in contact with the hypnotist while the remainder of the cortical activity is inhibited.

The experiments of sleep-learning have been rather extensively publicized in journals aimed at popularizing important scientific discoveries such as *Nauka i Zhizn (Science and Life)*. This popularization has aroused considerable criticism on the part of students of memory and linguists. (Hypnopedia is regarded by Bliznichenko as applied linguistics.) A. A. Leontev (1966) in particular ridiculed the claims of hypnopedists.

6

Emotions and Feelings

Though the subject will be returned to in the chapter on personality, the Soviet views on affective processes are presented under a separate heading. There are certain aspects to the study of feelings which do not fit into a general review of the Russian approach to personality.

Soviet psychologists have done strikingly little work in this field. As an illustration, the sole chapter in the two-volume *Psychological Science in the USSR* cites only 56 papers and books in the area of feelings as contrasted with the bibliographies of many hundreds of items for the chapters on thinking and learning. Soviet authors do in fact recognize their backwardness in the study of affective processes. Yakobson (1956), to whom further reference will be made as he is one of the most relevant writers in this area, frankly admitted: "Soviet psychology has so far done very little in the field of emotions and feelings. Apart from a few chapters in textbooks, nothing relevant was published" (p. 16). Yakobson's judgment is still applicable to current Soviet psychology, despite some publications which have been added since that time. Feofanov (1952) maintained that although Soviet authors emphasized the influence of emotions upon sensations, perceptions, thinking, imagination and will, they failed to indicate the extent of this influence and its parameters. He pointed out the need to integrate all the findings into a comprehensive theory which adheres to the methodological principles of Marxism-Leninism.

Yakobson, as a matter of fact, expressed his belief that Soviet psychology has in the Marxist methodology a solid basis for a fruitful investigation of affective processes. Moreover, he claimed that Marxism has uncovered many new and important aspects of human emotional life. Marxist ideology has imbued various findings with profound theoretical implications. The major proposition resulting from this approach is that human emotional experience represents a specific manner of reflection of objective reality. The characterization of feelings and emotions as a specific reflection of reality is, indeed, one of the main concerns of Russian writers. Much effort is made to differentiate this kind of reflection from intellectual reflection. Yet the attempt to link feelings with external objects and phenomena, on the one hand, and with the individual's needs, on the other, has resulted in little more than the formulation of vague propositions. There is no consistent theory based on the events of everyday life.

Rubinshtein compared the reflection of reality as it is manifested in perception with that expressed in emotions and feelings. While perception reflects the images of objects, feelings indicate changes in the internal state of the individual and his attitude toward the outside world. Both reflect reality. Rubinshtein (1959a) wrote that the source of emotions and feelings is the objective reality itself. Man is related emotionally to objects and phenomena of the real world and he experiences them differently according to their characteristics and to his objective relationship to them.

Emotions and feelings are considered by Russian authors to be related to man's basic attitudes towards the objects which he perceives and in connection to which he acts, towards other people and their actions, and towards himself and his own actions. Yakobson described three situations with regard to one's attitude towards his own feelings: (1) one tends to accept his feelings without any resistance; (2) one rejects his feelings for fear that they will become too strong; (3) one welcomes his feelings and allows them to develop in such a way as to prevent the occurrence of factors which would hinder the growth of the desired feeling. The following passage illustrates the rather simple approach to such a complex problem. Yakobson (1956) wrote:

> Man has varying attitudes towards his feelings; such variations result from the social evaluation of different feelings. These are not at the same level and constitute a certain hierarchy. Certain feelings are considered as superior and valuable and this tends to increase one's self-esteem. Such feelings are not only sanctioned but definitely approved by society. They conform to the ethical principles of that society . . . as well as to the ethical principles of the representatives of its progressive forces. Furthermore, these feelings are directly linked to one's ethical principles, ideals of behavior, etc. There are other feelings which, while not particularly approved by society, are not in contradiction with the ethical consciousness and are thus acceptable. Hence an individual does not fight against the occurrence of such a feeling. Finally, there are feelings which are regarded as inferior on the scale of moral values. Their occurrence is usually acutely experienced . . . the individual's moral consciousness is in conflict with his emotional experience. The intensity of such feelings tends to increase the feeling of contempt and this becomes the paramount experience which dominates the individual's behavior. The feeling of shame and dissatisfaction initiates a feeling of inferiority [pp. 133–134].

Following Pavlov's lead, Soviet authors classify the affective processes into emotions and feelings. Pavlov equated emotion with instinct as an expression of an unconditioned reflex with the cortical processes elaborated subsequently. On the other hand, he assumed that the nervous processes underlying feelings originate in the cortex. The different kinds of emotions were said to originate from a number of processes which include the various types of cortical inhibition, the effect of the substitution of familiar stimuli with unfamiliar ones, and the processes resulting from the transition from one nervous process to another. Accordingly, Yakobson discriminated emotions from feelings on the basis of the following criteria: an emotion is a reaction of varying degrees of intensity which manifests itself in vegetative symptoms as well as in facial and bodily expressions, whereas feelings are complex effects of man's attitude to various aspects of reality. Feelings are manifest in various emotional forms, coloring the individual's attitude towards situations. On the other hand, concrete emotional experiences are a necessary element for the occurrence and development of feelings. The latter always possess a particular content.

Rubinshtein has distinguished three levels of emotional reactivity. In the first place, there are elementary emotions of satisfaction and nonsatisfaction related directly to organic needs. These are the expression of a general organic state of the organism and are not related to a specific object. At the second level, feelings are related either to the perception of certain objects or to their utilization. In this instance, there is a kind of "objectivization" of feelings, which appear as a conscious experience. Intellectual, esthetic and moral feelings are generally considered to represent this level of reactivity. The third level represents generalized, abstract and stable feelings which are well integrated in the individual's outlook. These are the sentiments of the tragic, the sublime and the comic. Rubinshtein considered these levels as stages in the development of the emotional experience. The transition from one level to the other was related to the cognitive growth. The assimilation of human values, the acquaintance of the individual with various natural and social phenomena, were viewed as a prerequisite for the development of superior feelings. To Rubinshtein, the evolution of the forms of feelings indicates the changes of the relationships between the intellectual and affective processes. While primary emotions imply that the knowledge of reality is dominated by affect, the occurrence of specific feelings indicates that the knowledge of reality has become free of the affective process and itself begins to determine its content.

Soviet authors emphasize that feelings play an active role in the psychology of personality. Feelings are manifested in one's sensitivity and in one's capacity to react with emotions of a certain strength. These play an active role in the control of human behavior and should not be regarded as the mere shadow of an intellectual process, as an epiphenomenon. Thus, the feeling of pleasure serves as a conscious indication that a given need is in the process of being satisfied. This is not mere information but rather provides the necessary impetus towards the instigation of action having as its purpose the complete satisfaction of that need. Furthermore, feelings characterize the personality because of their close relationship to the individual's interests, inclinations and views. Hence the predominant feelings of an individual give an indication of the main psychological features of his personality.

The development of the individual's emotional life, as an expression of the growth of his personality, has been a main topic of Yakobson's writing. He described several kinds of changes in the emotional sphere. One kind consists of those changes resulting from the development of needs, inclinations and interests. One's emotional life becomes either richer or poorer, the sphere of reality towards which one reacts emotionally can become wider or more restricted, and new feelings may appear while others vanish. There are basic feelings related to the fundamental goals of life which tend to color one's entire emotional life in one way or another. These feelings influence other feelings which arise out of less significant circumstances. If the prevailing life conditions allow for the satisfaction of the basic needs, any secondary negative circum-

stances would evoke only a relatively weak emotional response. On the contrary, an unfavorable life situation producing frustration in the attainment of the primary objectives,
does not allow events of minor importance, though themselves
pleasant, to have any worthwhile effect on the emotional
state.

Both the content and characteristics of basic feelings change
at different stages of life. The particular content of these feelings at a certain stage, whether it be childhood, adolescence,
etc., determine the characteristics of one's emotional life. The
influence of emotional experiences on behavior may change
during the course of one's life. Such experiences may for example take the form of a transformation into a motive for action,
or may be experienced only as a sentiment. Finally, although
feelings generally stimulate activity, there are circumstances
in which they prove a hindrance. Thus, the possession of
a strong emotional reactivity together with insufficient internal resistance towards emotional experiences tends to characterize an individual who typically shirks responsibility. Such
an individual is particularly at the mercy of incidental feelings, as long as he lacks a guiding purpose.

Using material based on experience gained in Russian
schools, Yakobson has identified several situations from which
new emotional experiences are derived. In the first place, feelings provoked by the positive action of others tend to promote
attempts at transforming these actions into personal experience and in this way new feelings are developed. This could
be effectively utilized, in Yakobson's belief, as a method of
influencing and developing the child's emotional experience.
The sharing of a common interest with respect to social
events and human relationships, whether it be in the present
or in the past, is a further source of emotional experience. The
teaching of history, geography, literature, etc., is aimed at attaining this development.

Yakobson considered the ways in which new emotional

experiences are incorporated within the stable complex of attitudes. The educational implications of this process are obvious. Yakobson maintained that a newly acquired emotion is converted into an attitude which will have a bearing on the child's life, not only by virtue of its repetition, but primarily as a result of its becoming a motivational force in repeated actions. In order to achieve this, it is necessary to establish a set of situations in which the child has the chance to act while he experiences new emotions. The child's way of life has to be organized to include a set of requests and appraisals. Yakobson wrote:

> The development of feelings, unlike the accumulation of knowledge, does not consist of a mere addition of new feelings to those already existing. It consists essentially in the production of a certain change in current feelings. . . . A situation is remembered well when the individual has experienced an emotion in relation to it. That particular situation can be recalled without necessarily re-experiencing that emotion. But if the feeling itself is experienced again, that is, it is remembered, without the circumstances in which it occurred in the past, this repeated experience is not a mere shadow of the past emotion but it is a new emotion. To remember an emotion means to experience it again in a similar or changed form, with more or less the same intensity. In other words, the subjective world is again influenced. This is why the education of feelings . . . requires such actions on the part of the educator which are expected to produce a response of the whole personality. . . . The aim of such an educational policy involves the development of feelings which would lead to a change in the child's intellectual world and in his actions [pp. 45-46].

As a matter of fact, most Soviet studies on the subject of emotions and feelings are directly related to educational purposes. In many instances, however, the objectives are only very loosely formulated and the methodology to attain them is described in nothing more than vague prescriptions. In a recent book about the affective processes in school children, Yakobson (1966) wrote:

We need to know the characteristics of emotions and feelings first of all for the right development of the children's emotional life from the very beginning of our communication with them. For this, we have to solve the following educational problems: (1) As a result of the whole process of education, pupils of any age have to learn to react in emotionally appropriate ways to the influences to which they are subjected in their schools . . . families, or in communication with others. As a result of the pupil's appropriate reactions, there will be a development of such emotions, feelings and motives, corresponding to age, as will be in line with the social norms, tenets of communist ethics, views on beauty and our attitudes towards our fellow man. . . . (2) It is important to develop in pupils, during the process of their education, a positive *emotional responsiveness* to important life events. . . . Responsiveness means the capacity to react emotionally to everything which excites people in Soviet society, the ability to get involved in the tasks and goals of the Soviet people. . . . (3) It is important to develop in pupils a healthy correspondence between various feelings and emotions, to form a harmonious system of emotional responses. . . . (4) There is another task important to the formation of the emotional side of personality. It is the matter of limiting the role of negative feelings such as malice, envy, hostility, etc., in the emotional life of the child, teenager, youth, so that if these feelings should occur, they will dissipate quickly. . . . (5) Finally, it is important for a sound moral development to see to it that the pupil becomes a man who *possesses emotional maturity*, emotional culture [pp. 24-27].

Along a very similar line of reasoning, Myasishchev (1962), whose concept of personality will be discussed later, described certain personality features which represent a defense against the development of a neurosis and should be encouraged by educational methods. Such "antineurotic" features include the possession of a strong tendency towards positive emotions, the capacity to master the external manifestations of emotions as well as the ability to cope with them internally, the possession of broad interests, over and above narrow egoistic needs, the cultivation of a superior cultural outlook, an optimistic approach to life and a belief in justice.

With such an approach, it is not surprising that Soviet authors severely criticized psychoanalytic theory, regarding it as having reduced human behavior to the manifestations of biological needs and the richness of man's emotional life to a conflict between biological drives and the demands of society. Thus, typical of such thinking, Yakobson (1956) wrote:

> In Freud's well-known theory of emotions, we find the tendentious use of some limited propositions regarding human emotional life for purely reactionary ideological purposes. On the basis of the clinical study of a few neurotic cases, Freud unjustifiably ascribed what he observed . . . to the whole of man's emotional life. . . . The replacement of sociohistorical laws by fictitious psychological "laws" was one of the procedures used to build up a reactionary unscientific explanation of human emotions from fragmentary findings [pp. 14–15].

Soviet authors generally classify feelings as intellectual, esthetic and moral. Intellectual and esthetic feelings are related to natural phenomena, material and spiritual products of work, tastes and habits, inclinations and attractions. Moral and political feelings reflect certain demands and interests of a social class, social aspirations and relationships. The individual's attitude towards his own character also gains expression through these feelings. A close relationship is assumed to exist among different kinds of feelings. Thus, an individual who devotes himself to social service has a different attitude towards the products of human labor and towards the particular idiosyncrasies which make up his character than an individual who lacks all social conscience and is concerned with events only from the point of view of his own welfare.

As might be expected, relatively speaking, a great amount of attention has been devoted to the question of moral feelings. These are regarded as being related to the group to which the individual belongs, such as nation, class, party, etc., to social institutions, such as state, family, school, etc., as well as to social phenomena and events such as class struggle, war, scientific discoveries, etc. Yakobson wrote about a "moral receptivity," by which he meant that:

. . . certain tenets of the Soviet ethic with regard to the attitude that is to be taken towards social values, labor, people and their actions, as well as towards one's own behavior represent norms with which the individual . . . is in agreement. This means that he is not only *acquainted* with the demands of society but he wholeheartedly accepts them as a necessity. As a result, many factors become associated with an inner 'must' and 'must not.' Clear convictions are formed regarding what is good and what is bad, and a strong sense of morality and immorality . . . is developed [p. 184].

Elkonin (1960), a child psychologist, stated that moral feelings appear as early as in the preschool years. He rejected the view that children of this age are guided only by their own interests. In particular, it is believed that children develop feelings of duty. Zaporozhets (1964) studied childrens' understanding of the literature and noted the strong association that is formed with regard to the "positive" hero. Very young children are unaware of their attitude and are unable to evaluate the heroes whether they are good or bad. Older preschool children were already able to evaluate the social meaning of an act. These children identified with the positive hero, realizing the motives of his actions.

7

Will and Voluntary Activity

This subject, in fact, also falls within the topic of the psychology of personality. The concept of activity, however, holds so prominent a position in Soviet ideology that it shall be discussed separately. According to Soviet thought, activity is indeed the major source of human knowledge. The formation of psychical processes, in fact, their very existence, is seen as being essentially dependent on man's activity. As this point, the reader is reminded of the proposition about the link between consciousness and activity. Rubinshtein (1959a) wrote:

> The psychological research does not have to be concerned only with the internal, mental, intellectual activity, but also with the real, practical activity through which people transform nature and change the society, in its psychological aspect. . . . *The essence of the statement that consciousness and activity form a unity consists in the assertion that they are interconnected and interdependent:* man's activity determines the formation of his consciousness, of his psychical connections, processes and properties, and the latter, by their regulating the human activity, become the factor on which its adequate fulfillment depends. Man's activity is primarily a practical activity. Only thereafter is the theoretical and, generally, the internal, mental activity separated from it. The practical activity, however, also includes psychical components which reflect

the conditions under which this is fulfilled and which regulate it [pp. 250-251].

A study by Teplov, first published in 1945 and reissued in 1961, is illustrative in this respect. Teplov stressed the importance of practical thinking. He wrote that the process of thinking is generally studied as a theoretical activity. When practical thinking is investigated, the study is limited to processes linked with the direct manipulation of objects. While Teplov admitted that the introduction of the concept of a sensorimotor intellect was important, he thought that it should be distinguished from that of practical thinking. For instance, when a person is engaged in organizational work, he does not actually come into direct contact with concrete objects. On the other hand, an individual engaged in certain types of experimental work, either in physics or in chemistry, may have to deal with a sensorimotor activity. For Teplov, thus, theoretical thinking cannot be separated from practical thinking on the basis of the different mechanisms involved. Thinking is a unitary process and only the problems being dealt with are different. Practical thinking implies solving specific, concrete problems, while theoretical thinking connotes a search for general concepts. Theoretical thinking marks the transition from contemplation to abstraction, as distinct from practical thinking which is concerned with the second part of the process of gaining knowledge, that is with the application of abstract thinking as it relates to a certain problem. According to Teplov, theoretical thinking verifies the final results of practical solutions of problems. Whereas the theoretical thinker creates hypotheses which he can verify experimentally, the testing of practical hypotheses is more restricted. Because there is a time factor in practical thinking, Teplov considered the belief, that theoretical problems are more difficult to be a misjudgment. He wrote:

Moreover, if one is to establish any gradation of activities according to the complexity of their demands on the intellect, then one must admit that the diversity and occasional inner contradictions, as well as difficult conditions of the individual's practical activity places the superior forms of practical work in the forefront. Strictly speaking, the scientist's thinking is simpler, clearer and more contemplative—but not necessarily easier—than that carried on by a politician or a military leader. Such a gradation, however, is largely superficial. The main issue is not the scaling of the difficulty of practical tasks, but the evaluation of their psychological specificity, their significance and complexity [p. 255].

The main role ascribed to man's activity, in particular practical activity, resulted, however, in rather confused meanings. Man's activity was frequently identified with his adjustment to the environment. Moreover, it appears to be a general property of being, insofar as it is equated with the concept of reflection. Kovalev's (1965) monograph on the psychology of personality includes a chapter entitled "The activity of personality and its sources." The introduction reads as follows:

Activity is a property of every living thing. . . . Organic matter is part of natural phenomena and can exist only in constant interaction with the rest of nature. . . . The assimiliation of alien matter and its transformation in the organism in energy is dependent upon the organism's property of activity. . . . This property consists of the capacity of organic matter to become active when influenced by external and internal impingements . . . [p. 68].

The accurate reflection of reality is thus seen as being contingent upon active contact. The use of two words for activity—*deyatelnost* and *aktivnost*—is not too helpful to avoid confusion.

Confusion also surrounds the concept of motor activity. Soviet psychologists tend to regard psychical processes as a form of "activity," emphasizing the role of motor activity. They point to the involvement of muscular reactions in all kinds of activity. A statement by Sechenov (Undated) on the role of motor functioning has been frequently cited:

The infinite diversity of external manifestations of cerebral activity can be reduced ultimately to a single phenomenon—muscular movement. Whether it is the child's laughing at the sight of a toy, or Garibaldi's smiling when persecuted for excessive love for his native land, or a girl trembling at the first thought of love, or Newton creating universal laws and inscribing them on paper—the ultimate fact in all cases is muscular movement [p. 33]. [1]

Bernshtein (1966) made essentially the same statement:

Movement represents almost the only form of vital activity by which the organism not only interacts with its environment but also actively *influences* it, changing or endeavoring to change it towards its ends and needs. As far back as a hundred years ago, Ivan Mikhailovich Sechenov showed in his famous *Reflexes of Brain* the universal significance of movements. It has since turned out that movement is part and parcel of all sensory actions, of the development of sensory organs in early childhood, of the final active elaboration of the veridical *reflection of reality* in the brain, due to a controlled perceptual synthesis through practice. Thus, we can easily see how this factor was emphasized and became even more apparent in contemporary physiology [pp. 275-276].

Soviet authors have written about the transition from animal activity, as a process of adaptation, to human activity, as an expression of man's social existence. The first stage of such a transition makes sense. Human activity is seen as a transformation of man's environment according to needs, as distinct from animal activity which aims at the adaptation of the organism to its environment. At this point, however, the argument weakens. We are informed by Kovalev (1965) that human activity means

. . . participation in social work. An active person is a man who makes full use of his activity potential, one who takes part in the sociopolitical and ideological life of society. Such a person may be considered as an active worker for social development. . . . The activity of a person is determined by both his objective demands and those of the society. The

---

[1] Translated by the Foreign Languages Publishing House, Moscow.

individual is a human organism interacting with his social environment from the very first day of life, and his activity is conditioned by natural needs which develop genetically. Through his communication with others and the assimilation of the historical experience in the course of his activity, the individual develops into a personality with specific social needs, interests, inclinations and orientation [p. 70].

A related issue is that of the genetic development of man's ability to manipulate objects. Animal activity is said to be instinctive, oriented towards objects which either satisfy its needs directly, or are associated with the gratification of such needs. Changes in an animal's activity are dependent upon changes in stimuli, rather than upon changes in the relationships between environment and animal needs. Thus, the formation of a conditioned reflex does not imply the occurrence of a new need. On the other hand, human activity developed out of a gradual separation of action from the manipulated object. This resulted in man's realization of the relationship between the objective motive of his actions and the objects towards which the actions are directed. The individual's actions became meaningful precisely because he realizes this relationship. An individual, as part of a hunting team in a primitive society, can only act if he recognizes the relation between his action and the final outcome of the group action. The food to be won appears as a gratification of a need, regardless of the individual's own need at that particular time. This is not only realized in a practical fashion but is also recorded as a concept.

THE CONCEPT OF WILL

It is a tenet of Soviet ideology that human activity is predominantly conscious and voluntary. Yet, at the same time, this is seen as being determined by external reality. Marxist theory abounds in arguments attesting to the fact that dialectical materialism admits that man is governed by a blind necessity about which he is only partially aware. But it is strongly emphasized that man is able to perform deliberate actions. Voluntary activity is closely linked to the knowledge of objective reality and is performed in a conscious manner. Since the development of a conscious activity made possible man's relative detachment from directly impinging stimuli, his actions erroneously seemed to be independent of the external conditions, as if autonomous and only contingent upon subjective tendencies. Soviet writers have devoted considerable effort to combating these views.

Psychology set about to prove the conjectures mentioned above. The major argument revolves around the relationship between needs and actions. Activity is said to be oriented towards the satisfaction of needs, which are a particular kind of reflection of external and objective conditions. A need is an increased sensitivity towards a certain object. In its most elementary form, a need implies an increased drive towards unconditioned stimuli, i.e., objects which themselves satisfy the need. More complex needs implicate a relation to signaling stimuli, i.e., stimuli associated with those which satisfy the need. Need is expressed in a certain goal which may be either the attainment of an object, or the performance of a certain action. Although the latter may seem to possess a certain degree of autonomy, it is in fact also dependent upon external conditions. Biological needs lead to actions when the organism is subjected to a certain type of stimulation. Hunger, for instance, is due to interoceptive stimuli which produce a selective orientation of the organism towards specific objects. The stimulation itself, however, does not give rise to any action. Needs are experienced as wishes and inclinations, the latter functioning as a sort of signal for the occurrence of the need. The reach of objects satisfying needs represents the motives of actions. The subjective meaning of an action is somewhat identical to its motive. One has to distinguish between motives and goals. Although they may coincide in simple situations, in complex instances there can be a great deal of distance between motive and goal. The motives themselves range from immediate and partial motives to broad motives which are more stable and less dependent on circumstances. When a voluntary action is carried out, it is directed towards the attainment of a conscious goal. The realization of this goal represents the initial stage of a voluntary action. The second stage consists of the realization of the means of its fulfillment.

Along with a general characterization of human activity, as outlined above, one finds in Soviet works on this topic a more specific analysis of the relationship between the various aspects of human actions, with motivation being the main issue. In point of fact, the concept of motivation is almost exclusively linked to that of activity, and since the latter is seen as a manifestation of consciousness, one cannot expect to hear that motivation comes from the deep layers of the personality. Soviet authors do speak about unconscious motives but refer rather to a subconscious determination of actions in no relation to an analysis of the structure of personality. It is the matter of the changes taking place between the various components of a voluntary action in relation to its motives and goals. Leontev's school has been much concerned with this analysis. Activity is regarded as an assembly of processes expressing the individual's attitude. The stimulus of an action is its motive. For instance, when a student reads a book for his enjoyment, his interest in reading the book is the very motive of his activity. But if he reads the book in order to pass an examination the motive of his activity is different from his goal. The motive of a certain action is then not necessarily the goal of the whole activity of which the action is a part. In the given example, the purpose of reading the book is that of understanding its content, while the motive is passing the examination. A motive may turn into a purpose, in which case an action becomes an activity. A motive can be "only realized" or turned into an efficient stimulus of action. This transition takes place when the result of an action becomes more relevant than the motive which produced it. For instance, when a pupil does his homework quickly in order that he may go out and play, he may occasionally also find gratification in class for having done his lesson. This kind of reinforcement may result in the development of a higher motivation in direct relation to school tasks.

There are a diversity of relationships between an action and the operations by means of which the action is performed. While the action is related to the goal to be attained, the operations are contingent upon circumstances. Furthermore, a conscious operation occurs originally as an action and then turns into an operation and eventually into a skill. For a child's action to become an operation and a skill, he must be given a new task for the fulfillment of which he has to perform an action different from one with which he is already familiar. The previous action may then turn into an operation within the framework of the new action. Intellectual actions are similarly transformed into intellectual skills. For instance, the addition of two amounts is initially an action performed by adding unit to unit. Later, adding becomes an operation. Operations are said to consolidate the objective nonpsychological content of actions. Well-developed operations further the transition to more complex actions.

Soviet psychologists have been insistent that the automation of motor actions does not necessarily imply the separation between unconscious and conscious actions, but rather the consolidation of some operations through training. Puni (1960, 1964), a student of the psychology of sports, stated that being unaware of certain details of a complex, learned action does not imply that the whole of the action is unconscious. He pointed out the subject's ability to modify the performance of that action in a conscious fashion. In studying the movements of gymnasts, he observed that as the exercises became more familiar, the subjects themselves realized their faults.

The transfer of skills is another issue touched upon by Soviet authors. Some criticism was levelled against the view that the transfer implies the formation of associations of similarity between elements of the new skill and components of already acquired skills. Lisina (1960, 1962), who is well acquainted with the views of Western writers on this subject, pointed out that there are many instances of transfer to new skills which do not have common components with former ones. In her view, there was also a certain misuse of quantitative analysis. Despite the very rigorous analysis of the data, she felt that the actual process of transfer was not disclosed. Lisina considered that at the current level of knowledge on this subject, the main concern should be to determine specific mechanisms of transfer and not to attempt to study its general characteristics.

There is a noticeable tendency among Soviet psychologists to give a broad connotation to the concept of skill and to speak about intellectual skills. Chebysheva distinguished three groups of skills: intellectual, motor and sensory. She drew attention to the fact that today skills which were previously seen as motor acts have turned into intellectual actions. The behaviorist reduction of skills to the level of motor actions was criticized on the ground that it implies loosing sight of the psychical processes involved.

In view of the brief survey of some of the Soviet views regarding the structure of voluntary activity, the emphasis on volitional qualities of personality appears quite understandable. The concept of will is indeed very important to Soviet psychologists but its discussion hardly qualifies for psychological theory. What we read in textbooks differs very little from what is said on this subject in a propaganda pamphlet. The following features of will are characteristically mentioned in the *Pedagogical Dictionary:* (1) the capacity to subordinate one's behavior to a constant purpose; (2) the capacity to subordinate one's behavior to concepts and ideas; (3) the ability to make decisions and to fulfill them; (4) the capacity for self-control under any circumstances; (5) the capacity to act in accordance with social demands; (6) the capacity to act courageously, disregarding the danger to one's own life.

These vague formulations, however, did not prevent Soviet psychologists from doing interesting studies on the development of voluntary activity in children (Rahmani, 1966). Some of these studies were presented in English by Elkonin (1960) and Bozhovich (1969).

Physiological Bases of Voluntary Activity

This is a classical subject in Russian neuropsychology which gained importance with the new cybernetic approach. As a matter of fact, it is precisely in this area that the strongest attack has been made against the Pavlovian analytic approach.

Sechenov's work provided the basis for the Russian attempts to disclose the neurological mechanisms of voluntary activity. It is known that for Sechenov, a voluntary act, like any psychical act, has an initial stage consisting of a stimulation, an intermediary central link, and a final effector stage. Due to a central inhibition, the final stage, which represents the actual movement, may not occur. This is a result of the frequent repetition of associated learned reflexes which make it possible for man to coordinate as well as inhibit his actions. Thoughts, intentions and wishes comprise the first two thirds of psychical reflexes. They play an important role in controlling other reflexes.

Pavlov, following in the tradition of Sechenov, propounded the hypothesis that the cortical-motor region also represents an afferent system as is true of other analyzers.

8

Psychology of Personality

The study of personality is the least advanced of all fields of Soviet psychology. This situation is the result of three factors. First, an analytic approach concerned mainly with isolated aspects of mental life prevented any study of the personality as a whole. Second, a constant search for a biological basis of mental activity avoided any area not directly conducive to physiological study. Finally, it was assumed that psychologists could not add anything relevant to what the "classics of Marxism" had already dictated about personality. Quotations from these works were offered instead of genuine research. Some general socio-historical considerations about man substituted for the study of personality. Any attempt to go beyond such superficial statements in order to reveal deeper layers of the individual personality was discouraged. Such an attempt was not seen as being merely subjective guesswork, but as a considerable ideological error since it implied a substitution for the socioeconomic rules which are thought to govern human existence. Until the 1950's and over a period of about 20 years, Russian publications on this subject were very much geared along these lines and both the study of personality and of social psychology were practically nonexistent.

Since then significant changes have occurred as a greater awareness of the need to understand the individual personality developed (Kostyuk, 1970). The topic of social psychology was discussed for the first time in 1956. Many studies are still based on programmatic lines. There exists, however, a growing tendency to pass from the statement of purely theoretical positions to a more concrete and pertinent analysis. The Russians seem to have concluded that there is a need for the development of a system of concepts which would be able to express man's integral behavior. Selivanov (1964), an advocate of this position, wrote:

> Qualitative changes apparently only take place as a result of specific and socially significant complex stimulations, in accordance with the dominant needs of a personality at a given moment. One may speak about an integral response of personality, made up of a complex of emotions and actions, which cannot be reduced to one isolated action [p. 467].

The Biological Foundations of Personality

There has been a tendency to distinguish between mental processes and characteristics of personality which are influenced through education and the environment, from those processes and personality features which depend on biological and hereditary factors. Luriya (1962) has given an example of this approach. He compared the development of elementary visual memory, of memory for words, with and without the aid of corresponding pictures, in two groups of mono- and dizygotic twins. The subjects were presented with nine geometric figures which subsequently had to be recognized among 25 figures. The differences between dizygotic twins of preschool age were 3.3 times greater than the differences between monozygotic twins at the same age. At the school age, the coefficient fell to 2.5. In Luriya's view, these results indicated the relevance of the hereditary factor to the process of visual discrimination.

In a second study, the subjects had to recall 15 words. The difference within the dizygotic pairs of twins of the preschool age was found to be only 2.5 times higher than that of the other group of twins. The coefficient decreased to 1.75 at the school age. Luriya interpreted this finding as evidence for the increased influence of the environment on the tested function.

Then the subjects were asked again to remember 15 words which were presented together with corresponding pictures. The results at the preschool age were not significantly different from those of the previous experiment (2.3). But a considerably decreased coefficient of 0.8 was obtained at the school age. Luriya concluded that there was no significant difference between the pairs of mono-and dizygotic twins regarding mediated memory. New mental processes develop with age and the same tasks are accomplished in different ways. In other words, there is an essential change of the role of genotype in the performance of complex functions.

Platonov (1961, 1962, 1965), too, follows along the same line of reasoning when he describes four groups of personality characteristics: (a) socially determined characteristics, especially man's purposefulness and moral qualities; (b) biologically determined characteristics, such as temperament, instincts and elementary needs; (c) acquired experience—knowledge, abilities, skills, habits; (d) individual characteristics of mental processes. Platonov pointed out that both biological and social factors influence the various characteristics of personality but their roles are different. Thus, for instance, the biological conditioning of temperament is different from the role of the biological factor in producing carelessness. The social factors involved in forming one's philosophy is not the same as the social influence on the acquisition of skills and knowledge. The learning process is regarded by Platonov as an intermediary link between biological and social influences. The acquisition of knowledge makes up part of the structure of the personality, and thus learning must be taken into account when examining the sociohistorical nature of the personality. Various types of thinking determine what knowledge is acquired and this, in turn, determines the outlooks and beliefs which make up the personality. Acquired skills and habits, on the other hand, form the functional capacity of the personality.

Soviet psychologists have been particularly attracted to the problem of the relationships between characteristics of the nervous activity and features of personality, notably temperamental qualities, character traits and aptitudes (Teplov, 1961; Teplov and Nebylitsyn, 1969; Nebylitsyn, 1963, 1964, 1971; Ilina, 1963; Roshal, 1965; Kopytova, 1964; Perov, 1957). Many arguments have been waged over the definition of these concepts but, as in other instances, the appropriate empirical data have, for the most part, been lacking. A fortunate exception has been the study of temperamental features, especially Teplov's studies on individual differences.

Concerning the relationship between temperament and its underlying nervous activity, on the one hand, and character, on the other, Kovalev and Myasishchev (1963) distinguished four points of view: (a) temperament and character are basically opposed to each other, an opinion shared by Levitov (1964); (b) temperament and character are identical, a point of view upheld by Kretschmer which illustrated an incorrect tendency to overemphasize the biological side of the personality; (c) temperament forms the natural basis of character, an opinion shared by most Soviet psychologists, including Vygotskii, Rubinshtein, Kornilov, Teplov and Ananev; (d) temperament is one of the compounding elements of the character.

The third viewpoint was by and large suggested by Pavlov's proposition that the type of nervous system produced the genotype, while the character represented the phenotype. Teplov's extensive research has played an important role in the implementation of this assumption, as he discovered a diversity of correlations between the properties of the nervous processes of excitation and inhibition and individual characteristics of the personality. Gray (1964) has contributed a comprehensive presentation of Teplov's work.

Merlin's (1966, 1967) analysis of the relationship between general and individual characteristics of the personality is deserving of description at some length. He distinguished between features of personality which are of a social nature, that is, which express the assembly of attitudes towards social phenomena and events, and individual features. To the first category belong the individual's position towards other people, work, science, art, individual and social property, etc. as well as toward himself. These attitudes make up the individual's orientation. Their social nature consists in their being ultimately a product of social ideology and social psychology. A distinction has to be made between an individual's general personality attitude, and the motives of his actions in a certain concrete situation.

Merlin distinguished between two groups of individual characteristics, which differ in terms of their relationship to the individual's attitudes. The first group consists of the temperamental features and of the individual characteristics of mental processes, such as the accuracy of perception, the volume of memory, etc. While certain temperamental features also represent characteristics of mental processes, the latter are not temperamental features unless they determine the dynamics of the mental activity. This group of individual characteristics is not contingent upon the personality's orientation, that is, upon the attitude towards the collective to which the individual belongs, his work, etc. For instance, individuals with a positive attitude toward work may have a low work capacity related to a weak type of nervous system, and the other way around. Merlin explains the presence of individual characteristics which are independent of social conditions, by the diversity of the latter. Teaching methods, for instance, vary largely from one school to the other, although all of them serve the purposes of the same society or class. This independence, however, is relative. A child's negative attitude toward school may suppress the manifestation in school of some of his temperamental characteristics, such as strong emotional reactions. It was noticed that a responsible approach to work may inhibit one's lack of restraint. Merlin pointed out, however, that temperamental features of any nature may manifest themselves regardless of the individual's attitudes. He then raised the question as to whether individual characteristics of the temperament and of the mental processes are personality features. In Merlin's view, they are not, since personality is defined as the subject of an *activity* aimed at transforming the environment according to one's own purposes. Neither the temperament nor the characteristics of mental processes play a role in orienting the individual in any direction whatsoever.

The second group of individual characteristics are referred to by Merlin as features of individuality. Such features are the stable motives of action, or specific attitudes in certain situations, as, for example, the interest in music. These are fully determined by the conditions of development and education but are not related to any specific social group. Social attitudes expressed by the personality represent a system of motives among which there are hierarchical relationships. Thus, for instance, the attitude toward work includes ideological motives, self-esteem, dignity and the interest for a given profession. If the ideological or moral motives of duty, responsibility and creativity are dominant, then the entire system of motives is characteristic of the socialist attitude. Merlin maintains that there is no antagonism between a specifically individual aspect of personality attitudes and the social character of these attitudes. Such an antagonism occurs only if the same motive is shared by conflicting attitudes.

A major point in Soviet thinking is that man is a social being from the moment of his birth. Any assumption that the child's socialization occurs later has been flatly rejected. Piaget was particularly criticized for proposing that the child's behavior develops from autistic to social. Elkonin, a child psychologist, has stressed the close connection the child has with his parents during earliest infancy. To emphasize this, he refers to the fact that the infant reacts to his mother's face and voice as early as one month of age. Elkonin suggests that the child's inner world, including his own wishes, does not develop until after he has managed to communicate with adults. In contrast to Vygotskii's idea that the child develops from a social to an individual being, Elkonin sees each stage of the child's independent behavior as being linked to the acquisition of social experience. Thus, the child's development does not imply a reduction in his contact with the external world, but rather a change in the form of his communication and of his position in social relationships. Contrary to Piaget, who regarded the infant's play as egocentric activity, Elkonin considered it to be a social manifestation both in its content and genetically.

THE INDIVIDUAL AND SOCIETY

Soviet philosophers and psychologists have strongly emphasized that the individual's psychology is determined by the economic and social-class structure of the society. Marx's statement that the essence of the personality is the assembly of the individual's social relations has ben cited very frequently. Soviet writers rejected the idea that there are certain general psychological characteristics of human beings over and above their belonging to certain social classes. Furthermore, they have been critical of the view that certain developments in human society, like industrialization or automation, result in the appearance of certain feelings, notably that of alienation. They argue from a Marxist premise that the feeling of aloneness is not an unavoidable phenomenon but rather is peculiar only to capitalist society. Kremnev (1961) stated that the goals of capitalist and socialist societies with regard to automation are entirely different and that Western philosophers are actually defending capitalism when they claim that its drawbacks are due to industrialization. Mitin (1964) summarized the statements of Western philosophers at the third international congress of philosophy held in 1964, in Mexico, under the following points. (1) In the West, man's nature is considered in the light of existentialism and neo-Thomism. (2) The past is idealized and man's historical development is presented in abstract schemes. (3) Irrationalism and subjectivism predominate in the interpretation of social phenomena; objective relationships among people are subordinated to subjective and individualistic attitudes. (4) Any analysis of relevant social issues is all too readily dismissed. Similar critical views have been expressed by Oizerman (1964), Zamoshkin (1957, 1960, 1961, 1965, 1966) and others. The following summarizes the Soviet authors' own views on this issue.

Historically, in a uniform primitive society, where authority was in the hands of old men and blood kinsmanship was strong, the individual had no genuine personality. With the advent of master-slave society, people were divided for the first time into social classes: those engaged in physical and those in intellectual activities. This in turn lead to the development of varying personalities in the community. The social barriers, however, which came into existence at that time and were perpetuated by the feudal society, limited personal initiative and led to feelings of belonging to a stratified class. On this particular point, Soviet authors disagree with Fromm who contends that individuals did not have feelings of isolation in precapitalistic societies. In their view, Fromm has idealized the moral and psychological effects of feudalism. The degree of individuality of a human being under feudalism was relative, since man was not his own master and his value as an individual personality was negligible. As a matter of fact, capitalism originally led to the development of man's personality and initiative and it was only later that he lost his integrity. Man's personality was thus restricted to "professional idiocy" which finally resulted in his feelings of alienation. This feeling was associated with the attitude toward work which was now a strange and hostile part of life. Parygin (1965) pointed out that Fromm, in transferring the problem of alienation from sociology to psychology, has fundamentally taken the wrong line and this has led him to the mistaken assumption that alienation is produced by man's own irrational nature.

Expectedly, Soviet writers have emphasized that socialism has resulted in a maximum development of the personality and, implicitly, in the greatest decrease in feelings of alienation (Kurylev, 1964; Bueva, 1965; Frantsov, 1965; Naumova, 1965; Guryanov, 1965). Parygin (1965a), representing these views, wrote:

> The harmonious development and the multilateral manifestations shown by a free personality are only possible for an individual living in a genuinely collective society founded on the social relationships of communism. This result can only come into being after the long and hard process involved in changing the whole system of social relationships and the nature of man himself. In this process, the mental remnants of the old antagonistic classes of society will disappear and the communist social psychology will take shape [p. 128].

Soviet writers point out that in the socialist system in which there is collective possession of the means of production, a new kind of relationship is created between the individual and society, one which is essentially free from feelings of alienation. Thus we find fervent passages in praise of work (Platonov, 1962, 1965; Levitov, 1963; Zdravomyslov and Yadov, 1965a,b). The need to work under these conditions is not a mere habit, but an integral expression of the qualities of the personality, of man's social value and his moral makeup. Kovalev (1965) wrote:

> This is why the making of a worker under the conditions of our so-

ciety means the formation of a new man, with an all-around education, aware of his social duty [p. 147].

We read in Platonov's (1965) work, which is a publication of the Institute of Philosophy of the Academy of Sciences:

> Work is the most important factor in the formation of individual consciousness. Its significance stems firstly from the fact that through work the individual assimilates the social consciousness and, secondly, work is the most effective means of forming the individual consciousness corresponding to the purpose of building communism [p. 326].

One notices, however, a new tendency to take a broader approach to the individual-society relationship. There has been a call in recent years to revise what is said to be an overly rigid and dogmatic interpretation of Marxism. Two statements have been made which depart from the conventional formulations. In the first place, there is a plea for admitting that people share in common certain psychological features and endeavors which have been perpetuated from one society to another. This position is represented by Tugarinov (1962, 1965), a philosopher who writes about the relationships between personality and society. In his opinion, an individual's personality is a function of his reason which depends upon his historical development, his feeling of responsibility toward the society, his use of certain rights and liberties in accordance with his own likes, his contribution to the growth of the society, and the manner in which his own life corresponds to the ideals of the society, or the social class to which he belongs. Such features could be found in any society in varying degrees.

Hence, Tugarinov is opposed to the interpretation of Marxism as implying a denial of an universal concept of personality. It is apparent that the advocates of the latter position find support in a statement by Lenin that a scientific approach requires the elimination of the concept of personality from sociology. Tugarinov pointed out that Lenin's criticism of the subjective method in sociology is still valid but that this does not mean that Marxists must not tackle the problem of personality. Thus he wrote:

> The study of the individual has to have a place in science. After all, people not only create history, think about the laws of nature and the destiny of mankind. Man lives his *own* life, has *his* diseases, experiences *his* joys and sorrows, meditates about *his* life. . . . One can hardly conceive that the life, attitudes and consciousness of the individual in the primitive society . . . was fused with the collective, that is tribe, family, etc. It is less conceivable that in the future communist society individual and collective will become one [pp. 11–12].

While Tugarinov admitted that each socioeconomic formation has its own laws of development, he pointed out that there are general historical laws of development. He went so far as to emphasize that, after all, the goals of personality development and its ideals can be bourgeois and communist as well. The qualities of the "new" man represent a unity between general-historical and specific communist characteristics. Thus, there are personality features available in any society, which are developed in communism. Such features are rationality, responsibility, freedom, that is ". . . man's possibility to think or act not by external constraint, but in accordance with his own will" (p. 61), individuality and dignity. The editorial presentation of Tugarinov's monograph stated that "not everything in the book is undisputable."

Soviet psychologists have also recently made a strong plea for the concrete study of the individual's personality. One notices an increasing amount of publications on the personality that "not everything in the book is undisputable."

Soviet psychologists have also recently made a strong plea for the concrete study of the individual's personality. One notices an increasing amount of publications on the personality of the school-child, teenager, worker in relation to the nature of his work and scientist (Platonov, 1961, 1965; Zaporozhets and

Elkonin, 1964; Dragunova and Elkonin, 1965; Kovalev and Myas-ishchev, 1963; Kozyrev, 1965; Makhlakh, 1965; Valentinova, 1965; Ramul, 1965). These writers urge a move away from abstract formulations which are merely a restatement of the principles of dialectical materialism applied to society and the individual. Although this trend may appear as being opposed to Tugarinov's position, both points of view actually represent reactions to the dogma that only a class psychology exists.

Selivanov (1960) wrote:

> All Soviet psychologists mean by personality, not a man in general, but a concrete individual, a member of a certain society who has complex relationships to the other people. Such a concept of personality requires that the study be particularly concrete, in order to reflect the diversity of human life. . . . It is necessary to penetrate deeper into the Soviet man's life, to know his activity, behavior, mind as they are in reality . . . eventually without having to put forward to complex theoretical problems involved until the necessary material has been acquired [p. 38].

Selivanov mentioned three areas in which specific studies have to be carried out. First, it is necessary to study the psychological differences between individuals living in urban and rural areas. He made it plain that he did not mean primarily the different forms of socialist property in the city and in the country, notably in the collective farm—a topic traditionally discussed in Soviet publications—but rather, the influence of the characteristics of the industrial and agricultural production on the individual's personality. Selivanov remarked that Soviet developmental psychology is actually based on urban studies; the characteristics of rural children are overlooked. Second, national characteristics have to be taken into account. "The formula that the culture of the ethnic groups of the USSR is socialist by its content and national by its form has also to be applied on the psychological plane" (p. 40). Third, it is necessary to study the influence of the local conditions on personality development.

The following unconventional statement of Selivanov (1965) regarding the development of the child's personality in the collective farm is worth quoting:

> If parents in a *kolkhoz* work honestly, by their example they have a positive influence on their children. The preference for work in the kolkhoz to that in a private plot is early instilled in the child's mind. In most families in the kolkhoz, the childrens' work at home is seen as preparation for their later social duties. But for the child who works at home in a family possessing a private plot of land and where the collective work on the farm is an obligation and supplementary to the family's income, work has a different meaning. In such an atmosphere, work is linked in the child's consciousness with earning and narrow personal desires and needs. The school has to work hard to eradicate this incorrect attitude. . . . It is not only a matter of the important role of the family in the formation of the child's personality, but also of the fact that the family still retains the old mode of life, despite the considerable changes which have occurred, more so than any other collective and, thus, preventing the individual's progressive development. There is also the problem of the head of the family. The state is interested not only in his authority, but also in his being a progressive man. . . But it often happens that, because of the old tradition, the head of the family is the oldest man and he does not have a close contact with the kolkhoz [p. 462].

CHARACTERISTICS OF PERSONALITY

It is typical for Soviet publications to include in the psychology of the personality, the temperament, character, aptitudes, dominant feelings and motives as well as the individual features of mental processes such as perception, memory and thinking. The following definition of the psychology of personality is proposed in Kovalev's (1965) book on personality, one of the few works entirely dedicated to this topic.

> In a broad sense, the psychology of personality has to do with man's psychological life, notably, processes and states, properties and their system. In a more restricted sense, it means . . . man's various attitudes

and the ways of their manifestation which characterize the individual's moral-psychological physiognomy *(sklad)*. Some psychologists mean by the psychology of personality only the investigation of the individual's psychological characteristics. Such a restriction of the subject matter of the psychology of personality is incorrect. It has to include the moral *(dukhovnyi)* world of a concrete human personality which expresses the unity between general, particular and singular features. . . . The psychology of personality can be approached on both planes of general and individual psychology. The first deals with the general human psychological structures, while the second is concerned with the individual-typical characteristics of the personality; typological (temperament), characterological (typical features and types), aptitudes (general and special), typical and individual attitudes . . . [pp. 15–17].

Rubinshtein suggested a splitting off of the concept of personality from the concepts of individual and individuality. According to him, the individual is the bearer of general human psychical attributes and individuality is the result of peculiar developmental and educational conditions. Both these aspects were said to be involved in the concept of personality although they were not seen as its major features. Personality represents a broader concept and is a "unit" in the system of social relationships. Rubinshtein was inclined to think that personality was a sociological rather than a psychological concept. He described the mental life as a part of human existence: mental processes control the individual's activity which, in turn, produces behavior in accordance with external objective conditions.

Parygin, on the other hand, fought against this tendency to overemphasize the sociological aspects of the personality. He thought that in this way, the relative independence of the individual in his private life is underevaluated, with particular regard to his motives, resulting in the exclusion of any study of personality from psychology. Hence, Soviet definitions of personality generally emphasize the historical formation of the personality, its dependence on social conditions and the prevalent role of consciousness. One can hardly claim, however, that any of the suggested definitions is more than superficial. Nonetheless, in their criticism of the description of personality in Western psychology, in particular that of Allport, Soviet writers point out that these are merely formal definitions. They emphasize the lack of specific human features, above all consciousness. It was felt that Allport's definition could apply to almost any gregarious animal. We shall turn now to some specific issues in the psychology of personality discussed by Soviet authors.

Let us turn our attention to the relationship between personality and cognitive processes. Soviet textbooks have generally dealt with the topic of personality in their closing chapters. It is usual for the first part of the text to be concerned with the development of the psyche and the occurrence of consciousness, with subsequent chapters on the various cognitive processes, and terminating with personality features. Characteristically, there are only scanty paragraphs on the individual characteristics of these processes. Uznadze's set theory has been about the only attempt in Soviet psychology to approach the cognitive processes, notably perception and thinking, in close connection with the individual's orientation toward the involved material. This theory, however, was found to be ideologically suspect as it stressed factors other than external stimulation. It also showed the individual's readiness and inclination to perform certain actions in pursuit of the satisfaction of needs. Bzhalava (1966) wrote:

The stimulus operates on a subject, in this case a human being, and the changes which occur in the subject have obviously been produced by this operation. But the response is not merely a continuation of this operation and is not even necessarily related to this operation as is the case with cause-effect relationships. In analyzing a reaction, one has to take into account the state of the organism, "the intermediary variable" which has been called "motor task," "acceptor of effect," "preventing stimulation," set, attitude, *Einstellung, Aufgabe*, etc. . . . The personality, the bearer of certain needs, and not its psyche interacts directly with the environment. It is a living body *(zhivoe sushchestvo)* which must become an individual, a subject of behavior. The external reality acting upon him becomes a situation which satisfies his needs. . . . In other words, behavior as a purposeful reaction to external influences is mediated by the subject's state, by his past. The individual is not the sum total of psyche and body and likewise the change produced by the external influences is not a partial process but is an independent specific reality with its specific laws. It *precedes* the psychical and physiological processes and, as a matter of fact, cannot be reduced to either [pp. 30-31].

Certain Soviet psychologists use the concept of personality properties *(svoistva)*. Rubinshtein, for instance, assumed that the psychical processes are the construction material for man's psychical properties which represent the individual's capacity to respond to generalized influences of the environment by a certain mental activity. Kovalev, too, wrote about personality properties in the sense of stable structures which ensure a certain level of activity, or a behavior typical for a given individual. A personality property is both a potential factor and an actual capacity. Certain properties, such as organic needs, or temperamental characteristics express genetic features. Their majority, however, are the result of the ontogenetic development.

Levitov has been a long-time advocate of the concept of "psychical state," which he rather vaguely defines as a relatively stable psychical background on which take place the psychical processes. These states may become typical for a certain personality. Levitov proposed the following criteria of classification of the psychical states: (a) their specificity for the individual, i.e., are they typical or circumstantial; (b) their depth (e.g., passions are deeper than moods); (c) their influence on the individual's activity (e.g., enthusiasm has a positive effect, apathy—a negative one); (d) their persistence; (e) the degree of awareness. Kovalev accepted the term of psychical state by which he means a certain temporary functional level of the cortex reflecting the influences of the internal milieu or of the external environment and being manifest in the degree of mental activity. In terms of their stability, the psychical states hold a somewhat intermediary position between processes and properties. They include some states of an unconditioned-reflex nature such as hunger, thirst or for example, the anxiety related to heart conditions. Most psychical states are, however, of a social nature, as for instance one's mood at the usual work time. Perov (1957) considered the possibility of development of certain character traits from psychical processes and states. He provided, however, little evidence to support his assumption.

Myasishchev's theory about the individual's attitudes *(otnosheniya)* is ultimately the only Soviet theory which offers an integrated concept of personality since it takes into account a variety of factors from both normal and abnormal psychology, with particular reference to neuroses. Kovalev (1965), an associate of Myasishchev, appropriately formulated this concept.

> The personality takes shape in the system of objective relationships *(otnosheniya):* economic, moral-political and ideological. The personality's subjective relationships represent attitudes *(otnosheniya)* to society and people as well as to the self, namely to one's social and work commitments. These attitudes characterize the personality's moral constitution, its position in the society, in the collective. There are various attitudes not only with regard to their direction, but also to the level of the individual's awareness. We usually distinguish between attitudes of which the individual is acutely aware and attitudes of which he is barely conscious. An attitude of which the individual is fully aware is an attitude of principle which is . . . determined by inner convictions by the personality's moral ideal, his consciousness of duty and his commitments. The feelings of sympathy and antipathy belong to the second category [p. 14].

For Myasishchev, the individual's inner world consists of a unity between general, particular and individual human characteristics. The general features represent man's biological structure; the particular features express characteristics of the nation or of the social class. In Myasishchev's view, the study of personality should be concerned primarily with the general-human structure of the psyche and subsequently with particular and individual features. Man's attitudes are part of his relationships to the outside world and appear at various philo- and ontogenetic levels. The most elementary relationship takes place with the separation of the ego from the non-ego, which is linked to the feeling of belongingness to a collective body. Although moral relationships may take place at this early stage, their actual development is possible only at a later stage, since they are connected to the feeling of belongingness to a social class. The ethical attitude represents the highest form of man's relationship to his environment.

Myasishchev distinguished three levels of attitudes. The first is related to elementary needs. The second consists of the interplay of social-collective and individual-egoistic tendencies in interpersonal relations. Finally, there are attitudes toward certain objects or kinds of activity.

Social Consciousness and Group Psychology

The relation between individual consciousness and social consciousness has been a traditional topic in Soviet texts of historical materialism and psychology (Kelle and Kovalzon, 1959a, 1965a,b; Kornienko, 1962). Social consciousness was identified with the ideology consisting of politics, law, ethics, religion, science, art and philosophy. Thus there was no room for a study of the individual's belongingness to specific groups. The very existence of a social psychology was denied. Rubinshtein pioneered the harsh criticism which was to follow when he wrote in 1957 that the study of social psychology was favored by reactionary people and was but an attempt to introduce idealistic views into psychology. Kolbanovskii (1965), too, wrote:

. . . social psychologists in the USA rely on pseudoscientific theories in order to obscure the sharpness of contradictions of contemporary imperialism, in particular the acuity of the relations between classes, to neutralize and render harmless the increasing endeavor among workers to unite, to act jointly against the bourgeoisie. Social psychologists take an active part in presenting the employers' attitude toward workers as that of parents who care about their children [p. 130].

Kolbanovskii credited only a minority of American social psychologists with useful work. Others were said to be honest scientists who attempt to make an objective study of the phenomena of social psychology, but fail to do so because of their ignorance of the laws of social development and the wrong methodology. Soviet criticism of American social psychology can be summarized under the following points: (a) society is regarded as a conglomerate of individuals; (b) social development is seen as resulting from arbitrary needs, wishes, actions, etc. of individuals; (c) it overlooks the fact that the development of society is determined, in the last analysis, by the manner of production of material goods and not by the people's psychology; (d) it loses sight of the fact that ideology is the most important factor of the individual's consciousness and that progressive ideas and conscious actions of classes, organizations and individuals play a significant role in man's development; (e) it reduces man's complex psychology to a few unchangeable unconscious motivations and feelings which are seen as the propelling force of social development; (f) it regards the masses of people as a blind, amorphous and irrational force (Zamoshkin, 1957; Popova, 1961a,b; Baskin, 1952; Kremnev, 1961).

There is currently a clear tendency among Soviet authors to distinguish between social psychology in general, which has to be studied, and the Western idealistic theories in this field. In defense of such a study, Parygin (1962) wrote:

. . . bourgeois psychology is idealistic and reactionary . . . but one should not assume that social psychology is a science to be ignored. By the same token, one would not reject political economy, history and sociology because they are studied by idealistic, bourgeois thinkers. It is our belief that the elaboration of a materialistic social psychology by no means implies an agreement with the bourgeois psychology. On the contrary, this provides a possibility to offer opposition to the idealistic reactionary social psychology, with the only scientific social psychology—that of Marx [p. 108].

The revision of the former attitude is closely related to the reconsideration of the concept of social consciousness. A distinction is made between social consciousness and social psychology (Zhuravlev, 1961; Baranov, 1962; Kuzmin, 1963a,b; Parygin, 1962, 1963, 1965a,b; Kolbanovskii, 1965). Not surprisingly, divergent views were also expressed (Gak et al., 1960; Shorokhova, Mansurov, and Platonov, 1963b). The proponents of the above distinction pointed out that both ideology, that is, the social consciousness, as well as people's psychology, reflects the economic structure of the society. But whereas people's psychology is a direct expression of their lives, ideology is not. All ideologies reflect the economic, social and political relationships within the society through social psychology. The ideology represents a somewhat generalized view of the psychology of social groups of the society as a whole. In order to understand the ideology of social classes, it is not enough to be acquainted with the economic life of the society. One has to study the psychology of social groups. Kolbanovskii's (1965) argument is worth quoting:

> Social psychology as a direct reflection of social existence *(bytie)* is an amorphous *(massovidnaya)* form of social consciousness, whereas ideology reflects the social being in theoretical generalizations, laws, etc. We also have to keep in mind that social psychology also expresses the relations between people, their feelings towards each other, their needs and tastes, judgments and views, habits, manners and traditions which are relatively stable and confer a specific character to the group. . . . In this respect, due to the extent of its content, social psychology represents

a larger part of social consciousness. Ideology, however, plays the leading role in the development of a social consciousness, in the influence of the psychology of classes, or of the whole people [pp. 139–140].

Porshnev's (1965) position is also worth quoting at length:

Marxist social psychology does not intend at all to reduce its subject matter to the study of "irrational," "illogical" phenomena of the psychology of masses or groups. Such phenomena cannot be overlooked. Although they are important for theory, it would be wrong to build a Chinese wall between spontaneous, unrealized (neosoznavaemye) psychical phenomena and consciousness. . . . Our social psychology is against the opposition between the unconscious psyche of the crowd and the conscious psyche of its compounding individuals, but rather attempts to make of the process taking place in masses and gatherings, a property of their consciousness, of their understanding. Will the power of socialist competition decrease if every worker or member of a collective farm knows from the time of his school days the simple psychological rules which constitute the brigade's force? . . . Bourgeois sociologists put all the collectives in one bag; moreover, the most transient gathering of a few people linked by reciprocal sympathy (Moreno's sociometry) are given priority. This is only because these studies are based on idealism. Materialism does not deny at all the diversity of collectives, or that some of them are of a purely psychological nature. Materialism must strongly emphasize that only the collectives which correspond to the objective, materialist tendencies of economic development, of the class struggle, only those which are rooted in the social-political life are stable, long-standing and influential. The continuous appearance and disappearance of purely or predominantly psychological gatherings and collectives has served in history only as a mechanism of spontaneous development. Historical-materialism does not state that psychological phenomena in social life necessarily develop subsequently to economic and social changes, which they only reflect, sooner or later. The continuous occurrence of new transient social-psychological formations does not contradict materialism. . . . We should not throw away the material accumulated by bourgeois sociology about small and short-term groups, the economic and social basis of which is not apparent. The problem has to be turned upside down: not to see in them the principle and prototype of any collective, but a form without content, which is continuously sent out like a tentacle, a form which is filled up with a more or less objective content only under favorable circumstances [pp. 176-181].

Earlier Soviet publications used to claim that socialist living allowed man's higher moral qualities to manifest themselves under all circumstances. It was understood that a man who showed negative traits in his work, such as failure to increase his productivity, was also exhibiting negative personality features in his private life. Soviet psychologists currently admit that the individual does not automatically accept all the concepts and views of the society; rather these are transformed in his mind according to his own personality and specific conditions of life. This change of opinion and the renewed interest in the psychology of groups has been explained as being due to the disappearance of the class structure of the Soviet society. It is implied that since the people have for some time collectively owned the means of production, the differences between groups of the same social—worker—class have become more prominent. Olshanskii (1965) wrote:

> As long as there was a class struggle, it seemed evident that personality features depended upon the belongingness to a certain social class. Although "deviations" were unavoidable, they did not influence the historical trend and could be disregarded. When the society has the task of educating new people and leading them toward intellectual *(dukhovnyi)* completeness, moral purity and physical perfection, then not only the final outcome but also the whole course of the process and each decision assume a particular significance. . . . In order to control the formation of personality, we must know not only the major determining factors involved, but all the factors and the mechanism of their interaction [p. 473].

Hence, a trend is developing in Soviet psychology which takes into account the "group consciousness" and the group psychology for purposes of economic planning and ideological propaganda.

Soviet psychologists debate the subject matter of social psychology, the relations between the individual personality and the group, the characteristics of the latter and the methods of study. Kuzmin (1963a,b) suggested that social psychology concern itself with two questions: (a) what is the influence of social factors on the development of thinking generally and on the thinking of a certain individual; (b) what is the nature of interpersonal communication. Parygin (1965a) proposed defining social psychology as the science of the socio-historical typology of people, of their consciousness, individual characteristics and psychical processes. Since these characteristics develop within the framework of a certain group, social psychology becomes the study of the various forms of interpersonal relations. "It is the study of groups, societies and their characteristic structures, and the manifestations of groups in the ways of interpersonal communication" [p. 144].

Baranov (1962) attempted to define group psychology in terms of the reflection theory. He came up, however, with a statement which seems questionable from the perspective of Soviet epistemology:

> In his practical life, man deals not only with the material world, but with the spiritual world of his fellows, not only with the objective results of his activity, but also with the subjective opinions of other people. Certainly, the primary reflection of reality is vastly different from its secondary elaboration. When one elaborates the information received from other people, this is somewhat a reflection of the second order. Psychical processes, therefore, bear the stamp of a twofold subjectivity. This does not mean that knowledge acquired in an indirect way is less objective. On the contrary, the double processing of information enables a deeper penetration into the core of all phenomena. However, the tendency toward subjectivity is increased [p. 96].

Finally, Kelle and Kovalzon (1959b) also tried their hand in applying the Marxist theory of knowledge to this area, although their following statement attracted broad criticism (Gak et al., 1960). They wrote:

First, there is the cognitive process which is dependent upon man's practical interests and consists of the accumulation of objective knowledge about nature and society. Second, there is the ideological process which is dependent upon the interests of different groups. . . . The ideological process involves a cognitive aspect, while the development of knowledge includes the ideological aspect. But one should not confuse these two tendencies, since social consciousness cannot be reduced to either knowledge or ideology [p. 111].

While currently using the term "psychological group," Soviet authors are cautious as to its definition. They keep emphasizing the basic common features of socialist living. Selivanov (1968a) pointed out that no matter to which social group an individual belongs, the basic aims and endeavors are the same, pointing up the high moral qualities of the Soviet people. Other authors proposed to distinguish between the concepts of social group and psychological group. Osipov, for instance, stated that the formation of psychological groups is closely related to the consciousness of the members of the group, while social groups are formed as a result of economic necessity, independent of the will of their members. He made it clear, however, that the two types of groups cannot be absolutely separated since psychological groups are also contingent to some extent on economic factors. Finally, Olshanskii (1965) preferred the term "group consciousness" to that of "group culture" used in Western sociology. He felt that the latter confuses the material and cultural factors of social life and is likely to give rise to "idealistic speculations." Group consciousness implies a certain level of social consciousness above individual differences, such as personal experience, temperament, etc. By its very nature, the work-team produces a psychosocial group the members of which hold the same social position, the same attitude towards the means of production and the same role in the social organization of work. These factors produce a direct reciprocal influence among the members of the group. Olshanskii found that some of the opinions expressed by a group—workers in a factory—were in opposition to those expressed by the society in general. Thus, for instance, while the group admitted to adhering to marriage, accepted the importance of not being late at work without prior notification, it saw nothing wrong with swearing or drinking. The group had a system of "do's" and "don't's" and only after getting acquainted with it, could one understand why, at one time, the group defended one of its members who committed an offense, yet, on another occasion, supported the administration's position.

Olshanskii's study aimed at revealing some of the individual differences of the group members. His observations regarding their attitude toward religion are instructive. He noticed that only a few persons were actually believers, but that a great number of them had their children christened. This was because most of the workers grew up in a rural area, or had relatives living in country areas where their children spent vacations. In order to show how the individual's systems of values and goals influences his behavior and whether this can be changed through the group consciousness, a sociometric test was carried out. (Olshanskii put the word sociometric in quotation marks.) The experimenters engineered a rumour that the brigade was to be reorganized and that its members would have to change their places of work. An inquiry was made and each worker was asked to indicate the names of four workers whom he would wish to work with, giving the order of preference. The hypothesis of a relation between group values and individual values was confirmed. Olshanskii rejected the sociometric assumption that some people are preferred, while others, the "sociometric proletariat," are ignored. In his opinion, the choices were determined by group consciousness, the group appreciating those persons whose behavior corresponded to the collective values. Olshanskii acceded, however, that interpersonal relations were more complex than they appeared in his study and that the group's attitude towards its members represented only a statistical tendency.

A great deal of controversy exists as to the research methods of social psychology, especially with regard to sociometry (Kozyrev, 1965; Zdravomyslov and Yadov, 1965a,b; Kolominskii, 1963; Neimark, 1963; Tsentsifer, 1965; Sventsitskii, 1966). Some authors do not find any use for this method. Platonov (1965), who used it, felt that the same result could be obtained by other, more simple procedures. On the other hand, Kuzmin (1963b) wrote that the sociometric method is useful if it is isolated from Moreno's incorrect theory and methodology. He maintained that it gives a momentary accurate photograph of the inner relations among the members of a group, which although lacking in any explanation as to the causes of these relations, does provide a picture of the life of the collective.

Concluding Remarks

The closing pages of this work will consider the extent to which Soviet psychology represents a school of thought distinct from any Western trend. This topic is particularly relevant now in view of the recent developments in psychology in Russia, notably the acceptance of numerous findings of "bourgeois" psychology and the recognition of new areas of study as genuinely scientific and clearly under the influence of Western thought.

Three attitudes toward Western psychology may be distinguished in the history of Soviet psychology. In the first period of development of a distinct Soviet school of thought, some Western schools were regarded as compatible with Marxism. By contrast, a negativistic attitude prevailed between the end of the 1940's and the first half of the 1950's. The current period is characterized by the incorporation of specific theories of Western neurophysiologists, psychologists and students of related disciplines in the theoretical framework of a dialectical and materialistic psychology. Theoretical studies, such as for instance Leontiev's, include relevant references to Western works as support for views clearly emerging from the tenets of

Soviet philosophy. Thus, there is a remarkable rapprochement between Russian scholars and their Western counterparts. The neurocybernetic advances, the departure of some students of animal behavior from classical conditioning, the liberation from a dogmatic corticalism, the broader approach to the localization of cerebral functions, the intensive study of perception in terms of information processing, the flourishing of nonassociationistic approaches to problem solving and the willingness to use sociometric analysis are among the developments which have considerably broadened the platform on which Russian and Western scholars can meet.

A distinction should be made, however, between the current broader view on the part of the Soviets with regard to the achievements of their Western colleagues and their unchanged basic positions concerning such fundamental issues as the body-mind relationship, the "mirroring" nature of the cognitive and emotional processes and the relationship between the psychology of the individual and the class structure of the society in which he lives. Soviet authors may ally themselves with a particular Western school on some issues, and with another school on certain other issues. But as a whole, contemporary Soviet psychology constitutes a philosophical and theoretical framework clearly distinct from any other school.

How genuine are the Soviet psychologists in the expression of their philosophical credo? Is it more than compliance with the demands of officialdom? Such questions have been prompted by cases of self-criticism and retraction of former positions following ideological criticism. Rubinshtein's fluctuations provide the most prominent illustration of recantation. He was as convincing in his plea for the significance of Pavlovian theory on psychology as he had been in his arguments to the contrary. The typical commencement and/or conclusion of articles, particularly of those concerned with theoretical issues, with a philosophical or political statement (e.g., a reference to a passage by Lenin, to a speech by a Party leader, or to a resolution of a leading body of the Party), sometimes with remote connection to their content, has also contributed to raise doubts about the frankness of the authors involved.

It goes without saying that when Soviet psychologists deal with basic concepts, they are expected to be in agreement with the dialectical-materialistic philosophy and to couch their thoughts in a basically stereotyped language. For instance, among the objections levelled in 1948 against Leontiev's conjectures about the development of mind was the accusation that he used an unwieldy language. He failed, indeed, to follow the beaten track and departed from the stereotyped language of the textbooks of dialectical materialism. Furthermore, the authors of textbooks—which have to be approved by the Ministry of Education to be used in schools—are, by and large, simplified presentations of basic positions. They carefully avoid getting into any controversial depth. This is true even for the higher level of textbooks used by pedagogical institutes. The endeavor to echo the approved textbooks of philosophy is at its height.

However, one should not conclude that the expression of philosophical beliefs is a mere matter of lip service. The theoretical attempts of Soviet psychologists manifest in articles and monographs and their experimental efforts give evidence of their conviction that mind is a reflection of an external and objective reality and is the product of the evolution of the property of matter to reflect external influences, that it is imperative to investigate the material substratum of mind, that human consciousness is the highest level of reflection, that man is primarily a conscious and voluntary being and that the individual's psychology is largely a product of the economic structure of the society in which he lives. It is not infrequent that a conflict flares up between watchdogs of ideological purity—e.g., the editorial board of *Kommunist*—and scholars who have endeavored to substantiate Marxist tenets in specific propositions. Such conflicts were particularly acute in times when dogmatism prevailed (as in the late 1940's and the early 1950's) highlighting the genuine undertaking of psychologists to forward the Marxist approach to mind. Editorials in political journals claimed that the fundamental brain-mind problem had been solved in principle by the classics of Marxism and that the debate among psychologists was an indication that they did not assimilate the Marxist teaching and Pavlov's theory. The topic of a large number of theoretical articles was then the interpretation of statements by Marx, Engels, Lenin, Stalin and Pavlov. As a matter of fact, the authors of these articles have accepted the Marxist propositions, but their divergent attempts to go beyond the general statements were taken as misunderstanding of what Marx or Lenin had said. They apparently complied with the authoritarian demands by limiting themselves to an exegesis of what *Magister dixit*. In recent years, enjoying greater freedom of expression, Soviet authors have deepened the argument and tackled controversial issues in a drive to advance the materialistic and dialectical approach to mind. An extensive polemic currently taking place in *Voprosy Psikhologii*—too recent to be referred to in the body of the book—is illustrative in this respect. The participants to this debate thoroughly discuss the status of concepts of the traditional introspective psychology in a Marxist psychology. It is obvious that these writers do not merely comply with ideological demands.

It is important to keep in mind that although relevant Soviet works can be evaluated as such, without reference to their background, as if they could have been produced anywhere, they are part and parcel of the general endeavor to develop a materialistic psychology. Vygotskii's views are a case in point. The evolution of his thoughts on the role of "signs" in human behavior directly emerged from his purpose to overcome mechanist tendencies in the Russian psychology of the 1920's and formulate a theory based on Marx's proposition that man is a tool-producing being. Furthermore, the development of his conception by Leontiev, Luria and Galperin has been contingent upon the criticism of Vygotskii's theory. Another instance, Anokhin's work on the development of the organism's anticipatory adaptation, was explicitly inspired by the reflection theory. Other topics of experimental concern, such as for instance the nature of interoceptive conditioned reflexes, or the relationship between processes of analysis and synthesis in the course of solving a problem could readily be seen as having emerged from basic positions regarding the nature of mind.

To be sure, there are Russian works which make no reference to Marxism. For instance, no work of the "classics" of Marxism is listed in the bibliography of Glezer's monograph. Pavlov is mentioned only casually. The author's standpoint equally relies on Russian and Western works. (As a matter of fact, there are more Western than Russian references). But Glezer's position that visual images are largely the result of learning is consonant with the general Soviet view about the formation of mental images.

I have precisely attempted in this work to suggest the close relationship between general philosophical, and specific theoretical and experimental approaches to mind in the Soviet psychology. Although it currently presents a more diversified picture than in the 1920's, Soviet psychology appears as far more unitary than in that period. The meaning of the label "Soviet" psychology is thus basically different from that of "American" or "British" psychology. The achievements as well as the weakness of this school emerge from its philosophical-theoretical system.

Levy Rahmani

Boston, June 1972

References

Abramyan, L. A. (1961), *Signal and Conditioned Reflex. A Philosophical Study.* Erevan: Izd. Akad. Nauk Armyanskoi SSSR.

—— (1966), The basic concepts of semiotics. *Vop. Filos.,* 10:50–60.

Abuladze, K. S. (1961), *The Functions of Paired Organs.* Moscow: Medgiz.

Adrianov, O. S. & Rabinovich, M. Ya. (1960), On the mechanisms and localization of the connective function of the brain. In: *The Structure and Functions of Human Analyzers in Ontogenesis. Proceedings of a Symposium of the Brain Institute,* 11–13 December 1959, ed. I. N. Filimonov & L. A. Kukuev. Moscow: Medgiz, pp. 152–178.

Afanasev, V. G. (1960), *Fundamentals of Marxist Philosophy.* Moscow: Izd. Sotsialno-Ekonomicheskoi Literatury.

Airapetyants, E. Sh. (1952), *Higher Nervous Activity and the Receptors of Internal Organs.* Moscow-Leningrad: Izd. Akad. Nauk SSSR.

—— & Bianki, V. L. (1960a), The development of spatial analysis and of the conjugate functioning of the forebrain. In: *Problems of Comparative Physiology of Analyzers.* First Issue, ed. E. Sh. Airapetyants. Leningrad: Izd. Leningradskogo Universiteta, pp. 41–46.

—— et al. (1960b), The principle of convergence of analyzers in animal evolution. Ibid., pp. 7–24.

—— et al. (1960c), The physiological mechanisms for spatial analysis. *Sechenov Physiological Journal,* 8:1056–1067.

—— & Batuev, A. S. (1963), Sechenov's theory on the reflex nature of the reflection of space and its current development. *Zh. Vys. Nerv. Deyat.,* 5:831–844.

—— (1966a), Sechenov's hypotheses on internal analyzers and the current status of their study. In: *Consciousness and Reflex,* ed. E. Sh. Airapetyants, D. A. Biryukov & V. N. Chernigovskii. Moscow/Leningrad: Izd. Nauka, pp. 150–162.

—— & Batuev, A. S. (1966b), Sechenov's ideas about the role of the muscular sense for spatial orientation and their experimental design. Ibid., pp. 73–90.

—— ed. (1966c), *Problems of Comparative Physiology of Analyzers,* Second Issue. Leningrad: Izd. Leningradskogo Universiteta.

—— (1967a), Brain mechanisms and space analysis. In: *Researches on Brain Signaling Apparata,* ed. E. Sh. Airapetyants. Leningrad: Izd. Nauka, Leningradskoe Otdelenie, pp. 11–21.[1]

[1] A publication of the United Learned Board "Physiology of Man and Animals," Acad. Sci. USSR.

—— (1967b), Studies on the construction of the visceral cortex. Ibid., pp. 135–147.

Aizerman, M. A. (1962a), Experiments on teaching machines to recognize visual images. In: *Biological Aspects of Cybernetics*, ed. A. M. Kuzin et al. Moscow: Izd. Akad. Nauk SSSR, pp. 174–183.[2]

—— (1962b), Machines learn to recognize visual images. *Nauka i Zhizn*, 12:34–39.

Akchurin, I. A., Vedenov, M. F., & Sakhov, Yu. V. (1968), Methodological problems of mathematical modeling in biology. In: *Mathematical Modeling of Biological Processes*, ed. M. F. Vedenov et al., pp. 7–44.[3]

Akhlibinskii, B. V. (1966), *Cybernetics and the Enigmas of Psyche*. Leningrad: Lenizdat.

Aleksandrov, G. F. (1946), *The History of Western European Philosophy*, Second edition. Moscow: Izd. Akad. Nauk SSSR.

Aleksandrov, N. V. (1965), Problems of programmed learning. *Sov. Pedag.*, 6:3–11.

Alekseev, M. A. (1958), Some remarks on Anokhin's views of the afferent apparatus of the conditioned reflex. *Zh. Vys. Nerv. Deyat.*, 3:453–467.

Alekseev, N. G. (1963), Is the algorithmic approach to the analysis of learning warranted? *Vop. Psikhol.*, 3:137–142.

Amosov, I. M. (1965a), *Modeling of Thought and Psyche*. Kiev: Izd. Naukova Dumka.

—— (1965b), A possible approach to the modeling of human psychical life. *Vop. Filos.*, 2:49–56.

Ananev, B. G. (1931), Some problems of the Marxist-Leninist reconstruction of psychology. *Psikhologiya*, 3/4:325–344.

—— (1946), Toward a theory of internal speech in psychology. In: *Psychology of Sensory Cognition*. Works of members of the RSFSR Academy of Pedagogical Sciences. Moscow: Izd. Akad. Ped. Nauk, pp. 348–349, 1960.

—— (1948), The monocular localization of objects. Ibid., pp. 129–140.

—— ed. (1954), *Problems of General and Child Psychology*. Moscow: Izd. Akad. Pedag. Nauk.

—— (1955), *Perceptual Differentiation of Space*. Leningrad: Izd. Leningradskogo Universiteta.

—— (1958), The contribution of Soviet psychology to the theory of sensation. In: *Psychology of Sensory Cognition*, pp. 115–128.

—— et al. (1959a), *Touch in the Processes of Cognition and Work*. Moscow: Izd. Akad. Pedag. Nauk.

—— et al., eds. (1959b), Psychological Science in the USSR. vol. I and vol. II (1960). Moscow: Izd. Akad. Pedag. Nauk RSFSR.

—— (1960), *Theory of Sensation*. Leningrad: Izd. Leningradskogo Universiteta.

—— & Lomov, B. F., eds. (1961), *Problems of Perception of Space and Spatial Representations*. Moscow: Izd. Akad. Pedag. Nauk RSFSR.

—— & —— eds. (1963a), *Problems of General and Engineering Psychology*. Leningrad: Izd. Leningradskogo Universiteta.

[2] A publication of the Learned Board on the Complex Problem "Cybernetics" (Division of Biological Sciences), Acad. Sci. USSR.

[3] A joint publication of the Scientific Board on the Complex Problem "Philosophical Problems of Contemporary Natural Sciences," Acad. Sci. USSR and of the Division of Philosophical Problems of Biological Sciences, Institute of Philosophy, Acad. Sci. USSR.

_____ (1963b), Bilateral regulation as a behavior mechanism. Translated in: *Soviet Psychology and Psychiatry*, Winter 1964/65, 2:15-25.

_____ & Rybalko, E. F. (1964), *Characteristics of Spatial Perception in Children*. Moscow: Prosveshchenie.

_____ (1968a), The individual sensory-perceptual development. *Vop. Psikhol.*, 1:3-11.

_____ (1968b), Bilateral regulation of ontogenetic development in humans. Translated in: *Soviet Psychology*, Winter 1970, 2:138-156.

_____ Dvoryashina, M. D. & Kudryavtseva, N. A. (1968c), *Human Individual Development and Constancy of Perception*. Moscow: Izd. Prosveshchenie.

Andreev, I. D. (1959), *Fundamentals of Knowledge Theory*. Moscow: Izd. Akad. Nauk SSSR.

Andreev, N. D. & Zinder, L. R. (1963), On the concepts of speech act, speech, linguistic probability and language. *Vop. Yazykofnaniya*, 3:15-21.

Anisimov, S. & Vislobodkov, A. (1960), Some philosophical problems of cybernetics. *Kommunist*, 2:108-118.

Anokhin, P. K., ed. (1935), *Reports on the Problem of Center and Periphery in the Physiology of Nervous Activity. Experiments with Anastomosis of Nerves*. Gorkii: Gosudarstvennoe Izdatelstvo. (English resumé available).

_____ (1949a), *Ivan Petrovich Pavlov. Life, Activity and School*. Moscow/Leningrad: Izd. Akad. Nauk SSSR.

_____ ed. (1949b), *Problems of Higher Nervous Activity*. Moscow: Medgiz.

_____ (1956), Features of the afferent apparatus of the conditioned reflex and their importance for psychology. Translated in: *Recent Soviet Psychology*, ed. N. O'Connor. Oxford: Pergamon Press, pp. 75-103.

_____ (1957), Physiology and cybernetics. *Vop. Filos.*, 4:142-158.

_____ (1958), *Internal Inhibition as a Physiological Problem*. Moscow: Medgiz.

_____ (1961), A new conception of the physiological architecture of the conditioned reflex. In: *Brain Mechanisms and Learning*, ed. A. Fessard, R. W. Gerard & J. Konorski. Oxford: Blackwell Scientific Publications, pp. 189-227.

_____ (1962a), The theory of the functional system as a prerequisite for the construction of physiological cybernetics. In: *Biological Aspects of Cybernetics*, ed. A. M. Kuzin et al. Moscow: Izd. Akad. Nauk SSSR, pp. 74-91.

_____ (1962b), The anticipated reflection of reality. *Vop. Filos.*, 7:97-111.

_____ (1963a), Methodological analysis of crucial problems of the conditioned reflex. In: *Philosophical Problems of Physiology of Higher Nervous Activity and Psychology*, ed. P. N. Fedoseev, et al. Moscow: Izd. Akad. Nauk SSSR, pp. 156-214.

_____ (1963b), To dot the i's. In: *What Is Possible and Impossible in Cybernetics*, ed. A. Berg & E. Kolman (a scientific-popular series), pp. 95-103.

_____ (1964), Problems of modeling biological processes in physiology. In: *On the Essence of Life*, ed. G. M. Frank & A. M. Kuzin. Moscow: Izd. Nauka, pp. 204-210.

_____ (1966), Cybernetics and the integrative activity of the brain. *Vop. Psikhol.*, 3:10-32.

_____ et al. (1967), Biological and medical cybernetics. In: *Cybernetics in the Service of Communism*, vol. 5, ed. A. I. Berg. Moscow: Izd. Energiya, pp. 214-251.

_____ (1968), *The Biology and Neurophysiology of the Conditioned Reflex*. Moscow: Izd. Meditsina.

Antsyferova, L. I. (1961), *Determinism and Elementary Cognitive Activity*. Moscow: Izd. Akad. Nauk SSSR.

_____ (1963), Gestalt psychology. In: *Contemporary Psychology in Capitalist Countries*, ed. E. V. Shorokhova, Moscow: Izd. Akad. Nauk SSSR, pp. 90–148.

_____ (1964), The problem of perception in contemporary psychology in capitalist countries. *Sov. Pedag.*, 2:79–86.

_____ (1965), The neobehaviorist theory of thought and Piaget's operational conception. *Vop. Psikhol.*, 2:165–172.

_____ (1969), The principle of connection between consciousness and activity and the methodology of psychology. In: *Methodological and Theoretical Problems of Psychology*, ed. E. V. Shorokhova. Moscow: Izd. Nauka, pp. 57–115.

Arana, L. (1961), Perception as a probability process. *Vop. Psikhol.*, 5:47–62.

Arkhangelskii, L. M. (1964), The assessment of communist behavior. *Sov. Pedag.*, 8:65–72.

Arkhipov, V. M. (1954), On the material nature of the psyche and the subject matter of psychology. *Sov. Pedag.*, 7:67–79.

Artemov, V. A. (1928), The contemporary German psychology, First part, *Psikhologiya*, Seriya A., 1:66–94; Second part, Ibid., 2:32–58.

_____ (1929), On the problem of a social psychology. *Psikhologiya*, 2:165–178.

Ashby, W. R. (1950), *Design for a Brain. The Origin of Adaptive Behaviour*, Second edition. London: Chapman & Hall, 1960.

Asratyan, E. A. (1961), Some aspects of the elaboration of conditioned connections and formation of their properties. In: *Brain Mechanisms and Learning*, ed. J. F. Delafresnaye. Oxford: Blackwell, pp. 95–113.

_____ (1963), Conditioned reflex and related phenomena. In: *Philosophical Problems of Physiology of Higher Nervous Activity and Psychology*, ed. P. N. Fedoseev, pp. 323–357.

_____ (1965a), Some features of the formation, functioning and inhibition of conditioned reflexes with bilateral connection. In: *Reflexes of the Brain. An International Conference Dedicated to the 100 Aniversary of Sechenov's Work*, ed. E. A. Asratyan. Moscow: Izd. Nauka, pp. 114–126.

_____ (1965b), Conditioned reflex and contemporary neurophysiology. *Zh. Vys. Nerv. Deyat.*, 2:202–216.

_____ (1969), On the mechanism of formation of a conditioned reflex. *Zh. Vys. Nerv. Deyat.*, 5:741–751.

_____ (1970), A profound idea of Pavlov. *Zh. Vys. Nerv. Deyat.*, 2:269–279.

Aus der Resolution der Parteizelle des Instituts der Roten Professur für Philosophie und Naturwissenschaft in Moskau. Angenommen am 29 Dezember 1930. In: *Die Sowjetphilosophie. Wendigkeit und Bestimmtheit. Dokumente*, ed. W. Goerdt. Basel/Stuttgart: Schwabe & Co Verlag, 1966, pp. 237–248.

Avramenko, A. M. (1954), On the reflection theory of the psychical activity. *Sov. Pedag.*, 2:67–76.

Babosov, E. M. (1963), *Dialectics of Analysis and Synthesis in Scientific Knowledge*. Minsk: Izd. Akad. Nauk Belorusskoi SSR.

Baev, V. P. (1958), Dependence of functional features of internal speech on thinking activity. *Vop. Psikhol.*, 6:108–118.

Bailey, P. & Bonin, G. (1951), *The Isocortex of Man*. Urbana: University of Illinois Press.

REFERENCES

Bakhur, V. T. (1956), On some problems of the localization of functions. *Zh. Nevr. Psikhiat.*, 12:967–968.

Banshchikov, V. M. et al., eds. (1952), *The Physiological Teaching of the Academician I. P. Pavlov in Psychiatry and Neuropathology. Proceedings of a Conference Held in October 1951.* Moscow: Medgiz.

Baranov, A. V. (1962), On the topic of social psychology. *Vop. Psikhol.*, 2:92–100.

Baskin, M. P. (1952), The psychological trend in the American bourgeois sociology. In: *I. P. Pavlov's Teaching and Philosophical Problems of Psychology,* ed. A. S. Petrushevskii. Moscow: Izd. Akad. Nauk SSSR, pp. 457–474.

Basov, M. Ya. (1931), *Problems of General Pedology.* Moscow/Leningrad: Gosizdat.

Bassin, F. V. (1956), On some debatable problems of the contemporary theory of function localization. *Zh. Nevr. Psikhiat.*, 7:579–587.

—— (1960a), A debate on Freudianism: a critical analysis of Freudianism. *Soviet Review,* 1:3–13.

—— (1960b), A debate on Freudianism: a rejoinder to Professor Musatti. *Soviet Review,* 1:27–40.

—— (1962, On the problem of the "unconscious." *Vop. Filos.*, 7:112–123.

—— (1963), Consciousness and the unconscious. Translated in: *A Handbook of Contemporary Soviet Psychology,* ed. M. Cole & I. Maltzman. New York/London: Basic Books, pp. 399–420, 1969.

Batishchev, G. S., Trubnikov, N. N. & Sheptulin, A. P. (1964), Analysis of the dialectical path of knowledge in Lenin's *Philosophical Notebooks.* In: *Dialectics as Knowledge Theory; Studies in History of Philosophy,* ed. B. M. Kedrov. Moscow: Izd. Nauka, pp. 252–294.

Batuev, A. S. (1966), Cortical mechanisms of compensation after the exclusion of visual reception. In: *Problems of Comparative Physiology of Analyzers,* Second Issue, ed. E. Sh. Airapetyants. Leningrad: Izd. Leningradskogo Universiteta, pp. 25–45.

—— (1970a), The evolution of frontal lobes in mammals and the physiological basis of their pathology in man. *Zh. Nevr. Psikhiat.*, 6:847–852.

—— & Pirogov, A. A. (1970b), The neurochemical analysis of the primary response to flash stimulation in cats under nembutal anesthesia. *Fiziol. Zh. SSSR,* 3:297–304.

—— & Malynkova, T. V. (1971), Investigation of the role of the frontal lobes of the brain in complex forms of behavior in cats. *J. Evolutionary Biochemistry and Physiology* (published by Consultants Bureau), 4:352–358.

Bauer, R. (1952), *The New Man in Soviet Psychology.* Cambridge: Harvard University Press.

Bazhenov, L. B. (1964a), Some philosophical problems of modeling thinking by cybernetic devices. In: *Cybernetics, Thinking, Life,* ed. A. I. Berg et al. Moscow: Mysl, pp. 326–339.

—— Biryukov, B., & Shtoff, V. (1964b), Modeling. In: *Philosophical Encyclopedia,* vol. 3, ed. F. V. Konstantinov. Moscow: Izd. Sovetskaya Entsiklopediya, pp. 478–481.

Bein, E. S. (1948), On the constancy of perceived size. In: *Studies on Psychology of Perception,* ed. S. L. Rubinshtein. Moscow/Leningrad: Izd. Akad. Nauk SSSR, pp. 167–199.

Bekhterev, V. M. (1899), *Die Liestungsbahnen im Gehirn und Rückenmark.* Translated by R. Weinberg. Leipzig.

_____ (1908), *Psyche und Leben.* Second edition. Wiesbaden: Verlag von J. F. Bergman.

_____ (1913), *Objective Psychologie oder Psychoreflexologie; die Lehre von den Assoziationsreflexen.* Leipzig und Berlin: B. G. Teubner.

_____ (1917), *General Principles of Human Reflexology.* Translated by E. & W. Murphy from the Russian of the 4th edition (1928). New York: International Publishers, 1933.

_____ (1918), *La Reflexologie Collective.* Traduit du Russe Adapté et Complété par N. Kostileff. Neuchatel: Delachaux & Niestlé, 1957.

_____ & Shchelovanov, N. M. (1924), Toward the establishment of a developmental reflexology. Translated in: *Soviet Psychology,* Fall 1969, 1:7-25.

_____ (1925), *Advances in Reflexology and Physiology of the Nervous System.* Leningrad: Gosudarstvennoe Izdatelstvo.

_____ & Dubrovskii [4] (1926), Dialectical materialism and reflexology. *Pod Znamenem Marksizma,* 7/8:69-94.

Bekhtereva, N. P., ed. (1965), *Role of Deep Structures of Human Brain in Mechanisms of Pathological Reactions. Proceedings of a Symposium,* 10-12 June. Leningrad: Institute of Experimental Medicine of Acad. Med. Sci. USSR, and Sechenov Society of Physiologists, Biochemists and Pharmacologists, Leningrad.

Belyaev, B. V. (1929), The problem of the collective and its experimental study in psychology. *Psikhologiya,* Seriya A, 2:179-214.

_____ (1930), The beginning of the end of reflexology. Ibid., 2:134-144.

Berg, A. I. & Kolman, E., eds. (1963), *What Is Possible and Impossible in Cybernetics.* Moscow: Izd. Akad. Nauk SSSR.

_____ et al., eds. (1964), *Cybernetics, Thinking, Life.* Moscow: Izd. Mysl.

_____ & Novik, I. B. (1965), Development of knowledge and cybernetics. *Kommunist,* 2:19-29.

Beritashvili, I. S. [5] (1968), *Vertebrate Memory. Characteristics and Origin.* New York/London: Plenum Press (English edition, 1971).

_____ (1969a), Concerning psychoneural activity of animals. In: *A Handbook of Contemporary Soviet Psychology,* pp. 627-670.

_____ Bakhuradze, A. N. & Kats, A. I. (1969b), A study of image memory in lower primates. Translated in: *Soviet Psychology,* Fall 1970, 1:66-71.

Beritov, I. S. (1947), *General Physiology of the Nervous and Muscular Systems,* vol. I. Second edition. Moscow/Leningrad: Izd. Akad. Nauk SSSR.

_____ (1959), The mechanisms of spatial orientation in man. *Pavlov Journal of Higher Nervous Activity,* 9:1-10.

_____ ed. (1960), Gagra Symposia, vol. III: *Mechanisms of Formation of Neural Temporary Connections.* Tbilisi: Izd. Akad. Nauk Gruzinskoi SSR.

_____ (1961), *Neural Mechanisms of Higher Vertebrate Behavior.* Translation in 1965. Boston: Little, Brown, & Co.

_____ (1966), *General Physiology of Muscular and Nervous Systems,* vol. II. Third edition. Moscow: Meditsina.

_____ (1969), *Structure and Functions of the Cerebral Cortex.* Izd. Akad. Nauk SSSR, & Akad. Nauk Gruzinskoi SSR.

---

[4] First name is not mentioned.
[5] Beritashvili is Beritov's Gruzinian name.

REFERENCES

Bernshtein, A. N. (1947), *Organization of Movements*. Moscow: Medgiz.

_____ (1961), Current problems of the physiology of activity. *Problemy kibernetiki*, 6:101-160.

_____ (1962), Methods for developing physiology as related to the problems of cybernetics. In: *A Handbook of Contemporary Soviet Psychology*, New York: Basic Books, pp. 441-451.

_____ (1965), Towards a biology of active processes. *Vop. Filos.*, 10:65-78.

_____ (1966), *The Co-ordination and Regulation of Movements*. Oxford, New York: Pergamon Press, 1967.

_____ (1968),[6] Modeling problems in the biology of active processes. In: *Mathematical Modeling of Biological Processes*, ed. M. F. Vedenov et al., Moscow: Izd. Mysl, pp. 184-197.

Bertalanffy, L. (1968), *General Systems, Theory, Foundation, Development, Application*. New York: George Braziller.

Bianki, V. L. (1959a), Role of corpus callosum and the paired activity of the visual and skin analyzers in the rabbit. *Pavlov Journal of Higher Nervous Activity*, 1:101-110.

_____ (1959b), Interaction between the symmetrical cortical centers of the visual analyzer. Ibid., 6:782-791.

_____ (1960), New findings on the role of various brain areas in amphibians for the conditioned reflex activity. In: *Problems of Comparative Physiology of Analyzers*. First Issue, ed. E. Sh. Airapetyants. Leningrad: Izd. Leningradskogo Universiteta, pp. 46-65.

_____ (1967), *Evolution of the Paired Function of the Cerebral Hemispheres*. Leningrad: Izd. Leningradskogo Universiteta.

_____ Pokrovskaya, L. A. & Voevodenkova, M. A. (1969), Interhemispheric synthesis of antagonistic conditioned reflexes. *Zh. Vys. Nerv. Deyat.*, 6:928-936.

_____ (1970a), Interhemispheric synthesis of conditioned motor reactions elaborated at different angles. *Zh. Vys. Nerv. Deyat.*, 4:493-498.

_____ & Makarova, A. E. (1970b), The features of functional asymmetry of the hemispheres caused by different location of conditioning and control stimuli. Ibid., 1:50-58.

_____ & Moiseeva, L. A. (1970c), Binocular interaction in the visual cortex of rats related to change of time interval between monocular stimuli. *Fiziol. Zh. SSSR.*, 3:305-311.

_____ (1971a), A comparative hypothesis of orientation in space. *Fiziol. Zh. SSSR.*, 11:1595-1606.

_____ & Voevodenkova, M. A. (1971b), The influence of stage-by-stage splitting of the brain on the interhemispheric analytic-synthetic activity and hemispheric dominance. Ibid., 2:463-469.

Biryukov, B. V. & Tyukhtin, V. S. (1964), Philosophical problems of cybernetics. In: *Cybernetics, Thinking, Life*, ed. A. I. Berg et al. Moscow: Izd. Mysl, 76-108.

_____ et al. (1967), Philosophical problems of cybernetics. In: *Cybernetics in the Service of Communism*, vol. 5, ed. A. I. Berg. Moscow: Izd. Energiya, pp. 263-313.

[6] Published after Bernshtein's death.

_____ & Geller, E. S. (1968), On the cybernetic modeling of cognitive psychical processes. Introduction to I. B. Novik (1969), *Philosophical Problems of the Modeling of Psyche.* Moscow: Izd. Nauka, pp. 7–28.

Biryukov, D. A. (1962), Basic philosophical problems of the evolution of higher nervous activity. *Vop. Psikhol.*, 4:36–57.

_____ ed. (1966), *Problems of Physiology and Pathology of Higher Nervous Activity,* Issue III. Leningrad: Izd. Meditsina, Leningradskoe Otdelenie.

Blagonadezhina, L. V. (1952), On the reconstruction of psychology on the basis of I. P. Pavlov's teaching. *Sov. Pedag.*, 10:43–55.

Blakeley, T. J. (1964), *Soviet Philosophy. A General Introduction to Contemporary Soviet Thought.* Dordrecht-Holland: D. Reidel Publishing Company.

Blinkov, S. M. & Glezer, I. I. (1964), *The Human Brain in Figures and Tables.* New York: Basic Books (English edition, 1968).

Bliznichenko, L. A. (1966), *Remembering in Natural Sleep.* Kiev: Naukova Dumka.

Blonskii, P. P. (1925), *Pedology.* Moscow: Izd. Rabotnik Prosveshcheniya.

_____ (1927), *Psychological Essays.* Moscow/Leningrad: Gosudarstvennoe Izdatelstvo.

_____ (1935), *Memory and Thinking.* In: *Selected Psychological Works.* Moscow: Izd. Prosveshchenie, 1964.

Bobneva, M. I. (1964), Heuristic programs, "mazes" and some psychological problems. *Vop. Psikhol.*, 5:133–141.

_____ (1966), *Engineering Psychology.* Moscow: Izd. Nauka.

Bogoyavlenskii, D. N. (1951), I. P. Pavlov's teaching—the natural-scientific foundation of the psychology of comprehension. *Sov. Pedag.*, 12:28–39.

_____ (1957), *The Psychology of Acquisition of Spelling.* Moscow: Izd. Akad. Pedag. Nauk RSFSR.

_____ & Menchinskaya, N. A. (1959a), *Acquisition of Knowledge in School.* Moscow: Izd. Akad. Pedag. Nauk RSFSR.

_____ ed. (1959b), *Psychological Problems of Grammar and Spelling Acquisition.* Moscow: Izd. Akad. Pedag. Nauk RSFSR.

_____ (1962), Development of methods of intellectual work as a way of advancing and activating pupils' thinking. *Vop. Psikhol.*, 4:74–82

_____ (1969), Methods of intellectual work and their development in pupils. *Ibid.*, 2:25–38.

Boiko, E. I. (1952), Some problems of reconstructing psychology on the ground of I. P. Pavlov's teaching. *Vop. Filos.*, 1:162–168.

_____ (1958), On the double role of positioning reflexes in complex system reactions. In: *Orienting Reflex and Exploratory Behavior,* ed. L. G. Voronin et al., pp. 417–424. (English edition, 1965, ed. D. B. Lindsley. Washington D.C.: American Institute of Biological Sciences, pp. 417–424).

_____ (1959), Problems regarding the conditioned reflex foundations of higher psychological functions. In: *Psychological Science in the USSR,* vol. I, ed. B. G. Ananev et al. Moscow: Izd. Akad. Pedag. Nauk RSFSR, pp. 578–598.

_____ (1961), *Conterminous Problems of Higher Neural Dyanmics and Psychology.* Moscow: Izd. Akad. Pedag Nauk RSFSR.

_____ (1964), *Reaction Time in Man.* Moscow: Izd. Meditsina.

_____ (1967a), Modeling higher forms of temporary connections. *Vop. Psikhol.*, 4:107–114.

_____ et al. (1967b), Cybernetics and psychology problems. In: *Cybernetics in the Service of Communism*, vol. 5, ed. A. I. Berg. Moscow: Izd. Energiya, pp. 314-350.

_____ (1969), *Brain and Psyche. Physiology, Psychology, Cybernetics.* Moscow: Izd. Prosveshchenie.

Bondarenko, P. P. & Rabinovich, M. Kh (1959), A scientific conference on the ideological fight against contemporary Freudianism. *Vop. Filos.,* 2:164-170.

Bongard, M. M. (1961), Simulation of the process of recognition on a digital computer. *Biophysics* (English edition of *Biofisika*), 2:1-9.

_____ (1962), Simulation of the process of recognition on general-purpose computer. In: *Biological Aspects of Cybernetics*, ed. A. M. Kuzin et al. Moscow: Izd. Akad. Nauk SSSR., pp. 184-191.

_____ (1965), Simulation of the process of recognition. *Nauka i Zhizn*, 6:17-26.

_____ (1967), *Recognition Problems.* Moscow: Izd. Nauka.

_____ & Golubtsov, K. V. (1970), Types of horizontal interaction ensuring normal vision of images moving on the retina (modeling of certain functions of human vision). *Biophysics*, 2:383-396.

Borovskii, V. M. (1928a), Comparative psychology and pedagogy. *Psikhologiya*, Seriya A, 1:42-52.

_____ (1928b), On behaviorism and materialism. *Pod Znamenem Marksizma*, 8:207-215.

_____ (1932), Further development of the principle of adaptive economy. *Psikhologiya*, 4:77-89.

Botkin, S. P. (1899), *Clinical Lectures.* Second edition reprinted in 1950. Moscow: Medgiz.

Bozhovich, L. I. (1963), Formation of pupil's personality as related to educational problems. *Vop. Psikhol.,* 6:12-22.

_____ (1969), The personality of schoolchildren and problems of education. In: *A Handbook of Contemporary Soviet Psychology.* New York: Basic Books, pp. 209-248.

Braines, S. N. & Napalkov, A. V. (1959), Certain theoretical problems of self-controlling systems. *Vop. Filos.,* 6:148-154.

_____ (1961), Neurocybernetics. In: *Cybernetics in the Service of Communism*, vol. 1, ed. A. I. Berg. Moscow/Leningrad: Gosudarstvennoe Energeticheskoe Izdatelstvo, pp. 140-153.

_____ & Napalkov, A. V. (1964), *Neurocybernetics.* Moscow: Medgiz.

_____ et al. (1967), Bionics. In: *Cybernetics in the Service of Communism*, vol. 5, Moscow: Izd. Energiya, pp. 197-213.

Bratko, A. A. et al. (1969), *Modeling of Psychical Activity.* Moscow: Izd. Mysl.

Braverman, E. M. (1962), Experiments on teaching machines to recognize visual images. *Avtomatika i Telemekhanika*, 3:349-364.

Bronstein, A. A. (1960), Cyto- and histochemical study of the smell organ in mammals. *Tsitologiya*, 2:194-200.

Brožek, J. (1962), Current status of psychology in the USSR. *Ann. Rev. Psychol.,* 13:515-566.

_____ (1963), Soviet psychology. In: *Systems and Theories in Psychology*, ed. M. H. Marx & W. A. Hillix. New York, McGraw-Hill, pp. 438-455.

Brudnyi, A. A. (1961), Sign and signal. *Vop. Filos.,* 4:124-133.

Bruner, J. S., Goodnow, J. J. & Austin, G. A. (1956), *A Study of Thinking*. New York: John Wiley & Sons.

Brunswik, E. (1956), *Perception and the Representative Design of Psychological Experiments*. Berkeley: California University Press.

Brushlinskii, A. V. (1966), The cultural-historical theory of thinking. In: *Researches on Thinking in Soviet Psychology*, ed. E. V. Shorokhova. Moscow: Izd. Nauka, pp. 123-174.

_____ (1967), On the psychology of creativity; psychology of thinking instead of so-called heuristics. In: *Man, Creativity, Science, Philosophical Problems, Proceedings of the Moscow Conference of Young Scientists*, ed. F. V. Konstantinov, Yu. A. Levada, & Yu. V. Sakhov. Moscow: Izd. Nauka, pp. 13-40.

_____ (1969a), Some modeling methods in psychology. In: *Methodological and Theoretical Problems of Psychology*, ed. E. V. Shorokhova. Moscow: Izd. Nauka, pp. 246-273.

_____ (1969b), Problems of learning and thinking in S. L. Rubinshtein's works. *Vop. Psikhol.*, 5:130-136.

Brutyan, G. A. (1961a), *The Knowledge Theory of General Semantics. A Critical Analysis*. Erevan: Izd. Akad. Nauk Armyanskoi SSR.

_____ (1961b), A Marxist evaluation of the Whorf hypothesis. Translated in *ETC*, 2:199-220.

_____ (1963), The basic epistemological statements of Rapoport's "operational philosophy." In: *Marxist Philosophy and Neopositivism*, ed. T. I. Oizerman et al. Moscow: Izd. Moskovskogo Universiteta, pp. 379-395.

_____ (1965), The philosophical bearings of the theory of linguistic relativity. *ETC*, 2:207-220.

Budilova, E. A. (1960), *The Fight Between Materialism and Idealism in Russian Psychological Science (The Second Half of the 19th Century and the Beginning of the 20th Century)*. Moscow: Izd. Akad. Nauk SSSR.

Bueva, L. P. (1965), *The Formation of Individual Consciousness during the Transition to Communism*. Moscow: Izd. Moskovskogo Universiteta.

Bulygin, I. A. & Itina, L. V. (1960a), Comparison of conditioned reflexes elaborated on the basis of exteroceptive and interoceptive reinforcements. *Pavlov Journal of Higher Nervous Activity*, 3:392-400.

_____, _____ & Rapatsevich, E. S. (1960b), Comparative characteristics of exteroceptive and interoceptive reflexes. *Sechenov Physiol. J. of the USSR*, 8:1127-1138.

_____ Belorybkina, K. I., & Kulvanovskii, M. P. (1961), True sympathetic reflexes. Ibid., 3:315-324.

_____ (1962), The influence of receptors of the digestive apparatus on conditional and unconditional alimentary reflexes. In: *Brain and Behavior*, vol. II, ed. M. A. Brazier. Washington, D. C.: American Institute of Biological Sciences, pp. 349-369.

_____ (1963), Specific features of cortico-subcortical mechanisms of interoceptive and exteroceptive reflexes. *Zh. Vys. Nerv. Deyat.*, 5:845-858.

_____ (1967), Structural and functional features of ascending systems of external and internal analyzers. Ibid., 6:963-972.

_____ & Kachuro, I. I. (1970), Primary cortical responses as functional features of ascending systems of internal and external analyzers. Ibid., 1:115-122.

Bykhovskii, B. (1923), On the methodological foundations of Freud's theory. *Pod Znamenem Marksizma,* 11/12:158–177.
—— (1926), Freud's sociological views. Ibid., 9/10:178–194.
Bykov, K. M. (1944), *The Cerebral Cortex and the Internal Organs,* ed. W. H. Gantt. New York: Chemical Publishing Co. Inc. (English edition, 1957).
Byzov, A. L. (1962), Electrophysiological studies on the retina function. In: *Biological Aspects of Cybernetics,* ed. A. M. Kuzin et al., pp. 158–163.
Bzhalava, I. T. (1958), The nature of the contrast illusion. In: *Recent Soviet Psychology,* ed. N. O'Connor. Oxford: Pergamon Press, pp. 290–303 (English edition, 1961).
—— (1962), Contrast illusion or figural after-effect. *Vop. Psikhol.,* 5:57–69.
—— (1965), *Perception and Set.* Tbilisi: Izd. Metsinereba.
—— (1966), *Psychology of Set and Cybernetics.* Moscow: Izd. Nauka.
Chalin, M. L. (1959), Criticism of Jasper's existentialism. In: *Criticism of Contemporary Bourgeois Philosophy and Revisionism,* ed. M. A. Naumova, Kh. N. Momdzhyan and A. F. Okulov. Moscow: Izd. VPSh. i AON pri Tsk KPSS (Publishing House of the Party University and the Academy of Social Sciences at the Central Committee of the Communist Party), pp. 149–198.
Chelpanov, G. I. (1915), *Introduction to Experimental Psychology.* Moscow: Kushnerev.
—— (1924), *Psychology and Marxism.* Moscow: Russkii Knizhnik.
—— (1925), *Objective Psychology in Russia and America.* Moscow: A. V. Dumov i &.
—— (1926), *Psychology or Reflexology. Debatable Problems of Psychology.* Moscow: Russkii Knizhnik.
Cherkasov, V. I. (1962), *Dialectical Materialism as Logic and Knowledge Theory.* Moscow: Izd. Moskovskogo Universiteta.
Cheranovskii, R. (1928), Reflexology or psychology. *Pod Znamenem Marksizma,* 9/10:198–214.
Chernigovskii, V. N. (1962), The significance of interoceptive signals in the food behavior of animals. In: *Brain and Behavior,* vol. II, pp. 319–348.
—— (1965a), Some pathways in the evolution of interoceptive signalling. In: *Essays on Physiological Evolution,* ed. J. W. S. Pringle. A volume dedicated to the memory of Kh. S. Koshtoyants (1900–1961). Oxford: Pergamon Press, pp. 69–82.
—— ed. (1965b), *Problems of Contemporary Neurophysiology.* Moscow/Leningrad: Izd. Nauka.
Chikobava, A. S. (1967), The relationship between thinking and speech and their roles in communication. In: *Language and Thinking,* ed. F. N. Ilin. Moscow: Izd. Nauka, pp. 16–30.
Chkartishvili, Sh. N. (1967), The problem of will in psychology. *Vop. Psikhol.,* 4:72–81.
Cole, M. & Maltzman, I. eds. (1969), *A Handbook of Contemporary Soviet Psychology.* New York/London: Basic Books.
Conclusions of the discussion on reactology (1931). The resolution of the general assembly of the cell of the Communist Bolshevik Party of the State Institute of Psychology, Pedology and Psychotechnique, from 6/6, 1931. *Psikhofiziologiya Truda i Psikhotekhnika,* 4–6:387–391.

Conference on genetics and selection (1939). *Pod Znamenem Marksizma,* 11:86–215.

Danilova, N. N. (1961), The electrical reaction of the brain in response to light flicker at rates within range of alpha-rhythm frequencies. *Zh. Vys. Nerv. Deyat.,* 1:12–21.

Davidovich, V. E. (1962), *Society and Personality.* Moscow: Izd. Vysshaya Shkola.

Deborin, A. (1929), Hegel und der dialektische Materialismus. In: *Die Sovjet Philosophie,* ed. W. Goerdt, pp. 84–97.

Decision of the psychological conference (1952). *Sov. Pedag.,* 8:99–103.

Demirchoglyan, G. G. (1961), Mechanism of formation of the electroretinogram. *Biophysics,* 2:90–91.

_____ & Nagapetyan, Kh. O. (1968), Early receptor potential of the retina. Ibid., 3:646–649.

_____ (1969), Photo-electrical responses of the retina in vacuo. Ibid., 3:606–609.

Dmitriev, A. S. (1964), *Physiology of Higher Nervous Activity.* Moscow: Izd. Vysshaya Shkola.

Dobrogaev, S. (1947), *Speech Reflexes.* Moscow: Izd. Akad. Nauk SSSR.

Dobrynin, N. F. (1931), On reflexology. *Psikhologiya,* 1:109–127.

Dolin, A. O. (1962), *Pathology of Higher Nervous Activity.* Moscow: Izd. Vysshaya Shkola.

Dragunova, T. V. & Elkonin, D. B. (1965), Some psychological features of the adolescent's personality. *Sov. Pedag.,* 6:63–72.

Dubrovskii, D. I. (1968), Brain and psyche; on the philosophical denial of the psychophysiological problem. *Vop. Filos.,* 8:125–135.

_____ (1969), Regarding E. V. Ilenkov's paper. Ibid., 2:142–146.

Dvoryashina, M. D. (1964), On the constancy of perception in children. *Vop. Psikhol.,* 5:42–54.

Dzidzishvili, N. N. (1960), Remarks on the theory of temporary connections. *Gagra Symposia,* vol. III: *Mechanisms of Formation of Neural Temporary Connections,* ed. I. S. Beritashvili, Tbilisi: Izd. Akad. Nauk Gruzinskoi SSR, pp. 339–348.

Editorial (1929), A new phase; on the results of the Second All-Unional Conference of Marxist-Leninist Research Institutes. *Pod Znamenem Marksizma,* 5:1–5.

_____ (1954), On the philosophical problems of psychology. *Vop. Filos.,* 4:182–194.

_____ (1955), On the subject matter and tasks of psychology. *Sov. Pedag.,* 9:73–84.

_____ (1965), Marxism and pedagogy. Ibid., 9:67–94.

Elkin, D. G. (1956), Forgetting as a conditioned reflex. *Vop. Psikhol.,* 1:34–41.

_____ (1959), Perception of time. In: *Psychological Science in the USSR,* vol. I, pp. 193–206.

_____ (1962), *Perception of Time.* Moscow: Izd. Akad. Pedag. Nauk RSFSR.

_____ (1964), Perception of time and the anticipatory reflection. *Vop. Psikhol.,* 3:123–130.

Elkonin, D. B. (1951), Some problems of physiology of higher nervous activity and child psychology. *Sov. Pedag.,* 11:50–74.

_____ (1960), *Child Psychology. The Child's Development from Birth to Seven Years.* Moscow: Uchpedgiz.

Emme, A. M. (1964), Regarding the essence, origin and modeling of life. In: *On the Essence of Life,* ed. G. M. Frank & A. M. Kuzin, pp. 276–298.

REFERENCES

Endovitskaya, T. V., Zinchenko, V. P. & Ruzskaya, A. G. (1964), The development of sensation and perception. In: *Psychology of Preschool Children. Development of Cognitive Processes.* Moscow: Izd. Prosveshchenie, pp. 13-71.

Esakov, A. I. (1961), The afferent control of receptors (on the example of the chemoreceptors of the tongue). *Bull. Experim. Biol. Med.* (Published by the Consultants Bureau), 3:257-262.

Fadeeva, V. K. (1960), *Methods of Experimental Investigation of Higher Nervous Activity in Man: Child and Adult, in Health and Disease.* Moscow: Medgiz.

Fedoseev, P. N. et al., eds. (1959), *Philosophical Problems of Contemporary Sciences. Proceedings of an All-Unional Conference on Philosophical Problems of Natural Sciences.* Moscow: Izd. Akad. Nauk SSSR.

——— et al., eds. (1963), *Philosophical Problems of Higher Nervous Activity and Psychology.* Moscow: Izd. Akad. Nauk SSSR.

——— et al., eds. (1964), *Man and His Time.* Moscow: Izd. Nauka.

Feigenberg, I. M. (1963), Probabilistic prognosis in the brain's activity. *Vop. Psikhol.,* 2:59-67.

——— (1969), Probabilistic prognosis and its significance in normal and pathological subjects. In: *A Handbook of Contemporary Soviet Psychology.* New York: Basic Books, pp. 354-369.

Feldbaum, A. A. (1964), The processes of teaching men and automata. In: *Cybernetics, Thinking, Life,* ed. A. T. Berg et al., pp. 421-458.

Feofanov, M. F. (1952), Some problems of the psychology of feelings. *Sov. Pedag.,* 9:62-69.

Filipev, Yu. A. (1964), *Creativity and Cybernetics.* Moscow: Izd. Nauka.

Fleischer, H. (1961), On categories in Soviet philosophy. A survey. In: *Studies in Soviet Thought,* I, ed. J. M. Bochenskii, & T. J. Blakeley. Dordrecht, Holland: D. Reidel Publishing Company, pp. 64-77.

Frank, G. M., & Kuzin, A. M. eds. (1964), *On the Essence of Life.* Moscow: Izd. Nauka.

Frankfurt, Yu. (1928), Bekhterev's theory and Marxism. *Pod Znamenem Marksizma,* 6:48-79.

Frantsov, G. P. (1965), Socialist collectivism and the formation of personality. In: *Social Researches,* ed. N. V. Novikov, G. V. Osipov & G. A. Slesarev. Moscow: Izd. Nauka, pp. 39-54.

Frolov, Yu. P. (1936), *Pavlov and His School; The Theory of Conditioned Reflexes.* New York: Oxford University Press (English edition, 1937).

——— (1937), Descartes' physiological theory and I. P. Pavlov's theory of conditioned reflexes. *Pod Znamenem Marksizma,* 8:82-92.

——— (1938), A materialistic theory on the brain's work; on I. P. Pavlov's theory of conditioned reflexes. Ibid., 12:58-83.

——— (1952), *From Instinct to Reason. Outlines of a Behavior Science.* Moscow: Voennoe Izd.

——— (1961), The dialectics of animated nature and contemporary cybernetics. In: *Philosophical Problems of Cybernetics,* ed. V. A. Ilin, V. N. Kolbanovskii & E. Kolman, Moscow: Izd. Sotsialno-ekonomicheskoi Literatury, pp. 306-324.

Gaidenko, Yu. G. (1964), *The Role of Practice in the Process of Knowledge.* Moscow: Izd. Mysl.

Gaidukov, I. (1962), *What Is Consciousness?* Moscow: Moskovskii Rabotnik.

Gak, G. M. (1960a), *The Theory of Social Consciousness in Light of Knowledge Theory*. Moscow: Izd. VPSh i AON pri TsK KPSS.

———— et al. (1960b), Debatable statements in an interesting book. *Vop. Filos.*, 8:174–180.

Galperin, I. I. (1957), On the reflex functioning of controlling machines. Ibid., 4:158–168.

Galperin, P. Ya. (1953), An experimental study in the formation of mental actions. In: *Psychology in the Soviet Union*, ed. B. Simon. London: Routledge & Kegan Paul Ltd. (English edition, 1957).

———— & Talyzina, N. F. (1957), Formation of elementary geometrical concepts and their dependence on directed participation by the pupils. In: *Recent Soviet Psychology*, ed. N. O'Connor, Oxford: Pergamon Press, pp. 247–272 (English edition, 1961).

———— & Pantina, N. S. (1958), The dependency of the motor habit on the type of the task orientation. In: *Orienting Reflex and Exploratory Behavior*, ed. L. G. Voronin et al., pp. 425–433 (English edition, 1965).

———— (1959), The development of researches on formation of intellectual actions. In: *The Psychological Science in the USSR*, vol. I, pp. 441–469.

———— (1960), Some explanations concerning the hypothesis of intellectual actions. *Vop. Psikhol.*, 4:141–148.

———— (1966), The psychology of thinking and the theory of stages in the development of intellectual actions. In: *Researches on Thinking in Soviet Psychology*, ed. E. V. Shorokhova. Moscow: Izd. Nauka, pp. 236–277.

———— (1969a), Stages in the development of mental acts. In: *A Handbook of Contemporary Soviet Psychology*. New York: Basic Books, pp. 249–273.

———— (1969b), On the study of the child's intellectual development. *Vop. Psikhol.*, 1:15–25.

Gelfand, E. M., Gurfinkel, V. S. & Tsetlin, M. L. (1962), Physiology and the tactics for controlling complex systems. In: *Biological Aspects of Cybernetics*, ed. A. M. Kuzin et al., pp. 66–73.

———— & Tsetlin, M. L. (1964), Investigation of the cognitive activity. *Biofizika*, 6:710–717.

Gellershtein, S. G. (1930a), The status of the psychotechnical study of fatigue. *Psikhofiziologiya Truda i Psikhotekhnika*, 5:403–418.

———— (1930b), The problem of a vocational typology. Ibid., 6:489–502.

———— (1933), On the psychology of work in K. Marx's works. Ibid., 1:1–10.

Georgiev, F. I. (1961), *The Opposition between Marxist and Hegelian Views on Consciousness. Hegel's Theory of Consciousness*. Moscow: Izd. Vysshaya Shkola.

———— (1964), On the faulty vulgar-subjective view on the nature of psyche. In: *Dialectical Materialism and Contemporary Natural Sciences*, ed. V. N. Kolbanovskii et al., Moscow: Izd. Moskovskogo Universiteta, pp. 388–397.

———— et al. (1965), *Sensory Cognition*. Moscow: Izd. Moskovskogo Universiteta.

———— (1966), On the ideal nature of consciousness. In: *Lenin's Reflection Theory and the Contemporary Science*, ed. F. V. Konstantinov et al. Moscow: Izd. Nauka, pp. 224–244.

Gershuni, G. V. (1965), The afferent stream during discrimination of an external signal. In: *Reflexes of the Brain*, ed. E. A. Asratyan, pp. 202–217.

REFERENCES

_____ (1967), Temporal organization of the auditory system. In: *Electrophysiology of the Central Nervous System*, ed. R. W. Doty. New York/London: Plenum Press, pp. 145–153 (English edition, 1970).

Gertsberg, M. O. (1956), Regarding Sepp's paper on the localization of functions in the brain. *Zh. Nevr. Psikhiat.*, 12:963–966.

Glezer, I. I. & Zvorykin, V. P. (1960), A critical review of some theories on the evolution of brain. In: *Some Theoretical Problems of the Structure and Activity of the Brain*, ed. S. A. Sarkisov, I. F. Filimonov & L. A. Kukuev. Moscow: Medgiz, pp. 138–151.

Glezer, V. D. & Tsukkerman, I. I. (1959), The decision-making ability of the eye in light of the information theory. *Biofizika*, 1:55–63.

_____ (1960), Functional units of foveal vision. *Fiziol. Zh. SSSR*, 11:1325–1335.

_____ & _____ (1961), *Information and Vision*. Moscow/Leningrad: Izd. Akad. Nauk SSSR.

_____ Zyazina, Z. N. & Smolenskaya, L. N. (1962a), The changes of foveal receptive fields in man. *Biofizika*, 7:486–488.

_____ et al. (1962b), Recognition of visual images. In: *Biological Aspects of Cybernetics*, ed. A. M. Kuzin et al., pp. 164–173.

_____ & Nevskaya, A. A. (1964), Simultaneous and successive analysis of information in the optic system. *Prog. Acad. Sci. Biol. Sections*, March–April:280–282.

_____ (1966a), *Mechanisms of Recognition of Visual Images*. Moscow/Leningrad: Izd. Nauka.

_____ (1966b), The role of unconditioned and conditioned reflexes in the recognition of visual images. In: *Problems of Physiology and Pathology of Higher Nervous Activity*. Issue III, ed. D. A. Biryukov. Leningrad: Izd. Meditsina, pp. 109–131.

Glinskii, V. A. et al. (1965), *Modeling as a Scientific Method. A Gnoseological Analysis*. Moscow: Izd. Moskovskogo Universiteta.

Glushkov, V. M. (1963a), The gnoseological nature of informational modeling. *Vop. Filos.*, 10:13–18.

_____ (1963b), Cybernetics and economy planning. In: *What Is Possible and Impossible in Cybernetics*, ed. A. T. Berg & E. Ya. Kolman, pp. 194–204.

_____ (1964a), Thinking and cybernetics. In: *Dialectics in Sciences on Inanimate Nature*, ed. M. E. Omelyanovskii & I. V. Kuznetsov, Moscow: Izd. Mysl, pp. 499–520.

_____ (1964b), On cybernetics as science. In: *Cybernetics, Thinking, Life*, ed. A. T. Berg et al., pp. 53–61.

_____ (1966), *Thinking and Cybernetics*. Moscow: Izd. Znanie.

_____ (1970), Cybernetics: achievements and problems. *Kommunist*, 18:71–82.

Goerdt, W. (1966), *Die Sovjetphilosophie. Wendigkeit und Bestimmtheit. Dokumente*. Basel/Stuttgart: Schwabe & Co. Verlag.

Goryacheva, A. I. (1964), Social psychology and personality. In: *Problems of the Psychology of Personality and Social Psychology*, ed. A. G. Kovalev. *Uchenye Zapiski*, vol. 254, pp. 25–44. (A publication of the A. I. Gertsen State Pedagogical Institute in Leningrad.)

Grashchenkov, N. I. (1959), Lenin's reflection theory and the contemporary physiology of sense organs. In: *Philosophical Problems of Contemporary Natural Sciences*, ed. P. N. Fedoseev et al., pp. 341–364.

___ Latash, L. P. & Feigenberg, I. M. (1963), Dialectical materialism and some problems of contemporary neurophysiology. In: *Philosophical Problems of Physiology of Higher Nervous Activity and Psychology*, ed. P. N. Fedoseev et al., pp. 35-62.

___ & ___ (1964), Current problems of the organization and localization of brain functions. *Vop. Filos.*, 10:59-70.

___ & ___ (1965a), On the role of the orienting reaction in the organization of actions. *Vop. Psikhol.*, 1:21-42.

___ & ___ (1965b), On the active nature of the orienting reaction. In: *Reflexes of the Brain*, ed. E. A. Asratyan, pp. 263-274.

Gray, J. A. (1964), *Pavlov's Typology: Recent Theoretical and Experimental Developments from the Laboratory of B. M. Teplov*. London: Pergamon Press.

Grinshtein, A. M. (1956), The dynamic localization of functions in laboratory and clinic. *Zh. Nevr. Psikhiat.*, 12:949-962.

Gurevich, M. O. (1948), *The Neurological and Mental Disturbances in Closed Skull Trauma*. Moscow: Izd. Akad. Med. Nauk SSSR.

Gurevich, V. Kh. (1957), Proprioception in eye movements. *Doklady Akad. Nauk SSSR*, English edition of *Biological Science Section*, published by the American Institute of Biological Sciences (1958), vol. 115-117:754-757.

___ (1959a), The role of proprioception in the oculo-motor fixation reflex and in the functioning of the visual analyzer in man. *Fiziol. Zh. SSSR*, 11:1308-1316.

___ (1959b), Possible role of higher proprioceptive centers in the perception of visual space and in the control of motor behaviour. *Nature*, 185:1219-1220.

___ (1961), Universal features of the ocular fixation reflexes as a cybernetic model of purposeful behavior. *Biofizika* (Biophysics), English edition, pp. 95-101.

___ (1962), I. P. Pavlov's view on the role of "return connections" in the formation of conditioned reflexes. *Vop. Psikhol.*, 3:87-94.

Gurova, L. L. (1964), The interaction of thinking, visual and practical operations in solving problems. *Vop. Psikhol.*, 2:133-145.

___ (1968), The structural features of the heuristic processes and their formation as efficient components of solving problems. Ibid., 4:70-82.

Guryanov, S. T. (1965), The intellectual interests of the Soviet worker. In: *Sociology in the USSR*, vol. II, ed. G. V. Osipov. Moscow: Izd. Mysl, pp. 153-188.

Gutchin, T. B. (1967), *Formal Neurons in Bionics*. Moscow: Izd. Znanie.

Hebb, D. (1949), *Organization of Behavior*. New York: John Wiley & Sons.

Hubel, D. H. (1960), Single unit activity in lateral geniculate body and optic tract of unrestrained cats. *J. Physiol.*, 1:91-104.

Hyden, H. (1965), Activation of nuclear RNA of neurons and glia in learning. In: *The Anatomy of Memory*, ed. D. P. Kimble. Palo Alto: Science and Behavior Books, pp. 179-239.

Idashkin, Yu. V. (1959), On the problem of involuntary remembering. *Vop. Psikhol.*, 2:83-93.

Igitkhanyan, M. Kh. (1962), *The Power of Public Opinion*. Moscow: Izd. Znanie.

Ignatev, E. J., Ed. (1960), *Problems of the Psychology of Personality*. Moscow: Gosudarstvennoe Uchbno-Pedagogicheskoe Izdatelstvo Ministerstva Proveshcheniya RSFSR.

Ilenkov, E. V. (1968), Psyche and brain (a reply to D. I. Dubrovskii), *Vop. Filos.*, 11:145-155.

Iliadi, A. N. (1962), *The Practical Nature of Human Knowledge*. Moscow: Izd. Vys-shaya Shkola.

Ilin, V. A., Kolbanovskii, V. N. & Kolman, E. eds. (1961), *Philosophical Problems of Cybernetics*. Moscow: Izd. Mysl.

Ilina, A. I. (1963), The assessment of temperamental features in social psychology. *Vop. Psikhol.*, 3:47–54.

Istomina, Z. M. (1953), The development of voluntary memory in preschool children. *Doshkolnoe Vospitanie*, 4:31 ·39.

Itelson, L. B. (1963), Some theoretical problems of programmed learning. *Sov. Pedag.*, 9:117–131.

_____ (1965), Mathematical modeling in psychology and pedagogy. *Vop. Filos.*, 3:58–68.

Ivanov-Smolenskii, A. G., ed. (1930), *An Attempt at a Systematic Investigation of the Child's Conditioned-Reflex Activity. Transactions of the Laboratory of the Physiology of Higher Nervous Activity*, A. I. Gertsen Pedagogical Institute, Leningrad, vol. I. Moscow/Leningrad: Glavnauka. Rabotnik Prosveshcheniya. (English abstracts available.)

_____ (1933), *Methods of Studying Human Conditioned Reflexes*. Second edition. Moscow: Medgiz.

_____ (1950), *Essays on the Pathophysiology of the Higher Nervous Activity*. Moscow: Foreign Languages Publishing House (English edition, 1954).

_____ (1965), *Interaction of Experimental and Clinical Physiopathology of the Brain*. Moscow: Izd. Meditsina.

Ivanova, I. I. (1967), Symposium on the problem of consciousness. *Vop. Psikhol.*, 1:184–187.

Jung, R. (1962), Neuronal integration in the visual cortex and its significance for information. In: *Sensory Communication*, ed. W. A. Rosenblith. Cambridge, M. I. T. Press, pp. 627–675.

Kabanova-Meller, E. N. (1956a), Formation of representations during learning mechanical drawing by pupils. *Izvestiya Akad. Pedag. Nauk RSFSR*, 76:153–166.

_____ (1956b), Formation of geographical representations in pupils of 5th to 7th grades. Ibid., pp. 129–153.

_____ (1959a), Development of methods of intellectual work in pupils. Translated in: *Soviet Education*, 10:41–46.

_____ (1959b), The transition from "external" acts to mental acts during the acquisition of knowledge by pupils. *Vop. Psikhol.*, 3:44–45.

_____ (1962), *Development of Knowledge and Skills in Pupils. Methods of Intellectual Work*. Moscow: Izd. Akad. Pedag. Nauk RSFSR.

_____ (1968), *Development of Methods of Intellectual Work and Pupils Intellectual Growth*. Moscow: Izd. Prosveshchenie.

_____ (1970), The role of the image in problem solving. Translated in: *Soviet Psychology*, vol. IX, #4, Summer 1971:346–360.

Kairov, I. A., ed. (1960), *Pedagogical Dictionary*. Moscow: Izd. Akad. Pedag. Nauk RSFSR.

Kalmykova, Z. I. (1955), Processes of analysis and synthesis in solving arithmetic problems. *Izvestiya Akad. Pedag. Nauk RSFSR*, 71:3–112.

_____ & Lipkina, A. I. (1965), Symposium on optimisation of teaching. *Vop. Psikhol.*, 2:181–183.

Kedrov, B. M. (1959), The relationship between the forms of motion of matter in nature. *Vop. Filos.*, 4:44–56.

_____ (1963), *The Unity of Dialectics, Logic and Knowledge Theory.* Moscow: Gospolitizdat.

_____ (1964a), *The Subject Matter and Relationships of Natural Sciences.* Moscow: Izd. Akad. Nauk SSSR.

_____ ed. (1964b), *Dialectics as Knowledge Theory. Studies in History of Philosophy.* Moscow: Izd. Nauka.

_____ (1965), The general cognitive approach to nature. *Vop. Filos.*, 4:81–91.

Kekcheev, K. Kh. (1946), *The Role of Interoception and Exteroception for the Clinic.* Moscow: Medgiz.

Kelle, V. Zh. & Kovalzon, M. Ya. (1959a), *Forms of Social Consciousness.* Moscow: Gospolitizdat.

_____ & _____ (1959b), Regarding the problem of the relationship between social existence and social consciousness. *Vestnik Moskovskogo Universiteta, Seriya Ekonomika, Filosofiya, Prava*, 4:99–114.

_____ & _____ (1965a), The material production is the basis of social life. In: *Consultations on Teaching Philosophy*, ed. V. I. Ravzin. Moscow: Gospolitizdat, pp. 138–151.

_____ & _____ (1965b), Social consciousness and its forms. *Ibid.*, pp. 255–278.

Kerbikov, O. V. & Sarkisov, S. A. (1952), I. P. Pavlov's teaching and problems of medical science. *Vop. Filos.*, 1:216–219.

Kert, G. M. (1967), Regarding the problem of the relationship between language and thinking. In: *Language and Thinking*, ed. F. N. Filin et al. Moscow: Izd. Nauka, pp. 30–37.

Khananashvili, M. M. (1966), On the nature of the functional organization of the orienting reflex. In: *Problems of Physiology and Pathology of Higher Nervous Activity.* ed. D. A. Biryukov, pp. 30–42.

Khomskaya, E. D. (1962), Regarding the problem of the afferentation of eye movements; an investigation of eye movements by the photoelectric method. *Vop. Psikhol.*, 3:73–84.

Khromov, N. A. (1952), On the relationship between physical and psychical. In: *I. P. Pavlov's Theory and Philosophical Problems of Psychology*, ed. S. A. Petrushevskii. Moscow: Izd. Akad. Nauk SSSR, pp. 124–143.

Kobozev, N. I. (1966), On the physico-chemical modeling of the process of information and thinking. *Zh. Fizicheskoi Khimii*, 2:280–294; second part, pp. 784–794.

Koffka, K. (1932), Overcoming mechanistic and vitalistic trends in contemporary psychology. *Psikhologiya*, 3:59–69.

Kogan, A. B. (1961), On the structure of the circuit-closing apparatus of the conditioned reflex. *Zh. Vys. Nerv. Deyat.*, 4:654–659.

_____ (1964), Statistical probability principle of the neuronal organization of the functional system of the brain. *Proc. Acad. Sci. Biol. Sci.*, 154–156:139–142.

_____ (1965a), Inhibition of neuronal cell and of nervous center. In: *Reflexes of the Brain*, ed. E. A. Asratyan, pp. 103–113.

_____ (1965b), Probability-statistical model of the brain organization. In: *Progress in Brain Research*, vol. 17: *Cybernetics of the Nervous System*, ed. N. Wiener & J. P. Schadé. Amsterdam/London/New York: Elsevier Publishing Company, pp. 350–355.

REFERENCES

—— (1968a), The spatial organization of cerebral neuron ensembles. *Proc. Acad. Sci. Biol. Sci.,* 4:587–588.

—— (1968b), Correlation form of response of "idle" neurons. Ibid., 495–498.

—— (1968c), On the modeling of neural processes. In: *Mathematical Model of Biological Processes,* pp. 211–221.

—— & Kompaneets, E. B. (1969), Modeling of the adequate light signal by electrical irritation of the visual cortex of the brain. Proc. Acad. Sci. Biol. Sci., 4:587–588.

—— (1970), The probabilistic organization of complex physiological mechanisms. *Zh. Vys. Nerv. Deyat.,* 2:363–378.

—— & —— (1971a), Conditioned reflex differentiation of excitation mosaics provoked by direct electrical stimulation of the visual cortex. *Dokl. Akad. Nauk SSSR, Seriya Biol.,* 196(1):243–245.

—— Kuraev, G. A. & Chorayan, O. G. (1971b), Some characteristics of the informative processes in the visual analyzer. Ibid., 197(1):951–953.

—— & Tambiev, A. E. (1971c), On the structure of functional ensembles of neurons in the optic cortex. Ibid., 200 (2):1242–1245.

Kolbanovskii, V. N. (1932), Psychology in the service of the industry. *Psikhologiya,* 3:3–7.

—— (1939), Matter and consciousness. *Pod Znamenem Marksizma,* 8:39–61.

—— (1948), For a Marxist approach to problems of psychology. On Rubinshtein's *Fundamentals of General Psychology.* Translated in: *Soviet Psychiatry,* ed J. Wortis, pp. 286–294.

—— et. al., eds. (1964), *Dialectical Materialism and Contemporary Natural Sciences.* Moscow: Izd. Moskovskogo Universiteta.

—— (1965), The subject matter, methods and current problems of the Soviet social psychology. In: *Problems of Social Psychology,* ed. V. N. Kolbanovskii & B. F. Porshnev. Moscow: Izd. Mysl, pp. 127–170.

Kolman, E. Ya. (1955), What is cybernetics? *Vop. Filos.,* 4:148–159.

Kolmogorov, A. N. (1963), Automata and life. In: *What Is Possible and Impossible in Cybernetics,* ed. A. I. Berg & E. Ya. Kolman, pp. 10–29.

—— (1964), Life and thinking as special forms of existence of matter. In: *On the Essence of Life,* ed. S. M. Frank & A. M. Kuzin, pp. 48–57.

Kolominskii, Ya. L. (1963), A way of study and formation of personal relations among class mates. *Vop. Psikhol.,* 2:101–108.

Koltsova, M. M. (1958), *The Development of Higher Nervous Activity in the Child.* Leningrad: Medgiz.

—— (1967), *Generalization as a Brain Function.* Leningrad: Izd. Nauka, Leningradskoe Otdelenie.

Kon, I. S. (1964), *Positivism in Sociology. A Historical Study.* Leningrad: Izd. Leningradskogo Universiteta.

Kononova, E. P. (1962), *The Frontal Lobes.* Leningrad: Izd. Akad. Med. Nauk SSSR.

Konstantinov, F. V. et al., eds. (1966a), *Proceedings of a Conference on Contemporary Problems of the Materialistic Dialectics,* 7–9 April, 1965, vol. I: *Lenin's Reflection Theory and the Contemporary Science.* Moscow: Izd. Nauka.

—— et al., eds. (1966b), Idem. Vol. IV: *The Dialectic of the Material and Intellectual Life of the Society during the Transition to Communism.* Moscow: Izd. Nauka.

____ ed. (1968), *Personality and Socialism*. (A publication of the Institute of Philosophy, Acad. Sci. USSR). Moscow: Izd. Nauka.

Kopytova, L. A. (1964), The individual work style of adjusters as related to the strength of excitatory processes. *Vop. Psikhol.*, 1:25-33.

Korneeva, A. I. & Yakovlev, M. V., eds. (1961), *Criticism of the Contemporary Bourgeois Philosophy and Sociology*. Moscow: Izd. VShP i AON pri TsK KPSS.

____ (1962), *Criticism of Neopositivistic Views on the Nature of Knowledge*. Moscow: Izd. VShP i AON pri Tsk KPSS.

Kornienko, V. S. (1962), *The Nature of Esthetic Knowledge*. Novosibirsk: Izd. Akad. Nauk SSSR, Sibirskoe Otdelenie.

Kornilov, K. N. (1921), *A Theory of Human Reactions from the Psychological Point of View (Reactology)*. Moscow: Gosudarstvennoe Izd.

____ (1923), Contemporary psychology and Marxism. Paper read at the First All-Unional Congress of Psychoneurology, January 14, 1923. First part, *Pod Znamenem Marksizma*, 1:41-50. Second part, Ibid., 4:86-114.

____ (1924), The dialectical method in psychology. Ibid., 1:107-113.

____ Ed. (1925), *Psychology and Marxism*. Moscow: Gosudarstvennoe Izd.

____ (1926), The mechanical materialism in contemporary psychology: a reply to V. Struminskii. *Pod Znamenem Marksizma*, 4-5:185-212.

____ (1927), The current status of psychology in the USSR. Ibid., 10-11:195-217.

____ (1928), The comparative value of research methods in psychology and pedology in light of Marxism. *Psikhologiya*, Seriya A, 1:5-27.

____ (1929), The contemporary mechanical approach to the law of conservation of energy and psyche. *Psikhologiya*, 1:3-15.

____ (1930), Psychology in the light of dialectical materialism. In: *Psychologies of 1930*, ed. C. Murchison. Worcester, Massachusetts: Clark University Press, pp. 243-278.

____ (1931), Regarding the conclusions of the psychological discussion. *Psikhologiya*, 1:44-74.

____ (1946), *Psychology*. Moscow: Uchpedgiz.

____ Smirnov, A. A. & Teplov, B. M. (1948), *Psychology*. Third edition. Moscow: Uchpedgiz.

Korshunov, A. M. (1964), Model and reflection. *Vestnik Moskovskogo Universiteta, Seriya Ekonomika, Filosofiya*, 6:63-72.

____ (1969), Adequate images and active knowledge. In: *Problems of Reflection*, ed. F. I. Georgiev et al. Moscow: Izd. Moskovskogo Universiteta, pp. 37-54.

Koshtoyants, Kh. S. (1964), Some theoretical problems of contemporary physiology. In: *Dialectical Materialism and Contemporary Natural Sciences*, ed. V. N. Kolbanovskii, pp. 181-194.

____ (1965), I. M. Sechenov. In: *I. Sechenov, Reflexes of the Brain*. Cambridge, Massachusetts. The M. I. T. Press, pp. 119-139.

Kositskii, S. I. (1961), The subconscious, dreams and intuition. *Soviet Review*, 4:61-68.

____ (1962), Conscious and unconscious. In: *Philosophical Problems of Medicine*, ed. S. I. Tsaregorodtsev & A. D. Mikhailov. Moscow: Medgiz, pp. 147-189.

Kostyuk, G. S. (1949), Current problems of the formation of child's personality. *Sov. Pedag.*, 11:73-101.

____ Menchinskaya, N. A., & Smirnov, A. A. (1963), Current tasks of school and psychological problems of teaching. *Vop. Psikhol.*, 5:48-60.

_____ (1967), The child development in Soviet psychology. Ibid., 6:23–45.

_____ (1969), The development principle in psychology. In: *Methodological and Theoretical Problems of Psychology*, ed. E. V. Shorokhova. Moscow: Izd. Nauka, pp. 118–152.

_____ (1970), The development of Lenin's ideas in the Soviet psychology of personality. *Vop. Psikhol.*, 3:3–24.

Kovalev, A. S. & Myasishchev, V. M. (1957), *Psychological Features of Man*, vol. I *(The Character)*. Leningrad: Izd. Leningradskogo Universiteta.

_____ & _____ (1963), The psychology of personality and social psychology. *Vop. Psikhol.*, 6:23–34.

_____ (1964), People's interaction in the process of communication and the formation of personality. *Uchenye Zapiski*, 254:5–24.

_____ (1965), *Psychology of Personality*, Second edition. Moscow: Izd. Prosveshchenie.

_____ Stepanov, A. A. & Shabalin, S. N., eds. (1966), *Psychology. A Textbook for Pedagogical Institutes.* Moscow: Izd. Prosveshchenie.

Kozh, E. P. (1964), Selective disturbance of concrete generalizations in left posterior temporal lesions in man. *Zh. Vys. Nerv. Deyat.*, 4:587–594.

Kozhevnikov, V. A. & Chistovich, L. A., eds. (1965), *Speech. Articulation and Perception.* Moscow/Leningrad: Izd. Nauka.

Kozyrev, Yu. N. (1965), Methods of sociological study of the drop-out student. *Sov. Pedag.*, 10:84–90.

Krasilshchikova, I. D. (1956), On the stability of primary connections of memory. *Vop. Psikhol.*, 6:65–82.

Krasnogorskii, N. I. (1952), On the physiology of the development of childhood speech. *Zh. Vys. Nerv. Deyat.*, 4:474–480.

_____ (1954), *Studies of Higher Nervous Activity in Man and Animals.* Moscow: Medgiz.

_____ (1958), *Higher Nervous Activity in the Child.* Leningrad: Izd. Akad. Med. Nauk SSSR.

Kravkov, S. V. (1948), *Interaction of Sense Organs.* Moscow: Izd. Akad. Nauk SSSR.

_____ (1950), *The Eye and Its Work.* Fourth edition. Moscow/Leningrad: Izd. Akad. Nauk SSSR.

_____ (1951), *Color Vision.* Moscow: Izd. Akad. Nauk SSSR.

Kremnev, B. G. (1961), The relationship between society and individual in the contemporary American psycho-sociology. In: *Criticism of Contemporary Bourgeois Philosophy and Sociology*, ed. A. I. Korneeva & M. V. Yakovlev, pp. 162–203.

Krinchik, E. P. (1961), Information processing in man in a choice situation. Report I: The role of the significance of signals in the relation between choice reaction time and amount of information. *Doklady Akad. Pedag. Nauk RSFSR*, 5:73–76.

_____ (1962a), Idem. Report II: The relation between choice reaction time and amount of information in the range of 0 to 4 bits. Ibid., 2:65–70.

_____ (1962b), Idem. Report III: The relation between choice reaction time and amount of individual and average information. Ibid., 3:71–76.

_____ & Aleksandrova, L. N. (1966), The relation between incidental and alternative uncertainty in conditions of information processing in man. *Vop. Psikhol.*, 2:25–34

———— (1968), Determination of behavior by the probability structure of a situation. Translated in: *Soviet Psychology and Psychiatry*, Summer 1969, 4:37–47.

———— (1969), The probability of a signal as a determinant of reaction time. *Acta Psychologica*, 30:27–36.

———— & Mednikarov, P. D. (1970), On the mechanisms of the effect of signal probability on human reaction time. *Vop. Psikhol.*, 6:34–46.

Krushinskii, L. V. (1958), The biological significance of extrapolation reflexes. *Zh. Obshchei Biologii*, 6:457–466.

———— (1959), The study of extrapolation reflexes in animals. In: *Problems of Cybernetics*. Pergamon Press, pp. 586–654. (English edition, 1961).

———— (1960), *Animal Behavior, Its Normal and Abnormal Development.* New York: Consultants Bureau (English edition, 1965).

———— (1965a), Solution of elementary logical problems by animals on the basis of extrapolation. In: *Cybernetics of the Nervous System,* ed. N. Wiener & J. P. Schadé, pp. 280–308.

———— et al. (1965b), Express-informational associations as basis of complex forms of animal behavior. In: *Complex Forms of Behavior,* ed. A. D. Slonim. Moscow/Leningrad: Izd. Nauka, pp. 58–63.

———— (1970), The physiological-genetical study of elementary reasoning in animals. *Zh. Vys. Nerv. Deyat.,* 2:363–378.

Kryazhev, P. E. (1961), *Society and Personality.* Moscow: Gospolitizdat.

———— (1966), The dialectic of communication and alienation of the personality. In: *The Dialectic of Material and Ideal Values in the Period of Building Communism. Proceedings of a Conference on the Contemporary Dialectics.* 7–9 April, 1965, ed. F. V. Konstantinov. Moscow: Izd. Nauka, pp. 152–162.

Kudryavtsev, T. V. (1961), The interaction between theoretical knowledge and practical actions. In: *The Application of Knowledge in Pupils Practical Exercises.* ed. N. A. Mechinskaya. Moscow: Izd. Akad. Pedag. Nauk RSFSR.

———— & Yakimanskaya, I. S. (1964), Contribution to the study of technical thinking. *Vop. Psikhol.,* 4:3–19.

Kukuev, L. A. (1955), The cortical localization of motor functions. *Zh. Nevr. Psikhiat.,* 12:890–895.

Kulikov, V. N. (1964), The problem of hypnopedia. *Vop. Psikhol.,* 2:87–97.

Kupalov, P. S. (1960a), New findings on the formation of temporary connections. In: *Gagra Symposia,* vol. III, ed. I. S. Beritashvili, pp. 9–19.

———— ed. (1960b), *Problems of Physiology and Pathology of Higher Nervous Activity.* Leningrad: Medgiz, Leningradskoe Otdelenie.

———— (1962), The theory of reflex and of reflex activity and its development. *Vop. Psikhol.,* 4:9–35.

———— et al. (1964), *Place Conditioned Reflexes in Dogs in Normal and Pathological Conditions.* Leningrad: Izd. Meditsina.

Kurmanov, I. (1929), Reflexology or psychology. *Pod Znamenem Marksizma,* 6:127–145.

Kurylev, A. K. (1964), The multilateral development of personality and the distribution of labor in communism. *Sov. Pedag.* 8:43–54.

Kuzin, A. M. et al., ed. (1962), *Biological Aspects of Cybernetics.* Moscow: Izd. Akad. Nauk SSSR.

Kuzmin, E. S. (1963a), The subject matter of social psychology. *Vop. Filos.*, 1:142-145.

―― (1963b), The problem of social psychology. In: *Problems of General and Industrial Psychology*, ed B. G. Ananev & B. F. Lomov. Leningrad: Izd. Leningradskogo Universiteta, pp. 141-145.

Kuzmin, V. F. (1964), *The Philosophical Category of Consciousness and the Contemporary Science.* Moscow: Izd. Vysshaya Shkola.

Ladanov, I. D. (1964), Programmed teaching and behaviorism. *Sov. Pedag.*, 7:52-64.

Ladygina-Kots, N. N. (1959), *The Constructional and Instrumental Activity of Anthropoid Monkeys.* Moscow: Izd. Akad. Nauk SSSR.

―― (1965), *Prerequisites of Human Thinking.* Moscow: Izd. Nauka.

Landa, L. N. (1962), The cybernetic approach to learning theory. *Vop. Filos.* 9:75-87.

―― (1963), The algorithmic approach to learning is valid. *Vop. Psikhol.*, 4:143-152.

―― (1966), *Algorithms and Teaching.* Moscow: Izd. Prosveshchenie.

―― (1969), Some clarifications regarding algorithms and teaching. *Vop. Psikhol.*, 2:139-141.

Laptev, I. P. (1949), Bioelectrical phenomena in the lingual nerve under mechanical and thermic stimulations of the taste surface of the tongue. In: *Problems of Higher Nervous Activity*, ed. P. K. Anokhin. Moscow: Medgiz, pp. 131-147.

Lazarev, P. P. (1923), *The Ionic Theory of Excitation.* Moscow: Gosudarstvennoe Izd.

Lebedinskii, M. S. & Myasishchev, V. N. (1966), *Introduction to Medical Psychology.* Leningrad: Izd. Meditsina.

Leni, Zh. F. (1963), The problem of a materialistic social psychology. *Vop. Psikhol.*, 1:146-150.

Lenin, V. I. (1909), *Materialism and Empirio-criticism. Critical Comments on a Reactionary Philosophy.* Moscow: Foreign Languages Publishing House (English edition, 1952).

Leontev, A. A. (1963), *The Appearance and Initial Development of Language.* Moscow: Izd. Akad. Nauk SSSR.

―― (1966), *Linguistics and Psychology.* Moscow: Izd. Nauka.

―― (1967a), *Psycholinguistics.* Leningrad: Izd. Nauka, Leningradskoe Otdelenie. (A publication of the Learned Board for a Soviet Linguistic Theory, the Sector of Literature and Language of the USSR Acad. Sci.)

―― (1967b), Inner speech and the process of grammatical generation of utterances. *Soviet Psychology and Psychiatry*, Spring 1969, 3:11-16.

―― (1968), The psychological structure of meaning. Ibid., pp. 37-38.

Leontev, A. N. (1940), *Development of Psyche.* Excerpts of this work were included in *Problems of Psychical Development* (1959).

―― (1945), Contribution to the theory of the mental development of the child. Reprinted in: *Problems of Psychical Development.*

―― (1947), *Essay on Psychical Development.* Ibid.

―― & Rozanova, T. V. (1951), The dependence of the formation of associations on the content of actions. *Sov. Pedag.*, 10:60-78.

―― (1952), The materialistic and reflex theory versus the subjective and idealistic theory of psyche. Ibid., 7:50-65.

_____ (1955), The nature and formation of the human psychic properties and processes. Translated in: *Psychology in the Soviet Union*, ed. B. Simon. London: Routledge & Kegan Paul.

_____ & Luriya, A. R. (1956), Vygotskii's psychological views. Foreword to: L. S. Vygotskii, *Selected Psychological Works*. Moscow: Izd. Akad. Pedag. Nauk RSFSR, pp. 4-36.

_____ & Ovchinnikova, O. V. (1958), Analysis of the systemic structure of perception. V: The mechanism of tonal hearing. *Doklady Akad. Pedag. Nauk RSFSR*, 3:43-48.

_____ & Gippenreiter, Yu. B. (1959a), Idem, VIII: The influence of mother language on the development of hearing. Ibid., 2:59-62.

_____ (1959b), *Problems of Psychical Development*, Second edition. Moscow: Izd. Mysl, 1965.

_____ & Krinchik, E. P. (1961), The application of information theory to concrete psychological investigations. *Vop. Psikhol.*, 5:25-46.

_____ & _____ (1964a), Some features of information processing in man. In: *Cybernetics, Thinking, Life*, ed. A. I. Berg et al., pp. 227-241.

_____ (1964b), Thinking. *Vop. Filos.*, 2:85-95.

_____ & Galperin, P. Ya. (1964c), Learning theory and programmed teaching. *Sov. Pedag.*, 10:56-65.

_____ (1967a), The fight for consciousness in the development of Soviet psychology. *Vop. Psikhol.*, 2:14-22.

_____ (1967b) Some prospective problems of Soviet psychology. Ibid., 6:7-22.

_____ (1970), Sensory image and model in the light of Lenin's reflection theory. Ibid., 2:34-45.

Levandovskii, N. G. (1970), The structure of the character. Ibid., 3:51-61.

Levitov, N. D. (1963), *The Psychology of Work*. Moscow: Uchpedgiz.

_____ (1964), *Psychology. A Textbook for Teachers at Professional and Technical Schools*. Moscow: Izd. Vysshaya Shkola.

_____ (1967), Frustration as a psychical state. *Vop. Psikhol.*, 6:118-129.

Libenson, D. Ya. (1959), Cybernetics in the light of V. I. Lenin's *Materialism and Empirio-criticism*. English edition of Avtomatika i Telemekhanika *(Automation and Remote Control)*. Copyright by Instrument Society of America, 1960, pp. 973-982.

Linkovskii, B. & Smuglyi, S. I. (1964), Bionics, its methods and results. *Priroda*, 3:52-58.

Lisina, M. I. (1960), Some problems of transfer in the works of foreign authors. *Vop. Psikhol.*, 5:153-161.

_____ (1962), The influence of training on the formation of work skills in pupils. In: *Psychological Problems of Professional Training*, ed. A. A. Smirnov. Moscow: Izd, Akad. Pedag. Nauk RSFSR, pp. 7-47.

Livanov, M. N. (1960), The connection mechanism of conditioned reflexes. In: *Gagra Symposia*. vol. III, ed. I. S. Beritashvili, pp. 111-125.

_____ (1969), The application of electronic-computer techniques to the analysis of bioelectric processes in the brain. In: *A Handbook of Contemporary Soviet Psychology*. New York: Basic Books, pp. 717-734.

Logvin, M. A. (1959), I. P. Pavlov's criticism of Freudianism. *Vop. Filos.*, 9:140-150.

REFERENCES

Lomov, B. F. (1966), *Man and Technology. Studies in Engineering Psychology*, Second edition. Moscow: Izd. Sovetskoe Radio.

_____ (1971), The state and perspectives of development of psychology in the USSR in the light of the decisions of the 24th Congress of the Communist Party of the USSR. *Vop. Psychol.*, 5:3–19.

London, I. D. (1949), A historical survey of psychology in the Soviet Union. *Psychol. Bull.*, 4:241–277.

_____ (1954), Researches on sensory interaction in the Soviet Union. *Ibid.*, 6: 531–568.

Losskii, N. O. (1951), *History of Russian Philosophy*. New York: International Universities Press.

Luriya, A. R. (1926), Fundamental problems of contemporary psychology. *Pod Znamenem Marksizma*, 4–5:129–139.

_____ (1928), The system of behavior psychology. *Psikhologiya* Seriya A, 1:5–27.

_____ (1932), The crisis of bourgeois psychology. *Psikhologiya*, 1–2:63–88.

_____ (1959), Development of speech and the formation of psychological processes. In: *Psychological Science in the USSR*, ed. B. G. Ananev et al., Vol. I, pp. 516–577.

_____ (1961), An objective approach to the study of the abnormal child. *Amer. J. Orthopsychiat.*, 1:1–16.

_____ (1962), *Higher Cortical Functions in Man*. New York: Basic Books (English edition, 1966).

_____ (1963), *The Human Brain and Mental Processes*. New York: Harper (English edition, 1965).

_____ (1964), Brain and psyche. *Kommunist*, 6:107–117.

Lyapunov, A. A. (1964a), The structure of control systems in animated nature. In: *Cybernetics, Thinking, Life*, ed. A. I. Berg et al., pp. 177–181.

_____ (1964b), The control systems in animated nature. In: *On the Essence of Life*, ed. S. M. Frank & A. M. Kuzin, pp. 66–80.

_____ & Yablonskii, S. V. (1964c), Theoretical problems of cybernetics. In: *Cybernetics, Thinking, Life*, ed. A. I. Berg et al., pp. 62–75.

_____ (1968), The mathematical approach to biological phenomena. In: *Mathematical Modeling of Biological Processes*, pp. 65–101.

Lyublinskaya, A. A. (1960), Regarding the nature of the act in the theory of development of intellectual acts. *Vop. Psikhol.*, 3:136–141.

Maiorov, P. F. (1954), *The History of the Theory of Conditioned Reflexes*. Second edition. Moscow/Leningrad: Izd. Akad. Nauk SSSR.

Maizel, N. I. & Fatkin, L. V. (1962), A conference on philosophical problems of cybernetics. *Vop. Psikhol.*, 5:184–189.

Makhlakh, E. S. (1965), Methods for the study of the pupil's personality. *Sov. Pedag.*, 10:75–83.

Maksimov, V. V., Zenkin, G. M. & Byzov, A. L. (1965), Investigation of the functional properties of bipolars of two types in the frog retina. *Biophysics* (English edition of Biofizika), 1:154–161.

Malinin, V. A. (1966), The dialectic of tradition in social consciousness. In: *The Dialectic of Material and Intellectual Life of Society in the Period of the Construction of Communism*, ed. F. V. Konstantinov, pp. 200–211.

Maltsev, V. I. (1965), Semasiology and the theory of knowledge. *Vestnik Moskovskogo Universiteta, Seriya Ekonomika Filosofiya*, 6:55-61.

Mansurov, N. S. (1952), For the application and development of I. P. Pavlov's teaching in psychology. *Vop. Filos.*, 1:153-161.

_____ (1955), *I. P. Pavlov and the Fight for Materialism in Natural Sciences*. Moscow: Izd. Sovetskaya Nauka.

_____ (1965), Social psychology and the pedagogical science. *Sov. Pedag.*, 9:51-61.

Markov, A. A. (1964), The relationship of physical to biological laws. In: *On the Essence of Life*, ed. S. M. Frank & A. M. Kuzin, pp. 168-169.

Markova, A. K., Matyushkin, A. M. & Mukhina, T. K. (1970), The study of the mental development of the child as part of the theory of knowledge and dialectics. *Vop. Psikhol.*, 2:59-84.

Marr, N. I. (1925), Uber die Entstehung der Sprache. In: *Die Sovjetphilosophie*, pp. 202-236.

Maslina, M. N. (1948), The Leontev critique: for Bolshevist partisanship in questions of philosophy. In J. Wortis: *Soviet Psychiatry*, pp. 295-304.

Matveenko, I. I. (1966), The dialectical interaction between society and social consciousness. In: *The Dialectic of the Material and Intellectual Life of the Society in the Period of Construction of Communism*, ed. F. V. Konstantinov, pp. 174-181.

Matveev, B. (1934), The current status of Heckel's biogenetic law. *Pod Znamenem Marksizma*, 3:68-77.

Matyushkin, A. M. (1960), Analysis and generalization of relations. In: *Thinking Processes and the Laws of Analysis, Synthesis and Generalization*, ed. S. L. Rubinshtein, pp. 122-152.

_____ (1965), Some problems of the psychology of thinking. Foreword to: *Psychology of Thinking. Translations from German and English Works*. Moscow: Izd. Prosveshchenie, pp. 3-17.

_____ & Mikheev, V. I. (1970), Toward the modeling of the thinking process in a self-teaching system. *Vop. Psikhol.*, 1:70-78.

_____ (1971), Psychological problems of programmed teaching. Ibid., 3:68-83.

McCulloch, W. S. & Pitts, W. H. (1943), A logical calculus of the ideas immanent in nervous activity. *Bull. Mat. Biophysics*, 5:115-133.

Medvedev, N. V. (1964), On the nature of psyche. In: *Dialectical Materialism and Contemporary Natural Sciences*, ed. V. N. Kolbanovskii, pp. 341-352.

Megrabyan, A. A. (1959), *The Nature of Individual Consciousness under Normal and Pathological Conditions*. Erevan: Armgosizdat.

Meleshchenko, Z. N. (1960), *Neokantian Philosophy, the Basis of Revisionism*. Leningrad: Izd. Leningradskogo Universiteta.

Menchinskaya, N. A., Sokolov, M. V. & Shemyakin, F. N. (1952), Conclusions of the conference on problems of psychology. *Sov. Pedag.*, 8:88-98.

_____ (1955), *The Psychology of Teaching Arithmetic*. Moscow: Uchpedgiz.

_____ (1960), Concerning the theory of formation of intellectual acts. *Vop. Psikhol.*, 1:157-164.

_____ (1966), Thinking and learning. In: *Researches on Thinking in Soviet Psychology*, ed. E. V. Shorokhova, pp. 349-387.

_____ (1967), 50 years of Soviet learning psychology. *Vop. Psikhol.*, 5:51-70.

REFERENCES

Menitskii, D. N. (1966), Some aspects of the application of information theory to the study of higher nervous activity. In: *Problems of Physiology and Pathology of Higher Nervous Activity*, ed. G. A. Biryukov, pp. 91-108.

Merlin, V. S. (1966), Contribution a la théorie du tempérament. In: *Recherches Psychologiques en URSS*, ed. A. N. Leontev, A. R. Luriya & A. A. Smirnov Moscow: Editions du Progrès, pp. 284-306.

—— (1967), The relationship between social-typical and individual characteristics of the personality. *Vop. Psikhol.*, 4:34-43.

Mikhailov, F. T. & Tsaregorodtsev, S. I. (1961), *Beyond the Boundaries of Consciousness. A Critical Study of Freudianism*. Moscow: Gospolitizdat.

—— (1962), The gnoseological roots of Freudianism. In: *Philosophical Problems of Medicine*, ed. S. I. Tsaregorodtsev & A. D. Mikhailov. Moscow: Medgiz, pp. 203-232.

Mikhailov, M. (1954), The dialectical and materialistic versus the metaphysic views on psychical phenomena. *Sov. Pedag.* 5:77-84.

Miller, G. A., Gallanter, E. B. & Pribram, K. H. (1960), *Plans and the Structure of Behavior*. New York: Holt, Rinehart and Winston.

Mintz, A. (1958), Recent developments in psychology in the USSR. *Annual Review of Psychology*, 9:453-504.

—— (1959), Further developments in psychology in the USSR. Ibid., 10:455-487.

—— (1962), Introduction to contemporary Soviet psychology. In: *Some Views on Soviet Psychology*, ed. R. A. Bauer. Washington, D.C.: American Psychological Association, pp. 1-27.

Mitin, M. B. (1931), Current tasks on the philosophical front related to the conclusions of the discussion. *Pod Znamenem Marksizma*, 3:12-35.

—— (1934), Current problems of the reflection theory and Lenin's *Materialism and Empirio-Criticism*. Ibid., 4:21-51.

—— (1939), For a progressive Soviet genetical science. Ibid., 10:147-176.

—— (1963), The problem of the material and the ideal in the light of the dialectical materialism. In: *Philosophical Problems of Physiology of Higher Nervous Activity and Psychology*, ed. P. N. Fedoseev, pp. 13-34.

—— (1964), Man as a subject of philosophical research. In: *Man and his Time*, ed. P. N. Fedoseev et al. Moscow: Izd. Nauka, pp. 41-76.

Mkrtycheva, L. I. (1962), The electrical response of single neurons of the visual areas in frogs to colors. *Doklady Akad. Nauk SSSR*, 4:994-996.

Mogendovich, M. R. (1931), The final stage of Bekhterev's school. *Psikhologiya*, 1:78-100.

—— (1958a), *The Reflex Interaction of the Locomotor and Visceral Systems*. Leningrad: Medgiz.

—— (1958b), On the physiological foundations of sensation. *Vop. Psikhol.*, 2: 3-7.

—— (1961), On the neurological basis of Psyche. *Vop. Filos.*, 10:126-139.

—— ed. (1963), *Motor-Visceral and Viscero-Motor Reflexes. Researches on Physiology, Biophysics and Pharmacology*. Vol. V. Perm.

Moiseev, V. D. (1965), *Central Ideas and Philosophical Foundations of Cybernetics*. Moscow: Izd. Mysl.

Morozov, V. M. (1961), *Current Trends in Western Psychiatry and their Ideological Sources*. Moscow: Medgiz.

Moskaeva, A. S. (1965), Algorithms and the "algorithmic approach" to teaching. *Vop. Psikhol.*, 3:138–146.

Mshvenieradze, V. V. & Osipov, G. V. (1965), Basic trends and problems of concrete social researches. In: *Sociology in the USSR*, ed. G. V. Osipov, pp. 54–73.

Musatti, C. L. (1960), A debate on Freudianism: an answer to F. V. Bassin's criticism of Freudianism. *Soviet Rev.*, 1:14–27.

Myasishchev, V. N. (1960), On the methods of study of higher nervous activity in man and current problems of their development. In: *Problems of Physiology and Pathology of Higher Nervous Activity*, ed. P. S. Kupalov. Leningrad: Izd. Akad. Med. Nauk SSSR, pp. 119–146.

—— (1962), Mental hygiene and prophylactics as related to the pathogenetic prophylactics of neuroses. In: *Problems of Prophilactics of Neurological and Mental Diseases. Transactions of the Psychoneurological Institute V. M. Bekhterev in Leningrad*, vol. 27, ed. G. V. Zenevich. Leningrad.

—— (1969), The methodological value of medical psychology. In: *Methodological and Theoretical Problems of Psychology*, ed. E. V. Shorokhova, pp. 291–316.

Namitokov, Yu. K. (1955), Regarding Arkhipov's paper "On the material nature of psyche and the subject matter of psychology." *Sov. Pedag.*, 4:53–59.

Napalkov, A. A. (1961), Principles of information processing by the brain. In: *Cybernetics in the Service of Communism*, vol. I, ed. A. I. Berg, pp. 153–172.

—— (1962a), Information processing by the brain. In: *Biological Aspects of Cybernetics*, ed. A. M. Kuzin et al., pp. 134–144.

—— & Bobneva, M. I. (1962b), The analysis of information processing by the human brain. *Vop. Psikhol.*, 6:40–54.

—— (1964a), Elementary units of the brain. *Nauka i Zhizn*, 6:24–28.

—— (1964b), Information processing in biological systems. Ibid., 9:68–72.

—— & Turov, A. (1964c), Neural networks. Ibid., 8:36–41.

—— & Orfeev, Yu. V. (1965), Current problems of heuristic programming. *Vop. Filos.*, 6:61–72.

—— (1969), *The Informational Structure of the Brain*. Moscow: Izd. Znanie.

Narskii, I. S., & Suvorov, L. N. (1962), *Positivism and the Mechanistic Revision of Marxism*. Moscow: Izd. Vysshaya Shkola.

—— (1963a), The concept of formal analysis and dialectics. *Vestnik Moskovskogo Universiteta, Seriya Ekonomika, Filosofiya*, 1:39–51.

—— (1963b), The main ideas of the neopositivist knowledge theory. In: *Marxist Philosophy and Neopositivism*, ed. T. I. Oizerman et al., pp. 42–80.

—— (1968), The reflection of the properties of external objects in sensations. In: *Problems of Logic and Knowledge Theory*, ed. I. S. Narskii. Moscow: Izd. Moskovskogo Universiteta, pp. 3–76.

Natadze, R. G. (1969), Experimental foundations of Uznadze's theory. In: *A Handbook of Contemporary Soviet Psychology*. New York: Basic Books, pp. 603–624.

—— (1970), The categorical nature of perception. *Vop. Psikhol.*, 4:25–34.

Naumova, N. F. (1965), The social conditionality of the emotional attitude to work. In: *Sociology in the USSR*, vol. II, ed. G. V. Osipov, pp. 39–54.

Nebylitsyn, V. D. (1963), The basic properties of the nervous system. *Vop. Psikhol.*, 4:21–34.

—— (1964), The cortico-reticular relations and their role in the nervous system. Ibid., 1:3-24.

—— & Aleksandrova, N. I. (1971), Factor analysis of the relationship between the EEG quantitative parameters in the frontal and occipital lobes as related to the problem of general properties of the nervous system. *Fiziol. Zh. SSSR,* 11:1577-1586.

Neimark, M. Z. (1963), On the experimental investigation of the orientation of a personality. *Vop. Psikhol.,* 1:3-12.

Nepomnyashchaya, N. I. (1965), On the relationship between logic and psychology in Piaget's system. *Vop. Filos.,* 4:135-144.

Nevskaya, A. A. (1963), A method for the determination of the channel capacity of the human visual analyzer. *Fiziol. Zh. SSSR,* 7:892-896.

Nevskii, V. (1922), The political horoscope of an academician. *Pod Znamenem Marksizma,* 3:55-61.

Novik, I. B. (1963), The gnoseological specific of cybernetic models. *Vop. Filos.,* 8:92-103.

—— (1964a), The role of modeling in natural sciences and technical sciences. In: *Dialectics in Physico-Mathematical Sciences,* ed. M. E. Omelyanovskii & I. V. Kuznetsov, pp. 521-555.

—— (1964b), The unity between the subject matter and the methods of cybernetics. In: *Cybernetics, Thinking, Life,* ed. A. I. Berg et al., pp. 157-163.

—— (1964c), On the modeling of biological processes. In: *On the Essence of Life,* ed. G. M. Frank & A. M. Kuzin, pp. 66-80.

—— (1964d), *Philosophical Problems of Cybernetic Modeling.* Moscow: Izd. Znanie.

—— (1965), *The Modeling of Complex Systems.* Moscow: Izd. Mysl.

—— (1968), The role of cybernetic models for the knowledge of biological and psychical phenomena. In: *Mathematical Modeling of Biological Processes,* ed. M. F. Vedenov et al., pp. 152-167.

—— (1969), *Philosophical Problems of Modeling of Psyche.* (A publication of the Section of Philosophical Problems of Cybernetics, of the Learned Board on the Complex Problem "Cybernetics," the USSR Acad. Sci.

Novikova, A. L. (1957), Electrophysiological investigation of speech. In: *Recent Soviet Psychology,* ed. N. O'Connor, pp. 337-351 (English edition, 1961).

Novinskii, I. I. (1961), *The Concept of Connection in Marxist Philosophy.* Moscow: Izd. Vysshaya Shkola.

Nyuberg, N. D. (1962), The coding of color information in the retina. In: *Biological Aspects of Cybernetics,* ed. A. M. Kuzin et al., pp. 154-157.

—— (1968), [7] The cognitive possibilities of modeling. In: *Mathematical Modeling of Biological Processes,* ed. M. F. Vedenov et al., pp. 136-151.

Oizerman, T. I. (1958), The main trends of the contemporary bourgeois philosophy. *Vestnik Moskovskogo Universiteta, Seriya Ekonomiki, Filosofii, Prava,* 2:67-78.

—— et al., eds. (1963), *Marxist Philosophy and Neopositivism. A Criticism of the Contemporary Positivism.* Moscow: Izd. Moskovskogo/Universiteta.

—— (1964), Man and his alienation. In: *Man and his Time,* pp. 104-119.

[7] Published after Nyuberg's death.

_____ ed. (1966), *The Contemporary Existentialism. Critical Studies.* Moscow: Izd. Mysl.

Olshanskii, V. B. (1965), Personality and social values. In: *Sociology in the USSR,* vol. I, ed. G. V. Osipov, pp. 471-530.

Omelyanovskii, M. E. & Kuznetsov, I. V. Eds. (1964), *Dialectics in Physico-Mathematical Sciences.* Moscow: Izd. Mysl.

Oparin, A. I. (1957), *The Origin of Life,* Third edition. New York: Academic Press (English edition, 1957).

_____ (1964a), The essence of life and its origin. In: *Dialectical Materialism and Contemporary Natural Sciences,* ed. V. N. Kolbanovskii et al., pp. 140-158.

_____ (1964b), The relationship between life and other forms of matter in motion. In: *On the Essence of Life,* ed. G. M. Frank & A. M. Kuzin, pp. 8-34.

Orbeli, L. A. Ed. (1945), *Advances of Biological Sciences in the USSR in the Last 25 Years.* Moscow: Izd. Akad. Nauk SSSR.

_____ ed. (1949), *Mittwochkolloquien. Protokolle und Stenogramme Physiologischer Kolloquien,* 3 vols. German edition in 1955. Berlin: Akademie Verlag.

_____ (1962), *Selected Works in Five Volumes.* Second volume: *The Adaptive and Trophic Functions of the Nervous System.* Moscow: Izd. Akad. Nauk SSSR.

Orlov, V. V. (1962), *The Characteristics of Sensory Cognition.* Perm: Permskoe Knizhnoe Izdatelstvo.

Osipov, G. V. Ed. (1965), *Sociology in the USSR,* 2 vols. Moscow: Izd. Mysl.

Ovchinnikova, O. V. (1959a), Analysis of the systemic structure of perception. VI: The "sensory" training of tonal hearing. *Dokls. Akad. Pedag. Nauk RSFSR,* 1:79-82.

_____ (1959b), Idem, VII: Training hearing by the "motor" procedure. Ibid., 2: 55-58.

Panfilov, V. Z. (1957), On the relationship between language and thinking. In: *Thinking and Language,* ed. D. P. Gorskii, Moscow: Gospolitizdat, pp. 117-164.

Parachev, A. M. (1963), The algorithmic structure of active touch. *Vop. Psikhol.,* 1:69-79.

Paramonov, N. Z. (1960), Abstract and concrete as aspects of knowledge. In: *Problems of Knowledge Theory and Logic,* ed. I. D. Andreev. Moscow: Izd. Akad. Nauk SSSR, pp. 142-168.

Parin, V. V. (1961), Cybernetics in physiology and medicine. *Vop. Filos.,* 10: 92-104.

_____ & Baevskii, R. M. (1963), *Cybernetics in Medicine and Physiology.* Moscow: Medgiz.

_____ (1964), Biological and technological systems; problems of bionics. *Priroda,* 5:20-25.

_____ & Baevskii, R. M. (1966), *Introduction to Medical Cybernetics.* Moscow/Prague: Izd. Meditsina & Czechoslovak State Publishing House for Medical Literature.

_____ et al. (1969), *Problems of Cybernetics. Some Conclusions and Methodological Problems of Philosophical Studies.* Moscow: Izd. Znanie.

Parygin, B. D. (1962), On the subject matter of social psychology. *Vop. Psikhol.,* 5:107-112.

_____ (1963), A conference on social psychology. Ibid., 3:181-183.

REFERENCES

—— (1965a), *Social Psychology as a Science*. Leningrad: Izd. Leningradskogo Universiteta.

—— (1965b), Marx and Engels on social psychology. In: *Problems of Social Psychology*, ed. V. N. Kolbanovskii & B. F. Porshnev. Moscow: Izd. Mysl., pp. 11-51.

—— (1965c), Problems of social psychology in Plekhanov's works. Ibid., pp. 95-116.

—— (1965d), The nature and dynamics of general moods. Ibid., pp. 286-321.

Pavlov, I. P. (1897), *The Work of the Digestive Glands*. London: Charles Griffin & Co. (Second English edition, 1910).

—— (1916), The reflex of purpose. In: *Lectures on Conditioned Reflexes*, trans. and ed. W. Horsley Gantt in 1928: *Twenty-Five Years of Objective Study of the Higher Nervous Activity (Behaviour) of Animals*. London: Lawrence & Wishart, pp. 275-281.

—— (1917), The reflex of freedom. Ibid., pp. 282-286.

—— (1923), *Twenty Years Experience in the Objective Study of the Higher Nervous Activity (Behavior) of Animals*. In: *Collected Works*. Vol. III, Second Book. Moscow/Leningrad: Izd. Akad. Nauk SSSR. (Seventh edition, 1951).

—— (1927), Lecture XXIII: The experimental results obtained with animals in their application to man. In: *Conditioned Reflexes. An Investigation of the Physiological Activity of the Cerebral Cortex*, trans. and ed. G. V. Anrep in 1928. Oxford: Oxford University Press. Humphrey Milford, pp. 395-411.

—— (1934), Kritik der Gestaltpsychologie an Hand des Buches von Woodworth *Die Moderne Schule der Psychologie*. In: *Mittwochkolloquien*, vol. II, ed. L. A. Orbeli, pp. 536-550.

—— (1935), The conditioned reflex. In: *Lectures on Conditioned Reflexes*, vol. 2: *Conditioned Reflexes and Psychiatry*, trans. and ed. W. Horsley Gantt in 1941. London: Lawrence & Wishart.

Pavlov, T. D. (1966), Information, reflection, creativity. In: *Lenin's Reflection Theory and the Contemporary Science. Proceedings of a Conference on Current Problems of the Materialistic Dialectic*, 7-9 April, 1965, ed. F. V. Konstantinov et al., pp. 149-197.

Pavlov, V. (1966), *The Logical Functions of the Categories of Space and Time*. Kiev: Izd. Kievskogo Universiteta.

Payne, J. R. (1968), *Rubinštejn and the Philosophical Foundations of Soviet Psychology*. Basel/Stuttgart: D. Reidel Company.

Pekhterev, N. G. (1965), The authenticity of images and signals. *Vestnik Moskovskogo Universiteta, Seriya Ekonomika, Filosofiya*, 6:67-72.

Penfield, W. & Jasper, H. (1954), *Epilepsy and the Functional Anatomy of the Human Brain*. Boston: Little, Brown.

Perov, A. K. (1957), The development of psychical processes and temporary mental states into character traits. In: *Proceedings of the Psychological Conference*. Moscow: Izd. Akad. Pedag. Nauk RSFSR, pp. 79-89.

Petlenko, V. P. (1960), *Physiological Idealism and Some Philosophical Problems of Theoretical Medicine*. Leningrad: Medgiz.

Petrovskii, A. V. (1961), The major trends of Russian psychology in the early 20th century. In: *Aspects of the History of Russian Psychology*, ed. M. V. Sokolov. Moscow: Izd. Akad. Pedag. Nauk RSFSR, pp. 358-538.

____ (1964), Psychological problems in Blonskii's late works. *Vop. Psikhol.*, 3: 15-28.

____ (1967), *History of Soviet Psychology. The Development of Foundations of the Psychological Science*. Moscow: Izd. Prosveshchenie.

____ (1970), Some problems of research in social psychology. Translated in: *Soviet Psychology*, vol. IX, #4, Summer 1971: 382-398.

Petrushenko, L. A. (1967), *The Feedback Principle. Some Philosophical and Methodological Problems of Control*. Moscow: Izd. Mysl.

Petrushevskii, S. A. (1952), Pavlov's fight for materialism in physiology and psychology. In: *I. P. Pavlov's Teaching and Philosophical Problems of Psychology*, ed. S. A. Petrushevskii. Moscow: Izd. Akad. Nauk SSSR, pp. 33-88.

Pinkevich, A. P. (1929), *Fundamentals of Soviet Pedagogy*. Moscow/Leningrad: Gosizdat.

Platonov, K. K. (1961), *The Study of the Pupil's Psychology*. Moscow: Proftekhizdat.

____ (1962), *Problems of Work Psychology*. Moscow: Medgiz.

____ ed. (1965), *Personality and Work*. Moscow: Izd. Mysl.

____ (1969), The psychological principle of the individual approach. In: *Methodological and Theoretical Problems of Psychology*, ed. E. V. Shorokhova, pp. 190-217.

Poddyakov, N. N. (1965), The dynamicness of visual representations in preschool-age children. *Vop. Psikhol.*, 1:100-112.

Poletaev, I. A. (1958), *Signal*. Moscow.

Polyakov, G. A. (1960), The current status of the neuron theory. In: *Some Theoretical Problems of the Structure and Activity of the Brain*, ed. S. A. Sarkisov et al., pp. 22-48.

____ (1962), Current findings on the structure of the cerebral cortex. In: *Higher Cortical Functions in Man*, ed. A. R. Luriya.

____ (1964a), The system of analyzers as a universal apparatus of adequate reflection of reality. In: *Dialectical Materialism and Contemporary Natural Sciences*, ed. V. N. Kolbanovskii, pp. 285-326.

____ (1964b), Problems of regulation, control and orientation from the neurophysiological point of view. *Problems of Cybernetics*, 1:153-166.

____ (1965), The structural mechanisms of functional states of cortical neurons. In: *Reflexes of the Brain*, ed. E. A. Asratyan, pp. 434-442.

Ponomarev, Ya. A. (1960), *Psychology of Creative Thinking*. Moscow: Izd. Akad. Pedag. Nauk RSFSR.

____ (1967), *Knowledge, Thinking and Intellectual Development*. Moscow: Izd. Prosveshchenie.

____ (1971), Psychology and objective reality. *Vop. Psikhol.*, 6:131-139.

Popova, I. M. (1961a), The social background of the psychological orientation in the bourgeois sociology. *Vop. Filos.*, 3:86-95.

____ (1961b), Social psychology in American psychology. *Soviet Review*, 8:3-19.

Porshnev, B. F. (1965), Elements of social psychology. In: *Problems of Social Psychology*, ed. V. N. Kolbanovskii & B. F. Porshnev. Moscow: Izd. Mysl., pp. 171-195.

Preobrazhenskaya, N. S. (1957), Some problems of function localization. *Zh. Nevr. Psikhiat.*, 6:106-111.

Prezent, I. I. (1964), The essence of life as related to its origin. In: *On the Essence of Life*, ed. G. M. Frank & A. M. Kuzin, pp. 211-229.

REFERENCES

Protasenya, P. F. (1959), *The Origin of Consciousness and its Characteristics.* Minsk: Izd. Belorusskogo Universiteta.

— (1961), *Communication and Thinking of the Primitive Man.* Minsk: Izd. Ministerstva Vysshego, Srednego Spetsialnogo i Professionalnogo Obrazovaniya Belorusskoi SSR.

Puni, A. T. (1960), The formation of representation of movements. *Vop. Psikhol.,* 5:17-28.

— (1964), The nature of motor skills. *Ibid.,* 1:94-103.

Pushkin, V. N. (1965a), Toward a comprehension of the heuristic activity in psychology and cybernetics. *Ibid.,* 1:9-20.

— (1965b), *Operative Thinking in Large Systems.* Moscow: Izd. Energiya.

— (1967), *Heuristics—the Science of Creative Thinking.* Moscow: Politizdat.

— (1969a), The study of the thinking process. *Vop. Psikhol.,* 6:20-35.

— Pospelova, D. A. & Sadovskii, V. N., eds. (1969b), *Problems of Heuristics. Collection of Papers.* Moscow: Izd. Vysshaya Shkola.

Rahmani, L. (1963), Considerations on the Pavlovian theory in psychopathology. *J. Nerv. & Ment. Dis.,* 6:548-551.

— (1966), Studies on the mental development of the child. In: *Present-day Russian Psychology,* ed. N. O'Connor. Oxford: Pergamon Press, pp. 152-177.

Ramishvili, D. I. (1956), The inconsistency of the theory of an initial gestural language in the light of psychological laws of language. *Izvestiya Akad. Pedag. Nauk RSFSR,* 81:39-64.

Ramul, K. A. (1965), The psychology of the scientist, particularly of the psychologist. *Vop. Psikhol.,* 6:126-135.

— (1971), Wilhelm Wundt as psychologist. *Ibid.,* 1:114-121.

Rapoport, A. (1963), Letter to a Soviet philosopher. *ETC.,* 4:437-455.

Ravzin, V. I. ed. (1965), *Consultations on Teaching Philosophy.* Moscow: Gospolitizdat.

Razran, G. (1935), Psychology in the USSR. *J. Philos.,* 32:19-24.

— (1942), Current psychological theory in the USSR. *Psychol. Bull.,* 7:445-446.

— (1957a), Soviet psychology since 1950. *Science,* 125:1106-1113.

— (1957b), Recent Russian psychology. *Contemp. Psychol.,* 4:93-100.

— (1958), Soviet psychology and physiology. *Science,* 128:1187-1196.

— (1961), The observable unconscious and the inferrable conscious in current Soviet psychophysiology: interoceptive conditioning, semantic conditioning and the orienting reflex. *Psychol. Rev.,* 2:81-147.

Reich, W. (1929), Dialectical materialism and psychoanalysis. *Pod Znamenem Marksizma,* 7-8:180-206.

Reisner, M. (1923), The problem of psychology in the light of the theory of historical materialism. *Vestnik Sotsialisticheskoi Akademii,* 3:210-255.

— (1924a), The conventional symbols as a social stimulus. *Vestnik Kommunisticheskoi Akademii,* 9:175-197.

— (1924b), Freud and his school on religion. *Pechat i Revolyutsiya,* 1:40-60; second part: 3:81-106.

— (1925), *Problems of Social Psychology.* Moscow: Burevestnik.

Resolution of the congress of psychotechnique from 26 May 1931. *Psikhofiziologiya Truda i Psikhotekhnika,* 4-6:374-386.

Resolution of the CC of the Communist Party (b) on pedological distortions in the commissariats of education, taken on July 4, 1936. In: *Soviet Psychiatry*, J. Wortis, pp. 242-245.

Resolution of the conference on problems of psychology. *Sov. Pedag.*, 8:99-103.

Revzin, I. I. (1964), From structural linguistics to semiotics. *Vop. Filos.*, 9:43-53.

Reznikov, L. O. (1961), The role of signs in the process of knowledge. Ibid., 8: 118-132.

―― (1963a), The epistemology of pragmatism and Ch. Morris' semiotics. Ibid., 1:102-105.

―― (1963b), The positions of dialectical materialism and neopositivism regarding the relationship between language and reality. In: *Marxist Philosophy and Neopositivism. A Criticism of the Contemporary Positivism*, ed. T. I. Oizerman et al. Moscow: Izd. Moskovskogo Universiteta, pp. 427-445.

―― (1964), *Epistemological Problems of Semiotics*. Leningrad: Izd. Leningradskogo Universiteta.

Roitbak, A. I. (1960), Oscillographic data on the formation of temporary connections. In: *Gagra Symposia*, vol. III, ed. I. S. Beritashvili, pp. 149-165.

Rokhlin, L. (Undated), *Sleep, Hypnosis, Dreams. A Popular Exposition*. Moscow: Foreign Languages Publishing House.

Rosenblith, W. A. (1964), Postscript to I. Sechenov: *Reflexes of the Brain*. Cambridge, Massachusetts: The M. I. T. Press, pp. 43-45.

Roshal, B. N. (1965), The concept of type in physiology and psychology. *Vop. Psikhol.*, 6:170-173.

Rossolimo, G. I. (1922), French translation in 1929: *L'individualité de L'enfant*. Paris: F. Alcan.

Rozanova, T. V. (1959), Incidental memory for various aspects of a situation as a function of their role in activity. *Vop. Psikhol.*, 4:105-115.

Rozenberg, N. M. (1965), Teaching the algorithm of intellectual and practical acts. *Sov. Pedag.*, 8:59-69.

Rozental, M. M. (1963), *Lenin and the Dialectics*. Moscow: Izd. VPSh i AON pri Tsk KPSS.

―― (1966), The current development of Lenin's dialectic theory of knowledge. In: *Lenin's Reflection Theory and the Contemporary Science*, ed. F. V. Konstantinov et al., pp. 16-74.

Rubinshtein, S. L. (1914), *Eine Studie zum Problem der Methode. Absoluter Rationalismus (Hegel)*. In: *Philosophische Arbeiten*, vol. IX, ed. H. Cohen & P. Natrop. Giersen: Verlag von Alfred Töpelmann.

―― (1934), Psychological problems in Marx's works. *Psikhofiziologiya Truda i Psikhotekhnika*, 1:3-20.

―― (1943), Soviet psychology in war time. *Pod Znamenem Marksizma*, 10:45-61.

―― (1946), *Foundations of General Psychology*, Second edition. Moscow: Uchpedgiz.

―― ed. (1948), *Researches on the Psychology of Perception*. Moscow/Leningrad: Izd. Akad. Nauk SSSR.

―― (1952), Pavlov's teaching and psychological problems. In: *I. P. Pavlov's Teaching and Philosophical Problems of Psychology*, ed. S. A. Petrushevskii, pp. 194-228.

―― (1955), Questions of psychological theory. Translated in: *Psychology in the Soviet Union*, ed. B. Simon, pp. 264-278.

REFERENCES

_____ (1957a), *Existence and Consciousness.* Moscow: Izd. Akad. Nauk SSSR.

_____ (1957b), The relationship between language, speech and thinking. *Vop. Yazykoznaniya*, 2:42-48.

_____ (1957c), I. M. Sechenov's psychological views and Soviet psychological science. In: *I. M. Sechenov and the Materialistic Psychology*, ed. S. L. Rubinshtein. Moscow: Izd. Akad. Nauk SSSR, pp. 7-30.

_____ (1958), *Thinking and Ways of Its Investigation.* Moscow: Izd. Akad. Nauk SSSR.

_____ (1959a). *Principles and Paths of the Development of Psychology.* Izd. Akad. Nauk SSSR.

_____ (1959b), The determinism principle and the psychological theory of thinking. In: *Psychological Science in the USSR*, ed. B. G. Ananev et al., vol. I, pp. 315-356.

_____ Ed. (1960a). *Thinking Processes and the Laws of Analysis, Synthesis and Generalization.* Moscow: Izd. Akad. Nauk SSSR.

_____ (1960b), [8] Pressing problems of the psychological study of thinking. In: *Researches on Thinking in Soviet Psychology*, ed. E. V. Shorokhova, pp. 225-235.

Rudik, P. A. (1932), Bourgeois influences in the psychological measurement of the intellect. *Psikhologiya*, 3:3-7.

_____ (1962a), *Psychology. A Short Textbook.* Moscow: Izd. Fizkultura i Sport.

_____ Puni, P. Ts. (1962b), *Problems of Psychology of Sport.* Moscow: Izd. Fizkultura i Sport.

Rutkevich, M. N. (1959), *Dialectical Materialism.* Moscow: Sotsekgiz.

Rybnikov, N. A. (1928), Methodological problems at the First All-Unional Pedological Congress. *Psikhologiya, Seriya A*, 1:171-179.

Sakharov, L. G. (1930), The formation of concepts. *Psikhologiya*, 1:3-33.

Samarin, Yu. A. (1959), Regarding Galperin's theory of so-called "intellectual acts." *Vop. Psikhol.*, 5:154-160.

_____ (1962), *Studies on the Psychology of Intellect.* Moscow: Izd. Akad. Pedag. Nauk.

Sapir, I. (1926), Freudianism and Marxism. *Pod Znamenem Marksizma*, 11:59-87.

_____ (1929), Freudianism, sociology, psychology. Ibid., 207-236.

Sarkisov, S. A. (1957a), Some structural features of the upper sections of the central nervous system and their physiological role. *J. Nevr. Psikhiat.*, 1:15-23.

_____ (1957b), Regarding the conclusions of the debate on function localization. Ibid., 6:681-693.

_____ (1960a), The functional interpretation of certain cortical structures in the light of evolution. Ibid., 6:645-651.

_____ Filimonov, I. N. & Kukuev, L. A. eds. (1960b), *Some Theoretical Problems of the Brain Structure and Function.* Moscow: Medgiz.

_____ & Preobrazhenskaya, N. S. (1961), Individual variations in the structural characteristics of the human cortex. *Pavlov J. Higher Nervous Activity*, 5: 842-850.

_____ (1963a), Biological and philosophical problems of the contemporary brain science. In: *Philosophical Problems of Physiology of Higher Nervous Activity and Psychology*, ed. P. N. Fedoseev et al., pp. 275-298.

_____

[8] Theses of a paper prepared in January 1960.

_____ Bassin, F. V. & Banshchikov, V. M. (1963b), *Pavlovian Theory and Some Theoretical Problems of the Contemporary Neurology and Psychiatry.* Moscow: Medgiz.

_____ & Shorokhova, E. V., eds. (1963c), *Structural and Functional Foundations of Psychical Activity.* Moscow: Izd. Akad. Nauk SSSR.

_____ (1964a), Certain philosophical problems of the contemporary brain science. In: *Dialectical Materialism and Contemporary Natural Sciences,* ed. V. N. Kolbanovskii et al., pp. 234-257.

_____ (1964b), *The Structure and Function of the Brain.* Bloomington/London: Indiana University Press (English edition, 1966).

_____ ed. (1965), *Development of Child Brain.* Leningrad: Izd. Meditsina.

Schastnyi, A. I. (1957), Formation of cortical selective systems by substituting positive conditioned stimuli. *Zh. Nevr. Psikhiat.,* 2-3:278-284.

Sechenov, I. M. (1863), *Reflexes of the Brain.* Cambridge, Massachusetts: The M. I. T. Press (English edition, 1965).

_____ (1866), *Physiology of the Nervous System.* Partially reprinted in 1952. In: I. M. Sechenov, I. P. Pavlov & N. E. Vvedenskii: *Physiology of the Nervous System.* Selected Works, vols. II and III, ed. K. M. Bykov. Moscow: Gosudarstvennoe Izd. Med. Lit.

_____ (1878), *The Elements of Thought.* In: I. Sechenov: *Selected Works.* Moscow/Leningrad: State Publishing House for Biological and Medical Literature (English edition, 1935).

_____ (Undated), *Selected Physiological and Psychological Works.* Moscow: Foreign Languages Publishing House.

Selivanov, V. I. (1960), On the concrete study of the personality of the Soviet man. In: *Problems of the Psychology of Personality,* ed. E. I. Ignatev, pp. 38-43.

_____ (1964), The concept of will in Soviet psychology. *Vop. Psikhol.,* 1:83-93.

_____ (1965), The rural family and its influence on personality development. In: *Sociology in the USSR,* vol. I, ed. G. V. Osipov, pp. 458-470.

_____ (1968a), The concrete life conditions and the formation of personality. In: *Formation of Personality and the Volitional Process. Uchenye Zapiski,* vol. 59, ed. V. I. Selivanov. (A publication of Ryazan State Pedagogical Institute; works of the psychology department.) Moscow: Izd. Prosveshchenie, pp. 5-37.

_____ (1968b), On the question of the concept of will in psychology. Ibid., pp. 96-110.

Semenovskaya, E. N. (1959), Physiological laws and mechanisms of visual sensations and perceptions. In: *Psychological Science in the USSR,* ed. B. G. Ananev et al., pp. 84-113.

Sepp, E. K. (1955), On localization of functions in the cortex. *Zh. Nevr. Psikhiat.,* 12:881-889.

Severtsov, A. N. (1922), *Evolution and Psyche.* Reprinted in A. N. Severtsov: *Collected Works,* vol. III: *General Problems of Evolution,* ed. I. I. Shmalkhauzen. Moscow/Leningrad: Izd. Akad. Nauk SSSR, pp. 289-311.

Shalyutin, S. M. (1961), On cybernetics and its application. In: *Philosophical Problems of Cybernetics,* ed. V. A. Ilin et al., pp. 6-85.

_____ (1964), On basic possibilities of cybernetic modeling. In: *Cybernetics, Thinking, Life,* ed. A. I. Berg et al., pp. 347-362.

REFERENCES

Shapiro, S. I. & Umanskii, L. I. (1963), On the application of information theory to the study of human abilities. *Vop. Psikhol.*, 2:75-90.

_____ (1965), Pupils' individual characteristics in processing mathematical information. Ibid., 2:91-100.

Shchedrovitskii, G. P. (1957), The analysis of "verbal thinking." *Vop. Yazykoznaniya*, 1:56-68.

_____ (1964a), *Methodological Problems of Systemic Study*. Moscow: Izd. Znanie.

_____ (1964b), About the principles of analysis of the objective structure of thinking in terms of content-genetic analysis. *Vop. Psikhol.*, 2:125-132.

Shein, A. A. (1963), Bekhterev as representative of a materialistic psychology. *Vop. Psikhol.*, 5:152-158.

_____ (1964), P. P. Blonskii as psychologist. Ibid., 3:29-39.

_____ (1965), Vygotskii's early psychological investigations. Ibid., 6:7-15.

Shemyakin, F. N. & Germonovich, L. (1932), How Trotsky and Kautzky revise Marxism in psychology. *Psikhologiya*, 1-2:3-37.

_____ (1952), The problems of the relationship between language and thinking in the light of I. V. Stalin's works on linguistics. In: *I. P. Pavlov's Teaching and Philosophical Problems of Psychology*, ed. S. A. Petrushevskii.

_____ (1956), Memory "automatisms" and thinking; criticism of Levy-Bruhl's theory of memory as "substitute" of thinking. *Izvestiya Akad. Pedag. Nauk RSFSR*, 81:5-38.

_____ ed. (1960), *Thinking and Speech*. Moscow: Izd. Akad. Pedag. Nauk RSFSR.

_____ (1963), Certain problems of the contemporary psychology of thinking. In: *Thinking and Speech*, ed. N. N. Zhinkin & F. N. Shemyakin. *Transactions of the Psychological Institute*. Moscow: Izd. Akad. Pedag. Nauk RSFSR, pp. 3-46.

_____ (1969), V. I. Lenin and the historic development of thinking. *Vop. Psikhol.*, 4:3-14.

Shevarev, P. A. (1948), The problem of color constancy under changing illumination. In: *Researches on the Psychology of Perception*, ed. S. L. Rubinshtein, pp. 99-165.

_____ (1959a), Researches on perception. In: *Psychological Science in the USSR*, ed. B. G. Ananev et al., vol. I, pp. 114-139.

_____ (1959b), *Generalized Associations in Pupil's School Work*. Moscow: Izd. Akad. Pedag. Nauk RSFSR.

_____ ed. (1962), *Perception and Thinking. Transactions of the Psychological Institute. Izvestiya Akad. Pedag. Nauk* RSFSR, 120.

_____ (1966), Role of associations in the thinking process. In: *Researches on Thinking in Soviet Psychology*, ed. E. V. Shorokhova, pp. 388-437.

Shif, Z. I. (1935), *The Development of Everyday and Scientific Concepts*. Moscow: Uchpedgiz.

Shifman, L. A. (1948), On the problem of interaction of sense organs and sensory modalities. In: *Researches on the Psychology of Perception*, ed. S. L. Rubinshtein, pp. 42-93.

Shkolnik-Yarros, E. G. (1954), On the morphology of the visual analyzer. *Zh. Vys. Nerv. Deyat.*, 2:289-304.

_____ (1962), The structure of the analyzer and the problem of color vision. *Arkhiv Anatomii, Gistologii i Embriologii*, 2:12-30.

_____ (1965), Certain cortical apparata of interneuronal connections. *Zh. Vys. Nerv. Deyat.*, 6:1063–1071.

Shmaryan, A. S. (1949), *Cerebral Pathology and Psychiatry. Brain Tumors and the Theory of Localization of Mental Disturbances*, vol. I. Moscow: Medgiz.

Shnirman, A. L. (1928), Present-day tendencies in Russian psychology. *J. General Psychol.*, 3/4:397–404.

_____ (1930), Bekhterev's reflexological school. In: *Psychologies of 1930*, ed. C. Murchison, pp. 221–242.

Shorokhova, E. V. (1952), I. P. Pavlov's teaching on signal systems and Lenin's reflection theory. *Vop. Filos.*, 3:104–116.

_____ (1955), *I. P. Pavlov's Materialistic Theory on Signal Systems*. Moscow: Izd. Akad. Nauk SSSR.

_____ (1961), *The Problem of Consciousness in Philosophy and Natural Sciences*. Moscow: Izd. Sotsialno-Ekonomicheskoi Literatury.

_____ Kaganov, V. M. (1963a), Philosophical problems of psychology. In: *Philosophical Problems of Physiology of Higher Nervous Activity and Psychology*, ed. P. N. Fedoseev et al., pp. 63–105.

_____ Mansurov, N. S. & Platonov, K. K. (1963b), Problems of social psychology. *Vop. Psikhol.*, 5:73–82.

_____ (1966), I. P. Pavlov's theory on higher nervous activity and its meaning for the psychology of thinking. In: *Researches on Thinking in Soviet Psychology*, ed. E. V. Shorokhova, pp. 80–122.

_____ (1969), The determinism principle in psychology. In: *Methodological and Theoretical Problems of Psychology*, ed. E. V. Shorokhova, pp. 9–56.

Shpilrein, I. (1923a), The status and tasks of psychotechnique abroad in the USSR. *Vestnik Sotsialisticheskoi Akademii*, 2:114–129.

_____ (1923b), Wilhelm Stern's personalism and its relation to psychotechnique. Ibid., 3:200–209.

_____ (1928), Basic problems of the professional orientation and selection. *Zh. Psikhologii, Pedologii i Psikhotekhniki, Seriya B: Psikhofiziologiya Truda i Psikhotekhnika*, 1:31–40.

_____ (1930a), Elements of a theory of psychotechnique. Address to the 6th International Congress of Psikhotechnique. *Psikhofiziologiya Truda i Psikhotekhnika*, 4:237–242.

_____ (1930b), The subject matter and tasks of psychotechnique. Ibid., 6:461–466.

_____ (1931a), The situation on the psychotechnical front. Ibid., 2/3:103–111.

_____ (1931b), The problem of a psychotechnique theory. Ibid., 4–6:286–300.

_____ (1931c), A turning point in psychotechnique. Ibid., 4–6:247–285.

Shtoff, V. A. (1963a), *The Role of Models in Knowledge*. Leningrad: Izd. Leningradskogo Universiteta.

_____ (1963b), The characteristics of experiments based on models. *Vop. Filos.*, 9:40–50.

_____ (1966), *Modeling and Philosophy*. Moscow/Leningrad: Izd. Nauka.

Shumilina, A. I. (1949), The role of the frontal cortex in the conditioned-reflex activity of dogs. In: *Problems of Higher Nervous Activity*, ed. P. K. Anokhin, pp. 561–628.

Shvarts, L. A. (1954), Certain procedures of increasing the visual acuity. In: *Proceedings of the Psychological Conference. 3–8 July*, ed. A. N. Leontev et al. Moscow: Izd. Akad. Pedag. Nauk RSFSR, pp. 217–228.

REFERENCES

_____ (1960), Conditioned reflexes to verbal stimuli. Translated in: *Problems of Psychology*, 1/2:36-49.
Shvarts, L. M. (1931), Reflexological misinterpretations in the theory of the collective. *Psikhologiya*, 4:128-140.
Sidelkovskii, A. P. (1964), The algorithmic approach to the analysis of learning is valid. *Vop. Psikhol.*, 5:127-132.
Sitnikov, E. M. (1965), Alienation and the need for a party of communists. In: *Proceedings of the Second Regional Conference on Philosophical Sciences.* April 1965, ed. V. V. Orlov. Perm: Uralskii Gosudarstvennyi Universitet imeni A. M. Gorkogo; Permskii Gosudarstvennyi Universitet imeni A. M. Gorkogo, pp. 485-490.
Slavskaya, K. A. (1966), The determinism of the thinking process. In: *Researches on Thinking in Soviet Psychology*, ed. E. V. Shorokhova, pp. 175-224.
_____ (1968), *Thinking in Action. Psychology of Thinking.* Moscow: Izd. Politicheskoi Literatury.
Slobin, D. I. (1966), Soviet psycholinguistics. In: *Present-day Russian Psychology*, ed. N. O'Connor, pp. 109-157.
Smirnov, A. A. (1948), *Psychology of Remembering.* Moscow: Izd. Akad. Pedag. Nauk RSFSR.
_____ (1960), The experimental study of psychical reactions in Kornilov's works. In: *Problems of the Psychology of Personality*, ed. E. I. Ignatev. Moscow: Gosudarstvennoe Uchebno-pedagogicheskoe Izdatelstvo Ministerstva Prosveshcheniya RSFSR, pp. 21-37.
_____ et al., eds. (1962), *Psychology. A Textbook for Pedagogical Institutes.*
_____ & P. I. Zinchenko (1969), Problems in the psychology of memory. In: *A Handbook of Contemporary Soviet Psychology.* New York: Basic Books, pp. 452-502.
_____ (1970), Lenin's reflection theory and psychology. *Vop. Psikhol.*, 2:3-32.
Smirnov, V. P. (1969), Again about brain and psyche. *Vop. Filos.*, 2:137-142.
Snyakin, P. G. & Kurilova, L. M. (1961a), Some current problems of the physiology and pathology of sense organs. *Vestnik Akad. Med. Nauk*, 5:78-84.
_____ (1961b), Central regulation of the activity of sensory systems. *Sechenov Physiol., J. USSR*, 11:1-6.
_____ & Esakov, A. I. (1963), Problems of perception and the phenomenon of "attunement" of sense organs. *Vop. Filos.*, 2:61-70.
Sobolev, S. L., Kitov, A. I. & Lyapunov, A. A. (1955), The basic characteristics of cybernetics. *Ibid.*, 4:136-148.
_____ & Lyapunov, A. A. (1958), Cybernetics and natural sciences. *Ibid.*, 5:127-138.
_____ & _____ (1959), Cybernetics and natural sciences. In: *Philosophical Problems of Contemporary Natural Sciences*, ed. P. N. Fedoseev, pp. 237-267.
_____ (1963), Yes, this is very serious! In: *What Is Possible and Impossible in Cybernetics*, ed. A. I. Berg & E. Ya. Kolman, pp. 82-88.
_____ & _____ (1964), Cybernetics and natural sciences. In: *Dialectics in Physico-Mathematical Sciences*, ed. M. E. Omelyanovskii & I. V. Kuznetsov, pp. 86-103.
Sokhin, F. A. (1951), Some questions regarding the acquisition of the grammatical structure of language by children in the light of I. P. Pavlov's teaching. *Sov. Pedag.* 7:42-56.

_____ (1959), On the formation of linguistic generalizations in the process of speech development. *Vop. Psikhol.*, 5:112-123.

Sokolov, A. N. (1956), The speech mechanisms of mental activity. *Izvestiya Akad. Pedag. Nauk RSFSR*, 81:65-98.

_____ (1960), The dynamics and functions of internal speech (latent articulation) in the thinking process. Ibid., 13:149-182.

_____ (1963), Electromyographic analysis of internal speech and the problem of the neurodynamics of thinking. In: *Thinking and Speech*, ed. N. I. Zhinkin & F. N. Shemyakin, pp. 173-218.

_____ (1967), Speech-motor afferentation and the problem of brain mechanisms of thought. Translated in: *Soviet Psychology and Psychiatry*, Fall 1967, 1:3-15.

_____ (1969), Studies of the speech mechanisms of thinking. In: *A Handbook of Contemporary Soviet Psychology*. New York: Basic Books, pp. 531-573.

Sokolov, E. N. (1951), Perception in the light of I. P. Pavlov's theory of temporary connections. *Sov. Pedag.*, 7:27-41.

_____ (1952), Generalization in perception. Ibid., 52-61.

_____ (1954), Some problems in the study of memory. Ibid., 5:64-77.

_____ (1955), Higher nervous activity and the problem of perception. *Vop. Psikhol.*, 1:58-65.

_____ (1958a), *Perception and the Conditioned Reflex*. Oxford: Pergamon Press (English edition, 1963).

_____ (1958b), The orienting reflex, its structure and mechanisms. In: *Orienting Reflex and Exploratory Behavior*, ed. L. G. Voronin et al., pp. 141-151.

_____ (1958c), The measurement of sensitivity and reactivity of a conditioned reflex arc in connection with the interaction of orienting and defense reflexes. Ibid., pp. 222-237.

_____ (1959), The reflex mechanisms of perception. In: *Psychological Science in the USSR*, vol. I, ed. B. G. Ananev et al., pp. 57-81.

_____ (1960a), A probabilistic model of perception. *Vop. Psikhol.*, 2:102-116.

_____ (1960b), Neural model of the stimulus and orienting reflex. Ibid., 4:61-73.

_____ (1961a), Effect of darkness on the human electroencephalogram. *Pavlov J. Higher Nervous Activity*, 1:411-418.

_____ & Paramonova, N. T. (1961b), Extinction of the orienting reaction. Ibid., pp. 1-11.

_____ & _____ (1961c), Progressive changes in the orienting reflex in man during the development of sleep inhibition. Ibid., pp. 217-226.

_____ (1962), Perception. In: *Psychology. A Textbook for Pedagogical Institutes*, ed. A. A. Smirnov et al. Moscow: Uchpedgiz.

_____ (1963), Orienting reflex as a cybernetic system. *Zh. Vys. Nerv. Deyat.*, 5:816-830.

_____ (1964), On the modeling properties of the nervous system. In: *Cybernetics, Thinking, Life*, ed. A. I. Berg et al., pp. 242-279.

_____ (1965a), Neural mechanisms of habituation as the simplest form of a conditioned reflex. *Zh. Vys. Nerv. Deyat.*, 2:249-259.

_____ (1965b), Seminar dedicated to the modeling function of the nervous system. Ibid., 1:188-189.

_____ (1965c), Inhibition in the activity of analyzers. In: *Reflexes of the Brain*, ed. E. A. Asratyan, pp. 72-81.

REFERENCES

_____ (1969a), The investigation of memory at the level of macroreactions. *Zh. Vys. Nerv. Deyat.*, 3:441-452.

_____ (1969b), The modeling properties of the nervous system. In: *A Handbook of Contemporary Soviet Psychology*. New York: Basic Books, pp. 672-704.

Sokolovskii, M. A. (1965), The automation of production and the development of the Soviet worker's personality. In: *Proceedings of the Second Regional Conference on Philosophical Sciences*, ed. V. V. Orlov. Perm, pp. 269-276.

Spirkin, A. A. (1959), *The Origin of Consciousness*. Moscow: Gospolitizdat.

_____ (1961), On the nature of consciousness. *Vop. Filos.*, 6:118-126.

Stalin, I. V. (1950), *Marxism and Questions of Linguistics*. Moscow: Gosudarstvennoe Izdatelstvo Politicheskoi Literatury.

_____ (1952), *Economic Problems of Socialism in the U.S.S.R.* New York: International Publishers. Moscow: Gosudarstvennoe Izdatelstvo Politicheskoi Literatury.

Stankevich, I. A. (1960), Problems of evolution of the cerebral cortex and the wrong approach of some foreign authors. In: *Some Theoretical Problems of the Brain Structure and Function*, ed. S. A. Sarkisov et al., pp. 107-121.

Steklova, R. P. (1958), On the relationship between the change in light sensitivity of the eye and depression of alpha rhythm in the course of presentation of auditory stimuli. In: *Orienting Reflex and Exploratory Behavior*, ed. L. G. Voronin, et al., pp. 238-248.

Stempovskaya, V. I. (1958), *On the Role of Abstraction in Knowledge*. Moscow: Izd. Akad. Nauk SSSR.

Strakhov, I. V. (1930), Against formalism in psychology. *Psikhologiya*, 2:145-187.

Struminskii, V. (1926), Marxism and contemporary psychology. *Pod Znamenem Marksizma*, 3:207-233. Second part, Ibid., 4/5:140-184.

Sventsitskii, A. L. (1966), The interview as a research method in social psychology. In: *Problems of General, Social and Engineering Psychology*, ed. B. G. Ananev & B. F. Lomov, pp. 32-42.

Sviderskii, V. I. (1962), *On the Dialectics of Elements and Structure*. Moscow: Izd. Sotsialno-Ekonomicheskoi Literatury.

Szekely, L. (1950), Knowledge and thinking. *Acta Psychol.*, 7:1-24.

Talankin, A. (1931), On Prof. Kornilov's "Marxist" psychology. *Psikhologiya*, 1:24-43.

_____ (1932), Against the menshevik idealism in psychology. Ibid., 1-2:38-62.

Tarasenko, F. P. (1963), Regarding the definition of the concept of "information" in cybernetics. *Vop. Filos.*, 4:76-84.

Teplov, B. M. (1947), *30 Years of Soviet Psychological Science*. Moscow: Izd. Pravda.

_____ (1960), Kornilov's fight between 1923-1925 for the reorientation of psychology on a Marxist basis. In: *Problems in Psychology of Personality*, ed. E. I. Ignatev, pp. 8-20.

_____ (1961), *Problems of Individual Differences*. Moscow: Izd. Akad. Pedag. Nauk RSFSR.

_____ & Nebylitsyn, V. D. (1969), Investigation of the properties of the nervous system as an approach to the study of individual differences. In: *A Handbook of Contemporary Soviet Psychology*. New York: Basic Books, pp. 504-530.

Tikhomirov, O. K. et al. (1964), Application of information theory to the analysis of human problem solving. *Vop. Psikhol.*, 4:21–38.

_____ (1965a), The selectivity principle in thinking. Ibid., 6:16–32.

_____ (1965b), Some tendencies in American psychology. *Sov. Pedag.*, 10:143–155.

_____ & Poznanskaya, E. D. (1966a), An investigation of visual search as a means of analyzing heuristics. Translated in: *Soviet Psychology and Psychiatry*, Winter 1966–1967, 2:3–17.

_____ (1966b), Heuristics of man and machine. *Vop. Filos.*, 4:99–109.

_____ & Terekhov, V. A. (1967), Heuristics of man. *Vop. Psikhol.*, 2:26–41.

_____ & Telezina, E. D. (1969a), The analysis of the means=goal relationship as heuristics. Ibid., 1:75–90.

_____ & Terekhov, V. A. (1969b), Meaning and sense in the process of problem solving. Ibid., 4:66–84.

_____ (1970), Thinking as a psychical activity. In: *Contemporary Problems of the Dialectical Materialistic Theory of Knowledge*, vol. II, ed. M. B. Mitin et al. Moscow: Izd. Mysl, pp. 257–307.

Tonkonogii, I. M. & Tsukkerman, I. I. (1963), The use of drawings distorted by fluctuations for the study of disturbances of visual cognition. *Zh. Nevr. Psikhiat.*, 2:236–239.

_____ & _____ (1965), The study of perceptual disturbances in the light of information theory. *Vop. Psikhol.*, 1:83–92.

Tsentsifer, A. B. (1965), The study of the pupil's position in the collective. *Sov. Pedag.*, 11:57–64.

Tucker, R. C. (1963), Stalin and the uses of psychology. In: *The Soviet Political Mind.* New York: Praeger.

Tugarinov, V. P. (1962), *Communism and Personality. Vop. Filos.*, 6:14–23.

_____ (1965), *Personality and Society.* Moscow: Izd. Mysl.

Tyukhtin, V. S. (1959), On the problem of mental image. *Vop. Filos.*, 6:137–147.

_____ (1962), On the essence of reflection. Ibid., 5:59–71.

_____ (1963), *On the Nature of Image and Psychical Reflection in the Light of Cybernetics.* Moscow: Izd. Vysshaya Shkola.

_____ (1964a), The essence of reflection and information theory. In: *Cybernetics, Thinking, Life*, ed. A. I. Berg et al., pp. 309–317.

_____ (1964b), The "primary cell" of reflection and reflection as a property of the whole of matter. *Vop. Filos.*, 2:25–34.

_____ (1967), Reflection and information. Ibid., 3:41–52.

Uemov, A. I. (1964), Analogy as a research method of the relationship between machine and thinking. In: *Cybernetics, Thinking, Life*, ed. A. I. Berg et al., pp. 340–346.

Ukhtomskii, A. A. (1925), The principle of the dominant focus. In: I. M. Sechenov, I. P. Pavlov & N. E. Vvedenskii (1952), *Physiology of the Nervous System.* Selected Works, vol. III, ed. K. M. Bykov. Moscow: Gosudarstvennoe Izdatelstvo Meditsinskoi Literatury, pp. 262–279.

Ukraintsev, V. S. (1960), On the essence of elementary reflection. *Vop. Filos.*, 2:63–76.

_____ (1963), Information and reflection. Ibid., 2:26–38.

_____ & Platonov, G. V. (1966), Problems of reflection in the light of contemporary science. In: *Lenin's Reflection Theory and the Contemporary Science*, ed. V. N. Konstantinov, pp. 197–224.

REFERENCES

—— (1967), The categories "activity" and "purpose" in the light of basic cybernetic concepts. *Vop. Filos.*, 5:60–69.

Umanskii, L. I. & Vinogradova, M. G. (1964), Symposium on the problem of will. *Vop. Psikhol.*, 4:185–188.

—— & Shapiro, S. I. (1965), An experimental study of sensory-motor reactions in a probabilistic situation in relation to the strength and mobility of the nervous processes. Ibid., 5:18–27.

Uznadze, D. N. (1949), *Experimental Foundations of the Psychology of Set* (in Georgian). English edition in 1966 as *The Psychology of Set*, translation of the 1961 Russian edition. New York: Consultants Bureau, Plenum Press.

Vagner, V. A. (1923), *Biopsychology and Related Sciences*. Petrograd: Izd. Obrazovanie.

Vainshtein, I. (1924a), Review of A. Zalkind's: *Essays of a Culture of a Revolutionary Time. Pod Znamenem Marksizma*, 4/5:297–300.

—— (1924b), Marxist psychology or pathological Marxism. Ibid., 12:275–282.

Valentinova, N. G. (1965), On the characteristics of the worker's personality related to the content of work. In: *Sociology in the USSR*, vol. II, ed. G. V. Osipov, pp. 99–105.

Vasilev, G. A. (1956), Some remarks on Penfield's theory of cortico-subcortical relations and the memory mechanism. *Zh. Nevr. Psikhiat.*, 7:587–590.

Vasilev, L. L. (1962), *Distal Suggestion. Observations of a Physiologist*. Moscow: Gospolitizdat.

—— (1963), *Enigmatic Phenomena of Human Mind*, Second edition. Moscow: Gospolitizdat.

Vatsuro, E. G. (1951), I. P. Pavlov's teaching and some psychological problems. *Sov. Pedag.*, 9:50–59.

Vedenov, A. A. (1932), Regarding the subject matter of psychology. *Psikhologiya*, 3:43–58.

—— (1963), Problems of communist education and the psychological science. *Vop. Psikhol.*, 4:7–20.

—— (1964), Important questions of children's moral development and upbringing. *Sov. Pedag.*, 8:20–33.

Vedenov, M. F. et al. Eds. (1968), *Mathematical Modeling of Biological Processes*. Moscow: Mysl.

Vekker, L. M. & Lomov, B. F. (1961), The sensory image as a model. *Vop. Filos.*, 4:47–59.

—— (1964), *Perception and the Fundamentals of Modeling It*. Leningrad: Izd. Leningradskogo Universiteta.

—— (1968), The organizational levels of psychical processes as signals. Ibid., 4:58–69.

Vetrov, A. A. (1965), The subject matter of semiotics. Ibid., 9:57–67.

Vinogradova, O. S. (1961), *Orienting Reflex and its Neurophysiological Mechanisms*. Moscow: Izd. Akad. Pedag. Nauk RSFSR.

—— & Lindsley, D. B. (1963), Extinction of reactions to sensory stimuli in a single nerve cell of the cortex of the visual regions of an unanesthetized rabbit. *Zh. Vys. Nerv. Deyat.*, 2:207–217.

Vislobokov, A. D. (1965), *The Dialectical Process of Knowing Nature and Cybernetics*. Moscow: Izd. Mysl.

Voitonis, N. Yu. (1928), Behaviorism. *Psikhologiya Seriya A*, 1:95–114.

_____ (1929), The problem of "motives" of behavior and its study. Ibid., 2:227–253.

_____ (1949), *The Prehistory of Intellect. The Problem of Anthropogenesis.* Moscow: Izd. Akad. Nauk SSSR.

Volkov, N. N. (1948), On the constancy of perception of shape and size. In: *Researches on the Psychology of Perception,* ed. S. L. Rubinshtein, pp. 201–254.

_____ (1950), *Perception of Objects and Drawings.* Moscow: Izd. Akad. Pedag. Nauk RSFSR.

Volkov, P. P. & Kochergin, A. N. (1969), Modeling the psychical activity as a complex problem. *Vop. Filos.,* 4:154–157.

Volkova, V. D. (1953), Some features of the formation of conditioned reflexes to verbal stimuli in children. *Fiziol. Zh. SSSR,* 5:540–548.

Volume Dedicated to Vladimir Mikhailovich Bekhterev at his Anniversary of 40 Years of Teaching (1885-1925). Leningrad: Izdanie Gosudarstvennoi Psikhonevrologicheskoi Akademii i Gosudarstvennogo Refleksologicheskogo Instituta po Izucheniyu Mozga (1926).

Vorobev, N. N. (1964), Philosophical problems of the game theory. In: *Cybernetics, Thinking, Life,* ed. A. I. Berg et al., pp. 157–163.

Voronin, L. G. (1952), *Analysis and Synthesis of Complex Stimuli in Higher Animals.* Leningrad: Medgiz.

_____ et al., eds. (1958), *Orienting Reflex and Exploratory Behavior,* ed. D. B. Lindsley. Washington, D.C.: American Institute of Biological Sciences (English edition, 1965).

_____ (1962), Some results of comparative-physiological investigations of higher nervous activity. *Psychol. Bull.,* 3:161–195.

_____ (1965), *Lectures on Physiology of Higher Nervous Activity.* Moscow: Izd. Vysshaya Shkola.

_____ (1969), Pavlov and the contemporary brain physiology. *Zh. Vys. Nerv. Deyat.,* 6:911–920.

Vostrikov, A. V. (1965), *The Knowledge Theory of Dialectical Materialism.* Moscow: Izd. Mysl.

Vulfzon, B. L. (1965), Freudianism and the bourgeois pedagogy. *Sov. Pedag.,* 8:124–135.

Vygotskii, L. S. (1926), *Educational Psychology. Short Textbook.* Moscow: Izd. Rabotnik Prosveshcheniya.

_____ (1927), The biogenetic law in psychology and pedagogy. In: *Large Soviet Encyclopedia,* ed. I, vol. 6, pp. 275–279.

_____ (1931a), The problem of relationship between psychology and pedology. *Psikhologiya,* 1:78–100.

_____ (1931b), Psychotechnique and pedagogy. *Psikhofiziologiya Truda i Psikhotekhnika,* 2/3:173–184.

_____ (1932), The problem of consciousness. In: *Psychology of Grammar,* ed. A. A. Leontev & T. V. Ryabova. Moscow: Izd. Moskovskogo Universiteta, pp. 182–196, 1968. [9]

_____ (1934), *Thought and Speech.* English edition: *Thought and Language.* Cambridge, Massachusetts: The M. I. T. Press, 1962.

[9] An informal talk at a gathering of his associates.

—— (1956), *Collected Psychological Investigations.* Moscow: Izd. Akad. Pedag. Nauk RSFSR.

—— (1960), *Development of Higher Psychical Functions.* Moscow: Izd. Akad. Pedag. Nauk RSFSR.

Watson, J. B. (1927), Behaviorism. In: *Large Soviet Encyclopedia,* vol. 6, ed. O. Yu. Shmidt et al. Moscow: Aktsionernoe Obshchestvo "Sovetskaya Entsiklopediya," pp. 434–443.

Wortis, J. (1950), *Soviet Psychiatry.* Baltimore: The Williams & Wilkins Co.

Yakobson, P. M. (1953), Psychological problems of the education of feelings. *Sov. Pedag.,* 6:39–53.

—— (1956), *Psychology of Feelings.* Moscow: Izd. Akad. Pedag. Nauk RSFSR.

—— (1960), The problem of the psychology of emotions. In: *Psychological Science in the USSR,* vol. II, ed. B. G. Ananev et al., pp. 168–189.

—— (1966), *The Pupil's Emotional Life. A Psychological Study.* Moscow: Izd. Prosveshchenie.

Yarbus, A. L. (1961), The eye movements in the scrutiny of complex objects. *Biofizika,* 2:202–212.

—— (1965), *Eye Movements and Vision.* English edition, 1966, ed. L. A. Riggs. New York: Plenum Press.

Yaroshevskii, M. G. (1960), Helmholtz, Sechenov and the determinism of the neuropsychical activity. *Vop. Psikhol.,* 5:3–16.

—— (1961), *The Determinism Problem in the Psychophysiology of the 19th Century.* Tbilisi: Izd. Dushanbe.

—— (1968), *Ivan Mikhailovich Sechenov (1829–1905).* Leningrad: Izd. Nauka.

—— (1970), V. I. Lenin and the crisis of psychology at the turn of the century. *Vop. Psikhol.,* 2:46–58.

Yorish, Ya. S. (1969), Psyche is biological as well as social. *Vop. Filos.,* 2:147–148.

Yurinets, V. (1924), Freudianism and Marxism. *Pod Znamenem Marksizma,* 8/9: 51–93.

Zagorovskii, P. L. (1951), I. P. Pavlov's teaching and problems of the child's mental development. *Sov. Pedag.,* 4:74–86.

Zak, K. E. (1967), Qualitative changes and structure. *Vop. Filos.,* 1:51–58.

Zakharov, A. N. (1959), Comparison between theoretically possible and actual procedures in problem solving. *Vop. Psikhol.,* 6:110–118.

Zalkind, A. V. (1924a), *Essays of a Culture of a Revolutionary Time.* Moscow: Izd. Rabotnik Prosveshcheniya.

—— (1924b), Nervous Marxism or pathological criticism. *Pod Znamenem Marksizma,* 12:260–274.

—— (1930), *Basic Questions of Pedology.* Moscow: Izd. Rabotnik Prosveshcheniya.

—— (1931), The psychoneurological front and the psychological discussion. *Psikhologiya,* 1:17–23.

Zamoshkin, Yu. A. (1957), A critical study of the "psychological orientation" in sociology. *Vop. Filos.,* 2:101–109.

—— (1960), Contemporary capitalism and the individual's intellectual life. Ibid., 6:43–57.

—— (1961), The bureaucratisation of bourgeois society and the individual's fate. Ibid., 4:71–85.

—— (1965), The crisis of bourgeois ideology and the individual. Ibid., 4:29–38.

—— (1966), *The Crisis of Bourgeois Individualism and the Individual.* Moscow: Izd. Nauka.

Zankov, L. V. (1951a), The problem of memory in the light of I. P. Pavlov's teaching. *Sov. Pedag.,* 6:59–79.

—— (1951b), On the introduction of I. P. Pavlov's teaching in pedagogy. Ibid., 10:3–15.

Zaporozhets, A. V. (1958), The role of the orienting activity and of the image in the formation and performance of voluntary movements. In: *Orienting Reflex and Exploratory Behavior,* ed. L. G. Voronin et al., pp. 434–440.

—— & Elkonin, D. B., Eds. (1964), *Psychology of Preschool-Age Children. The Development of Cognitive Processes.* Moscow: Izd. Prosveshchenie.

—— & —— (1965), *Psychology of the Personality and Activity of Preschool-Age Children.* Moscow: Izd. Prosveshchenie.

—— et al. (1967a), *Perception and Action.* Moscow: Izd.Prosveshchenie.

—— (1967b), Development of perception and activity. *Vop. Psikhol.,* 1:11–16.

Zavadovskii, B. (1925), Darwinism and Lamarckism and the problem of inheritance of acquired characteristics. *Pod Znamenem Marksizma,* 10/11:79–114.

Zavalishina, D. N. & Pushkin, V. N. (1964), On the mechanisms of operational thinking. *Vop. Psikhol.,* 3:87–100.

Zavalova, N. D., Zukhar, V. P. & Petrov, Yu. A. (1964), Regarding the problem of hypnopedia. Ibid., 2:98–102.

Zdravomyslov, A. G. & Yadov, V. A. (1965a), The attitude toward work and the individual's priorities. In: *Sociology in the USSR,* vol. II, ed. G. V. Osipov, pp. 189–208.

—— & —— Eds. (1965b), *Work and the Development of Personality.* Leningrad: Lenizdat.

Zenkin, G. M. & Petrov, A. V. (1967), System of image analysis and recognition of objects against a complex background. *Biophysics* (English edition of *Biofizika*), 3:564–574.

Zetkin, C. (1925), *Reminiscences of Lenin.* New York: International Publishers (English edition, 1934).

Zhdanov, A. A. (1947), On philosophy; speech at the conference of Soviet philosophical workers. In: *On Literature, Music and Philosophy.* London: Lawrence & Wishart, pp. 76–112.

Zhdanov, D. A. (1969), *The Genesis of Abstract Thinking.* Kharkov: Izd. Kharkovskogo Universiteta.

Zhinkin, N. I. (1956a), The development of written speech in third to seventh graders. In: *Izvestia Akad. Pedag. Nauk RSFSR. Transactions of the Psychological Institute,* ed. D. N. Bogoyavlenskii: *Acquisition of Grammar and Spelling and Development of Writing.* 78:141–250.

—— (1956b), New findings on the functioning of the speech-motor analyzer and its connections with the auditory analyzer. In: *Izvestiya Akad. Pedag. Nauk RSFSR,* ed. F. N. Shemyakin: *Psychological Problems of Thinking and Speech.* 81:169–295.

—— (1959), Ways of studying the speech mechanism. In: *Psychological Science in the USSR,* ed. B. G. Ananev et al., vol. I, pp. 470–487.

—— (1963), On vocalization theories. In: *Thinking and Speech,* ed. N. I. Zhinkin & F. N. Shemyakin. pp. 219–271.

REFERENCES

_____ (1964), Code transfer in internal speech. *Vop. Yazykoznaniya,* 6:26–38.

Zhukov, N. I. (1963), Information in the light of Lenin's reflection theory. *Vop. Filos.,* 11:153–161.

Zhuravlev, V. V. (1961), *Marxism-Leninism on the Relative Independence of Social Consciousness.* Moscow: Izd. Vysshaya Shkola.

Zinchenko, V. P. (1958), On the problem of the formation of an orienting image. In: *Orienting Reflex and Exploratory Behavior,* ed. L. G. Voronin et al., pp. 441–449.

_____ (1961), *Involuntary Remembering.* Moscow: Izd. Akad. Pedag. Nauk RSFSR.

_____ Chshi-Tsin, V. A. & Tarakhanov, V. V. (1962), Formation and development of perceptual operations. *Vop. Psikhol.,* 3:3–14.

_____ (1967), Perception as action. *Vop. Psikhol.,* 1:17–24.

Zinovev, A. A. (1960a), Regarding the definition of the concept of connection. *Vop. Filos.,* 8:58–66.

_____ & Revzin, I. I. (1960b), The logical model as a means of scientific research. Ibid., 1:82–90.

Zotov, A. V. (1965), The Marxist knowledge theory. In: *Consultations on Teaching Philosophy,* ed. V. I. Ravzin, pp. 98–119.

Zukhar, V. P. et al. (1965), An experiment of collective hypnopedia. *Vop. Psikhol.,* 1:143–148.

Zurabashvili, A. D. (1957), On the centro-encephalic theory and our findings on the development of thalamic nuclei in man. *Zh. Nevr. Psikhiat.,* 6:701–705.

_____ (1958), On cybernetics and psychiatric questions. Ibid., 10:1259–1264.

_____ (1961), *Clinical-Theoretical Researches in Psychiatry.* Tbilisi: Izd. Gruzinskoi Akad. Nauk.

_____ (1964), *Current Problems in Psychiatry.* Tbilisi: Metsinereba.

Zvegintsev, V. A. (1961), Neopositivism and recent linguistic trends. *Vop. Filos.,* 12:92–100.

_____ (1963), Neopositivism in linguistics. In: *Marxist Philosophy and Neopositivism,* ed. G. V. Osipov, pp. 116–153.

Name Index

Subject Index